AF798642

WINNICOTT'S THEORY OF THE MATURATIONAL PROCESSES

WINNICOTT'S THEORY OF THE MATURATIONAL PROCESSES

Elsa Oliveira Dias

Routledge
Taylor & Francis Group
LONDON AND NEW YORK

First published 2016 by Karnac Books Ltd.

2 Park Square, Milton Park, Abingdon, Oxfordshire OX14 4RN
52 Vanderbilt Avenue, New York, NY 10017

Routledge is an imprint of the Taylor & Francis Group, an informa business

First issued in hardback 2019

Copyright © 2016 by Elsa Oliveira Dias

The right of Elsa Oliveira Dias to be identified as the author of this work has been asserted in accordance with §§ 77 and 78 of the Copyright Design and Patents Act 1988.

All rights reserved. No part of this book may be reprinted or reproduced or utilised in any form or by any electronic, mechanical, or other means, now known or hereafter invented, including photocopying and recording, or in any information storage or retrieval system, without permission in writing from the publishers.

Notice:
Product or corporate names may be trademarks or registered trademarks, and are used only for identification and explanation without intent to infringe.

British Library Cataloguing in Publication Data

A C.I.P. for this book is available from the British Library

ISBN-13: 978-1-78220-364-3 (pbk)
ISBN-13: 978-0-367-32965-5 (hbk)

Typeset by V Publishing Solutions Pvt Ltd., Chennai, India

In memory of my mother

To my dearest children Sandra, Claudia, and Paulo Manoel, who made me a mother each in their own way

"[…] We do need to try to get at a theory of normal growth so as to be able to understand illness and the various immaturities, since we are now no longer contented unless we can cure and prevent. We do not accept childhood schizophrenia any more than we accept poliomyelitis or the condition of the spastic child. We try to prevent, and we hope to be able to lead the way to cure wherever there is abnormality, which means suffering for someone".

—*Winnicott*, 1965b, p. 67

"Leave man undisturbed from the cradle on! Do not drive him out of the tightly closed bud of his being, out of the small hut of his childhood! Do not do too little, and thereby he shall not dispense with you and thus distinguish you from himself; do not do too much, and thereby he shall not feel your or his power and thus distinguish you from himself; in short, do not let man know until late that there are men, that there is anything else outside of him, for only thus shall he become a man. But man is a god as soon as he is a man. And when he is a god, he is beautiful".

—*Hölderlin*, Hyperion, p. 106

CONTENTS

ACKNOWLEDGEMENTS

This book would not have been the same without the contribution of the colleagues and friends who read the first draft of this study, accompanied its development and helped it with valuable suggestions.

I would like to thank the Marsh Agency Ltd., incorporating Paterson Marsh and Campbell Thomson & McLaughlin for their permission to quote many excerpts (around 500 words) from Winnicott, D. W. (1988) *Human Nature*.

Many thanks also to my translators, Regina de Barros Carvalho and Jonathan Morris, for the dedication, skill, and rigour with which they undertook the translation of my book into English, each of them with their respective talents, sensitivity, and linguistic skills which they brought to the task of translation.

I would like to thank Meire Gomes, who revised the references in the text and their links to the final references, for her indispensable assistance.

Many thanks to Loris Notturni, Suze Piza, and Teresa Mendonça, for their diligent assistance in tracking down quotations in English.

Once again, my thanks to Zeljko Loparic, my life and working companion, for his characteristic boldness of thought and partnership in the task of teaching and research which expanded enormously, as well as for the enthusiasm with which he has incorporated Winnicott into his acute philosophical reflection.

Lastly, I would like to express my special thanks to and affection for my children, Sandra, Claudia and Paulo Manoel, for the joy which they, together with my grandchildren, André, João and Francisco, have brought to my life, for confirming my faith in human nature and for giving me a profound sense of continuity. I am particularly grateful to Claudia for being an alert and inquisitive reader of my work and a valuable conversation partner regarding Winnicott's theoretical and clinical work.

ABOUT THE AUTHOR

Elsa Oliveira Dias, PhD, is a clinical psychologist, psychoanalyst, and co-founder of the Brazilian Society of Winnicottian Psychoanalysis. She is also Deputy-Chairperson of the International Winnicottian Psychoanalysis (IWA), and the author of a number of books, including *A teoria do amadurecimento de D. W. Winnicott*, *Sobre a confiabilidade e outros estudos*, and *Interpretação e manejo na clínica winnicottiana*, as well as many articles on Winnicott.

PREFACE TO THE ENGLISH EDITION

The possibility of publishing a book in Winnicott's own language and with the publisher who traditionally edited a large part of his work, while he was alive and posthumously, has been a great joy to me. I have thus been delighted to devote myself to the task of preparing the English edition of *A teoria do amadurecimento de D. W. Winnicott*, published by Karnac Books.

The book is the corrected and expanded version of the first part of my doctoral thesis, submitted in 1998, to the Pontifical Catholic University of São Paulo (PUC-SP). Its objective was to present Winnicott's theory of psychoses in a coordinated and extensive way, highlighting the originality of his contributions to psychoanalytic thought, including the fundamentally temporal and relational nature of human beings, his new criterion for classifying psychic disorders, primarily maturational and only secondarily symptomatological, the fact that in his theory, creativity is a diagnostic criterion for distinguishing between sickness and health and the fact that he highlighted the existence of environmental deficiency disorders, as is the case for psychoses, related to the importance of the environment in constituting the individual and the idea of dependence. At the same time, and contrary to many of his commentators, I have attempted to show the extraordinary theoretical unity of thought and its clinical consequences, fully aligned with his new approach, in particular, his introduction of the concept of care-cure and management.

Considering the close connection established by Winnicott between the nature of psychic disturbances and their point of origin (aetiology) in the line of maturation, I found myself obliged, above all, to explain the stages of the maturation process, emphasising and describing the tasks and achievements which characterise each stage, so as to open the field in which the various types of emotional disturbances may be configured, in particular, psychoses. In dealing with these latter disturbances, like Winnicott, I have given priority to the early stages, since it is during these that the foundations of an integrated personality and psychic health are established, and for this very reason, it is here that the risk of this type of disorder lies.

Winnicott formulated this theory which, in his own view, forms the backbone of his work and thought, but not in the systematic manner which I present here after collecting its constituent conceptual elements which are scattered across his work; in these, however, the theory is absolutely clear and internally consistent, as I intend to demonstrate in my book, with this indeed being one of the reasons why I have included so many direct citations of the author. This is a theory of health or perhaps, more precisely, of fundamental human needs, from the start of life and throughout the entire process as well as of the way in which the environment, in a specifically Winnicottian sense, favours or fails to favour the processes by which a baby, who is initially immature and heavily dependent, becomes a viable person, capable of establishing relations with external reality, of identifying with it without an excessive loss of spontaneity, of finding some sense in the fact of being alive and being reasonably able to take care of herself. All in all, this is the subject matter of this book.

Published in 2003, by the Brazilian publisher Imago, *A teoria do amadurecimento de D. W. Winnicott* was favourably received by the Brazilian public, having become work of reference in Winnicottian studies, among both psychoanalytic and academic institutions. It represented one of the first systematic studies in Brazil of the central theoretical component of the Winnicottian paradigm, his theory of maturational processes. The first edition, which was reprinted several times, was followed by a second edition in 2012 and a third edition in 2014, both published by DWW Editorial, the publishing company of the *Sociedade Brasileira de Psicanálise Winnicottiana* (Brazilian Society of Winnicottian Psychoanalysis) (SBPW). Also in 2012, the book was translated into Spanish with the title *La teoria de la maduración de D. W. Winnicott* and made available in electronic form. A translation into French by Loris Notturni is in preparation and should be completed by mid-2017; another translation into Chinese is also in progress, under the coordination of Dr. Zhao Chengzhi, with the participation of Dr. Ling Sunang, by way of evidence for the growing international reception of the book and research programme which it follows.

The text which I am presenting here to an English-speaking public is based on the third Brazilian edition. The changes made reflect the inherent difference between the two languages and their forms of expression, as well as corrections to the text and references, with the inclusion of various footnotes.

I have not made any amendments or additions for the purpose of updating results, in particular, I have left unchanged the sections "The relevance of the study of the theory of maturational processes", and "Brief discussion of divergent readings", of the Introduction, in which I compare my own interpretation of Winnicott with those of his commentators, whose works were published in those years. The most recent studies of Winnicott's work have certainly made new and significant contributions. I nevertheless consider that this book remains timely, since it presents Winnicott's central contribution to psychoanalytic theory and clinical practice in a unified and comprehensive form, notably his theory of maturational processes, organised around the ideas of a tendency towards integration, the realisation of this tendency by virtue of environmental facilitation, at the same time as it reveals the possibilities of failure or even breakdown of this integration process.

The reader who reflects on these themes will be able to understand more readily what Winnicott had in mind when, already at the end of his life, he expressed the following wish: "I am asking for a kind of revolution in our work. Let us examine what we do" (Abram, 2013, p. 312). The reader will also understand that the revolution for which Winnicott was arguing had already been initiated and partially achieved by him. He will also note that works which attempt to clarify the nature of this revolution began to be realised several years before his request was made public in 2013, by a number of institutional groups of clinicians and researchers in various countries, who, going against the dominant minimising interpretations, independently noted the momentous advances which psychoanalysis owes to Winnicott.

What I desire, above all, with this publication in English is that an increased dissemination of this study will help to provide debate on the crucial questions which Winnicott introduced to psychoanalysis and the study of human nature.

PREFACE TO THE SECOND EDITION

It has been with great satisfaction that I have prepared the second edition of this book, which was first published in 2003 by Imago. The fact that the first edition, which went through several reprints, is once again out of print shows that it has achieved one of its objectives: the broad dissemination of Winnicott's psychoanalysis among the Brazilian public.

Developing a unified reading of Winnicott's work, which clarified the unity of his thought, was the goal of my doctoral thesis; its partially rewritten first section constitutes this book. Already at that point, it seemed to me that a coordinated presentation of Winnicott's thought around one of its main axes, the theory of maturational processes, would facilitate understanding and consequently, the acceptance of his highly complex and innovative theoretical perspective, resulting in far-reaching and highly effective clinical practice. In addition to this dissemination, I also had another objective: that of drawing the attention of specialised public to the fact that Winnicott, in addition to being an uncommon clinician, had developed a consistent unified theoretical framework, which represents a decisive step in the progress of psychoanalysis and which could be seen as a new paradigm within that discipline. Despite giving the impression of looseness or of a certain dispersion, Winnicott's work has an unrivalled internal organisation and consistency, which allows a radically renewed psychoanalytic vision of health, illness, and the clinic to be extracted from it without great effort, together with teachings of capital importance, applicable to areas which are not strictly clinical. After 2003, I developed some of these viewpoints in a series of articles, basically written to be read at conferences. Some of them are now gathered in my book *Sobre a confiabilidade e outros estudos* (On reliability and other studies) (DWW editorial, 2011).

The favourable reception of *A teoria do amadurecimento de D. W. Winnicott* (D. W. Winnicott's theory of maturation) made the book a work of reference in the disciplines of the Winnicottian School of Psychoanalysis, taught by the Winnicott Centres of the Brazilian Society of

Winnicottian Psychoanalysis (SBPW). I was also delighted to observe that the book began to be used in a number of other courses on Winnicott and became the object of study by various research groups. Dissertations and theses for Postgraduate Programmes at various universities refer to the book. Several of the articles in the review *Natureza humana* (Human Nature) and of *Winnicott e-Prints* take up and develop the viewpoints which I articulated. The results achieved by some of these authors may be found in the collection *Winnicott na Escola de São Paulo* (Winnicott in the School of São Paulo) (DWW editorial, 2011). The book was also the object of specialist reviews, including those of Edna Vilete and Ricardo Rodulfo. The emergence of interest in the book outside Brazil provided an impetus for translations, which are currently in preparation, in order to meet the demand which we have received from our foreign colleagues.

The book took an important step in the direction of providing theoretical support and promoting, as far as possible and in different contexts, the application of Winnicott's psychoanalysis both to the treatment of difficult clinical cases, especially those which, according to traditional psychoanalysis, fall outside their areas of expertise, and in different not strictly clinical fields, such as those relating to prevention policies in mental health, to adolescents in conflict with the law and to manifestations of anti-social tendencies, in broader fashion.

For this second edition, undertaken by DWW editorial, the publisher of SBPW, which is primarily devoted to publishing works on Winnicott and related topics, corrections and modifications were made to spelling, in accordance with the recent reform, and to bibliographic references, as well as alterations aiming at improving the clarity of the phrase, with a number of theoretical additions to the text which were suggested to me and/or which I understood to be necessary. Some footnotes were omitted and other new ones added. As a result, the pagination of the book was slightly modified relative to the first edition. As a consequence, the references listed in the index were amended.

Once again, I would like to thank Zeljko Loparic for his partnership in the project which has grown enormously in scope, and for the enthusiasm with which he articulates Winnicott with his acute philosophical reflection. I would like to express my gratitude to all of my friends and colleagues who took the trouble to read the first steps in this study, long ago, as well as its development, which they aided with valuable suggestions. In this second edition, I would like to thank Meire Gomes for her meticulous revision and Simone Novo for patiently scanning for errors in the references and citations. I also want to thank Claudia Dias Rosa for her readiness to help, Daniela Guizzo and Roseana Moraes Garcia for organising the index. I would also like to record my thanks to all of my colleagues who have shared the joy with me of discovering and using Winnicott's precious legacy and who have not only made valuable use of my study but have also advanced it in numerous directions. I would especially like to thank my beloved children Sandra, Claudia, and Paulo Manoel, whose existence in my life fills me with joy as I work, study, and write, and for giving me a deep sense of continuity. I am particularly grateful to Claudia, for being an attentive and inquisitive reader of my writings and a valued partner on Winnicottian paths; and Sandra, for using her talent for creating the book cover so well and affectionately.

Elsa Oliveira Dias

PREFACE TO THE THIRD EDITION

With the second edition of this book having sold out in only two years, I am extremely satisfied to be preparing this third edition, again with DWW editorial. The publisher and I decided that rather than simply reprinting, a new edition would be necessary, as it was necessary to correct errors of spelling and standardisation detected in the second edition and to introduce changes aiming to improve the clarity of one or other phrase or to refine the formulation of others.

Until recently, the idea of maturation was not regarded as central to Winnicott's work, even by scholars studying the author, both within Brazil and abroad, let alone as the horizon from which his thought is unified and from which it is possible to develop a theory of health and another of psychic disorders, with both phenomena endowed with a sense of maturation.

Already today, at least in Brazil, on the basis of the work of research, teaching, and dissemination that has been undertaken, this idea is being discovered and used, apparently to great advantage, in theoretical work, as a guide to clinical practice, in the guidelines and supervision of different institutional fields and for preventive policies in mental health. In study and research, rather than the habit of simply highlighting isolated concepts, more care has been taken in contextualising it in the whole of Winnicott's work or in locating the described phenomenon, within the line of maturation.

Scholars from other countries are also expressing interest in deepening the proposed reading and by virtue of this demand, this book has been translated into Spanish, with this edition now available as an e-book. Other translations are being undertaken into French and English, which are expected to be finalised soon.

I would like to express here how happy I am to enjoy the good fortune of being able to coexist with and rely on colleagues and contacts with whom I share the pleasure of studying, reflecting, and discovering the richness of Winnicott's thought, in ever greater detail, as well as of placing this richness and its clinical acuity at the service of therapeutic work of all kinds.

In this third edition, I would again like to thank Meire Gomes for her meticulous revision, Loris Notturni, my French translator for his thorough collecting of minor errors and inaccuracies, as well as Gabriela Galván who, on the basis of her translation into Spanish, has been indefatigable in detecting imprecise phrases or terms.

Elsa Oliveira Dias

INTRODUCTION

The theory of maturational processes in Winnicott's work[1]

Winnicott formulated a theory of *personal development*, which he subsequently termed the "Theory of Maturational Processes", based on the ideas that every human being has an innate tendency towards maturation and that no aspect of human existence, whether healthy or unhealthy, can be understood independently of the moment of the process to which it belongs or from which it originates. He regarded this theory as the backbone of his theoretical and clinical work.[2] The emphasis of this theory is on the initial stages, since it is during this period that the basis of personality and of psychic health is formed. By shedding light on what goes on in the special relationship between a mother and her child, Winnicott describes the fundamental human needs, which persist throughout life, from the most primitive stages until the death of the individual, and the environmental conditions which facilitate the gradual constitution of the unitary identity that every baby should achieve, with the ability to relate to the world and to external objects as well as to establish interpersonal relationships.

Winnicott's theory of maturational processes conceptualises and describes the different tasks, achievements, and difficulties inherent to the developmental process at each stage of life. It thus serves as a practical guide for understanding the phenomena of health and for early detection of emotional difficulties. His theory is useful not only for psychoanalysts and psychotherapists but also for parents seeking to assist the personal development of their children, for professionals whose work affects the emotional development of babies, children, adolescents, and adults in some way as well as for anyone made aware of the need for a reflection on preventive activities and policies in the field of psychic health.

Important in itself, the theory of maturational processes also provides the theoretical framework from which different aspects of the study of human nature can be developed, such as those related to cultural achievements and the entire field of creativity. It also forms the theoretical basis, both in Winnicott's own work and in the research project including this book, which allows a clarification of concepts of general psychic disorders, due to their intimate connection with the stages of development.

In order to understand the perspective from which Winnicott develops his theory of maturational processes and psychic disorders, we should underline that he was a paediatrician who became a psychoanalyst due to his conviction, confirmed by his clinical practice, that most of the problems which brought mothers and their babies to his office resulted from extremely primitive emotional difficulties. As his thinking evolved, he defined these as difficulties in establishing the relationship between mother and baby in the earliest stage of life. Once he had become a psychoanalyst, Winnicott devoted himself to the treatment and study of psychotic pathologies, albeit without ever abandoning paediatrics. In the parallel exercise of both clinical practices and in simultaneously observing psychotics and babies with their mothers, he came to realise that emotional development during the very early stages of life related to exactly the same phenomena as those which emerged from the study of the various forms of adult schizophrenia. In this way, the in-depth investigation of an individual of any age with a disorder of a schizophrenic type "becomes an intimate study of that individual's very early development" (1953a, p. 222). In essence, the difficulties shared by infants and psychotics concern the constitution of the self as a unitary identity and the contact with reality. In babies, these difficulties are due to extreme immaturity; in psychotics, to the fact that at some point they have strayed from the path leading to maturity.

The theory of maturational processes is thus the central point of Winnicott's analytical thought. The need for such a theory and the essential connection which exists between this theory and that of psychic disorders were made explicit by the author in 1962, a decisive year for the development of his new concepts, when he stated that:

> […] we do need to try to get a theory of normal growth so as to be able to understand illness and the various immaturities, since we are now no longer contented unless we can cure and prevent. We do not accept childhood schizophrenia any more than we accept poliomyelitis or the condition of the spastic child. We try to prevent, and we hope to be able to lead the way to cure wherever there is abnormality, which means suffering for someone. (1965e, p. 67)[3]

As the theoretical *background* for the understanding of psychic disorder, the theory of maturational processes is an intrinsic part of therapeutic action:

> The only companion that I have in exploring the unknown territory of the new case is the theory that I carry around with me and that has become part of me and that I do not even have to think about in a deliberate way. (1971c, p. 6)

This book proposes to study and to present the concepts of Winnicott's theory of maturational processes in a unified way, clarifying its premises and providing an organised description of the various stages, their respective tasks and achievements. This study shall concentrate on the early stages, just as Winnicott did, since in the author's view, it is psychoses and not neuroses that form the paradigm of human illness. Referring to the fundamental tasks of the beginning of life, psychotic disorders derive from an environmental failure in facilitating the accomplishment of these tasks and in transforming them into achievements of maturation. In addition, Winnicott's thought demonstrates that it is from the observation and treatment of psychosis that a perspective emerges, which allows us to glimpse essential aspects of human existence that would otherwise be inaccessible when studying a healthy or even a neurotic individual.

The development and application of the theory of personal development for the characterisation of Winnicott's theory of psychic disorders shall be presented in a forthcoming study (in preparation), which refers specifically to psychoses. This more general project, of which this book is the first step, will consist of a unified presentation of Winnicott's theory of schizophrenic psychosis in the light of the theory of maturational processes, with an emphasis on the initial stages of life.

Although Winnicott insisted on the central role of the theory of maturational processes throughout his entire work, he did not go as far as presenting it in a systematic or organised fashion. The only book that offers a more explicit global presentation of the process of personal development was *Human Nature* (1988), which remained unfinished. With the exception of this book, which was conceived as a complete work, Winnicott's books are collections of independent articles, originally written as lectures for different audiences. Since Winnicott took account of the specific character of his public, these articles repeat the same principal theses, albeit from different perspectives, in the light of which one or other specific aspect of human existence is analysed. All of this makes it difficult to grasp the unity of his thought. The objective of this book is to present the various conceptual elements which constitute his theory of maturational processes in a unitary and organised manner. In order to achieve this, we have found it necessary to group and compare the most diverse texts, since the author refers to different stages in different parts of his work, without ever presenting them as a whole.

This study is based on a close reading of the whole of Winnicott's work directed towards the proposed theme. As in any other reading, the one made here has its own premises. The principal ones shall be explained in this Introduction; others will become clearer in the course of the exposition. Essentially, I shall use the classical principle of hermeneutics, according to which, each part of a work must be understood in the light of the whole of this work while, on the other hand, its structure must be reconstructed, taking into account each of its components.[4] In this case, I do not intend to offer an exhaustive reading of Winnicott's work as a whole, but to reconstruct its most central section: the theory of maturational processes. Applying the methodological principle of hermeneutics to this particular task, I shall proceed in such a way as to understand Winnicott's statements about the issue in question, in the light of the totality of his thought. This, as a consequence, will be illuminated as a whole, on the basis of his theory of maturation. I shall subsequently do the same for the theory of psychoses.

Some principles made explicit by Winnicott himself shall also be used, one of which, for example, recommends that an understanding of psychoanalysis in general and of one's own should be achieved by considering the historical route taken in seeking solutions for the problems raised. This is the reason why, for psychoanalytical topics,

> [...] the reader must form a personal opinion in these matters, after learning what is taught as far as possible in the historical manner, which is the only way that the theory of anyone moment becomes intelligible and interesting. (1988, p. 42)

Unifying the general hermeneutic principle and this advice from Winnicott, the work will have, from a methodological viewpoint, the character of *internal and historical analysis* of the text. According to this procedure, I shall not attempt to justify Winnicott's theses, any more than he did himself. Nor shall I make a comparative study except in order to highlight the specificity of some of his points of view. This shall be done, above all, in relation to Winnicott's main interlocutor, traditional psychoanalysis, *but always starting from his own position*.[5] I shall not aim at exhaustiveness in these comparisons, but shall limit myself to questions regarding the theory of maturational processes.

Such a task, even within the indicated limits, has its difficulties. One of these is always considering the historical evolution of his thought. In general, leaving aside the texts from the 1930s, during which he wrote as a paediatrician, we may distinguish three phases of his work: the one from 1940 until the publication, in 1951, of his seminal article on transitional objects; the 1950s, during which the decision to develop his own theoretical perspective becomes more explicit; and finally, the phase starting from the 1960s, above all with the publication of the 1962 article "Ego integration in child development" (1965n), in which he introduces the central concepts of the innate tendency to maturation and of the subjective object.[6] The evolution of his thought shall be considered, albeit not in a systematic way, since such task would require another study, despite remaining limited to the presentation of the central theme.

The relevance of the study of the theory of maturational processes

In addition to the fact that the theory of maturational processes constitutes Winnicott's central contribution to psychoanalysis, its study is justified by the fact that, until now, the secondary literature has approached the theme without fully exploring its theoretical and clinical consequences. Furthermore, despite the fact that the author has stated, above all from the 1960s onwards, that this theory is the necessary theoretical horizon for understanding the concepts relating to psychic disorders and their classification, this point has not been emphasised by his commentators.[7]

The same is true of the various general introductions to Winnicott's works.[8] In most of these, we find careful and dense interpretations of aspects of his work but not the internal articulation of his thought as a whole, in a way that clarifies the conceptual key that gives it unity and coherence. There is no emphasis on the importance of the theory of psychoses (with no highlighting of the originality of his approach to the theme and of the fact that the fundamentals of human existence are revealed through the study of psychoses), or any mention of the intrinsic connection between this theory and the theory of maturational processes (i.e., the fact that the latter is the basis of Winnicott's conception of the nature and aetiology of psychoses). Since these are presentations which, while succinct, are intended to provide a general overview of the author, the fact that the core of his thought is not mentioned becomes incomprehensible.

We should consider a few examples.[9] In *Boundary and Space: An Introduction to the Work of D. W. Winnicott* (1981), one of the first general presentations of Winnicott's work, the authors Madeleine Davis and David Wallbridge expose the central concepts of Winnicott's thought, but these are not articulated in terms of the maturational processes, as a function of its basic temporality.[10] There is no reference to the fact that the theory of maturation is the theoretical foundation required for understanding and classifying psychic disorders. I found only one reference to the aetiology, which, moreover, is the only one made explicit by Winnicott when, while describing the false self, the authors say: The aetiology of the false self is to be found particularly in the failure in object presenting at the stage of absolute dependence (Davis & Wallbridge, 1981, p. 65). However, there is one passage in this work, in the item "Adapting to Shared Reality", in which the authors present a sequence that may suggest the various stages of development to the attentive reader.

A critical appreciation in the same vein would apply to the book *The Work & Play of Winnicott* (1990) by Simon Grolnick, which despite emphasising the developmental character of Winnicott's work, does not specify the singularity of what Winnicott understands by development, nor does it contemplate the essential internal articulations with the theory of psychic disorders.

In the preface to *Le Paradoxe de Winnicott* (Winnicott Paradox, 1987), Anne Clancier and Jeannine Kalmanovitch[11] assert that the work, made possible by the collaboration of "a profoundly Winnicottian team, *but a very objective one* [*sic*], takes up the highly original notions of this creative psychoanalyst […]" (p. xiv, preface). The 250-page book dedicates a chapter of only eight pages to an aspect undoubtedly central to the theory of psychoses: the fear of breakdown. In this chapter, there is allusion to psychoses *en passant*. There is no mention to the central character of the theory of maturational processes and its connection to a theory of psychic disorders. That is not surprising since the entire interpretation of Winnicott's thought is based on Freudian psychoanalytic theory, especially Kleinian theory.

In 1981, Claude Geets published her study *Winnicott*. The author describes Winnicott's concepts most properly, above all those which characterised his originality, for example, questions relating to primary creativity, to playing and to transitional phenomena. Since, however, the author does not consider the global theory of maturation she presents the concepts in an isolated manner, as if they were timeless, that is, without expanding the different meanings that they acquire according to the moment in the personal development process. As, in Winnicott's view, the language that is appropriate for describing one stage becomes *wrong* when used for another stage, since the tasks involved are of different natures, the indiscriminate use of terms promotes the impression that his theory is incomprehensible or inconsistent. In addition to the lack of distinction between the different stages, there is also some backsliding into the traditional theory. The following example demonstrates both problems. Geets begins an item called "From object relation to object usage" (De la relation d'object à l'utilization de l'object) with the following sentence:

> *The adaptation of the child to reality* may thus be described as this long path from subjectivity to objectivity. The *opposition* between me and not-me is supported by the *fantasy* (fantasme) of an *internal* reality, located in the body […]. The child has an "inside" in which he may accumulate

> things and his growth is based on the form of an exchange between him (the internal reality) and the world (the external reality) [...] the progressive achievement of objectivity is *favoured by the inevitable frustrations.* (Geets, 1981, p. 100; my italics)

However, for Winnicott, in the first place, the child does not initially *adapt* to reality; if he does so, and it would not be to reality but to the environment, this could be the start of the formation of a pathological false self. In normality, *it is the environment that adapts to the baby*, and as the baby grows, in the presence of the facilitating environment, he *creates* not only one, but many senses of reality. Secondly, bearing in mind that the author announces that she is referring to the passage from the subjective to the objective, which as she herself concedes, is a "long path", it is necessary to discriminate the different stages of this long path. However, in dealing with the beginning of the process, the author not only goes straight to the end (speaking immediately of the "opposition" between me and not-me) but also interprets and uses terms that are alien to Winnicott (for the author, this is a question of *separation* between the me and not-me and not of opposition). The author also discusses the inside and the outside of the infant, when Winnicott clearly affirms that at the start of the process, the senses of internal and external realities have not yet been established and the baby lives in a subjective world, which is neither inside nor outside. Furthermore, the me/not-me separation is not supported by any fantasy (fantasme), nor is it favoured by frustrations, but is initiated by the experience of *no anger* destructiveness, which creates the externality of the world at the stage of object usage.

Adam Phillips, with his book *Winnicott* (1988), is largely an exception in this panorama. Emphasising the originality of Winnicott's theory of personal development, as well as the difference that separates it both from the Freudian theory of the development of sexual functions and the Kleinian "positions", he asserts that Winnicott not only introduced significant innovations into psychoanalytical theory and practice, but that his theory leads to "radical departures from Freud". The main point of this rupture consists of the fact that Winnicott "would derive everything in his work, including a theory of the origins of scientific objectivity and a revision of psychoanalysis, from this paradigm of the developing mother–infant relationship" (Phillips, 1988, p. 5). Phillips uses the term paradigm in the sense of "model" and not in the technical sense used by Thomas Kuhn, who, as we shall see below, uses this term to designate the exemplary problem and solution brought together by a scientific discipline.

In any case, what Phillips indicates is that Winnicott has constructed a theory that is not limited to enriching psychoanalysis with new contributions to an old model, but starts from another point crucial for the study of human nature, namely the initial vulnerability of the dependent infant and the importance of the environment. According to the commentator, these new propositions lead Winnicott to issues that had never been formulated by traditional theory, such as: "what do we depend on to make us feel alive, or real?" (cf. Phillips, 1988, p. 5). However, even this commentator, whose work appears to me to be one of the most significant expositions of Winnicott's thought to date, states that the theory of maturational processes seems to be vague and lacking in solid foundations. In a passage which highlights that, in Winnicott's view, "a too militantly knowing psychoanalysis had usurped, or simply lacked confidence in, what he called 'essentially natural process'" (ibid., p. 98), Phillips asks:

> But were such "natural process" simple or complicated? What do we need to know about them in order to adjust to them when, in Winnicott's view, "if the parents have succeeded as parents they are unaware of the things in themselves that have made for success"? (Phillips, 1988, p. 99)

On the other hand, Phillips continues, Winnicott

> comes to increasingly complex and often obscure formulations about the earliest "natural" stages of infant's development that involve him in a radical revision of the kinds of instinct-theory that psychoanalysis had been traditionally based on. (Phillips, 1988, p. 99)

The fact is that having glimpsed Winnicott's theoretical strength and originality, neither the meaning of maturation, nor the meaning of what Winnicott understands by natural processes or even the status of the theory of maturational processes are clear to an acute interpreter like Phillips. Perhaps it is for this reason that he did not refer in this work to the articulation of the stages of personal development to the theory of psychic disorders.

We have another example in Michael Jacobs, in his book *D. W. Winnicott* (1995). The author states the central character of the concept of development in Winnicott's work, highlighting it as the mark of the decisive influence of Darwin on him, but, nevertheless fails to indicate their profound differences; the fact that, in Winnicott, maturation is not reducible to the biological evolutionism, and the essentially personal character with which Winnicott endows his concept of development. There are two chapters in this book "Major Contributions to Theory" and "Criticisms and Rebuttals", in which we might expect a mention of the link between the theory of maturational processes and the study of psychic disorders, but there is none. In the last chapter, Jacobs declares that in Winnicott, "there is also little even in the way of a more theoretical position [...] that can be debated as readily as, for example, Freud can be on instinct theory, the unconscious, the centrality of sexuality" but concedes, in parentheses "(...) except perhaps his theory of the development of the self" (Jacobs, 1995, p. 99). What would be an introduction to the theory of maturational processes is contained in an item named "From dependence towards independence" (p. 37). In it, not considering the specific character of development, Jacobs declares: "just as Winnicott moves away from a strict Freudian tripartite division of personality, so too he has little to say about the Freudian threefold development scheme of oral, anal and phallic or genital stages of sexuality"; also with the proviso that "like that of Freud, Winnicott's scheme contains three categories [*sic*] (rather than stages, although they are similarly progressive): absolute dependence, relative dependence and the phase 'towards independence'" (ibid., p. 37). That is, juxtaposing Winnicott and Freud, Jacobs does not conclude that there are differences in the theories, but that the former has a debt to the latter.

Although it is a dictionary and not an introduction to Winnicott's work, it is appropriate here to mention Jan Abram's book *The Language of Winnicott: A Dictionary of Winnicott's Use of Words* (1996). Abram selected twenty-two items that she regarded as the main themes of Winnicott's thought. In addition to making explicit, for each one of the chosen items, the main orientation of Winnicott's thought, she enumerates a list of contents in which she points out related themes, weaves her own comments and, as is appropriate to a dictionary of this kind, presents extensive citations of the original texts. The quality of the conceptual analysis of themes is uneven: in some of them the author keeps to what is essential in the theme, maintaining Winnicott's theoretical position accurately. In others, the analysis is vague, losing itself in secondary ideas. Despite being quite successful in the task of establishing links between the concepts, with this making her dictionary a kind of general introduction to Winnicott's work, the book suffers from a lack of a unitary interpretation of his thought. This becomes clear above all since the author has not considered the theory of the maturational process in a consistent fashion, making only isolated references to the connection between the stages of maturation and psychic disorders. This lack of a unitary interpretation also appears in the absence of certain fundamental concepts from the main list, for example, the theory of personal development itself, the subjective object, imaginative elaboration, unthinkable agonies, psychoses, family, Oedipus complex, and the establishment of morality. Psychoses, for example, do not appear in the central themes, being considered within the theme "environment", with the author highlighting the articulation of such disorders with the failure of the environment to provide the baby, during the initial stages, with the satisfactory conditions which permit the continuity of personal growth. Another reference to the aetiology of psychosis is found under the item "antisocial tendency".[12]

I shall now refer to Julio de Mello Filho, with his book *O ser e o viver* (Being and living), of 1989. This book, which marks the beginning of Winnicottian studies in Brazil, is also a rewarding surprise regarding the principal point: the reading of Winnicott's thought presented in it is made with a fearless appreciation of the originality of Winnicott's theory, even if the author does not always extract all of its implications, and demonstrates a vast knowledge of the subject. In the first chapter, "The man, the life and the work", Mello Filho provides what he describes as a bird's eye view, that is, a general and concise introduction, albeit very well elaborated, of a number of points which he regards as basic. In this chapter, what seems important to me and revealing of this scholar's understanding of Winnicott is his initiative of extending and I would say, correcting the list of Winnicott's contributions to psychoanalysis made by André Green, in a 1977 article. Green had distinguished seven theories in Winnicott's thought, including a "theory of pulsions", which was evidently an error. Green also mentions "the theory of development" as one of the theories and not as the theoretical horizon of all the others, in addition to mentioning it last. Correcting the French commentator, Mello Filho begins the list of Winnicott's contributions with the theory of development, leading us to believe that he has prioritised it. At the same time, neither the central position of this theory nor the interrelationship between the stages of maturation and psychic disorders are explicitly emphasised in the work. He also adds several other theories to the list which indeed deserved to be mentioned: for example, a theory of the self, a theory of psycho-somatics[13] and a theory of regression, in addition to re-describing those already mentioned by Green in a way which seems to me to be more faithful to Winnicott than Green himself had previously done. Lastly, he rightly modifies Green's note regarding the nature of a theory of pulsions in Winnicott, proposing a Winnicottian theory of impulses (the term used by Winnicott is *drives*).

Despite the fact that Mello Filho highlights important aspects of the theory of maturational processes here and there, it is mentioned only as a theoretical position to be described, without taking maturation itself into consideration. For example, in the second chapter, "Human development and the analytical situation", the author mentions "the three main processes which accompany the development of the infant: integration, personalisation and adaptation to reality", without distinguishing the stage when they begin. Shortly afterwards, without discussing the entire process and the various challenges which, from this point onwards, must be overcome in order to ensure integration into a unity, he states: "According to Winnicott, through the *conjunction* of the three described processes, [the baby] begins to distinguish a 'me' from a 'not-me', separated by the skin, operating as a limiting membrane" (Mello Filho, 1989, p. 37; my italics).

Brief discussion on the divergent readings

As a result of its subject and methodology, the present characterisation of Winnicott's theory of maturational processes offers a general view of his work that, while not completely new, differs considerably from some other existing readings. As there are several different ways in which Winnicott's work is read and evaluated regarding the extension of his contribution to psychoanalysis, the question here is of knowing exactly of what this contribution consists?

Some challenge the notion that Winnicott is an original thinker. Proponents of this reading deny the existence of a typically Winnicottian "theory" on any significant subject and, as a rule, include his contributions within the theoretical framework of traditional psychoanalysis (Freud & Klein). There is no shortage of this type of assimilation. Already in the title of Chapter Two, "L'enfant et ses fantasmes" (The child and his fantasies) (in Winnicott Paradox, by A. Clancier and Kalmanovitch, cited above) a concept of fantasy (*fantasme*) is used, which belongs to Klein's theory and which is totally alien to Winnicott. In this same chapter, which describes the baby-mother unity, the authors reproduce Winnicott's graphic illustrations of the baby as an isolated being, of the baby discovering the environment, etc.[14] Following this, by way of a caption they say:

> The emergence of id impulses makes it easier for the child to face the outside world. If the good breast realizes this experience of itself, all will go well. When the two do not meet, there will be a split. (Clancier & Kalmanovitch, 1987, p. 26)

In other words, everything here is Kleinian. The only Winnicottian element in this phrase is the movement towards an encounter but even in this case, the direction of the movement is wrong.[15]

Another good example in the same line is Luiz Meyer's 1994 article. Commissioned by the review *Percurso* to encourage reflection on the motives of a possible failure in psychoanalytical training, the article analyses the famous letter from Winnicott to Melanie Klein of November 1952. From any perspective, this letter is an alert regarding the uneasiness and the paralysing atmosphere for the evolution of psychoanalytical thought, resulting from the intransigence, sectarianism and abuse of power by the Kleinian group of the time, through the imposing of clichés and other types of constraint on thought. Meyer is prepared (se dispõe) to consider "the specifically Winnicottian concepts" in the letter, but only to analyse the precise nature of the criticism directed by Winnicott against Klein and particularly against the Kleinians. From this point onwards, Meyer skilfully and subtly undermines Winnicott's thought, shifting away from Winnicott's own concepts to a point outside the scope of the questioning which gave rise to them. This denaturing or even disfiguring reaches a crescendo until, in the final part of the text nothing of Winnicott is left, merely an anonymous and mimetic figure delivering Kleinian ideas.

Most commentators nevertheless do not hesitate in granting Winnicott a notable originality. An example of such an appreciation is provided by Geets (1981): "Winnicott's position in the field of contemporary psychoanalysis is original [...] his work has progressively imposed itself through the novelty of its language and the wealth of its perspectives [...]" (p. 15). In the article "Le concept de limite" (The borderline concept), Green himself states that Winnicott is specifically the analyst of borderline cases, pointing out that the apparent simplicity of the concepts of the British author frequently fails to note the subtle complexity of his discoveries (cf. Green, 1976).

Some interpreters, while acknowledging Winnicott's originality, deny that he is a theoretical thinker, insisting that his richness lies precisely in the fact that he is not "theoretical" or "systematic". Among those who seem to prefer this reading is Pontalis. In an interview with Clancier, the French psychoanalyst claimed that:

> [...] One can trace back Freud's thought, one can expound Melanie Klein's theory, one can systematize Lacan's theories even more. If you try to do that with Winnicott, you lose what is best in him. What I have been and remain sensitive to is the Winnicott effect.[16]

Rogério Luz, emphasising the fact that Winnicott's manner of theorising may result in this kind of approach, acknowledges that it leads to a narrowing down of his contribution. In a 1989 article, Luz points out the way in which Winnicott's text:

> [...] in approaching everyday language and since it refuses a scholarly systematisation, at times is seen merely as an expression of brilliant intuitions, linked to clinical practice, but incapable of responding to the demands of a theory of the subject and his relation to culture. (Luz, 1989, p. 26)

In the same sense, it also postulates the importance of not immobilising a thought that is rich and in continuous flux. For example, Claude Geets, draws attention to the risk of "paralysing a thought in incessant motion, of fixing within a rigid conceptualisation what, in principle, lends itself to being seen and heard as a clinical experience" (Geets, 1981, p. 17) a risk that would be particularly formidable in Winnicott's case. Part of this danger would be the possibility that Winnicott's thought could be transformed into a dogma if it were formulated into a theory. According to Geets, nothing would be more extraneous to the author's mentality than "the dogmatism of a system applied to living reality; detached from the experience that witnessed its birth, theory loses its sense and sheds its skin to become doctrine" (Geets, 1981, p. 17). A number of questions arise regarding this legitimate fear: why would conceptual clarity, unity, and rigour of theory become dogma specifically in Winnicott? If any work, once made public, is necessarily at the mercy of the reading that it receives, which is the equivalent of saying that the subjective world always interferes in the perception of objective reality, why enthrone this structural truth and recommend this subjective reading specifically in Winnicott's case? How can we establish a genuine dialogue with the author if what we do is use his name and language to dress up our old theories? Or also: which is the greater risk? Trying to understand exactly what Winnicott wanted to formulate (which ultimately is what we try to do with our patients) and so many times defended, using the enshrined method of reading and comparing his texts, or decreeing that his thought should be left to the discretion of every and any type of interpretation?[17]

I believe that it is the same kind of anxiety as that expressed by Geets that leads José Ottoni Outeiral, one of the most active disseminators of Winnicott in Brazil, to declare in his "Introduction to the Brazilian edition" of Winnicott's *Psychoanalytic Explorations* that in order to read Winnicott's work,

> it is necessary to do as he suggests in the *Squiggle Game*, with reader and author jointly creating a 'personal reading', a transitional space in which the reader 'will discover' as a personal finding what D. W. Winnicott wrote. (Outeiral, 1994, p. viii)

It is hard to agree with this reading method suggested by Outeiral. Firstly, in view of the same considerations as those made above with regard to Geets and secondly because the construction of a theory or the formulation of a concept is not a spontaneous gesture (which does not deprive them of creativity) as is required in the squiggle game. This game is a therapeutic method, a procedure for interpersonal communication that is entirely different from the procedure for constructing theories, which consists, as we shall demonstrate, of the elaboration and testing of hypothesis, which characterise the scientific activity of problem-solving. Furthermore, it does not seem to be legitimate for a reader to appropriate the ideas of an author without acknowledging his due merits; it is not fair to make a "personal finding" of what Winnicott wrote before trying to know what he actually wrote, forgetting that he was the one who wrote it. This would mean establishing a relationship with Winnicott's work, which had become a subjective object, which, according to the author, represented a "dead-end communication", a monologue instead of a dialogue; it would be to deny the fact that Winnicott and his work belong to external reality, with which each of us must deal if we hope to reach maturity. As was already mentioned, Winnicott actually recommends that "the reader must form a personal opinion in these matters", but only "after learning what is taught as far as possible [...]" (1988, p. 42).

Curiously, this is not always Outeiral's position. Considering the subject of the father in Winnicott's thought, he concedes that "an extensive and unsystematic work [...] complicates an in-depth study of certain issues" (Outeiral, 1997, p. 91). In another text, declaring that he was inspired by Hartmann, who once told Masud Khan that everybody referred to his work, but that nobody actually read it (cf. Khan, 1958, p. xxxi), Outeiral explains to the reader that the excessive number of citations of Winnicott in his article has the function of "preserving the true meaning of his ideas and not [favouring] a personal interpretation of them" (Outeiral, 1991, p. 133, note 1).

To the same group of interpreters, belong all those who acknowledging Winnicott as a great clinician, insist on the merely suggestive character of his work highlighting his preference for expressing himself in everyday and even poetic language as a proof of the non-existence of a theoretical interest.

The tendency to consider Winnicott uniquely from the perspective of a brilliant clinician or a "free" or "poetic" thinker is sometimes due to circumstantial reasons. According to Daniel Widlöcher, Winnicott counterbalanced in France, "a slightly intellectualist formalism" derived from Lacan's work, with those works which, on the contrary, gave priority to the therapeutic relationship and the feelings.[18] Having represented an alternative to Lacan's hyper-systematisation in France, in England, Winnicott served as an antidote against the dogmatism and sectarianism of the Kleinian group, not only in the theoretical plane, but also in the political-institutional and scientific one.

There are also those who, without necessarily denying the theoretical originality of Winnicott's texts, note their unscientific character and theoretical weakness. For example, Greenberg and Mitchell remarked that Winnicott's central themes "are generally presented in the form of evocative paradoxes that entice the reader playfully. The arguments are more discursive than tightly reasoned" (Greenberg & Mitchell, 1983, p. 189).

For his part, Jacobs, certainly supported by the absence of an unitary interpretation of Winnicott's thought, observes that although the name of Winnicott may be proverbial in the field of counselling,

> [...] his ideas attract little actual debate [...] within that related profession. [...]; if behaviourism [...] continues to have running battles with psychoanalysis, Winnicott does not attract any specific fire [...]. There may be reasons why there is little major criticism of his whole work. It is possible, for example, that the nature of his writing is such that debate is necessarily quite limited. He may have written prolifically, but he published little that was presented as a comprehensive theory [...]. There is no clear scheme in Winnicott, with the possible exception of *Human Nature*. (Jacobs, 1995, p. 98)

Rycroft, who is a prominent figure in the *Middle Group* laments the absence of a consistent theorisation in Winnicott's works. He concedes that the idea of a transitional reality "is perhaps the most important contribution made to psychoanalytic theory in the last thirty years" (Rycroft, 1985, p. 145). He nevertheless also states that "in spite of the occasional use of abstract nouns", Winnicott's theses are always:

> [...] a personal statement, too idiosyncratic to be readily assimilated into the general body of any scientific theory. He often sounds like a voice crying in a wilderness that is in fact inhabited, or like a visionary who is disguising himself as a thinker. (ibid., p. 144)

Finally, there are some who defend the existence of a profound originality in Winnicott with regard to his theory. In an even more radical way than Phillips, who, as we have seen, acknowledges the character of a break in Winnicott's thought with regard to traditional theory, Zeljko Loparic (2001b, 2006/2011) states that Winnicott's work introduces a new paradigm in the framework of psychoanalytical theory. In order to do so he starts from the idea that if psychoanalysis wishes to be scientific, then approximately in the same way as a mature factual science, it constitutes

> the framework within which *an activity of problem solving* develops that is similar to puzzles. The internal structure of this framework is characterised by a way of seeing the world and of talking about it that is shared by an institutionalised group and that is structured as a paradigm or a disciplinary matrix. (Loparic, 2006/2011, p. 29)

The notion of paradigm implied in it is that of Kuhn in his book *The Structure of Scientific Revolutions* (1970). Kuhn holds that a scientific discipline is defined by its "paradigms" and he already defines them in his first work on the issue as "universally recognized scientific achievements that for a time provide model problems and solutions to a community of practitioners" (Kuhn, 1970, p. viii). "A paradigm" consists of two kinds of paradigm. Paradigm I, composed of exemplary or paradigmatic problems, "concerning facts accessible in some form of experience (observation, experimentation, clinical practice) followed by their solutions" (Loparic, 2006/2011, p. 29). Paradigm II, also known as "disciplinary matrix" or "theoretical commitments", consists of the different theories which were formulated to solve exemplary problems. These theories are a) guideline generalisations, used as guides to the research in question; b) the ontological model of the studied domain; c) the methodological model and d) the values involved, including the epistemological ones: internal consistency, plausibility, etc. (cf. Loparic, 2006/2011, pp. 29–30). Paradigm II thus contains the group of hypotheses which serves as a theoretical basis for normal research, that is, for the resolution of problems in progress. Scientific research devotes itself to detecting and solving new problems and usually, the procedure consists of formulating the new problems on the lines of the exemplary or paradigmatic problems, solving them in the light of paradigmatic solutions. While it is capable of encompassing and solving the majority of the emerging problems, the paradigm (I and II) is maintained; however, as a large number of problems emerge which resist solution by an established paradigm, the so-called anomalous problems, a crisis begins which, in general, is slowly engendered. Little by little, research ceases to be "normal" and becomes "revolutionary", in the sense that now its effort is to find or to test a new paradigm capable of solving both the old problems and the new and anomalous ones.

According to Loparic, it is this situation of a change in paradigm that characterises Winnicott's work within psychoanalysis. To traditional psychoanalysis the exemplary problem is the Oedipus complex and the guiding theory is the theory of sexuality. The paradigmatic solution to the exemplary problem consists of the identification of the boy with the father, which means the resolution of the fear of castration and the abandonment of his intention of occupying the father's place as husband of the mother. "The new example proposed by Winnicott", the philosopher says,

> is the baby in the mother's lap, who needs to grow, that is, constitute a basis for continuing to exist and integrating itself into a unity. The most important guiding generalisation is the theory of maturational processes, of which the theory of sexuality is only a part. (Loparic, 2005, p. 314)

This is the new problem, which is anomalous for traditional psychoanalytical theory and refers not to issues of a pulsional order related to incestuous desire, but to the constitution of a sense of reality of the self and of the world. However, Loparic continues, besides altering the exemplary problem,

> Winnicott altered the disciplinary matrix as well. He rejected or significantly modified the use of fundamental concepts such as subject, object, object relation, pulsion (will, impulse), mental representation, mental mechanism, pulsional force. In their place and that of the theory of sexual development, he placed the theory of human development, as well as a series of new basic concepts to be used from that point onwards, in studying new and old problems. (Loparic, 2005, p. 314)

The attribution of the status of paradigmatic revolution to the psychoanalytical work of Winnicott is a polemical thesis of Loparic, surrounded by debate. For example, Roberto Graña, in the introduction to the 1997 Brazilian edition of *Thinking about Children* (1996a), disagrees with the philosopher, saying that this is a "statement which is difficult to maintain" (Graña, 1997, p. xi). Firstly, he says, because of the "inappropriateness of applying the Kuhnian method to the *Geisteswissenschaften*" and secondly, since Winnicott declared in many occasions that he was a Freudian psychoanalyst. Graña's first argument is incorrect, for the very reason that Freud himself declared that psychoanalysis is not a science of the spirit but a natural science.[19] Furthermore, although the main field to which Kuhn applies the notion of paradigm is that of natural sciences (physics, chemistry, biology, etc.) he maintains that *it can be equally applied to the social and human sciences*, with a difference: in these latter fields, the situation must be said to be pre-paradigmatic, since a paradigm I has not yet been established in an unambiguous way and research is seeking to do precisely this. In the field of the human sciences, however, if there is a science for which the paradigm has remained clear, it is psychoanalysis. Even if we were to consider psychoanalysis to be in a pre-paradigmatic situation, it is nevertheless important to read Kuhn when he says:

> [...] the members of all of the scientific communities, including schools of the "pre-paradigmatic" period, share the types of elements which I have collectively labelled as "a paradigm". What changes with the transition to maturity is not the presence of a paradigm but rather its nature. (Kuhn, 1970, p. 179)

In any case, the issue regarding the nature of Winnicott's contribution to psychoanalysis is a fertile discussion, which is still in progress. Graña's second argument concerning Winnicott's explicit affiliation to Freudian psychoanalysis is not convincing, since in addition to failing to resist an analysis of Winnicott's theoretical positions, as we will see in the current study, it refers to a declaration that was more political than theoretical. As Winnicott's thought evolved and he felt more free to express it, what we find is a highly critical analysis of Freud and Melanie Klein's positions, above all when it comes to the claimed breadth of the body of theory of these authors for understanding psychic disorders in general. This does not mean that Winnicott ceases to be a psychoanalyst but, believing psychoanalysis to be an evolving field of knowledge, he carries on with his task as researcher and modifies the theory in the light of new discoveries and from this perspective, he is indeed a follower of Freud.

Rogério Luz is another commentator on Winnicott who, without completely postulating a new paradigm, indicates the radical change that his work represents: "Winnicott introduces into psychoanalysis not only a new object, phenomenon or activity, but provokes a rearrangement of its field of problems and consequently, of its concepts" (Luz, 1989, p. 32).

Clarification of the overall vision of Winnicott's work

My starting point is the conviction that Winnicott's original contribution to psychoanalytical thought lies in the fact that he proposed a theory of the maturational processes of human beings and a theory of psychic disorders, especially psychoses, which are articulated internally and which are interconnected with each other. I also share the position of those who acknowledge that a series of Winnicott's concepts are radically new and extrapolate the available metapsychologies and even the philosophical tradition to which they belong, possibly announcing the emergence of a new paradigm for psychoanalysis as a whole. It is not my purpose to adduce the reasons why I accept this viewpoint. I shall limit myself to highlighting some aspects of Winnicott's procedure, not always noted, which prepare the way for the type of reading elaborated in this study. These observations concern forms of theorising practiced by him, in particular, (1) his conception of psychoanalysis and scientific work; (2) the dialogue which he maintains with the various areas of science; (3) his relationship with language; (4) the use that he makes of poetry and art in general; and finally, (5) the way in which he relates to non-scientific areas of knowledge, such as philosophy and theology (and religion, in general).

We shall initially look at aspects of his theoretical elaboration and in particular of his conception of scientific work. Winnicott always insisted on the fact that what he wrote derived from his own work and on how incapable he was of drawing up an inventory of an inheritance, of working from another person's conception. "My mind does not work that way", he affirmed (1945d, p. 145). In a letter of 1957 to Augusta Bonnard, he mentioned that it was of no importance to him whether or not he was the first to say a certain thing or whether it had already been said (cf. 1987b, p. 116) and also, "I'm not concerned either with being original or with quoting from other writers and thinkers (or even Freud)" (1968c, 193). The need to use his own language to elaborate his theories or as he put it, to formulate "my latest brain-child" in the most personal way is also well-known and has been stated on many occasions. This is undoubtedly due to the unusual freedom of thought that he practiced and of which he was an implacable defendant. His contemporaries are unanimous in affirming his extraordinary capacity to be himself, his aversion to dogmas or to any constraint on thinking.[20]

At the same time, he is the author who, by making explicit the fundamental paradox on which any access to reality is based, that the baby creates what he encounters, makes creativity pay tribute to tradition: "[…] in any cultural field it is *not possible to be original except on a basis of tradition*" (1967b, p. 134). When we are healthy, he says, we only create what we discover, that is, what is already there to be found. Even in the arts, "we cannot be creative into the blue unless we are having a solo experience in a mental hospital or in the asylum of our own autism" (1986h, p. 53). Creativity does not consist of an autistic invention, but "I mean seeing everything afresh all the time" (ibid., p. 41). Winnicott's originality does not come out of the blue and the same is true of scientific creativity; his ideas were forged from observation and within the debate with related areas: paediatrics, child psychiatry, and psycho-somatic medicine.[21] At the same time, his main interlocutor was traditional psychoanalysis. Winnicott always considered himself a psychoanalyst and acknowledged his debt to Freud and Klein on several occasions. Such acknowledgement is in full agreement with his conception of creativity. He states: "I am a product of the Freudian or psychoanalytic school. This does not mean that I take for granted everything Freud said or wrote" (1965i, p. 21).[22]

One of the aspects which Winnicott prised most highly in Freud's intellectual inheritance was the fact that the latter started a scientific approach to the problem of human development and created a method which allows for analysts to check the observations of others and contribute with their own (cf. 1965i, p. 21). A few years later, he would state that Freud gave us a method which we can use and which certainly leads us to something: "it's an objective way of looking at things and it's for people who can go to something without preconceived notions, which, in a sense, is science" (1989f, p. 574).

Winnicott leaves no doubts as to his choice of a scientific approach to the study of human development. Psychology, he stated as early as 1945, makes "no claim to priority in regard to the understanding of human nature, except in one respect: that is to say, in the making of this study a science" (1945b, p. 4). In the first part of *Human Nature*, we also find the formulation that the main objective of the book was to point out the ways in which emotional development was considered to be complex, albeit susceptible to investigation by scientific method (cf. Winnicott, 1988, p. 12).

As a student of human nature, however, with this conceived as essentially temporal, and in seeking to describe the stages of the maturational process, which refers to what is strictly personal in the human being, Winnicott nevertheless cannot accept any type of science and certainly does not accept the natural science to which Freud affiliated his psychoanalysis. What Winnicott rejects in the human sciences are the attempts to build closed systems or to reduce human life to physical entities or to quantifiable categories. He knows that such a science "boggles at the problem of human nature, and tends to lose sight of the whole human being" (1965f, p. 173). He also rejects the claim of a definitive solution for scientific problems. He manifests a singular indignation at Joan Rivière's declaration, in her Introduction to Melanie Klein's book, that the latter had produced an integrated theory which, while still in draft form, "nevertheless takes account of all psychical manifestations, normal and abnormal, from birth to death, and leaves no unbridgeable gulfs and no phenomena outstanding without intelligible relation to the rest" (1989b, p. 460). Winnicott remarks that this was: "A sentence which Melanie would have disallowed had she been truly a scientist" (idem).[23]

For him, there is the danger of science itself, when it is built on foundations which lead to the objectification of the human being and there is the danger of false science, or more precisely, of scientific praxis which is false, since instead of devoting itself to the ever greater clarification of its field of studies, it places itself in the service of "loyalties" and the preservation of power groups. All of this specifically legitimates the need *not to abandon* the task of

> […] making the study of human nature a science, a process characterized by observation of facts, by the building of theory and the testing of it, and by modification of theory according to the discovery of new facts. (1945b, p. 5)

In this sentence, Winnicott seems to indicate the need to construct a new manner of doing science, adapted to the study of human nature, albeit while maintaining the essential character of the scientific spirit. His work gives us a sample of how to do it and, in this sense, constitutes a legacy and a responsibility.[24] Maintaining what seems to him to be fundamental in Freud's creation, the fact that any transformation in a person occurs within a human relationship, Winnicott formulates new exemplary problems and places the procedures of observation and description at the service of the phenomena which emerge in this new environment of interrogation. Since the rigour of a science consists precisely of the fact that its methodologies and procedures are adapted to its object of study, it is to be expected that a science dedicated to the study of human nature will be governed by another criterion of objectivity and rigour. Objectivity in human questions cannot in any way follow the standard of research in the physical or natural sciences; we cannot conceive of the human being on the basis of categories formulated for the study of natural and measurable entities. The research material for a science of human nature "is essentially the human being … being, feeling, acting, relating and contemplating" (1965f, p. 175). Furthermore, objectivity, in this field, says Winnicott, "is a relative term because what is objectively perceived is by definition to some extent subjectively conceived of" (1971g, p. 88).[25]

The main thing to be preserved consists of the fact that in scientific research, the gap in knowledge is accepted as a challenge and does not lead the scientist to indulge in supernatural explanations. Ignorance is assumed, and around this, a research programme is devised. What matters to the scientist is to formulate questions; the answers which arise merely lead to new questions. Compared to the certainty of religion, it will be seen that science is completely different. "Religion replaces doubt with certainty. Science holds an infinity of doubt, and implies a faith. Faith in what? Perhaps in nothing; just a capacity to have faith" (1986c, p. 14).

In another text, he again emphasises that "the scientific approach to the phenomena of human nature enables us to be ignorant without being frightened, and without, therefore, having to invent all sorts of weird theories to explain away the gaps in knowledge" (1945b, p. 6). Psychoanalysis, he continues,

> […] turns out to be a fine new instrument by which human beings may study themselves and their interpersonal relationships; but it does remain an instrument of scientific research or a therapy, and it never makes a direct philosophical or a religious contribution. (1945b, p. 11)

In a text of 1948, on mentioning, from an historical perspective, some of the theoretical developments which followed the pioneer work of Freud, he states that now

> […] a highly complex theory of the emotional development of the human being has been worked out, so that with all our terrible and at the same time exciting ignorance, we now have useful working hypotheses, hypotheses, that is to say, that really work. There is now sufficient material available for attempts to be made to formulate things about infants which concern equally the psychiatrist and the children's physician, and I want to be one of those trying to say these things. (1948, p. 157)

The method which Winnicott recomends is essentially that of observing and recording phenomena in detail, testing new hypothesis within the perspective of the theory of personal development. We must not forget the example, as he states, of great masters of clinical medicine who loved to observe and to record, living in our minds and affections due to their belief in the value of carefully noting and collating small details (cf. 1969f, p. 255). In this regard, we should note, for example, that his much praised ability to observe and record what happened in his consultations with babies and their mothers, as well as in the clinical relationship with adults, was fed by two other capacities: that of being in actual personal contact with the individual whom he was treating and that of seeing phenomena which only became visible in the light of the theory of maturational processes. On account of the very nature of the phenomena which he studied, Winnicott was convinced that personal contact, far from going against the demands of rigour and objectivity of observation, was precisely what made them possible. These were the peculiarities which enabled him to describe aspects of human nature that had never been "seen" before. Perhaps without understanding the specific quality of Winnicott's clinical observation, but perceiving its result, the editors of his last book *Thinking about Children* (1996a) declared in the preface that

> [...] a striking feature of Winnicott's work was his great power of observation and description so that what he writes has an air of extraordinary familiarity—*one feels that one already has known what he reports all along*. (Shepherd, Johns, & Robinson, 1996a, p. xv; my italics)[26]

Another point which is convergent with what we have just outlined refers to the *sui generis* relation that Winnicott developed with language. In order to make explicit the phenomena that he intended to describe, Winnicott resorted to a language based on common language. In the introduction to the book *Through Paediatrics to Psychoanalysis* (1958a), Masud Khan asserts, not without a certain irony, that Winnicott

> [...] wrote as he spoke: simply and to relate. Not to incite conviction or indoctrinate. He made his idiom so much that of the ordinary cultured and common usage that everyone was illusioned into the make-believe that they have always known what he was saying. (Khan, 1975, p. xii)

In so proceeding, Winnicott often introduced concepts which were central to his theory, without showing a concern with defining, justifying, or providing a foundation for them through a conceptual abstraction. This is the case with "continuity of being", "feeling of real", "essential aloneness", "mutuality", "falling forever", etc. This does not imply that these concepts are lacking in analysable meaning, but rather that their sense must derive from the concrete situation, from the context in which they emerge. This, for example, is the case of "*good-enough* mother", where the "enough" cannot be explained in terms of rules of conduct and even less so is it quantifiable. On this point, Winnicott is incisive: the mother's knowledge derives from her ability to identify with the baby on the basis of her own experience of having been cared for; such knowledge cannot be learned from books or in lectures; regulating it is the same as destroying it, that is, depriving it of its main attribute, its relation to the personal nature and spontaneity of the mother. Defining his concepts by *use*, Winnicott's language is much more indicative than propositional. He allows the word itself to touch us; if this does not happen, it is no use explaining. It is more a question of a communication experience than the production of a verbal meaning intended for a purely intellectual understanding. He says, for example, that: "We can use words as we like, especially artificial words like counter-transference. A word like 'self' naturally knows more than we do; it uses us, and can command us" (1960a, p. 158).

The fact that the analyst, like the good enough mother, is affected by the patient is so intrinsic to the relationship that creating a concept to describe it appears to him to be totally artificial. Furthermore, on some occasions, in order not to misrepresent the phenomenon to be described or to violate it or cover it with a false and precipitated clarity, a certain degree of obscurity must be maintained. In a passage in his work in which a concept was particularly difficult to explain, Winnicott reflected that "just here one must allow obscurity to have a value that is superior to false clarification" (1989k, p. 240).

I would thus like to suggest that the singularity of Winnicott's language is not due solely to his freedom or need to be personal in everything that he did, but knowingly or not, to a well-established theoretical and methodological need, arising from his new perspective. The simplicity of Winnicott's language, at times poetic, is not literary charm, nor does his creativity reside in it; it is a need imposed by the phenomenon which he was able to see. When theorising about the achievements peculiar to the initial stages of development, Winnicott acknowledged that the language available in the context of psychoanalysis, and even in the human sciences, as well as within the framework of the philosophies that govern them, is not capable of addressing the specific nature of the phenomena which he intended to describe, without distorting them. In 1957, he had already stated that

> [...] a writer on human nature needs to be constantly drawn towards simple english and away from the jargon of the psychologist, valuable as this jargon may be in contributions to scientific journals. (1957a, p. 127)

Dealing with issues relating to human experience and not to a psychic apparatus, describing relations between persons and not between psychic agencies (*Instanzen*), indicating details of the mother/baby relation, in the "magic of intimacy" that governs it, Winnicott had to create another language. This is not merely a question of his idiosyncrasy, nor of neglecting descriptive rigour. It is a matter of extreme importance to know whether the language of metapsychology is adequate for describing the nature of human experience. His discussion with Freud and with metapsychology is not political, but methodological. With regard to Freudian psychoanalysis, we may perceive that Winnicott distinguishes two theories in Freud: an empirical one based on experience and another speculative one. These correspond to two types of language: the descriptive type, when Freud speaks of orality, anality, interests, rivalry of the boy with his father, etc.; and the language of metapsychology, which consists of abstract conceptual conventions, which he used to investigate clinical phenomena and to organise the results of those investigations: life and death pulsions, protophantasies, libido, cathexis, etc. Winnicott seems to accept Freud's descriptive theory very readily, while his profound suspicion regarding metapsychology is explicit. In a letter to Anna Freud, mentioning his tendency to say things in his own language instead of using the terms of metapsychology, he wrote:

> I am trying to find out why it is that I am so deeply suspicious of these terms. Is it because they can give the appearance of a common understanding when such understanding does not exist? Or is it because of something in myself? It can, of course, be both. (1987b, p. 58)

A philosophical benchmark for understanding and assessing Winnicott's difficulties with Freudian metapsychology can be found in Loparic's texts on the philosophy of psychoanalysis. Starting from his semantic interpretation of Kant's transcendental philosophy (Loparic, 2000c) and from the reconstruction of Kant's speculative method (Loparic, 1983) Loparic defends the thesis that: (1) Freud, as well as other members of the neo-Kantian School of Helmholtz, fall within the Kantian program of the critique of pure theoretical reason, (2) the basic concepts of Freudian metapsychology have the character of fictions introduced for heuristic reasons, (3) Freud's metapsychological propositions which employ these concepts are undecidable, (4) Freud's speculative method is a version of Kant's speculative method (Loparic, 1985). The philosopher writes:

> We find in Freud different series of observations that may serve to justify the *thesis of the impossibility of deciding about propositions that aim at determining the true nature of the unconscious.* They are all Kantian in inspiration. Firstly, Freud explicitly accepts the non-identity, established by Kant, between *the phenomenal world* given in unempirical experience and the *noumenal world* introduced by understanding, in order to satisfy the internal needs of its operation, in which Freud locates his unconscious [...] Furthermore, he accepts the Kantian thesis of the unknowability of the noumenal world, that is, the impossibility of deciding all of the propositions regarding the properties of noumenal objects [...]. In this way, Freud could only conclude that the problem of knowing what is the true nature of the unconscious is an insoluble one. (Loparic, 1985, p. 34)[27]

Loparic is not alone in adopting this position. In 1966, in a lecture to the British Psycho-Analytical Society, H. J. Home demarcated the theme of the article that he was going to present, saying that it was a philosophical text, which aimed to reflect on the following questions: what exactly does the psychoanalytical theory address and which types of theories can validly be constructed on the basis of it? Anticipating the conclusion, namely that psychoanalytical theory presents "serious logical difficulties, that many of its concepts are ill-defined and many terms in regular use for clinical description ambiguously employed" (Home, 1966, p. 42). Home affirms that the motivation for this study came to him from several scientific meetings with psychoanalysts and from his perplexity regarding the incomprehensibility of clinical articles, written in what was frequently called "technical language", and at what seemed to him to be "the philosophical naiveté of the theoretical papers" (ibid., p. 42). In order to illustrate this point, Home used a passage from Sandler's book "On the concept of superego", which states: "The two techniques of restoring a feeling of being loved (of increasing the level of libidinal cathexis of the self) [...]". Home comments: "The first part of this sentence seems to me completely comprehensible, the second part is, I believe, meaningless" (ibid., p. 42). One of the conclusions to be drawn from Home's article is the incapacity of metapsychological language, which is clearly metaphysical, to cope with the object of its study, the meaning of human experience.[28]

Continuing, Home writes that when, in 1954, Winnicott wanted to present his clinical experiences of regression to dependence, which could certainly be described by common use of language, as they indeed were, he realised that they did not fit either of the two already enshrined categories. "This meant", states Home, "that, strictly speaking, it could not exist as regression so far as psychoanalytic theory was concerned" (ibid., p. 46). That is, *there are human phenomena that cannot be encompassed by psychoanalytical theory, once it circumscribes its knowledge within the limits of the metapsychology language.* In this way, by insisting on using his own language to describe phenomena that had not yet been configured by the traditional theory and in stating, as it was mentioned before, that "a writer on human nature needs to be constantly drawn towards simple English", Winnicott was, even without knowing it, responding to a requirement imposed on thinking by the object of study itself.[29]

We should now highlight the importance ascribed by Winnicott to artistic modes of experience and to the poet who exists in all human beings, in performing the task of understanding human nature and its problems. Always preserving the value of scientific procedures in the building of knowledge, Winnicott never dismissed the fact that there are phenomena that can only be apprehended by the poetic gaze and voice. This refers in particular to his acknowledgement of a poetical truth about the human being, a truth that naturally is included in his theory of the individual personal maturation. Referring to the intimacy and the peculiar communication that develops within the unity baby–mother—central to the clinical work—he maintains that "it would be a pity to give examples lest this should seem to indicate that anyone but a poet could put into words that which has infinite variability" (1970a, p. 85).[30]

Manifesting a concern with the incessant eradication of poetic truth in current civilisation, Winnicott is aware of the danger that the power of technology represents for humankind, the objectifying power of which sweeps away all human sense from things, from the world, and from men and women themselves, with the aim of manipulating and controlling. In his text from 1969, "The Pill and the Moon", he recounts that one night while observing the moon, he raged at the recollection that there is an American flag stuck on it. The idea of a scientific exploration of the moon obscures "the waxing and waning of it and the majesty of it and the mystery" (1986i, p. 207). He continues: "if we can get back to the poetry and recover from the American landing on the moon, before it starts up on Venus, we might feel that there's some hope for civilization" (ibid).

At the same time, when he writes, Winnicott does not make poetry: at the most he places poetic truth at the service of knowledge. Moreover: at different points in his work, Winnicott imposed clear restrictions on a psychoanalytical work built exclusively on poetic truth, which can undoubtedly offer profound satisfaction and, he says, when an old truth encounters a new expression, there is an opportunity for a creative experience in terms of beauty. He nevertheless warns: it is very difficult to use poetic truth directly, since it is about feelings and not everybody feels the same with regard to a certain problem. In one of his most famous and important texts, "Fear of breakdown", he begins by stating that if there is any truth in what he is going to say in that article, the poets of the world would certainly have already addressed it. He nevertheless continues "[…] the flashes of *insight* that come in poetry *cannot absolve us from our painful task of getting step by step away from ignorance towards our goal*" (1974, p. 87; my italics).

For a student of human nature, the procedure is clear: it is about "moving step by step" as is proper to science, "the construction of a better, more accurate, and more serviceable theory of the emotional development of the individual human being" (1984f, p. 64). The scientific procedure "is not a matter of proving this or that by statistics", but instead "it is a matter of being free from knowing in advance. (Knowing in advance belongs to poetry)" (1996b, p. 236). Ivone Accioly Lins makes this point very well when she highlights that despite the evident affinity between Winnicott's ideas and the thought of the Romantic poets, "it would be a mistake to attribute the novelty of his conceptions only to this affinity" (Lins, 1997, p. 22). Unlike the poets, Winnicott was convinced of how necessary and painful the scientific task is and, Accioly continues, "although his research was animated by a poetic spirit, the type and the means of investigation were clinical and scientific" (Lins, 1997, p. 22).

Also with regard to intuition, generally so highly praised in him, Winnicott indicated the restrictions, especially in his classes for students in the field of health: "True intuition can reach to a whole truth in a flash (just as faulty intuition can reach to error) whereas in a science the whole truth is never reached" (1945b, p. 5). In this way, although we value this glimmer of truth that intuition can provide, we must always remember that "our feelings and our imaginings may get out of hand and may take us anywhere" (ibid., p. 5). There is also an ethical issue, in terms of professional responsibility, since intuitive understanding of human nature may prove unreliable as a guide in the field of social living.

> It might enable a doctor to be brilliantly understanding of a patient who was a thief, but unless the psychology of delinquency is studied as a science, intuitive understanding will not prevent doctors as well as other people from doing and saying all sorts of useless things when decisions have to be taken in a practical way, as, for instance, in a juvenile court. (ibid., p. 5)

Winnicott leaves no doubt about his position: in a lecture to paediatricians on child neurosis, he enumerates a few methods for treatment and says that he can "only stress that *intuition is not good enough in psychological practice*". Shortly afterwards, he asserts that "There *must* be those who dislike psychoanalysis, because of the fact that it studies human nature objectively; it invades the realms where previously belief, intuition, and empathy held sway" (1958k, p. 321). As a result of all of this, he concludes that

> […] what is important in science is a construction of a satisfactory road towards the truth. That is why a scientific training is so important for everybody; it enables you and me to test our own little bits of the world satisfactorily. (1945b, p. 5)

In 1946, in reply to a letter from Ella Sharp, Winnicott once again addressed the relation between psychoanalysis and art, stating that he was not sure whether he agreed with Sharpe's thesis that psychoanalysis is an art and that he preferred what he understood as the true psychoanalytical work, since in psychoanalysis, art occupies less space than technique based on scientific considerations (cf. 1987b, p. 10). Some years later, he would declare that the idea of psychoanalysis as art must gradually give way to a study of environment adaptation regarding to the regressions of patients, albeit while pointing out that "while the scientific study of environmental adaptation is undeveloped, then I suppose analysts must continue to be artists in their work" (1955b, p. 291). However, even if the psychoanalyst may be a good artist, "what patient wants to be someone else's poem or picture?" (ibid).

The therapeutic ability of the psychoanalyst, whose paradigm is the good enough mother clearly does not rest on purely intellectual knowledge, but above all on his personal sensitivity and ability to identify with the patient and understand his or her needs. However, apart from the fact that the analyst, unlike the mother, does not have twenty-four hours a day to be with the baby and to get to know him, he cannot count on the natural advantage of primary maternal concern. He may do better than the patient's own mother, but some humility is required in order to know that "[...] the clumsiness of the psycho-therapist as compared with the mother makes it inconceivable that regression to dependence even in a carefully controlled treatment is pleasurable" (1988, p. 159).

On the contrary, a period of regression to dependency requires that for a long period of time, analysts keep themselves within the strict limits dictated by the patient and, during this period, "the strain can be terrific" (1987b, p. 182). It is necessary, for example, to be prepared for the event which occurs when the patient, regressing to dependence, "goes mad" increasingly, while in search of the cure. In these cases, "if the analyst understands what is going on he or she is able to tolerate the very considerable tension that belongs to this kind of work" (1989q, p. 129). In this way although it is the patient who constantly teaches the analyst—who is capable of learning—about her own needs, as Winnicott points out, the analyst:

> [...] should be able to know, theoretically, about the matters that concern the deepest or most central features of personality, else he may fail to recognise and to meet new demands on his understanding and technique. (1989o, p. 169)

On account of all of this, in his specialised work and above all in cases of patients with difficulties of a schizophrenic type, the analyst "must have a working theory of the emotional growth of the personality" (1968c, p. 194), learning to see, listen and understand through it. "That theory", says Winnicott, "is always there in the background" (1954c, p. 114), serving to shed light on the phenomenon and guide imagination, sensitivity and intuition. Starting from the observation of facts, we need to continue developing the theory "to arrive at an accurate and valuable theoretical statement, without which we are stuck" (1996c, p. 212).

The theory of maturational processes should not be understood as a merely intellectual tool to be applied to each case. On the contrary, highlighting the way in which it participates in clinical practice, Winnicott points out, as has already been mentioned, that his only company when facing the unknown territory of a new clinical case, is the theory which he carries with him, which, in this way, became such a part of himself that he does not even need to think about it in conscious fashion. He simply sees through it. Shortly afterwards in the same text, Winnicott compares himself to a cello player, who first works on the *technique* and then actually begins to play the *music*, most certainly using the technique (cf. 1971c, p. 6).

In an article from 1950, Winnicott expresses the hope that babies who have been offered a satisfactory presentation of external reality by their mothers, in small doses and in a comprehensible way, will grow up and develop "to be capable of making a scientific approach to phenomena", even being able to "carry a scientific method into the study of human affairs" (1965i, p. 28). This task is necessary since if what is good and natural in human nature and in the management of human beings in development is to be protected from being squashed out by science, it can only come about "by an extension of scientific inquiry into the whole field of human nature" (1965i, p. 28).

Another point to be considered refers to the fact that in order to clarify points with which he is dealing, Winnicott repeatedly refers his readers to philosophical and theological theses and even to religious and mystical practices. Some of these concepts effectively require an approximation to philosophy and many of them constitute fundamental philosophical themes.[31] Sometimes this occurs amid descriptions which seem to be restricted to the simplest everyday life. At a certain point, for example, Winnicott describes how the support of the maternal ego facilitates the organisation of the baby's ego. "Eventually", he says, "the baby becomes able to assert his or her own individuality and even to feel a sense of identity." And later: "There is the beginning of everything, and it gives meaning to very simple words like *being*" (1987e, p. 11). This is the text highlighted by Loparic (1995b) in his article "Winnicott and post-metaphysical thought". His philosophical reading leads him to perceive that,

> [...] suddenly, in a context which appeared only to concern mothering, the problem of identity emerges, which is one of the most difficult in philosophy. Moreover, the idea also arises that in the two-in-one of baby and mother, semantic questions are decided. Not the semantics of nipples and milk, nor even of the good and bad breast, but a semantics that metapsychology ignores, the semantics of the simple words, such as the word "being". Everything occurs as if, even for a philosopher thinking seriously, that is, not academically, about what the word "being" means, its original meaning would only be determined by a return to the original simplicity of the human being, initially experienced in the intimacy of the relationship between mother and baby. (Loparic, 1995b, p. 47)

As we have seen in Home's article, the description of what happens in the intimacy of the peculiar baby–mother relation cannot be made in an abstract language, built for dealing with systems. Winnicott accomplishes the not at all easy task of formulating his theme conceptually, without "insulting the delicacy of what is preverbal, unverbalised and unverbalisable, except perhaps in poetry" (1967a, p. 151).

All of the highlighted points deserve detailed analysis, although this is not what we intend to offer here; they were only enlisted in order to open the way and to outline the framework of interpretation. In the light of what has been set forth, we can only regard Winnicott as a scientific thinker. If this were not the case, it would lead us to an explicit contradiction with his text. On the other hand, we must acknowledge that his conception of scientific theorisation does not fit without further ado into the commonly held conceptions of what scientific work might be. This should not be understood, as the divergent interpretations mentioned here do, as a sign of lack of interest in scientific theorisation, of theoretical weakness, of inclination towards the poetic, etc. It instead means that in addition to his other scientific contributions, Winnicott introduced innovative proposals for the very way in which psychoanalytical knowledge is constituted.

It is perhaps also for this reason that some authors maintain, as we have seen, that his work constitutes a paradigm shift in the field established by Freud, including the form of theorisation. The paradigm shift frequently implies a change both in the scientific criteria which define a scientific discipline as a body of knowledge, and in the philosophical framework into which this body of knowledge is inserted. It is this direction that Rodman seems to tread, in the introduction to the book that assembles Winnicott's correspondence, when he writes that:

> Freud the great system builder probably meant less to Winnicott than Freud the originator of a method to plumb the human soul. One has the sense that Winnicott did not set his sights on Truth with a capital T, but on truths that would not stay still, the truth that is contained in the continuous interplay of people. He did not seem to require what Nietzsche has called "metaphysical solace", of the sort one may get, for example, from a convincing philosophical system. Yet this feature of his thought constituted a kind of philosophy in itself. (Rodman, 1987, p. xxvii)

On this point Rodman appears to align with Loparic when the latter states that Winnicott's theory of personal development constitutes a deliberate attempt to break with the metaphysics embedded in the language of Freudian metapsychology and for that reason, in the central body of traditional psychoanalysis.

In summary, if Winnicott certainly was not a "systematic thinker", he did not avoid the effort of articulating his thought internally. What characterises his thought, apart from its *total rejection of the objectification of the human being*, is absolutely not the rejection of any theorisation, but of *theories that are closed, definitive and unquestionable, susceptible to transformation into dogmas.* It is from this aversion that his much vaunted anti-dogmatism derived. Winnicott did not permit schools to develop around himself, since he understood that they tend towards proselytising and political games, to the detriment of a reflection based on experience. He even feared that some of the terms he created would become empty "Winnicottian" *slogans*, or impersonal applications of his conceptual findings, without the participation of the psychoanalyst's creativity. We can also observe in him a deep mistrust of abstract conceptualisations, unrelated to experience, which retreat from a commitment to life's intimate truth. We should not forget that his rejection of closed, abstract systems did not prevent him from seeking original theoretical paths, independent of those of Freud and Melanie Klein, rejecting traditional concepts that seemed unacceptable to him, from outlining his theoretical field with well-defined conceptual frontiers and from defending it effectively.

Notes

1. Until early 1960s, the expression most frequently used by Winnicott to refer to his central theme and theory was "emotional development". He took great care to clarify that the development which he was interested in did not concern just the growth of body and mental functions, but in the first place their integration in one individual person. In a paper published in 1960, Phyllis

Greenacre used the expression "maturational processes" in her considerations regarding the parent–infant relationship. She was not the first or the only one to use the expression, but the fact that she emphasised the role of maternal contact and care in these processes appealed very much to Winnicott. The point that interested him was not exactly that of Greenacre's. He nevertheless realised that this was the expression which he needed to make more accurate what he understood by "development": that it consists of several integrated maturational processes, and that the integration requires a facilitating environment in order to take place. Maturational processes thus imply dependence. Not only do we find Winnicott referring to his theory of "maturational processes" more and more frequently from 1960 onwards, but he also included the expression in the title of his very important book *"The Maturational Processes and the Facilitating Environment"*, published in 1965. In attempting to preserve the specific meaning of the language of Winnicott, I have chosen to name my study "Winnicott's Theory of Maturational Processes". However, I shall follow Winnicott and use the expressions "emotional or personal development" and "maturation" or "maturational processes" as synonymous.

2. Besides affirming on many occasions and throughout his work, that the theory of maturational processes is a central feature of his thought, Winnicott uses the decisive expression "backbone" in 1984e, p. 184.
3. Please note that all the quotations without an author's name are from Winnicott.
4. The procedure of text reading outlined here is that of the classical hermeneutical method, introduced by Schleiermacher in his reading of the Scriptures and restated by Dilthey for the study of Human Sciences in general. In Heidegger's early works and in Gadamer, Hermeneutics is raised to the condition of descriptive procedure par excellence. On all issues related to the method, cf. Hans Georg Gadamer (1976), especially the second section of Part Two.
5. I shall call traditional psychoanalysis the one represented by Freud and Melanie Klein, whose work may be considered as the matrix for that discipline. The naming is owed to Winnicott himself, who particularly dwelled on the discussion with these authors, referring to both their work with the expression "traditional", "classical" or "orthodox". Cf. Winnicott, 1969d, 1970b.
6. In a text from 1967, discussing his theoretical trajectory, Winnicott mentions that his view, constituted along the 1920s and 1930s while he worked as a paediatrician and started his psychoanalytical training, was reformulated in the 1940s when, he affirms in another text: "[...] I began to have my own way of stating the essential stages of the intertwined physical and emotional development of the human infant" (1968a, p. 218). Today, however, the historical perspective of the entirety of his work allows us to affirm that it was only from 1960 onwards, the year of Melanie Klein's death, that Winnicott felt himself freer to expose the new orientation of his thought clearly and incisively. Surely, the texts written in the 1940s already introduce a conceptualisation of his own, related to aspects of human nature that had not been considered by traditional psychoanalysis. However, because his ideas were not well established or for political reasons, or both, he expressed them timidly or, as Jan Abram puts it (1996, p. 1) "obliquely", sometimes even denying the originality that characterised them.
7. The only clear mention from others in this respect is found in the introduction to the first part of *Deprivation and Delinquency*, written by the organisers of the work: Clare Winnicott, Ray Shepherd and Madeleine Davis. (cf. Winnicott, C., Shepherd, & Davis, 1984).
8. I shall only mention the works which aim to introduce Winnicott's thought as a whole, leaving aside books or articles that linger over one or another aspect of his work.
9. The examples are restricted to the works in existence at the time of the first edition of this book, in 2003. There would be other references to be made today certainly.

10. This historical perspective does not appear even with reference to the development of Winnicott's work. In Chapter One, the section "The evolution of the theory", the authors, having already in hand most of the material that would only appear in public at a later date, refer only to the evolution from Winnicott's admiration of Darwin, while the former was still a student, to his discovery of psychoanalysis; from his fascination with Freud and then with Melanie Klein to his criticism of the Kleinian theory of jealousy. No reference is made to the gradual formulation of the theory of personal development, to the slow elaboration of the concepts of subjective object, of self and false self, to the new way of formulating the concepts of subjective object and object objectively perceived as respectively being and doing, to the last findings about destructiveness in terms of object usage, etc.
11. J. Kalmanovitch was the French translator of Winnicott's work *Maturational Processes and the Facilitating Environment.*
12. A more detailed analysis of Jan Abram's book may be found in the reviews by Dias, 2001 and by Bogomoletz, 2001.
13. In his text on psycho-somatic disorders (1966) and throughout the work, Winnicott uses the term "psycho-somatic" with a hyphen, to indicate that this compound expression is necessary to distinguish two domains of the whole person, the psyche and the soma, which cannot be reduced to each another, but through the specific tendency which characterises human nature, tend towards integration. This integration is not automatic and only takes place if there is environmental facilitation. It is an achievement of maturity. The hyphen, says the author, both unites and separates the two aspects of human nature; it is not a good sign when it merely separates them.
14. Cf. Winnicott, 1953a, p. 223.
15. According to Winnicott, when the care is good enough it is not the breast which makes the movement, imposing contact, but rather the baby, who by making the spontaneous gesture, encounters the breast, creating it. There are many examples of this kind of assimilation, which are equated in the same language and obscures the originality of Winnicott's proposals. In the same work, the authors, who are completely indifferent to Winnicott's insistence on the fact that reality is subjective and not internal at the beginning of life, named the next item of Chapter Two "From internal reality to external reality". A current way of assimilating Winnicott into the traditional theory without facing the questions that arise from his new conceptions, as if they belonged to the same theoretical horizon or, as Loparic puts it, to the same paradigm, is to say that Winnicott complements one single analytical theory, of which Freud would have described the more advanced cases, Melanie Klein, the more primitive disorders and Winnicott, those even more primitive. I shall attempt to show that this thesis is indefensible.
16. Cf. Pontalis' interview with Anne Clancier, in Clancier & Kalmanovitch, 1987, p. 143.
17. Some of Winnicott's commentators, defending the "free" interpretation of his thought, that is, without paying greater attention to what he actually wrote or defended, claim to be supported by a statement of Masud Khan in the preface to *Collected Papers: Through Paediatrics to Psychoanalysis.* Mentioning that he had never met someone "so inevitably himself" as Winnicott, Khan affirms that this is what allowed him to be multiple, and for everyone "to have his *own* Winnicott." If this was true, however, besides being inevitable with regard to Winnicott as a person, it is certainly not with regard to his theory, which he consistently defended whenever it was an object of distortion. Cf. among other examples, 1963a, p. 255/256, 1987b, letters 60, 74, 82, 89, and 125.
18. Cf. D. Widlöcher's interview to Anne Clancier, in Clancier & Kalmanovitch, 1987, p. 148.
19. Cf. Freud, 1933a (lectures 34 and 35) and 1940b.
20. Cf., in particular, the letter dated November 1952 to Melanie Klein (1987b, p. 33).

21. As a psychoanalyst and paediatrician, Winnicott had long debates with medical psychiatry, paediatrics, and academic psychology, spread throughout his works, on various themes, such as human nature, the relation between mind and body, human growth and the issue of health and illness. Several moments of this debate are the subject of a detailed analysis in Chapter One.
22. To say that Winnicott was influenced or that he started from one idea or another, is not the same as to state, for example, like Adam Phillips does, that "his work, in fact, cannot be understood without reference to Klein" (Phillips, 1988, p. 9) or, as Luiz Meyer affirms: "In fact, we need to think about Winnicott starting from Melanie Klein" (Meyer, 1994, p. 83).
23. Cf. Winnicott, 1989b. In this same text, Winnicott refers to the fact that scientific discussion and the advancement of knowledge are often prevented not only by our "fear of doubts", but also by the play of "loyalties", frequent in groups inclined towards sectarianism, which, being more concerned with power than with the true discussion of ideas, stagnate thought and inhibit free expression. In this respect, cf. also Winnicott's letter to Melanie Klein, November 1952, in 1987b, p. 33.
24. Often in his work, Winnicott urges psychoanalysts to go on researching and increasing their understanding of phenomena which can be seen in the light of the theory of the maturational processes. "The analyst", he affirms in 1967, "has a great responsibility for the teaching of theory and for the development of theory according to what the patients are all the time trying to teach us [...]" (1996b, p. 252). The theory, Winnicott says, is too complex and "there are great gaps in our understanding" (1989q, p. 119); hence, any study which clarifies the nature of the infant at the time of birth and the first feed is welcome. (cf., 1988, p. 150).
25. It is interesting to note that the need both of a new science and the rigour that must characterise it finds a parallel in Heidegger. In the *Zollikon Seminars* (1987), addressing a group of doctors and psychiatrists interested in finding another way (not the scientific-natural one) of thinking about human issues related to the practice of their profession, Heidegger affirms that the rigour of a science resides in the fact that it corresponds to its object both in its project and in its method. However, he says, "Yet not every rigorous science is necessarily an exact science. Precision is merely a specific form of the science's rigour, for precision exists only where the object is posited as something that can be calculated before hand. But if there are matters that resist calculability due to their nature, then any attempt to measure them according to the method of an exact science is inappropriate" (Heidegger, 1987/2001, p. 132). Some time afterwards, bearing in mind the project of edifying a science of care for the man who falls ill, in the light of existential analytics, Heidegger would say: "Science means the systematic ordering of interpreted experience. Each science is rigorously bound to its subject domain, but everything rigorous does not involve exactitude *[Exaktheit]* in a [natural science's] calculative sense. The unifying pole in psychotherapeutical science is the existing human being" (Heidegger, 1987/2001, p. 207).
26. By emphasising Winnicott's profile as a scientist, the editors of the book *Thinking about Children*, neglected the fact that the science valued by him must not be understood in the terms of positivist or naturalistic science, but must be adapted to the study of human nature (cf. Shepherd, Johns, & Robinson, 1997).
27. Loparic also pointed out that Freud was familiar with the work of Ernst Mach, whose empiricism continued many aspects of Kant's criticism (cf. Loparic, 1984 & 1985). Details of the relationship between Freud and Mach were explained by Loparic in "Freud: contemporary of Brentano and Mach," a lecture delivered at the colloquium "Vienna in the beginning of the Century: a paradigm of modernity" (CLE, Unicamp, November 1985).

28. In a passage from *Zollikon's Seminars,* Heidegger says: "the whole starting point within the psychic and the point of departure from a consciousness is an *abstraction* and a *nondemonstrable construct [eine nicht ausweisbare Konstruktion].* The relationships of a thing to the surrounding world *[Umwelt]* do not require explanation; they must simply be seen [in a phenomenological sense]" (cf. Heidegger, 2001, p. 162).
29. Although Winnicott did not clarify exactly what he understood by that, he knows that the metapsychology is metaphysical. He says: "Freud was able to develop the theory on which psychoanalysis is based very far indeed in his own lifetime, and this theory is usually called metapsychology (on the analogy with metaphysics)" (1986c, p. 15).
30. Ivone Accioly Lins points to the influence that English poets such as Wordsworth and Keats exercised on Winnicott's thought. In a passage from her article, she wrote: "Through the notion of 'negative capacity', Keats highlights the capacity to remain in uncertainty, in mystery, in doubt, without the 'irritating search for the facts or the rationale, that is, without the irritable flight to explanatory or scientific systems. Winnicott asks for the paradox to be tolerated and respected, instead of being resolved by intellectual processes" (Lins, 1997, p. 21).
31. As in the case of science, it is not any philosophy that addresses the questions raised by Winnicott's thought. The thinker who, in my view, favours the understanding of Winnicott's work the most, and who offers a philosophical foundation for some of his fundamental concepts, is Martin Heidegger, especially in his first phase, of *Being and Time* (1974). It is not the purpose of this study to explain the possible approximations between Winnicott's thought and that of Heidegger, and still less to apply Heidegger to Winnicott. It is nevertheless difficult, when studying Winnicott, not to observe Heideggerian resonances. Heidegger's ontology of finitude will be hence a background for the examination of certain aspects of Winnicott's thought which could not otherwise be understood by the traditional theory of psychoanalysis or philosophy. I shall mention it occasionally, when it appears opportune to me, in order to facilitate the understanding of the concept. Such approximation is entirely my responsibility, and is corroborated by the philosopher Zeljko Loparic, who has since developed a series of works around this fertile affinity (cf. Loparic, 1995a, 1995b, 1998, 1999b, 1999c, 2001). After having conceived this link, I found it in the book *De l'enfant à l'adulte* (1979), by the French psychiatrist Georges Amado. His interpretation of Winnicott and Heidegger, as well as the approximation that he made between them nevertheless diverge from my own to such an extent that I ultimately have not used his work in the context of this book. There is no evidence that Winnicott ever read Heidegger. The only possible proximity, highly indirect, is that Winnicott was R. Laing's supervisor before the latter went down the route of anti-psychiatry that was clearly influenced by Sartre. Adam Phillips, biographer of Winnicott and commentator on his work, states that the *Middle Group* was "obliquely influenced by existentialism" (Phillips, 1988, p. 11), without providing any further information. It would appear that this existentialism refers to the current created by Sartre in France. Nor there is any sign of Sartre in Winnicott's work; indeed, Sartre was not a follower of Heidegger, even if he wished to have us believe so. Moreover, Heidegger always rejected the epithet of existentialism for his philosophy.

CHAPTER ONE

Winnicott and the debate with related areas

Historical aspects of Winnicott's intellectual background

In examining Winnicott's conception of psychic health and illness in general, and of psychoses in particular, it is important to highlight some aspects of his professional and intellectual life that strongly influenced his theoretical positions. It will be equally useful to review the implicit or explicit debate within his work with the related areas of psychiatry, academic psychology, and traditional psychoanalysis. We may perceive the trend in the evolution of his thought through which certain concepts emerged and were consolidated as responses to the conceptions of his time which he judged to be inadequate and even unacceptable, starting with the general outlines of this debate.

At several points, Winnicott refers to the importance for his thought of his medical training. On the one hand, he had the obvious advantage of medical knowledge, which allowed him to identify clinical states with an active physical factor, which generated secondary psychological symptoms, or which allowed him to determine that a sick child was not suffering from a physical disorder, which indicated a psychological disturbance or a depression in the mother which manifested itself as an excessive concern for the child. Probably, however, his greatest debt to his medical training and practice lay in his clarity about what *not* to think or do in treating someone's health. Having lived among paediatricians and psychiatrists, Winnicott experienced the inadequacy of thinking about health and illness in purely organicist terms at first hand. He seems to have realised at a very early stage that health, and even more importantly, the feeling of being alive, could not be reduced to the effective functioning of the body and its organs and that the separation of the physical from the psychic was intellectually possible, but highly artificial.

In 1920, during his medical training, Winnicott was already firmly convinced of the impossibility of diagnosing disorders of relevance to paediatrics without considering their psychological aspects. While he was still a student, he encountered a work on Freud by the Swiss pastor Oskar Pfister and was delighted with the possibility offered by psychoanalysis of approaching psychic illness and somatic disorders from a predominantly psychological viewpoint. In a letter of 1919 to his sister Violet, he enthusiastically describes his discoveries regarding the Freudian theory of the psyche (cf. 1987b, p. 1). In 1923, he became an assistant doctor at the Paddington Green Children's Hospital, a position he held for forty years.[1] Having decided to include psychoanalysis in his training, he began analysis with James Strachey in the same year, which would last for a decade. The clinical care at the hospital gradually evolved from paediatrics to child psychiatry with an analytical orientation.

In the paediatric practice, carried out in terms of child psychiatry, Winnicott succeded in verifying that most of the problems which brought mothers with their babies and children to a clinic were due to primitive emotional disorders. Furthermore, he observed that not only children but also physically healthy babies could already be emotionally ill during the first weeks of life. He was impressed by the precocity of the disorders and by the importance of psychic factors in their emergence; at the same time, the nature of these factors was not yet clear to him and in approaching psychoanalysis, he sought the field *par excellence* for investigating them. He indeed located them, albeit with the proviso that he would very soon realise that he did not agree with what the established traditional theory understood as psychic.

The discovery of the existence of these precocious emotional disorders decisively influenced the evolution of his analytical thinking. As a result of this finding, Winnicott could never be persuaded of the centrality of the Oedipus complex proposed by Freudian psychoanalysis. In 1967, during a lecture in which he presented a sort of intellectual autobiography to his analyst colleagues, he noted:

> When I came to try and learn what there was to be learned about psycho-analysis, I found that in those days we were being taught about everything in terms of the 2-, 3-, and 4-year-old Oedipus complex and regression from it. It was very distressing to me as someone who had been looking at babies—at mothers and babies—for a long time (already ten to fifteen years) to find that this was so, because I knew that I'd watched a lot of babies start off ill and a lot of them become ill early. (1989f, p. 574)

Marked by this evidence, Winnicott's theoretical efforts moved in the direction of clarifying what happens to babies at the very outset of life and the specific nature of the difficulty faced by or afflicting them.[2] In 1935, at Strachey's suggestion, he contacted Melanie Klein, who was already known for her interest in the more primitive anxieties of childhood. Regarding the study by Klein as being extremely important, Winnicott followed the path initiated by her, becoming her supervisee between 1935 and 1940 or 1941.[3] He soon realised that Klein knew a great deal and much more than he did about the topic and even during subsequent phases, when he decisively distanced himself from Klein's theoretical line, he always affirmed that he had learned much from her. There had nevertheless been theoretical differences between them from the start, which gradually deepened and became clearer as the basic conceptual elements of his theory became more precise, ultimately revealing a fundamental incompatibility between their respective theories. We shall examine some of these conceptual differences in greater detail below.

It was nevertheless during this period, at the end of the 1930s, that another professional experience decisively influenced the theoretical direction of his thought. During the Second World War, Winnicott was appointed psychiatrist-consultant to the Government Evacuation Scheme of one reception area in the UK and, according to Clare Winnicott, who was a member of his team as a social worker, this position had a profound effect on him, since he found himself facing a large scale and concentrated disruption of households and a massive disintegration of family life, allowing him to observe the effects of separation and loss on children and adolescents. In addition to the global situation, there was also the fact that the children for whom Winnicott became responsible were exactly those who, having already presented difficulties at home before the war, required special arrangements and could not be introduced into ordinary households which would "adopt" them, in accordance with the evacuation plans. Winnicott further observed that for such children, war was not only secondary but beneficial, as they found themselves removed from an intolerable situation in their own homes, for which they had not found an exit and were placed in a new situation, in which they could possibly obtain help. This was the experience that provided Winnicott with material for formulating his theory on delinquency and character disorders, clinical manifestations included in what he termed the *antisocial tendency*. From this point onwards, certain specific theoretical aspects of an as yet incipient theory of maturational processes were gradually outlined with greater clarity, with these relating to the importance of the environment in the aetiology of psychic disorders.

Until this point, character disorders such as delinquency and juvenile violence were seen by psychoanalytic theory as manifestations of the anxiety or guilt resulting from the inevitable unconscious ambivalence between love and hate, from the conflict which arises when the desire to destroy is specifically directed at the loved person. If the guilt cannot be repaired or sublimated, the individual is compelled to act out so as to give it a concrete outline. The aetiology of delinquency basically consisted of an intrapsychic conflict. For Winnicott, data from experience again led towards another hypothesis, namely, that the environmental factor was aetiologically decisive in these issues, with this undoubtedly already a tendency of his thought. This becomes clear, for example, in Winnicott's early texts from the 1930s, in which he describes several paediatric cases treated during the 1920s, for the elucidation of which he was already starting to use psychoanalytical theory. Although these articles point out unconscious conflicts that could form the origin of particular physical disorders, he did not fail to demonstrate the importance of environmental factors in the aetiology of the problem.[4] In 1967, when presenting a retrospective of his intellectual trajectory to his colleagues at the British Psycho-Analytical Society, Winnicott referred to the characteristic position of traditional psychoanalysis of emphasising internal factors and neglecting environmental aspects; he noted that for ten or fifteen years, psychoanalysts were the only ones who accepted the existence of anything other than the environment and that although everybody claimed that the delinquency of a particular boy was a consequence of his father's alcoholism, etc., psychoanalysts continued to attribute the problems to the constitution of the boy and to research into his internal conflicts (cf. 1989f, p. 577).[5] On several occasions, Winnicott tried to talk to Melanie Klein and to some Kleinians about the environmental factor, met with complete disinterest, if not suspicion. Soon afterwards, he stated that anyone interested in the care of children ran the risk of being considered "traitors to the cause of the internal processes" (1965h, p. 126).

In 1945, four years after leaving Klein's supervision, Winnicott wrote the article "Primitive emotional development", in which he made a number of statements indicating that he had decided to follow his own path. While he had always been interested in the child patient, he stated that he had decided to study psychosis and that he now had much to add to the current theories and "perhaps this paper may be taken as a beginning" (1945d, p. 145), that is, the beginning of the development of his own theory. In order to present his contribution, he nevertheless had to prepare the ground and would hence try "to describe *different types of psychoanalysis*" (ibid., my italics). At this point, Winnicott already seemed to be aware that both the Freudian version and the Kleinian revision of traditional psychoanalysis, which sought to cover psychoses, were incapable of dealing with the type of problem present in these serious disorders, especially those of a schizophrenic nature, which required an adjustment to the theory.

The debate with paediatrics

During the 1930s, as his psychoanalitical training progressed, Winnicott undertook to persuade paediatricians to abandon certain procedures resulting from a merely organicist background and to learn about psychological aspects in evaluating disorders in children. Although traditional psychoanalysis was his main point of reference over the whole of his intellectual life, Winnicott never ceased to address paediatricians, obstetricians, nurses, and nursery specialists in order to alert them to certain discoveries, which seemed to be essential to him, regarding child care and the implementation of health. During this period, he wrote several articles, as a paediatrician to paediatricians, in which he presented the emotional disorders which could form the basis of certain clinical situations typical of childhood and urged specialists to ensure that they were prepared to investigate the psychological motivations of such disorders.[6]

Winnicott was familiar with his potential readers and the traditional conceptions of illness and health which had dominated medical theories and practices since the start of the modern era. It was not only true that paediatrics and child psychiatry concerned themselves unquestioningly with their respective and traditionally separate fields, the body and the mind, but both areas also represented recent specialisations in medicine and general psychiatry which were still in the process of consolidating their specific characters. In addition, physical medicine had always tended towards a study of the classification of diseases, regardless of the age at which these occurred. Paediatrics became a necessity and was established as a specialist discipline in the mid-nineteenth century, when it became clear that there are morbid states specific to each age group and diseases typical of childhood. Even when syndromes are common to both childhood and adulthood, age imposes a peculiar characteristic from the perspective both of the etiological circumstances and of the clinical aspect.

At the same time, paediatrics limited itself to the physical and physiological aspects of growth. The paediatrician was a somatist whose specialisation was above all in terms of physiology. It was very hard, Winnicott observed in 1958, to find a paediatrician who did not restrict himself to the physical aspect. His background obliged him, for example, to be aware of the mental illnesses deriving from the rubella contracted by the mother during the second month of pregnancy, of orthopaedic malformations, of blood incompatibility between the mother and the baby, or of the damage caused to the meninges as a result of a delayed birth, etc. In the 1950s, many things had already changed in paediatrics theory and practice. These modifications, which included an incipient interest in the psychological aspects of development, were due in part to progress in research, to public sanitation, and to a general improvement in living conditions, which released doctors from a complete dedication to the study and treatment of primary diseases. Indeed, Winnicott conceded, until that point much specialised work had been necessary. In the mid-nineteenth century, he reported, the situation was even worse and the urgent task for the whole pioneer generation of paediatricians in the United Kingdom was to ensure an appropriate classification of the various physical illnesses peculiar to childhood and to try to eradicate them:

> In those days there was not much time or place for the consideration of health as such, nor for the study of the difficulties that beset the physically healthy child through the fact of growing up in a society that is composed of human beings. (1988, p. 9)

This quotation includes one of the main elements of Winnicott's conception of health and illness, a topic of his discussion with the entire medical field, from which important theoretical positions derived: the idea that health is a complex state which carries its own demands and must be conceived in its own right. Both in paediatrics and in psychiatry, health is generally conceived as the absence of illness, with Winnicott finding this negative definition grossly inadequate. On the other hand, illness was regarded as an evil to be eradicated. In the article "A note on normality and anxiety", Winnicott held that although from a purely physical viewpoint any deviation from health could be regarded as abnormal, "[...] it does not follow that physical lowering of health due to emotional strain and stress is necessarily abnormal" (1931b, p. 3). Reporting the case of a boy aged two and a half who had a strong adverse reaction to the birth of a brother, Winnicott stated that if the baby had not been born, the child would have been spared but would nevertheless have missed out on a real experience at an appropriate age. Such an occurrence, he continues, "justifies the statement that it can be more normal for a child to be ill than to be well" (ibid., p. 4).

The quotation highlighted above not only indicates the need to consider health as a state with its own profile but also contains the statement which permeates the whole of Winnicott's thought and has more extensive implications than may be apparent at first sight, namely, that, from the outset, *life itself is difficult* and the task of living, of continuing to be alive, and of maturing is a permanent struggle. It is thus necessary to study the difficulties that beset the physically healthy child through the fact of growing up in a society that is composed of human beings (1988, p. 9).

Furthermore, although paediatrics and child psychiatry began to take account of the psychological aspect of these phenomena and their specific character according to the stage of development, all of this refers to childhood from when children can already speak and not to babies. Neither specialisation viewed the baby as a human being capable of emotional states and of being affected by the environment. At birth, it was seen merely as an organism. Despite having observed babies becoming ill precociously, Winnicott himself admitted to having taken a long time to see them as human beings. He became capable of this through his own analysis, stating that this was indeed the principal result of his first five years of analysis with Strachey. In 1957, the author stated that he had observed an evolution in the attitude of health specialists towards babies and small children. Perhaps, he said, parents had considered the baby as a person for longer than specialists had done, sometimes seeing in him much more than was actually there, a potential little man or woman. This had initially been neglected and even rejected by science and, for a long time, children were considered as beings that were hardly human until they started to speak, but that recently, "it has been found that infants are indeed human, though appropriately infantile" (1957d, p. 107).

The contribution of psychoanalysis to this evolution had been decisive. Around the end of the Second World War, many research studies were being conducted on the normal emotional development of babies and children of different ages. This entire advance, Winnicott noted, was attributable to Freud, who proved, with the theory and treatment of neurotic disorders, that the analyst reaches the child in the adult. Winnicott stated that he had never abandoned paediatrics, since he understood that child psychiatry with a psychoanalytical orientation was an intrinsic part of it (cf. 1988, p. 1). His frequent assimilation of child psychiatry and psychoanalysis was due to the fact that the former has found its main stimulus during the second half of the twentieth century, in such research studies with a psychoanalytical orientation.

Convinced that psychic health is established in the early days of childhood and that as soon as the baby is born, he is already a human being, thrown like all of us to the task of living, Winnicott was concerned with advancing the work of those in contact with the infant and who could in some way facilitate or hinder the process of maturation. Since they occupied a privileged place in medicine, paediatricians are the only ones who, while specialising in one or other field, could monitor the process of maturation from the outset, when the baby's possibilities were still merely potential. In performing their duties, paediatricians were capable of detecting, if observant and alert, not only an incipient child neurosis which has already taken root, but also a latent tendency towards neurosis, which could become manifest at some point in adult life. And if this was true for neurosis, it was even more so for psychoses. The prevention of the illness which leads to the psychiatric hospital, says Winnicott, "(...) is in the hands of the paediatrician. It is safe to assert, however, that the paediatrician does not know it, and his life is thereby made sweeter" (1958k, p. 317).

By and large, paediatricians failed to use this privilege because they lacked training in psychology and would tend to provide guidance to parents without having the necessary knowledge of the difficulties relevant to emotional development.[7] It was nevertheless unlikely that a paediatrician already established in her carrier and relatively satisfied with the tools of an organicist approach would follow the path of an analytical training. One of the main obstacles to this is the fact that when someone studies psychology, even of a baby, this study brings the specialist back to herself as a person. Winnicott nevertheless stated that there were no shortcuts and there never would be any. The time would come when no further expansion of somatic paediatrics would be necessary and young paediatricians would be pushed towards child psychiatry. "I long for this day, and have longed for it throughout three decades" (1988, p. 10). The danger is nevertheless of avoiding the painful side of the new development and attempting to find a way round; theories will be reformulated, implying that the psychiatric disorder is a product not of emotional conflict but of heredity, constitution, endocrine imbalance, and crude mismanagement.

> But the fact is that life itself is difficult, and psychology concerns itself with the inherent problems of individual development and of the socialisation process; moreover in childhood psychology we must meet the struggles that we ourselves have been through, though for the most part we have forgotten these struggles or have never been conscious of them. (ibid., p. 10)

Winnicott not only disagreed with organicist theories (hormonal imbalances) and academic psychology (brutal environments) but also repudiated theories that conceived of psychic disorders in terms of constitution and heredity. In the latter case, he addressed not only psychiatry but traditional psychoanalysis as well.

Limits of academic psychology

During the 1950s, the new generation of medical students in England claimed a knowledge of psychology in order to deal with the task of which they were becoming increasingly aware, namely the close connection of the emotional factor with disorders of children. What they were offered, however, was knowledge of academic psychology, which did not have the answers to what was required and presented a real danger that the superficial aspects of child psychology would be overvalued. One of these refers to elements intended for the understanding of mental manifestations which, while psychological, were actually related to physical growth. When, for example, the academic psychologist studies the age at which the child is able to walk, he does not take into account the fact that a child may be led to walk earlier than the average or be delayed in this achievement due to emotional factors. The same occurs with research into skills, for which, using intelligence tests and measurement of intellectual capacity based on the quality of the brain as a functional organ, the academic psychologist isolates every single emotional factor that may interfere with the "pure" results. In other words, in the exercise of his functions, *the psychologist isolates the psyche in order to study the mind and the brain;* for Winnicott, however, dealing with and knowing the intellectual field was not the same as knowing the "psyche" of psycho-somatic existence.[8]

The major problem was nevertheless that in attempting to make explicit the role played by the environment in structuring the child's personality, academic psychology distorted the whole phenomenon, tending to concentrate on describring situations of brutality, effective abandonment and cruelty, constituting traumas which would, par excellence, be the causes of mental disorders, without considering the counterpart, the effective and necessary participation of the environment *in the establishment of health.* Psychoanalysis nevertheless specifically opposed this type of simplistic reductive conception, which saw human beings as products of the environment, and in this sense, Winnicott thought, it was not surprising that psychoanalysts were reluctant to consider the environmental factor, since

> [...] those who wished to ignore or deny the significance of the intrapsychic tensions chiefly stressed the bad external factor as a cause of illness in child psychiatric. However, psychoanalysis is now well established, and we can afford to examine the external factor both bad and good. (1963 a, p. 251)

This quotation is from a text of 1963 and it becomes clear that when referring to psychoanalysis in general, Winnicott was actually mentioning his own contribution, knowing that it was far from being accepted. In a letter to an editor of *New Society* whose name was not revealed, he wrote:

> I shudder lest my work should be taken as a weighting on the environmental side on the scales of argument, although I do hold the view that psychoanalysis can afford now to give full importance to external factors, both good and bad, and especially to the part played by the mother at the very beginning when the infant has not yet separated out the not-me from the me. (1987b, p. 141)

In Winnicott's work, the concept of environment, or of an external factor, is extremely complex and in the same way that it constitutes one of the main keys to the understanding of his thought, it is also one of the major sources of mistakes, if misunderstood. When referring to the initial stages and taking into account what the baby's viewpoint would be, the author speaks of the external environment, which is only external from the observer's perspective. At the beginning of life, the environment is subjective and, in this sense, is neither external nor internal. Insofar as it is subjective, the environment participates intrinsically in the constitution of the self and is not merely an *external influence*. It is only during the maturational process that the child will be able to achieve a sense of externality. Only then can the environment be seen as external and even then, not entirely or always.

The debate with psychiatry and with child psychiatry

Winnicott's dialogue with psychiatry revolves around the conceptions of health and illness, of the body/mind dichotomy and its consequences for theory and clinical work, and the conception of the aetiology of disorder from which the nature of the proceedings and the care provided to the patient derive. To these points we add one relating to child psychiatry: its need to protect its own specific field of research and to avoid being driven by the parameters of adult psychiatry.

The mind/body opposition may well be the oldest and most controversial of the distinctions to which the health specialist is subjected and has also been one of the most persistent in philosophy. It is sufficient to recall here the endless series of discussions both scientific and philosophical rekindled in the West by Cartesian dualism and the physicalist medicine based on it. For classical psychiatry, above all of the pre-psychoanalytic kind, psychiatric disorders are interpreted as symptoms of pathological processes of the organism, relating to an acquired organic dysfunction or to hereditary transmission. Psychiatry, which understands itself as a science of the somatogenesis of the psyche, views the psychic disorder as a "symptom".

This psychiatry is a specialised discipline of scientific clinical pathology, based on the body considered as an aetiological field.[9] Even when classical psychiatry adheres to certain psychogenic hypotheses, in reality, this psychogenesis continues to be somatogenesis, since what is termed psychic refers to the brain and to brain tissue. In medical psychiatry, the concept of mind, opposed to that of body, was assimilated with the concept of psyche, with the entity mind/psyche being located in the brain. When a patient, as a result of problems in the maturational process, develops a defensive hyper-mentalisation, which tortures him or her and points to a schizophrenic picture, the psychiatric diagnosis assumes that there is something wrong with his brain, since, in scientific medical thought, the brain has been equaled with the mind. The type of patient mentioned feels the mind to be an enemy, something that persecutes him inside the cranium. With this,

> [...] the surgeon who does a leucotomy would *at first* be doing what the patient asks for, that is, to be relieving the patient of mind activity, the mind having become the enemy of the psyche-soma. (1954 a, p. 253)

In Winnicott's conception, mental activity whether compulsive or not, has nothing to do with the brain. In this way, says Winnicott, one cannot claim that the patient is helped by a lobotomy through the visible relief of his suffering, since

> [...] there is no such thing as relief of suffering *in vacuo*; some person who suffers can be relieved; but it does not seem possible (to one holding my view on this point) to take responsibility for changing the person from one who suffers into quite something else, a part-human that does not suffer but which is not the original person who was brought for treatment. (1988, p. 53)

From the mid-1940s onwards, Winnicott engaged in a genuine campaign against shock therapies and, above all, against the practice of lobotomy, sending letters to the health authorities and writing articles in specialist magazines. In 1967, still involved in this struggle, he wrote that he would simply ignore those specialists who intended to provide physical treatment for psychic disorders, since

> [...] there will still be the patients there, persons like ourselves, with a history in each case of the onset of the disorder, and with a load of personal striving and suffering, and with an environment that is simply bad or good or else confusing to a degree that can be bewildering even to relate. (1968c, p. 194)

Another of Winnicott's objections to psychiatry concerns the fact that, just like the medical area in general, it only sees the illness and not the individual. This is a long tradition and even when, under Kraepelin's influence, in the late nineteenth and early twentieth century, classical psychiatry admits the heterogeneity of madness and starts to distinguish and divide the different categories of mental illnesses into groups, it does so with regard to the illnesses and not to individuals in their relations and in their history.[10] It is thus not surprising that health is not an interesting state to study and has a purely negative definition. In this way, all that matters is symptomatology and it is around it that the nosographic entities are built.

It is probable that from Kraepelin onwards, the new task of observing, describing, and recording the acts and symptoms of patients in order to match them to the label or diagnosis provided by his classification aroused a desire on the part of the specialist to know the hows and whys of those acts and symptoms, with this leading him to explore the patient's biography. The fact is that at a certain point, this became a mandatory part of the psychiatric file. Since a well-organised biography leads to the beginning of the patients' life, in the early twentieth century, psychiatry for the first time began to take an interest in childhood. This was nevertheless a biographical, retrospective interest, which failed to establish a direct relationship between childhood events and the sick individual who appeared and whose history was never examined from the perspective of the nature and meaning of his primitive experiences. It was Freud who revolutionised this situation. Around 1890, when the majority of Kraepelin's work was published, the incipient Freudian psychoanalysis began to introduce a dynamic conception in opposition to the static or nosographic psychiatry of the previous era. Recovering the meaning of the symptoms, psychoanalysis opened the field to studying the psychiatric disorders *of individuals* according to their history and unlike the psychiatrist, who catalogued symptoms, the psychoanalyst became a specialist in obtaining the life history of the patient.[11] In Winnicott's view, this was one of the great contributions of psychoanalysis to psychiatry: the suppression of the old idea of nosological entities. Mental illnesses cannot be considered illnesses in the same sense as rheumatic fever or scurvy; it is false to label psychic disorders in a manner characteristic of the classification in physical medicine.[12]

Another point relates not only to the debate but also to Winnicott's struggle to preserve the specific character of child psychiatry. This only emerged as a branch of specialised study in the early twentieth century; until then, with a few rare exceptions, psychiatry saw the child, who could already speak, as an adult in miniature and applied to him or her the clinical and psychopathological criteria of general psychiatry. There was no place, for example, for the conception of child psychosis and even less for disorders of that nature in babies. At this point, adult psychosis was defined as the degeneration of mental processes, with this definition not applicable to children.[13]

The fact is that all of nineteenth century psychiatry, under the influence of the dismemberment of Pinel's notion of idiotism, in the idiocy-dementia distinction established by Esquirrol and also with the advent of psychometrics and its premature generalisation to grave intellectual deficiencies, viewed child mental pathologies, especially those disorders understood today as child psychosis, as a form of mental deficiency or disorders of character. Even during the second half of the nineteenth century, as Misès noted, any reference to child psychosis was still inconceivable, "madness in children lies in the realm of the inconceivable", the famous Moreau de Tours supposedly stated in his classical treaty *La folie chez les enfants* (1888). Madness in children "can only exist exceptionally, as an acute transient phenomenon or the expression of some neurological disorder, such as epilepsy" (Misès, 1969, p. 10).[14]

In the early twentieth century, when Sancte de Sanctis (1908) described the most precocious cases found until then, he created an autonomous morbid entity, *dementia praecocissima*, the characteristics of which are close to precocious dementia of adults, characterised by Kraepelin in

1899. Misès highlighted, with regard to this new nosographical entity, the frequent observation "how a clinical picture in children which associated delirium, hallucinations and catatonia in children as a simple projection of adult pathology seemed artificial" (Misès, 1969, p. 11).

It was only very gradually that child disorders gained a specific place. Around 1912, researching children between the ages of eight and thirteen, Chaslin "sensed a particular meaning of certain morbid developments in retarded patients, epileptics, wayward children, wondering whether they should not be considered as hebephrenics" (Aubin, 1975, p. 14). It was nevertheless Bleuler who suggested the notion of schizophrenia without the implication, present in Kraepelin's precocious dementia, of loss of affectivity and of fatal evolution towards dementia. This, says Aubin, "opened the doors to child psychosis, the future of which is not one of inevitable despair [...]" (idem).

Even though child psychiatry had established itself as a specific field of study, a tendency remained to observe and understand child disorders, or those prior to puberty, in accordance with the parameters constructed for adult psychopathology. In the article "Psychoses and child care" (1953a), Winnicott mentions M. Creak's book *Psychoses in Childhood*, published in 1951, as an example of this. The author described a psychotic picture, without making an effort to research situations of immaturity in children, in which an organised introversion occurred, with consequent bizarre behaviour patterns and secondary physical disorders; he then applied this framework to a type of child undoubtedly familiar to child specialists. If matters were this simple, Winnicott argued, it would be possible to apply any type of adult nosological entity to countless childhood situations: states of melancholy, manic-depressive psychoses, hypomanic agitation, confusional states, etc.

Despite all of the advances in psychoanalytic research and its influence on general psychiatry, Winnicott observed major resistance among the latter to considering, firstly, the existence of a disorder of schizophrenic type which was entirely psychological, that is, which could be prevented and cured; secondly, to regarding schizophrenia as a disorder which established itself in the earliest stages of childhood, and consequently, which should be studied within the categories of child psychiatry, psychoanalytically oriented by the theory of maturational processes. Psychiatrists remained and are still averse to a study which shows that the aetiology of the illness is not entirely dependent on heredity, even if heredity and constitutional factors may often be important. Winnicott nevertheless points out that even in the case of progressive general palsy, a disease caused by an organic disturbance in the brain, it is possible to find in the psychology of the patient, "an illness which belongs specifically to that patient and his personality and character, and the details relate to the patient's early history" (1989q, p. 123). It is this conviction that leads Winnicott to assert that *the psychic diseases* to which a hereditary or constitutional character is usually attributed *are not diseases in the usual sense of the term.* This aetiological hypothesis is not acceptable even when constitution is considered in psychological terms, as is the case with traditional psychoanalysis. *Psychosis is not defined by the heritage of a family degenerative process and neither is it the fruit of an unbalanced constitution of the pulsional forces.* The aetiology is not that simple:

> For those psychiatrists who are interested not so much in people as in diseases—diseases of the mind, they would call them—life is relatively easy. But for those of us who tend to think

> of psychiatric patients not as so many diseases but as people who are casualties in the human struggle for development for adaptation, and for living, our tasks is rendered infinitely complex. (1961a, p. 72)

Winnicott evidently acknowledges the existence of psychological disorders related to physical abnormalities. Lesions or chemical alterations may occur in the brain, which is the organ on which the mind depends in order to function. Malfunctions which affect the apparatus may be hereditary, congenital, caused by infectious disease, by a tumour or by degenerative processes, such as arteriosclerosis. The problem consists of failing to draw a distinction between psychiatric disorders, that is, those which present psychological manifestations deriving from physical diseases or lesions and which must be considered as such, and those which are fundamentally psychic, that is, which relate to failures in the maturational processes. It is not a question of denying the existence of hereditary factors, but rather of supplementing them with aspects that may prove more vital to the life of the individual than the disorder itself (cf. 1965n, p. 58). When the psychiatrist fails to pay attention to this distinction and an organic disorder is detected, all of the individual's difficulties are attributed to it, everything is due to the "nosological framework", with no consideration of the environmental factor. It follows from this, and this is the worst consequence, that the psychological approach is abandoned in favour of a biochemical and neurological one. Even with regard to tuberculosis, Winnicott said that much was lost when the treatment for this condition became purely chemical, with the long period of special care humanely provided to the patient being dismissed as unnecessary.

According to the author, however, at the time, psychiatry drew a distinction between the two classes of disorders, which could present similar and confluent symptomatology but which were nevertheless radically different in nature.[15] What could indeed occur was the conjugation of these two factors, since a mother who was capable of being good enough to a physically healthy baby, might not stand the tension of taking care of a baby with cerebral complications.

Generalising to the whole of psychoanalysis what was in fact the theoretical perspective of his own contribution, Winnicott asserted that the psychoanalysis tended to understand schizophrenia as a reversion of the maturational process of early childhood. That is, if every individual is endowed with an innate tendency towards maturation, disease consisted of the reversal of this tendency, in its paralysis at a point when absolute dependence was already a fact. Instead of developing, the baby came to a halt. If this perspective became widely accepted, this could bring

> [...] schizophrenia into the realm of the universal human struggle and would take it out of the realm of specific disease process. The medical world urgently needs this bit of sanity in so far as it is true, because disorders arising out of the human struggle should not be housed along with disorders secondary to degenerative processes. (1965f, p. 178)

Winnicott left no room for doubt: he was interested in people and not in things endowed with properties, which carried intrinsic determinations in themselves; his question was the suffering or the imprisonment of people due to their inability to live, and not the entities, mechanisms or forces operating inside people, despite themselves, which could be studied as natural and quantifiable entities. It is always possible to clarify mechanisms of functioning of living matter, but in so doing, we will make specific structures of this matter explicit and this in no way reveals the essence of life itself.

Winnicott's discussion with traditional psychoanalytical theory

Even though he has always declared that he could only think and write from his own experience, and in his own language, Winnicott did not abstain from discussing with his contemporaries. On the contrary, spread all over his work and correspondence, there are comments and appreciations on almost everything that has been written in psychoanalysis in his time and prior to it. From Jung to Lacan, from Anna Freud to the Kleinians, among whom Meltzer, Esther Bick, Susan Isaacs, and Joan Rivière, from Spitz to Erick Erickson, from Hartmann and other authors in ego psychology to Balint and Bowlby, from Virginia Axline to Harold Searles, Winnicott debated with almost all authors who, from different lines, sought to extend the theoretical field of psychoanalysis.

His main interlocutors were, however, Freud and Melanie Klein. It was especially to the work of these two authors that Winnicott referred when, while formulating his ideas, he tried to distinguish his own original contribution. For this reason, this is the debate that we are interested in resuming here, since while there have been developments in the psychoanalytical theory and even new lines (such as Lacan), we may say that no divergence or significant alteration was traced regarding the basic theoretical assumptions formulated by Freud that would justify what is now justifiable, namely, the assertion that Winnicott's contribution constitutes a new paradigm for psychoanalysis. The modifications introduced by Klein (or Lacan) are not really revolutionary in the specific sense of Thomas Kuhn, since they do not really alter, as we saw in the Introduction, the oedipal paradigm which guides the research in the traditional theory.

Just like other analysts and commentators of Freud, Winnicott also considers the existence of two different types of theorisation in the Freudian work, which leads his discussion with Freudian psychoanalysis to develop in two interdependent levels: the first level concerns the metapsychology as theoretical supra-structure; the second one refers to Freud's dynamic psychology, that is, the empirical-descriptive theory that interprets individual clinical phenomena. The latter, more pertinent to the theme under examination here, shall be detailed as it appears in the course of this study. I shall approach especially the structural differences, which are important to characterise the theoretical framework to which this study belongs.

For Winnicott, Freudian psychoanalysis undoubtedly went beyond the organicist hypothesis of psychiatry and the environmental positions of academic psychologists. The psychoanalysts were the ones who drew attention to the internal conflict which lies at the basis of psychoneurosis, and it was, above all, under the influence of psychoanalysis that psychiatry started to consider the psychogenesis of psychic phenomena in addition to the somatogenesis. Always affirming his filiation to psychoanalysis and the inestimable value of Freud and Melanie Klein's contributions to the understanding of psychic disorders, what Winnicott certainly appreciates and maintains of the psychoanalytical tradition is both the conception that psychic illnesses are fundamentally of a psychological origin and the fact that psychoanalysis, in the hands of Freud, has established itself as a method of research and treatment oriented by the scientific spirit, which means that the theories and practices are permanently subjected to revision. For this reason and precisely in order to advance the psychoanalytical knowledge, Winnicott sees no inconsistency in remaining a psychoanalyst while, at the same time that supported by his parallel experience with babies and psychotic patients, he proposes a radical questioning of the Freudian meta-psychological super-structure. Imposed by the new clinical phenomena, this questioning aims to raise the issue of theoretical differences in the conception of psychic illness and health which, in turn, were founded on the conceptual differences regarding the psyche and the human nature.

A first and more general point refers to the fact that Freudian psychoanalysis was built along the lines of a natural science and that Freud has never abandoned the idea of settling his findings on biology, having maintained a close connection to this science in many aspects of the theory. As Laplanche and Pontalis have well observed (1967, p. 126), it is the biological functions which provide the basic model for the functioning of the primitive psyche and this is showed, for example, in the way how the progression of the erogenous zones which mark the phases of sexuality was formulated.

The difficult and complex articulation between body and psyche was resolved by Freud by means of the concept of pulsions, understood as psychic representatives of physical forces, with the dualism of the pulsional forces setting the psyche in motion.[16] By the very definition of pulsion, one can affirm that Freudian psychoanalysis remains tied to the physical model of the psyche, with force as its central concept. Although Freud's interpreters differ as to which principle fundamentally rules the elaboration of the Freudian metapsychology, the fact is that the whole discussion remains in the ambit of forces or of libidinal investments. According to Loparic, the central methodological principle in the elaboration of the metapsychology is the dynamic viewpoint.[17] For Richard Simanke, the economical point of view is primordial, assuming the character of a necessary principle, albeit not sufficient, for the Freudian explanation of the psyche; and particularly in moments of impasse in the theory, says Simanke, when it is necessary to reformulate it, Freud relies on the quantitative criterion.[18] Also Laplanche and Pontalis affirm that it would not be possible for the father of psychoanalysis, the complete description of the psychic process without the appreciation of the economy of the investments.[19]

Winnicott shows that he is perfectly aware of the theoretical foundations on which the general ideas of Freudian psychoanalysis were developed:

> Freud is here dealing with human nature in terms of *economics*, and deliberately simplifying the problem for the purpose of founding a theoretical formulation. There is an implied determinism in all this work, an assumption that human nature can be examined objectively and can have applied to it the laws that are known to apply in physics. (1958e, p. 16)[20]

In addition, given his debt to the German philosophical tradition of the nineteenth century and the development of neurophysiology, Freud was led to build a model of mental functioning on the lines of a machine. Recognising the limits of this key to the understanding of human nature, Masud Khan states that:

> One has to admit the fact that the climate of neuro-physiological research at the end of the 19th century biased Freud to conceptualise human psyche and its functioning on the model of the machine: hence his theories of the psychic apparatus, energic cathexes and intrapsychic structures, where he diagrammaticaly traced out as the ego, the id and the super-ego; plus the topografical schema of the conscious, the preconscious and the unconscious. (Khan, 1958, p. xxxvi)

Loparic points to the affiliation of the basic notions of Freudian psychoanalysis, the mind and the psychic apparatus, to the "project of mechanising the image of the world and of the human being, which began in Ancient Greece and was made explicit by Nietzsche, as the will to power" (Loparic, 1997c, p. 99). He also notes that "in Freud, the mind makes use of an instrument [*Instrument*] or device [*Apparat*] in order to execute its actions or performances [*Leistungen*]. The mind also makes use of the energy termed libido, which drives the device" (ibid., p. 98).

As a result of this theoretical position, illnesses as described by the Freudian metapsychology are disorders of the functioning of the forces within an "apparatus" which, while psychic, belongs to the same context as the objects of the physical sciences: it is driven by forces and mechanisms. Health is also only describable in metapsychological terms. In "Finishable and unfinishable analysis", Freud says that

> It is impossible to define health except in metapsychological terms: i.e. by reference to the dynamic relations between the agencies of the mental apparatus which have been recognized—or (if that is preferred) inferred or conjectured—by us. (Freud, 1937c, vol. 23, p. 226, note 2)

Starting from another conception, in which abstract categories are absent and which includes the refusal to objectify life, Winnicott does not accept that the foundation of human nature may rest on the causal deterministic principle of the intensities of pulsional forces or any other quantifiable entity. It is not the conflicting pulsional forces that set life in motion; the baby lives from the fact that it "is alive" and has someone who responds to this fact in a satisfactory way; it develops since it is endowed with an innate tendency towards maturation and because there is someone facilitating the accomplishment of that tendency. A psyche where fantasies, mental mechanisms and repressed contents coexist is not given, but acquired; it is itself an achievement of the maturational process. "The psychoanalyst, more than any other type of careful observer, finds himself in the position of being certain from clinical experience that the individual's psychological life is not exactly adjusted to the time of birth" (1987c, p. 54). In addition to the fact that this position, averse to the concept of pulsional forces, is fully inferable from Winnicott's thought as a whole, it is clarified in a letter to Roger Money-Kyrle, in which he comments that it is unfortunate that Melanie Klein had made such an effort to reconcile her opinion with the pulsions of life and death, "which are perhaps Freud's one blunder" (1987b, p. 42). Likewise, in another article, "A personal view of the Kleinian contribution", after listing Klein's "positive contributions", he alludes to the "*doubtful* contributions", one of which is "retaining a use of the theory of the Life and Death Instincts" (1965g, p. 178).

Regarding the metaphysical framework within which Freud moves, it is possible to distinguish two aspects of Winnicott's criticism of Freudian psychoanalysis. On the one hand, there is the mode of theorisation. Loparic, who has dealt extensively with the theme, indicates that the considerations of a metapsychological type

> [...] prohibit access or even disfigure essential moments of the maturational process of human nature [...]. This is a question of opposing what is manifested to what is merely thought, observations to constructions, phenomena to fictions, in short, description to metapsychological speculation. (Loparic, 1995b, p. 44)

The fact is that the process which derives from the innate tendency towards maturation has nothing to do with biology or with any other physical substratum; it has to do with human nature and the capacity for existence.[21] This does not mean that the author has ignored the biological aspect. On the contrary, Winnicott takes it into account as it is, without trying to humanise it and this is why he uses the word "instinct" instead of "pulsion". Considering something which is a condition, that is, without which no human relation can be achieved, nevertheless does not mean taking the condition as the cause or foundation. For him, with regard to instinctuality, human beings are not radically different from animals; what makes them different is the fact that all of their bodily functions, including the instincts, go via the strictly human route of imaginative elaboration.[22] The brain is also the condition for the functioning of the psyche, but this does not entail that the psyche may be conceived on the basis of the categories governing the study of the brain.

Another of Winnicott's objections to Freud was that the latter had thought his theory on the nature and dynamics of neuroses could be the key to understanding all psychic disorders, and furthermore, that the study of neurosis could lead to a deep understanding of human nature. Even when, in an attempt to respond to the theoretical impasses presented by his theory of narcissism, Freud became interested in psychoses, the questions which he formulated derived from the same field that he had demarcated for understanding neuroses. For Winnicott, however, "a claim that the healthy child can be completely understood on the basis of a study of neurosis and its origins in childhood would be absurd" (1988, p. 37). Winnicott's argument rests on the conviction that the bases of psychic health are established at the beginning of life, the moment when the cornerstones of personality are being established. In this way, for a child to reach the point of a disorder of a neurotic type, we must assume that he has successfully completed the more primitive stages, with the basic achievements which, once the child has integrated into a unity and separated the me from the not-me, render him vulnerable to the type of conflict which is inherent to the triangular relationships.[23] For the psychotic individual, the interpersonal problem within the neurotic disorder simply does not make sense and he does not reach the point of being emotionally affected by it.[24] From Winnicott's perspective, neurosis in this very specific sense means health and this is the meaning of his claim that if primitive development is disturbed, then the child will not be "healthy enough" to reach neurosis (cf. 1988, pp. 38–39).

All of these questions relating to the establishment of the bases of personality could not even have been formulated within the theoretical horizon of classical psychoanalysis. Having founded his field of reflection on the internal dynamics of the psyche and taking for granted the feeling of real and the capacity for establishing relations with external reality, all that was left to do was to analyse the pulsional quality of the relations and not their existence or reality, or the existence and reality of the baby and the external world.[25] In this way, when the psychoanalyst becomes a specialist in obtaining the history, it still remains to be asked *which history* and what scope does it have for understanding phenomena, for example, of a psychotic type. In traditional psychoanalysis, the history is the development of the sexual functions, with the Oedipus complex as the basic plot. For Winnicott, however, *there is a pre-history in which the little individual, who already is a human being capable of being affected by the environment, has not yet reached himself;* the baby is only beginning the process of maturation which leads to the integration into a unitary me and if the process fails, this baby may never achieve a me with a history to tell.[26] Achieving the point of having a history depends on processes that do not belong to the domain of sexuality and largely antecede it, such as, for example, the constitution of a personal memory related to a process of temporalisation of the baby. The gradual integration of the baby into a time and a space cannot possibly be understood in terms of pulsions. Time and space are not objects; and neither are they goals or forces. Without time and space, however, one cannot find objects and even less desire them.

Another even more specific aspect derives from this, the difference between Winnicott's thought and traditional theory: since the latter conceives of health and illness in terms of categories constructed in order to understand neuroses, illness can only be conceived in terms of the pulsional conflicts regarding the Oedipus complex and, as a result, health consists of the state of defences of the ego. It is the rigidity of these defences which are erected against the anxiety resulting from the pulsional conflict that constitutes an indication of disease. A healthy individual is one who is relatively free from a massive repression and inhibition of instinctual impulses.

Despite the fact that for the author, these criteria remain valid in cases of neurosis which offer no doubt as to the integration of the personality—which is not easy to diagnose quickly—they do not permit an understanding of cases in which the personality was not established in integrated form, notably since after Winnicott's formulation of the defensive formation of the false self type, in which there is a psychosis underlying the neurotic symptomatology, we must be alert to the basic aspects of the personality, which *are not instinctual in nature.* For all of these reasons and given the knowledge now available, it is no longer acceptable to continue to access health in terms of what is traditionally termed the positions of the id, that is, instinctuality. Researchers and analysts must be prepared to examine the process of personality structuring from the outset. While it is certainly easier to describe the maturation in terms of instinctual functioning than in terms of the ego and its complex evolution, there is no longer any way to avoid the second alternative (cf. Winnicott, 1971f, p. 21).

One aspect of the question regarding the structuring of the ego may illustrate the way in which Winnicott makes ego achievements prevail over sexual functions, as well as how the development of the ego is seen as a condition for the possibility of instinctual life. According to the author, the initial hypothesis of Freudian psychoanalytical theory referred both to the id, active since the beginning, and the defence mechanisms of the ego, especially repression. The ego mechanisms organise themselves in order to avoid the anxiety deriving from object loss or from instinctual tensions, which are already felt as belonging to the me. This necessarily presupposes a separation from the self, an ego structure and perhaps a personal body scheme, meaning that the child has reached a sophisticated degree of maturation, having already achieved some independence and a defensive personal organisation. From the perspective of Winnicott's theory of maturational processes, however, *this can no longer be assumed* and a central aspect of the discussion, which derives from the observation of psychoses, consists precisely of this point: it is not the instinctual tension and the resulting formation of defences which force the structuring of the ego, but on the contrary, it is this structuring which, facilitated by good environmental conditions, generates the anxiety of instinctual tension or of loss of the object. It is only insofar as the instinctual phenomena can be experienced, catalogued, and interpreted by the functioning of the ego that the instinctual anxiety may make any sense. There is no id before the ego, says Winnicott, and it is only on the basis of this premise that an exhaustive study of the ego is justifiable. At the point when the constitution of the self is taking place, the anxiety is not that of castration or of separation but of the possibility of annihilation of the incipient self. In this respect, Winnicott considers that Melanie Klein added a great deal to the Freudian theory. By emphasising the earliest childhood, she clarified the interrelation between primitive anxieties and defence mechanisms. Winnicott nevertheless finds the Kleinian premise that the relation to external objects is already established as soon as the baby is born to be unacceptable, since it cuts off any possibility of a discussion on the origin of psychoses at the root.[27]

One of the consequences of this position of traditional theory is that health is again conceived in negative terms. This point of Winnicott's objection constitutes a blind spot in psychoanalytical theory, with the author clearly stating that when, as is generally the case, we start from the defences of the ego against the anxiety arising from instinctual life, health is conceived in terms of the state of defences of the ego, whether or not they are rigid, etc. "But we seldom reach the point at which we can start to describe what life is. That is to say, we have yet to tackle the question of *what life itself is about*" (1967b, p. 133).

The conception of health as the absence of illness and, in this case, as the absence of neurotic symptoms, ignores the fact that a state of good health must have a quality of its own, which cannot be described in merely negative terms, and that there is a "health" which is symptomatic, defensively constructed, and infused with fear of the various madnesses which traverse the life of every individual. It is thus of paramount importance to acknowledge openly, says Winnicott, *"that absence of psychoneurotic illness may be health, but it is not life"* (1967b, p. 134; my italics). The place from which psychoanalysts research human experience is thus a partial one which eludes the primordial issues of existence; this is the meaning of Winnicott's claim that:

> [...] psychoanalysts who have rightly emphasized the significance of instinctual experience and of reactions to frustration have failed to state with comparable clearness or conviction the tremendous intensity of these non-climactic experiences that are called playing. (1967b, p. 132)

Health includes the capacity for playing, which is the prototype of creative living; it refers to the possibility of inhabiting the potential space and of surrendering oneself there to an experience which is sustained by the basic illusion; it also refers to the freedom to transit via the various worlds created during maturation, which embraces the capacity for establishing relations with the world objectively perceived without a major sacrifice of personal spontaneity.

In conceiving of health in terms of ego defences, traditional theory ignores the fact that there are individuals who fail to establish egoic defences since an ego capable of defending itself has not been formed. The problem here lies not in rigid defence organisations, but in a failure *of formation of egoic type defences.* Psychoses refer to "not so much the individual's organized defences as [to] the individual's failure to attain the ego-strength or the personality integration that enables defences to form" (1963c, p. 220). In psychoses, there are indeed defences. In fact, psychoses are themselves defensive organisations, but not of a repressive type, in which the individual, who has already achieved a unitary identity with an already established internal psychic reality, suffers from conflicts both of instinctuality—which is already endowed with personal sense and relates to interpersonal relations—and the restrictions imposed by censorship. In psychoses, defences are of a nature which paralyses the innate tendency towards maturation, preventing the constitution of the self. For all of these reasons and in particular, since in Winnicott's view, neuroses were not the paradigm for psychic illness, the theory of the development of the sexual functions, which forms the basis for the theory of neuroses, ceased to be the theory *par excellence* of the constitution of the individual.[28]

Winnicott's debate with Melanie Klein reiterates these points, in that while she had made significant modifications to the Freudian theory of the most primitive stages of life, I do not perceive any significant difference in the field of theoretical foundations between her and Freud. Having examined primitive pre-oedipal anxieties at length, Klein did not modify but instead stressed their alleged oedipal character, extending the Oedipus complex backwards in time and resolving the theoretical impasses through abstract constructions such as the symbolic equations. Among Winnicott's objections to Melanie Klein, two, of a general character, stand out. The first one goes against Klein's resorting to the constitutional factor, with pulsional intensities determining fundamental aspects of human nature and maturation. By this route, the dynamics of development is predetermined and moves along phylogenetically traced paths. The endogenous is reduced to the regressive tendency and the only difference separating neurosis from psychosis is the radical and deep character of the regressions.

The second objection relates to the fact that Klein formulated the individual development of the human baby in exclusively intrapsychic terms, without reference to the environment. These differences in premises led to radically different theoretical and clinical paths: while Winnicott concerned himself with describing the personal needs of the infant and the various types of failures of the environment in responding to these needs, Melanie Klein continued to describe the baby's primitive mental mechanisms and to configure the psychic internal and phantasmatic conflicts, with a total contempt for external reality.[29]

Winnicott considered the theory of the depressive position as Klein's most valuable contribution to psychoanalysis, above all appreciating the fact that this achievement was conceived as an acquisition of normal development, which was a sign of health. For this reason, he had reservations about the term "*depressive* position", which led to thinking in terms of a disorder when it was a gain in maturity and health. By incorporating it into his theory of maturational processes, calling it the achievement of the capacity for guilt and responsibility at the stage of concern, Winnicott indicated that his description of this achievement, formulated in his own language, was the result of his own work, in the knowledge that Klein would certainly disagree with various details. This redescription was nevertheless necessary since Klein's formulation of the depressive position was based on a conception of aggression incompatible with Winnicott's own. When, in 1945, Klein formulated the schizo-paranoid position and above all, the postulation of innate envy, it became clear to him that he could not accept her theoretical framework: the constitutional factor is present in full force, providing easy explanations of manifestations that would demand an accurate study of the infinite and subtle details of the *sui generis* relations of the baby with the environment during the initial stages.

In this way, the discussion of many highly complex problems was discarded when, for example, Klein claimed with regard to the roots of aggression that there was an innate quantity of death pulsion. Winnicott could not accept any such theses. He is undoubtedly referring to her and to the Kleinians when he speaks of researchers who cannot conceive of a maturational process in which the baby is a being already capable of experiences at the outset and that the quality of these experiences depends on the encounter with the facilitating environment. For those researchers who do not take the environment into account, the phenomenon of babies who are very difficult and startled at birth can only be explained by the constitutional factor; in this case, a paranoid one (cf. 1988, p. 150). From Winnicott's perspective, this line of argument ignores the baby's pre-history, his immaturity and initial environment. Since a human being capable of experiences is already present, even in the uterus, he may have suffered several interruptions to the continuity of being while *in utero*, during the birth process, or immediately afterwards and may have reacted to these intrusions, leading to a paranoid state which, no matter how precocious, is due to the environmental factor and not to constitutional inheritance.

In his scientific practice, Winnicott was also intolerant and almost merciless to "anyone who treats psychoanalytic theory as if it were a religion, or a political view with religious overtones" (Rodman, 1987, p. xxv). There was something dogmatic, proselytising, and even religious in what might be called the Kleinian movement, which he particularly disliked. In 1956, after listening to the reading of Melanie Klein's article on envy, Winnicott wrote to Joan Rivière "the only thing that can happen is that those who like to support Melanie produce, as we could all do, clinical material or quotations from the Bible which support her theme" (1987b, p. 95). One of the problems related to scientific communication and his complaint, repeated on several occasions, was that the Kleinian group used terms which should have been descriptive but which ultimately became partisan slogans, the use of which was mandatory. In a letter to Bion from 1955, he stated that

> [...] the Society gets awfully bored with the plugging of terms. In the last six months the words "projective identification" have been used several hundred times. Of course we are in for a few months in which the word "envy" will be brought in everywhere. [...] There is something wrong here and I believe and hope that you will take part in the attempt we must make if the Society is to survive to get behind these disruptive tendencies, which are of the nature of a plugging of theme-songs. (1987b, p. 92)[30]

Winnicott glimpsed a religious bias not only in the group's stance but also in the Kleinian conceptualisation, which, in some aspects, made this theory a reaffirmation of the principle of original sin.[31] This situation introduced a certain sectarian politics into the British Psycho-Analytical

Society, which became an obstacle to freedom of thought, communication and to progress in psychoanalytical science.[32]

The debate with traditional psychoanalysis did not end there; on the contrary, it could form the object of an entire book. Although this theme falls outside the scope of this study, I would like to mention in broad terms Winnicott's theoretical rapprochement to the psychoanalytical school termed ego psychology. What often leads us to believe that his thought lies in this theoretical direction is that he was genuinely interested in some of the propositions of this school, particularly those stressing the importance of the environment in the constitution of the individual. This nevertheless does not mean that the general orientation of American ego psychology was akin to his own thinking.

For example, Winnicott appreciates Hartmann's concept of "average expectable environment", which, he affirms, is approximately the same thing that he himself termed the "ordinary devoted mother". Other analysts have also used similar terms in order to describe an environment whose qualities made the child's maturational process effective (cf. 1984e, p. 187), but Winnicott seems to have a particular liking for Hartmann, since he includes the term "expectable", the meaning of which approximates it to the central characteristic of the good enough environment, which is that of being reliable in the sense of being predictable.

Despite the different theoretical foundations on which they are based, there are several other theoretical affinities between Winnicott and ego psychology. One of them consists of the idea that the ego cannot possibly derive from the id. According to Hartmann, mental development is not simply the result of the struggle with impulses, objects, with the super-ego, etc. We must assume that this development "is served by a psychic apparatus which functions from the start of life" (Hartmann, 1958, p. 15). These are the "primary autonomous apparatus" or "innate ego apparatus", which would supposedly develop into functions, such as perception, object comprehension, intentionality, thought, language, memory, all of which are potentialities of the organism, in a "conflict-free zone". The conception of innate ego apparatus is very close to Glover's concept of "ego nuclei", which suggested to Winnicott the state of non-integration regarding the stages of absolute dependence. Despite the affinity of the general idea, Hartmann's theory nevertheless fails to draw the distinction between the mental and the psychic which is essential to Winnicott's thought and is based on the idea of apparatus, which is entirely foreign to Winnicott.

Hartmann's idea that the ego cannot possibly derive from the id relates to another one, that a theory of instincts is incapable of explaining the access to reality, with which Winnicott agreed. Hartmann's hypothesis nevertheless includes a concept of adaptation, primarily defined as a reciprocal relationship between organism and milieu. It is not difficult to grasp, however, that Winnicott did not see the baby as an organism and that in the initial stages, we cannot think in terms of a reciprocate relation, since the baby is not yet a unity capable of relating and is merely a part of the mother–baby unit; the adaptation derives exclusively from the mother.

The authors also agreed on the autonomous development of the egoic functions with regard to the id; Winnicott certainly accepts the sense of Hartmann's concept that the ego develops in a "zone free from conflicts", since he also held that the structuring of the ego is not subjected to the vicissitudes of instinct. In Hartmann's view, on the other hand, the conflict-free ego sphere was linked to inherited tendencies, whereas in Winnicott's, it depended on the quality of environmental care.[33] These differences are substantial and if a few modifications to the traditional theory, introduced by the psychology of the ego, were in line with Winnicott's positions, this does not mean that his thought can be regarded as ego psychology.

Notes

1. Referring to his work at the Paddington Green Hospital, Winnicott points to the fortunate influence of Guthrie, a paediatrician who despite failing to make a significant theoretical contribution, created a special atmosphere for exercising a type of paediatrics that was not merely organicist, but which considered psychological factors. Winnicott subsequently learned that his nomination as Guthrie's replacement in order to continue the work of his department was due to his own manifest interest in psychology.
2. In this same lecture of 1967, Winnicott remembers that around 1935 he could not find an interlocutor for his question on primitive emotional difficulties, unless they were interpreted as regressions and mentions having thought: "I'm going to show that infants are ill very early, and if the theory doesn't fit it, it's just got to adjust itself. So that was that" (1989f, p. 575).
3. Cf. Winnicott, 1955c, p. 262.
4. Cf. in the article "A note on normality and anxiety" (1931b) the case of Veronica, who started to wet her bed every night, after her mother had been away in hospital for a month, as well as the case of Francis, who presented episodes of violence associated with his mother's depression.
5. Winnicott was not entirely alone in this perspective. Some years before the war, another psychoanalyst, John Bowlby, working at the Child Guidance Clinic, had researched the history of disturbed children and, in a formal study of 150 cases with varied problems, had established a direct link between theft and deprivation, with the latter primarily understood as separation from the mother during the first years of childhood. Both men conducted a broad campaign in the UK to alert the health authorities to the serious problems resulting from the evacuation of children during the Second World War as well as the need to ensure emotionally safe conditions for them.
6. Cf. "A note on normality and anxiety" (1931b) and "Fidgetiness" (1931a); cf. also Winnicott, 1969a, Chapters Thirteen, Fourteen, Nineteen, Twenty, Twenty-one, and Twenty-two.
7. Winnicott warned on many occasions of the way in which doctors and nurses hindered the healthy mother and failed to assist the sick mother to deal with her baby. An example of this may be found in Winnicott, 1965c.
8. The question referring to the distinction between psyche and mind will be resumed in Chapter Two, sub heading "Psycho-somatic existence: the soma, the psyche and the mind". Cf. also Winnicott, 1954a and 1988 (part I).
9. Despite an entire current that asserts the heuristic fecundity of this conception and which remains extremely active and confident of its hypothesis, its very authors admit that the genetic derivation of the psychic phenomena from body sources remain scientifically problematic. Kronfeld, for example, states that one can already see that "certain psychic modifications depend on certain physical modifications, but it is not possible to explain them" (Kronfeld, 1927, cited in Tellenbach, 1961/1980).
10. L. Kanner, creator of the term "autism", states that the curisosity of psychiatrists was directed toward the mental illnesses of individuals rather than mentally ill individuals (cf. Kanner, 1935).
11. This is not due only to Freud. Also Jaspers, in his *General Psychopathology*, observed that the fundamental theme of psychiatry was man as man and that "Not everything that hapens in a psychic illness can be explained by using the criteria of science. Human beings are creators of

culture, they develop beliefs and moral standarts and constantly transcend their own empirical human self which is the only self that scientific research can recognise and grasp [...]. The most vital part of the psychopatologist's knowledge is drawn from his contact with people. What he gains from this depends upon the particular way he gives himself and as therapist partakes in events, whether he illuminates himself as well as his patients" (Jaspers, 1959/1997, pp. 8 & 21).

12. Much has changed since then in psychiatry and it is probable that psychoanalysis is reaping the fruits of its own contribution. With regard to the old question of putting the disease before the patient, Henri Aubin, a psychiatrist of the Solliès-Pont Hospital, specialist of the World Health Organization, affirms in his book *Les psychoses de l'enfant*, that "Our concern will never be to place a label on a patient, to classify him, to submit to a kind of botanical study but to take a first step towards the *understanding* of a case and towards a therapeutic treatment. I think that the vast majority of practicing psychiatrists see things in this way" (Aubin, 1975, p. 10).
13. According to some historians of child psychiatry, the first occasion for which it is possible to discern retroactively the first incursion in the field of child psychosis was the so-called "wild boy of Aveyron", who seems to have been "the first significant observation of a psychotic child" (Aubin, 1975, p. 13). According to Misès, this observation and the essay of the re-education of little Victor by Dr. Itard, a doctor at an institution for deaf-mutes, imposed "the notion of evolving personality disorders and retroactively raised the question of psychosis in children as a manifestation of a deficit" (Misès, 1969, p. 10).
14. Cf. also Misès, 1969, p. 11. Some historians of psychiatry consider the frequent attribution of this assertion to Moreau de Tours to be a mistake. Aspects of this polemic, which go beyond the limits of this present work, may be found in Aubin, 1975, p. 12.
15. Cf. for example, Winnicott's review (1963e) of the book *Childhood Schizophrenia*, by William Goldfarb, in Winnicott, 1996a, Chapter Twenty-four. In these cases, it may be necessary to medicate the patient in order to neutralise the inertial physical-chemical imbalances of the organism, but it is still left to psychotherapy to take care of the disorders that resulted from the environmental failure in promoting the maturational processes, failures that might imply the mother's difficulty in taking care of a child with physical problems satisfactorily.
16. For a detailed exam of the concept of pulsion (*Trieb*) in philosophy and in psychology, cf. Loparic, 1999a.
17. Already in his article from 1985, "Resistances to psychoanalysis", Loparic shows that Freud's inference, starting from the phenomenon of resistence to the affirmation of the existence of forces of repression, presupposes the additional methodological thesis that all causal explication in psychology must be dynamic. The philosopher says: "It may be clearly understood that this was the Freudian conception of scientific explanations, on the basis of the following extract from *Conferences*: 'We seek not merely to describe and to classify phenomena, but to understand them as signs of an interplay of forces in the mind, as a manifestation of purposeful intentions working concurrently or in mutual opposition. We are concerned with a *dynamic view* of mental phenomena. On our view the phenomena that are perceived must yield in importance to trends which are only hypothetical' (1916–1917, p. 86)" (Loparic, 1985, p. 32).
18. Simanke highlights section IV, of "The unconscious" (Freud, 1915e, AE, vol. 14, p. 178), as one of the passages of the Freudian work in which the prevalence of the economic principle over the topical and the dynamic is made clearer. (cf. Simanke, 1994, p. 171).
19. Cf. Laplanche & Pontalis, 1967, p. 125.
20. This appreciation is entirely in agreement with Heidegger who, having read Freud at Medard Boss's insistence, saw that "Freudian metapsychology is the application of Neo-Kantian

philosophy to the human being" (Heidegger, 1987/2001, p. 207). According to the philosopher, the Freudian theory is supported on one hand on the natural sciences and on the other, on the Kantian theory of objectivity; it is based on the postulate of "the complete explanation of psychical life", which is "not derived from the psychical phenomena themselves but is a *postulate* of modern natural science" (Heidegger, 1987/2001, p. 208).

21. An example of this stance may be found in the article "Primary maternal preoccupation" (1958h), in which Winnicott initially salvages some of the references to the nature of the relation between mother and baby in the work of other psychoanalysts. In addition to mentioning Anna Freud's studies, he discusses Margaret Mahler's expressions "homeostatic equilibrium" and "symbiotic relationship" (1952 & 1954), noting that: "I think that these various concepts need joining together and the study of the mother needs to be rescued from the purely biological. The term symbiosis takes us no further than to compare the relationship of the mother and the infant with other examples in animal and plant life—physical interdependence. The words homeostatic equilibrium again avoid some of the fine points which appear before our eyes if we look at this relationship with the care it deserves" (1958h, p. 301). In other words, both the term "symbiosis" and the expression "homeostatic equilibrium" are not specific to the nature of the human relationship and may be used for human or feline babies.
22. A detailed examination of Winnicott's conception of human instinctuality and of imaginative elaboration of the bodily functions is made in Loparic, 2000b.
23. For Winnicott, the term "deep", which refers to unconscious fantasy or repressed contents is not a synonym for "early", because "an infant needs a degree of maturity before becoming gradually able to be deep" (1958i, p. 111).
24. With regard, for example, to the jealousy between siblings, which is updated in the analytical situation as hate for other patients, Winnicott says that those individuals who suffer from a psychotic problem and regress to dependence "either have no objection to there being other patients or else they cannot conceive of there being another patient" (1955b, pp. 288–289).
25. Certain authors maintain that this position stems from the fact that for classical psychoanalysis, which falls within the metaphysical tradition of Cartesianism, reality, whether external or internal, has only one meaning: something already given, peopled by objects, the access to which, also unique, occurs via representation. From this perspective, there is no idea of a constitution of the senses of reality, inherent to the modes of being which unfold during development and throughout life (cf. Loparic, 1997a).
26. For more detail on this point, cf. Loparic, 2001b.
27. Melanie Klein, at the beginning of her famous article "Notes on some schizoid mechanisms" states: "I have often expressed my view that object relations exist from the beginning of life" (Klein, 1946, p. 2).
28. Cf. Loparic, 1997a.
29. Cf. Winnicott, 1989a, Chapter Fifty-three, part two.
30. Winnicott was extremely cautious with regard to this tendency, which we might call media-oriented. He was extremely cautious when proposing terms to designate a number of phenomena which became visible in the light of his theory, fearful that they would eventually be used as clichés, as "Winnicott's things", emptied of the experiential meaning that they should contain. For example, in distinguishing "object-mother" from "environment-mother", he warned that these expressions should not become empty slogans and "develop a rigidity and an obstructive quality" (1963b, p. 102).

31. Cf. Winnicott, 1971g, p. 95. Winnicott is not alone in this assessment. Pontalis also asserts that the Kleinian theory of envy and guilt attributed to the most primitive childhood, "was no more than a psychoanalytical transcription of the myth of original sin" (Pontalis, 1981, p. 95).
32. Cf. Winnicott's letter to Melanie Klein, of November 1952, in Winnicott, 1987b.
33. For Masud Khan, there is a bridge between Winnicott's work and Hartmann's research on this sphere of the ego free from conflicts (Khan, 1975, p. xviii) in the concept of "the period of hesitation" described by Winnicott in his article "The observation of infants in a set situation" (1941).

CHAPTER TWO

Basic concepts of the theory of maturational processes

Maturation as an innate tendency towards integration

Winnicott's theory of maturational processes is founded on two basic conceptions or, in other words, the personal maturacional process fundamentally depends on two factors: the innate tendency towards maturation and the continuous existence of a facilitating environment. We shall start with the first one.

According to Winnicott, every human being is endowed with an innate tendency towards maturation. This conception is based on another one, that man is essentially a temporal being. A human being, the author says, "is a time-sample of human nature" (1988, p. 11).[1] All human phenomena are an unfolding in time of human nature, in such a way that they cannot be described, at any level, as something substantial, under penalty of distorting the fundamental nature of man: of being a form of temporalisation. Winnicott's theory of personal maturational processes is the explanation in time, in the form of phases or stages, of the various tasks imposed by the innate tendency towards maturation on the individual throughout his life.

What does Winnicott understand by human nature? Human nature, which is "almost all we have" (ibid., p. 1), consists essentially of *an innate tendency towards integration into a unit* throughout a maturational process. As a time-sample of human nature, each human being is endowed with a *tendency* towards *maturation*, that is, a *tendency towards integration into a unitary whole.* This is her most important inheritance. "The individual inherits a maturational process" (1974, p. 89; 1984f, p. 62). Every individual is *destined to mature* and that means: becoming unified and bearing responsibility for a me. As a function of this, what fails in the process and is not integrated through experience is not just a nothing, but a perturbation.

The notion that maturation is governed by the tendency towards integration into a unit resulted from a long evolution in Winnicott's thought. The idea that development is always in progress was already established in the 1940s, as was the fact that there are difficulties relating to maturation itself. In a text from 1959, we find the statement that what is most important in heredity "is the individual's inherent tendency to grow, to integrate, to relate to objects, to mature" (1965h, p. 137); we may perceive that at this point, the fundamental direction of maturation as a tendency towards integration into a unity is still vague. It is in a late text, from 1968, that Winnicott spells out that *the state of unity is the basic human achievement for health in the emotional development of every human being* (cf. 1984f). In 1969, he reaffirmed the existence of something "*universal* in the emotional development of the individual, namely, the integrative tendency that can bring the individual to a *status* of unity" (1989i, p. 244; my italics).[2]

We should not attribute an essentialist character to Winnicott's thesis that human nature consists of an innate tendency towards integration into a unity. This is not an eternal essence, says Loparic,

> [...] for Winnicott understands that "human nature evolved, just as human bodies and beings evolved, in the course of hundreds of thousands of years". He does not dispute the *phylogenesis* of the human species, that is, of the tendency towards integration itself, even if he has nothing to say about this subject. At the same time, however, Winnicott notes that "there is very little evidence that human nature has altered in the short span of recorded history" [...]. Winnicott's concept of human nature may therefore be understood as designating the fixed structure of our *ontogenesis* or, in a less biologising language, more characteristic of Winnicott, of our personal or emotional development, which is governed by the innate tendency towards integration. (Loparic, 2000b, p. 355)[3]

In order to arrive at this final formulation, that the unitary status is the basic achievement for health in the emotional maturation of every human being, Winnicott had to overcome two ideas established by traditional psychoanalysis: first, the one which assumes that the constitution of the primitive me and the capacity for contacting reality are already given. Second, the idea that division, the essential "dynamic" of humans, could be described in terms of pulsions. Attentive to babies and psychotics, Winnicott introduced an initial phase in which there is not yet an established me, but rather, a non-integrated being who emerges from a state of essential aloneness. This aloneness, which will be partly overcome, remains throughout life in the depths of every individual. There is indeed an essential splitting, but it is not related to pulsions; inherent to human nature, it consists of the gap between the tendency to open up to relations with the other and the world, and the primordial isolation of the human being.[4] A successful process of integration will lead to the coexistence and transit between these two extremes within the individual: the essential aloneness, on the one hand, and the communication and encounter with the other and with external reality, on the other.

Maturation and the facilitating environment

Despite being innate, the tendency towards integration does not happen automatically, as if the mere passage of time were enough. This is a tendency, not a determination. In order for it to be achieved, *the baby depends fundamentally on the presence of a facilitating environment which provides good enough care.* The fact of dependence, which is absolute in the initial stages, is essential to Winnicott's theory: "Human infants cannot start to *be* except under certain conditions" (1960b, p. 43). No baby, no child can become a real person, *unless it is under the care of an environment that provides support and facilitates maturational processes.* Babies who do not receive this good enough care "do not fulfil themselves, even as babies. Genes are not enough" (1968d, p. 94). Since the absolute outset, the fundamental need of the human being is to be and to go on being. The individual must not only arrive at a beginning, so that entry into life may occur, but he must also keep himself alive throughout life: "It is a constant struggle to get to the starting point and to keep there" (1965j, p. 192). There are physically healthy babies who die because they do not find a basis for being from the outset. Others do not necessarily die; they are persuaded into "feeding and living, although the basis for living is feeble or absent" (1988, p. 107).

All this means that becoming unified and real and reaching the unitary identity (which implies the separation between the me and the not-me, demarcating the end of the initial stages) may never occur. For psychotics, whose disorders derive from the most primitive stages of life, this is precisely what they were unable to achieve. For this reason, their difficulties and problems are particularly afflicting, since these are "not so much a part of life as a part of the struggle to reach a life [...]" (ibid., p. 80). Such patients, permanently hovering between living and not living, force us to face this kind of problem, which actually relates to all human beings and which boils down to the following question: what is life about and what makes it worth living? (cf. 1967b & 1971g).

Hence, in *personal maturation* it is not isolated functions that are at stake, whether biological, mental or sexual, but human life itself, in what is strictly personal to it: the feeling of being, of being real, of existing in the real world as a self. None of this is given by biological conception or birth. Even when the cerebral and biological structures are intact, the fact of having been born does not guarantee the achievement of the feeling of being alive, of feeling real and of being able to have experiences that are felt as real. Throughout maturation, all of the human dimensions must be gradually integrated into the personality, but always starting from the personal sense of existence, a sense that, initially, is the mere continuity of being. Moreover, the drive to live, to stay alive and to develop is not described in terms of forces: it is not the libido that passes through various phases or object fixations, but human nature which temporalises itself as a result of its innate tendency towards growth, and gradually generates a self that is integrated both internally and with the environment.

General characteristics of maturational processes

The maturational process begins at some point after conception and continues throughout the individual's life until his natural death, with this being the last event to be integrated, the last task of health.

The process unfolds in stages, or steps, that can be briefly and generically enumerated as follows.[5] The primitive stages of absolute dependence include: (1) the essential aloneness, the experience of birth and the stage of the theoretical first feed. The initial stages of relative dependence include: (2) the stage of disillusion and beginning of mental processes; (3) the stage of transitionality; (4) that of object usage; and (5) the stage of I AM. After this, the baby moves on "towards independence": (6) the stage of concern. Next, are the stages of relative independence: (7) the oedipal stage; (8) the latency stage; (9) adolescence; (10) the beginning of adulthood; (11) adulthood; (12) old age and death. In old age, something of absolute or relative dependence returns.

The chronological age to which these stages correspond cannot be located accurately, but only approximately, for which reason, we refer much more to stages than to ages. To the different stages correspond tasks and achievements of different natures, which are imposed on the individual throughout development by the innate tendency towards integration itself. If the baby succeeds in accomplishing the task which corresponds to the phase, this fact becomes an achievement of maturation. As development proceeds, tasks become more complex, and if the individual is healthy, he is able to become involved and deal naturally with the tasks specific to his age group. Gradually, over time,

> [...] the infant becomes the man or the woman, not too early, not too late. Middle age arrives in due course, with new appropriate changes, and eventually old age curbs the various functions till natural death follows as the final seal of health. (1988, p. 12)

From a global perspective, maturation can be described as a journey that starts with *absolute dependence*, passes through a period of *relative* dependence, reaches the stages which move *towards independence*, until it reaches *relative independence*, the stage at which the healthy individual remains regularly throughout life. It should be noted that the terms are relational, always implying the existence of another human being. At the beginning of the process, however, the "relation" has a *sui generis* character, due to the fact that the baby is not yet a unity. The unity is the mother–baby pair, with the mother being felt by the baby as part of himself, that is, as a subjective object.

The essential tasks and achievements of emotional development take place during the most primitive stage of life, when the baby lives in a state of absolute and then relative dependence on the mother's care. This results not only from the precocity of the moment, but also from the nature of the tasks and achievements that are inherent to it. These primitive stages may therefore be called fundamental in the literal sense that it is during this period that the fundamental bases of existence are being established, that is, the foundations of personality and of psychic health. This is achieved through the resolution of three tasks in which the baby is involved: integration in time and space; gradual indwelling of the psyche in the body and the beginning of object relation or of contact with reality. As these tasks are being achieved, there is a fourth one in progress: the self is being constituted through the continuous repetition of small experiences of integration; gradually, the integrated state becomes increasingly more stable in such a way, that the baby moves towards integration into a unit.[6]

It is also possible to describe development in terms of the sense of reality that the individual is able to create at each stage and of the nature of the relation that he establishes with the environment at a given moment in development. The baby initially lives in a world which is conceived subjectively; he then moves on to an intermediary form of reality, that of transitionality, which is halfway between the subjective and the objective; after that, he moves towards constituting the me as an integrated identity, separate from the not-me, being then able to start to perceive the external or shared world objectively.

> At first the relationship is to a subjective object, and it is a long journey from here to the development and establishment of a capacity to relate to an object that is objectively perceived and that is allowed a separate existence, an existence outside the omnipotent control of the individual. (1963c, p. 224)

If it is possible to say that the human individual has a beginning, this must be thought of as a sum of beginnings (cf. 1969e). In the above quotation, the achievement of the me as an identity separated from the not-me demarcates a beginning of the individual, probably the main one, when he becomes able to relate to external reality; however, everything depends on other previous beginnings having been successful. When speaking of psychic health, Winnicott is referring, above all, to the fact that a child has accomplished the initial tasks satisfactorily and has managed to reach a unitary status, which is the basic condition for the beginning of the establishment of relative independence. From this point onwards, with the foundations established, the individual may suffer psychic disorders but he does not run the risk of becoming a psychotic.

The achievement of unity in an integrated *me* occurs around the age of one year to eighteen months, in the stage rather appropriately termed "I AM". The me that is achieved is the initial self itself, which, after becoming integrated in various levels and aspects throughout the initial stages, has now separated from the mother. This unitary status is not a cohesive whole, without fractures or exempt from conflicts, but a state of spatio-temporal integration, in which "there is one self containing everything instead of dissociated elements that exist in compartments, or are scattered around and left lying about" (1971g, p. 90). In this achievement, there is a completion and a beginning, since the I AM state, the feeling of being real and of existing as an identity, "is not an end in itself, it is a position from which life can be lived" (1989h, p. 435).

We must not think of a baby in his "long journey", as a car that starts from a pre-existing point to arrive at another equally pre-existing one. There is no ready-made place from which he can start or at which he may arrive, that of objectively perceived reality, which is waiting to be discovered, nor is there an already determined path. Despite the limitations and dangers of such images, the baby is much more like the road, which builds itself, without losing the previous sections. The individual who develops progressively establishes his self like a path.[7]

Since the sequential presentation of the stages of the maturational processes[8] and the very term "stage" may lead to the idea of separate steps, each one following the other, it is necessary to highlight that despite being so presented, *the process is not linear*. Firstly, because in life, the different stages with their respective tasks partially overlap; secondly, because in Winnicott's conception, development is not a synonym for progress: developing includes the possibility of regression, whenever life demands rest, in moments of overloading and tension, or in order to return to points which have been lost. This is due to the fact that no achievement provides a guarantee: once reached, it may be lost, then reached again and then lost again.[9] This is why it is possible to find all kinds of needs in a person of any age, from the most primitive to the latest ones. People are not exactly their age; "they are to some extent every age, or no age" (1984c, p. 81).

The incompleteness of the maturational achievements is especially true with regard to the tasks at the start of life. These fundamental tasks are never left behind as completed or sorted out; they are never established as definitive achievements, since "they are matters which are and which go on being the basic task of every human being throughout life" (1988, p. 83).

However, despite the non-linearity of the process, we cannot neglect the fact that some achievements (and this refers, above all, to the primitive ones) can only be reached after others have been, which are their prerequisite, their condition of possibility.[10] That means that, achieving the tasks of each stage depends on having successfully achieved the tasks of the previous ones. If there is failure, new tasks will keep emerging, but the individual, having missed the previous acquisition, will lack the maturity required to address the new ones; he may even sort them out intellectually, but they will stand on false ground and will not become an intrinsic part of him or herself as personal acquisitions. Regarding the achievement pertinent to the stage of concern, for example, Winnicott says:

> [...] the earlier stages must have been successfully negotiated either in real life or in the analysis, or in both, if the depressive position is to be reached. To reach the depressive position a baby must have become established as a whole person, and be related to whole persons as a whole person. (1955c, p. 264)[11]

That is, for a child to be able to take responsibility for his instinctual impulsiveness, he must already be a me; only a me is capable of being concerned and worried about the consequences of instinctuallity. If this does not happen, then the child cannot achieve the capacity for guilt. He will simply go on without it, albeit with a distorted personality. It is probable that schizoid individuals, whose problems derive from very primitive stages, prior to the one in which they already have sufficient maturity to achieve the capacity for guilt and responsibility, will make no significant achievement regarding concern, and, for them, "magical re-creation has to be exploited in default of what is described as reparation and restitution" (ibid., p. 264).

When there is failure in the achievement of one or another stage of development, an emotional disorder is established. *The nature of the disorder relates to its point of origin on the line of development, that is, to the nature of the task in which the baby, or child, was involved at the time of the environmental failure.*

The theory of maturational processes thus constitutes the necessary theoretical horizon for the consideration and understanding of human phenomena that we encounter in clinical practice. According to this theory, any phenomenon that we wish to consider, be it in illness or in health, can only be duly appreciated if we consider the entire development process of the individual, starting from the most primitive stages, and if we can locate the stage at which the phenomenon originated, in other words, if we are alert to *the emotional age relating to the phenomenon or disorder* which arises. Only in this way, can we understand the "nature" of the problem with which the individual is involved, arrive at the classification of the disorder and provide specific care according to his needs. We must "always think in terms of the *developing individual.*

This means going back very early and looking to see if the point of origin can be determined" (1984c, p. 81).

It follows from this that in a particular clinical case, there is always a dominant difficulty, which refers to a task which was not resolved at a specific stage. This is the reason why diagnosis is so important. One of the main difficulties with the analytical technique, says Winnicott, is to know *the age of the patient at a specific moment of the analytical relationship*, so that we may provide care concerning the specific need that he or she presents and which varies with the emotional age of the patient (cf. 1958f).

Regarding the initial stages, if the baby does not resolve the task relating to his current maturational stage, there is an interruption to the process of personal maturation. Everything built from this point on will be distorted at the root, will acquire a defensive character and will have no personal value for the individual.

Psycho-somatic existence: the soma, the psyche, and the mind

Winnicott distinguishes personal maturation from bodily growth. The former is related to life experiences which, facilitated by the environment, permit the constitution of the unitary personality; the latter depends largely on genetic factors. However, even in this latter case, the environment factor is decisive, in so far as physical growth may be seriously affected by problems related to maturation.

Whatever human phenomenon is being considered, we must take account of the *total person*, in which the *soma* and *psyche* exist. Human nature, writes the author, "is not a matter of mind and body—it is a matter of inter-related psyche and soma" (1988, p. 26). Mind "is of an order special to itself, and must be considered as a special case of the functioning of the psyche-soma" (1988, p. 11). Although there are operational differences between psychic and bodily functions, on account of their very nature and the tendency towards integration, psyche and *soma* are closely interconnected. *Human existence is essentially psycho-somatic.*

It is always possible for an external observer to distinguish the physical, the psychic and the mental aspects in a human being, but this means looking from a certain point of view at the total, psycho-somatic, person, aiming at the consideration of one of the elements. This distinction is nevertheless superfluous for an individual whose mother took care of him as a whole, as a potentially psycho-somatic existence, during the initial stages. When the baby is held properly, he

> [...] does not have to know about being made up of a collection of parts. The baby is a belly joined on to a chest and has loose limbs and particularly a loose head: all these parts are gathered together by the mother who is holding the child, and in her hands they add up to one. (1969e, p. 568)

The soma is the *living body*, which is gradually personalised as it is *imaginatively elaborated by the psyche*. This living body is undoubtedly physical but not merely physiological or anatomical; it is certainly not the physical machine, autonomous with regard to the psyche, with which classical medicine deals; in this way, it is not a body that may be studied through corpses. The living body is an aspect of the individual's "aliveness"; breathing, temperature, motility are an intrinsic part of his vitality, in addition to the vitality of tissues, since as a living body, "the tissues are alive and they are part of a whole animal, and are *affected* by the varying psyche states of that animal" (1988, p. 26; my italics).[12] There are situations of anxiety in which the child's metabolism is practically reduced to zero and, in this case, "sores sometimes do not heal simply as a result of a general lack of interest on the part of the child, and of the tissues, in living" (1931b, p. 17).

The psyche encompasses everything that, in the individual, is not the *soma*, including the mind, understood as a specialised mode of psycho-somatic operation. The psyche starts as "the *imaginative elaboration of somatic parts, feelings, and functions*, that is, of physical aliveness" (1954a, p. 244).[13] The psyche, *without ever losing this original function*, develops throughout maturation into ever more advanced functions, which include all of the mental operations that can be covered by the different meanings of the word *to think*. The central task of the psyche is nevertheless the gradual constitution of human temporality and hence, the manifestation of the sense of history in human life. Starting from the baby's primitive temporality, which is that of the body itself, at the start of life, the psyche is responsible for both the imaginative elaboration of bodily experiences of all kinds, and the storage and gathering of the memories of those experiences. As development proceeds, these become increasingly more sophisticated and the psyche gradually interconnects "past experiences, potentialities, and the present moment awareness, and expectancy for the future" (1988, p. 19). It is this operation that gives sense to the feeling of self and justifies "our perception of an individual there in that body" (ibid., p. 28).

The first task of the psyche is, as mentioned before, the imaginative elaboration of bodily functions. The body that is imaginatively elaborated is the living body of someone that breathes, moves, searches for something, suckles, kicks, sucks its thumb, rests, is cuddled, changed, surrounded by the bathwater, etc. Whatever is being experienced, and everything is initially experienced in the body and through the body, *is being personalised by the imaginative elaboration*. Since from the time of birth, the baby already has a life that, while restricted, is already personal, any experience is lived not as an anodyne and simple physical sensation, but with a *sense*.[14] That is, *the direct experience that a baby has of the functioning, of the sensations and of the movements of the body* has for him a sense, because of the fact that it is imaginatively elaborated. Despite the fact that this sense cannot be directly observed, it will become manifest later, in playing and/or in clinical situations of regression to dependence.

This "creation of meaning"[15] as Loparic states, and this is the central point for the understanding of the concept of imaginative elaboration, *precedes the mental operations of representation, verbalisation and symbolisation*, operations for which the baby is still too immature. Referring to the fact that one of the various forms of integration in the human being in development is "a satisfactory working arrangement between the psyche and the soma", Winnicott adds: "This starts prior to the time when it is necessary to add the concepts of intellect and verbalisation" (1971d, p. 270).

It is because of the concept of imaginative elaboration that Winnicott is able to make many statements, such as the following ones: We already have good evidence that in intrauterine life, both the movement phase and the rest phase are significant (cf. 1988, p. 21). Or that when it is a full-term birth, the baby feels that it was his impulse "that produced the changes and the physical progression, usually head first, towards an unknown and new position" (ibid., p. 144). He also notes that "the *imaginative* feeding experience is much wider than the purely physical experience", demanding "something more in infant life than sleeping and getting milk, and something more than getting instinctual gratification from a good feed taken in and kept down" (1993e, p. 17). It is precisely the things that the baby does while suckling, and that are not those which makes it gain weight, that corroborate the fact that it "is feeding and not just *being fed*, is living a life and not just responding to the stimuli we offer" (idem). Sucking the thumb is also a highly elaborated action for the human baby, since it means "being in control of the thumb which stands for all other objects which are gathered together in this way and put into relationship with the mouth, etc., etc." (1987b, p. 122). It also consists of the attempt by the baby to situate the object (breast, thumb, etc.), keeping it halfway between the inside and the outside, which constitutes "a defence against loss of object in the external world or in the inside of the body, that is to say, against loss of control over the object" (1945d, p. 156).[16]

In a definition of the concept of imaginative elaboration which is still vague, Winnicott says this is "a crude form of what later we call the imagination" (1993e, p. 17). In the earlier texts he sometimes uses the term fantasy to refer to what he will later more specifically term imaginative elaboration. We must nevertheless highlight that this "imagination" which elaborates the somatic functions from the outset and is responsible for the mutual interrelationship of psyche and soma *is not yet a fantasy* in the traditional sense of the term, as we shall see below. In a letter from 1954 to Betty Joseph, Winnicott writes: "I am trying to draw attention to the very early stages, quite apart from the fantasy" (1987b, p. 59).

Winnicott's substitution of the traditional concept of psyche, understood in the same sense as mind, for a psyche in which the mind is only one aspect of this psyche has the same character as his substitution of the concept of "fantasy" for that of imaginative elaboration, with regard to the early stages. The reasons are as follows: in the traditional theory, fantasy is a *mental* function that develops into mental mechanisms, such as introjection and projection, which, according to this theory, are in full operation since the beginning of life. For Winnicott, however, the baby's extreme immaturity does not allow us to suppose such a sophisticated operation. He pleads for an entire initial period when the work of the psyche, through imaginative elaboration, leads to a *schematisation* of the body, to a personal appropriation of the sense of anatomy, sensations, movements and the body functioning in general, without the participation of the mind.[17] In Winnicott's perspective, fantasy as a mental operation developing in an inner world that has already been constituted, *belongs to a later moment in development* and is not a direct elaboration from reality like imagination, but rather a creation from memory; it thus requires that a certain temporalisation has already been established, which has not yet occurred at the start of life.

Furthermore, the term "imagination" may itself lead to the wrong idea that images participate in imaginative elaboration, which would make it another mental mechanism. A clarification on this point is contained in a footnote in which Winnicott makes explicit his use of the term "fantasy", highlighting its peculiarity when it refers to the initial stages:

> It occurs to me that I may be using the word "fantasy" in a way that is not familiar to some of you. I am not talking about fantasying, or about contrived fantasy. I am thinking of the whole

> of the child's personal or psychic reality, some of it conscious, but mostly unconscious, and *including that which is not verbalized or pictured or heard in a structural way because it is primitive and near the almost physiological roots from which it springs.* (1989p, p. 69; my italics)

It is possible to say that the primary psychic function, the imaginative elaboration of bodily functions, which includes what is neither verbalised *nor pictured* and is close to "the physiological roots from which it springs"—is the necessary basis so that fantasy, in the sense of a mental mechanism, may become a later acquisition in the development of the individual. This moment, starting from which the individual becomes capable of fantasising, in the traditional sense, is clearly indicated by the author: at the stage of object usage, when the baby starts to destroy the mother as subjective object, in order to expel her from the area of omnipotence, in other words, into the externality of the world; if the mother survives, the child will find "a new meaning to the word love, and a new thing turns up in the baby's life which is fantasy" (1969b, p. 31).[18]

It is nevertheless important to emphasise that the imaginative elaboration does not disappear with the advent of the capacity to fantasise. This function remains so throughout life at the same time as it becomes "infinitely complex" as mental functions are included and both growth and maturation impose new tasks, deriving from anatomical transformation and from new forms of functioning, organisation and sensitisation of tissues, organs and the brain. In a text from 1958, Winnicott provides a list, ordered chronologically according to the successive stages of development, of the tasks incumbent on imaginative elaboration, clarifying that the primary psychic function plays an essential role in the main achievements of the process (cf. 1958j).

Imaginatively elaborated since the start of life, all of the bodily functions of the baby, motor, sensory and instinctive, are simultaneously *organised*, in other words, they are articulated and integrated by the "functioning of the ego". The result is the "experience of ego". It is by virtue of this organising function, in which the imaginative elaboration of the bodily functions participates, that the experiences of the id, that is, instinctive ones, are not lost, but brought together in all of their aspects. And it is because of this that Winnicott affirms: "There is thus no sense in making use of the word 'id' for phenomena that are not covered and catalogued and experienced and eventually interpreted by ego-functioning" (1965n, p. 56).[19]

For this same reason, Winnicott was able to affirm that in theory and in normality, the baby's ego is based on a bodily ego. The ego nevertheless only develops from the bodily ego if the baby is getting good enough maternal care, which favours the integrative tendency of the indwelling of the psyche in the body. Recalling that Freud, decades previously, had also stated that the ego was based on a corporeal ego, Winnicott comments: "Freud might have gone on to say that *in health* the self retains this apparent identity with the body and its functioning" (1966, p. 112). In this way, for Winnicott, unlike for Freud, the integration of the psyche in the body does not happen automatically, as an inevitable *a priori* of the maturational processes but requires the facilitation of the supporting environment. Since this latter is an imponderable element, the achievement may or may not happen. Neither the concepts of hysterical conversion and somatisation grasp the issue of the difficulty of establishing the psycho-somatic relation and the threat of breaking it.

The differences between Freud and Winnicott regarding this question nevertheless do not end there. Having conceived the body as the place from where the sensations both internal and external may arise, Freud was able to affirm that "the ego is first and foremost a bodily ego; it is not merely a surface entity, but is itself the projection of a surface" (Freud, 1923b, vol. 11, pp. 364–365). In a footnote, specifically added to this sentence, in the English translation of the text, *Ego and id*, Freud also explains that

> the ego is ultimately derived from bodily sensations, chiefly from those springing from the surface of the body. It may thus be regarded as a mental projection of the surface of the body, besides, [...] representing the superficies of the mental apparatus. (Freud, 1923b, vol. 11, note 2, p. 365)[20]

Commenting on this note, Loparic concludes:

> Like the ego and the id, Freud's corporeal ego, a speculative entity, related to the *surface of the body*, is essentially different from Winnicott's, which is based on the effectively experienced imaginative elaboration of the *whole body*. (Loparic, 2000b, p. 382)

Winnicott's thesis that human existence is essentially psycho-somatic does not imply a monism that obscures the specific features of soma and psyche, assimilating one with the other.[21] In fact, what we have is a dualism. He states: "There are the soma and the psyche" (1988, p. 11); or also: "There is no inherent identity of body and psyche" (ibid., p. 123). We must distinguish these two contexts, not only in order to be able to consider that both are intimately interconnected and tend towards integration. From the point of view of the developing individual,

> [...] the self and the body are not inherently superimposed, the one on the other, and yet it is necessary for health that such a superimposition should become a fact, so that the individual can become able to afford to identify with what is, strictly speaking, not the self. (1988, p. 123)

However, Winnicott's dualism, which tends towards integration, can in no way be approximated to the Cartesian mind/body dichotomy. First, because, in the latter, mind and body are understood as substances and not aspects of being. Furthermore, these substances are of an irreconcilable nature; between the *res cogitans* and the *res extensa* there is no possible association or integration. This is the meaning of Winnicott's statement that the terms mental and physical "are not descriptive of opposed phenomena. *It is the soma and the psyche that are opposed*" (1988, p. 11; my italics). Second, because from the Cartesian perspective, mind assimilates and dominates the whole of the psyche. For Winnicott, however, the psyche is far from being restricted to the functioning of the mind. With regard to Winnicott's preservation of dualism, in terms other than those of Descartes, Loparic says:

> In Winnicott's thought, the *substantial difference* between mind and body, introduced by Descartes, is not denied for the sake of reductionism, whether materialistic or spiritual; it is replaced by the *operational difference* between bodily functions and psychic ones. By analogy, the *problem of the union* of mind and body is replaced by the *problem of the integration* of the

> bodily functions by the psychic ones, with each one of these two groups of functions being treated as irreducible to the other. (Loparic, 2000b, p. 360, note 20)[22]

At the same time, as the living body is in some way an element of the external world and has its own modes of growth and its own temporality, it must be said that there is always something of the physical body left that is not integrated and that when it sickens, it reveals its autonomy and opacity, as something that escapes the individual's omnipotence and cannot be fully covered by the work of the psyche.[23] It is thus always important to examine "the infant's original mix-up of the body itself with the feeling and ideas about the body" (1988, p. 95). If Winnicott had not preserved the body autonomy, he would not have been able to affirm that "it is distressing that healthy persons may have to live in deformed or diseased or old bodies, or may be starving or in great pain" (1971f, p. 29).

Where does the mind fit into the psycho-somatic existence? The mind, says Winnicott, "means something quite distinct from psyche" (1958j, p. 7); It constitutes an order special to itself (cf. 1988, p. 11). When environmental care facilitates the psycho-somatic partnership, the mind does not exist as a separate entity, being merely a *special way of functioning of the psyche-soma*, a specialisation for intellectual functions, its culminating point, "as a flourish on the edge of psycho-somatic functioning" (1988, p. 26).

The mental functions span the different meanings of the word "thinking". At the very outset, they exert the functions of cataloguing, comparing and classifying: "It is a function of mind to catalogue events, and to store memories and classify them" (1958j, p. 7). As these develop, they make use of time as a measurement, to measure space, relate cause and effect and to make predictions.[24] In health, the baby's mind is driven to exert its specialised functions as a natural development of the increasing psycho-somatic cohesion, starting from the stages where the de-adaptation of the mother begins, that is, when dependence shifts from absolute to relative. Intellectual processes equip the baby for dealing with the gaps in adaptation, for understanding and anticipating the environmental failures characteristic of this period, with this enabling him to continue in the direction of independence. This development occurs in its own time and while it has a defensive function, it is not pathological since it does not arise as a reaction to invasions which exceed the maturational capacity.

At the right moment, when the mental functions begin, the baby, by virtue of repeated experiences of adaptive care, already "knows" many things *through non-mental ways*. It is absolutely vital, for the psychic health of the little individual that this pre-cognitive knowledge is already established at the stage when intellectual processes effectively begin to function; this knowledge constitutes an essential basis for existence. Throughout life, above all at crucial moments, it is on this that the individual draws when he requires reassurance about himself or the world in which he lives.

Despite the fact that the right time for the beginning of mental functioning, which will not overwhelm the baby is the passage from absolute to relative dependence, it is already possible to observe the use of some mental functions at the start of the maturational process in a sort of "precognitive ordering of incipient thought" (1989s, p. 154), of which very little is yet known. We may thus speak of a "rudimentary mind", which is pre-representational and which is still not sufficiently mature for perception.[25] This kind of rudimentary mental functioning belongs to this moment of development; being natural and not impelled by pressure or invasion, it does not overload the baby. It must not be mistaken for the phenomenon consisting of the baby's mind being made to function prematurely as a result of his defensive need for alertness, preventing failures that may derive, for example, from environmental instability. The good enough mother, in spite of delighting in the "intelligence" or "cleverness" of her baby, always takes his emotional immaturity into account, so that she does not prematurely exploit the ability that he certainly has to understand and tolerate failure. If the mother abandons her protective function and neglects her adaptive behaviour to the infant's needs and begins to count on his intelligence for failing beyond that which is tolerable to a particular baby, a premature development of the ego may occur, which, as we shall see, is pathological and in these cases, the mind becomes an entity in itself.

Conceived as an operation mode of the psyche-soma and not as an entity in itself, the mind is not localised in the body. In popular thinking, however, people tend to place mental activity inside the head, or even outside of it, albeit in some special relation to the head.[26] Winnicott states that he cannot answer why the head is the place where individuals tend to situate the mind, but sees in this common understanding the fruit of one of the imaginative elaborations characteristic of the psyche itself regarding somatic functioning. Perhaps this is due to the fact, he suggests, that since the human baby has an absurdly huge head, this is affected and compressed during birth, exactly when the still rudimentary mind starts to function in "furiously active" fashion, cataloguing and memorising the many discontinuities that the process of birth entails.[27] Despite the fact, however, that it depends on the functioning of the brain, in terms of psycho-somatic existence, the mind is not necessarily linked to a given point in the body. We nevertheless indulge

> in a fantasy that there is a place, which we call the mind, where the intellect works, and each individual places the mind somewhere, and there feels muscular straining or experiences vascular congestion when trying to think. (1988, p. 53)

We all know that sometimes the mind knows things "in its gut" and that it is without doubt at the fingertips of the virtuoso pianist at the moment of the concert.

Heritabilities

The word "heritability" is used by Winnicott in two senses, which must be rigorously distinguished from each other: firstly, the innate tendency towards maturation, which in his view is the main inheritance of the human being; second, biological inheritance. My purpose in this section is to examine his position regarding the participation of genetics in the maturational process, in the constitution of the individual and in the aetiology of psychic disorders, and to examine how the two senses of heritabilities relate to each other.

On the one hand, we thus have the innate tendency towards integration. Having stated in a text from 1954 that there is a biological drive behind the progression contained in the tendency towards integration (cf. 1955b, p. 280), Winnicott never elucidated whether, due to this participation of biology, we are authorised to think of variable degrees of tendency towards integration.

It is nevertheless possible to affirm that this tendency is not reducible to any genetic inheritance. On the other hand, we have hereditary or congenital factors that are organic: lesions or acquired illnesses[28] which determine certain psychological disorders or tendencies of the personality: "There are genes which determine patterns and an inherited tendency to grow and to achieve maturity" (1969c, p. 187). In the same sense is the affirmation that "inheritance of personality traits and tendencies towards psychiatric types and disorders belongs to the physical, and limits are set to psychotherapy by inheritance" (1988, p. 19). We must thus distinguish between *genetic patterns*, which determine anatomical and biological patterns and the innate tendency to grow and to mature, which may or may not occur naturally, *within these patterns*. The meaning of this is not "to deny the existence of hereditary factors, but rather to supplement them in important respects" (1965n, p. 59).

An accurate examination of any psychic disorder must take all of the factors into account, both the inherited and the environmental ones. First, however, we must recall that, from a purely psychological perspective, "inherited *factors are environmental, i.e. external to the life and experience of the individual psyche*" (1989q, p. 124; my italics). People in general are surprised, the author says, when they hear that a baby's inherited tendencies are factors that are external to him, but they are just as clearly external or alien to the baby as is, for example, the capacity of the mother for being good enough or her tendency to become depressed (cf. 1968d).[29] They will only become part of the baby's personality if he appropriates them through experience.

Moreover, what Winnicott observes, on the basis of his clinical experience with psychotics, is that in the majority of cases, the hereditary factor is non-existent or irrelevant. There are cases of schizophrenia, says he, in which "a hereditary tendency to psychosis is strong, whereas in others it is not a significant feature" (1965l, p. 62). In a case in which the hereditary factor is active, we will be dealing with secondary psychological complications resulting from a disorder that is physical. We must nevertheless distinguish these psychological disorders, with a somatic basis, from *psychic disorders*, a term reserved by the author for disorders of the development process, which may also manifest themselves.

What must be considered is that somatic disorders, with their inevitable psychological complications, may (and usually are) accompanied by disorders relating to the development process. This occurs due to the additional difficulty of the parents in performing their role with a child whose development is arduous and impaired by organic-cerebral problems.

In this way, although it is necessary to consider the participation of physical heredity, it should not be regarded as a decisive factor. When studying, for example, the use that a specific individual makes of his mind, we generally carry out routine intelligence tests, that is, an assessment of his or her intellectual capacity, with regard to the quality of the cerebral tissue, which is hence basically hereditary. Such tests are useful and necessary, but, the author says, are "no basis, however, for the assessment of a personality or of personal emotional growth" (1988, p. 140).

This issue, relating to intellectual function, is a good example of how to include organic heredity in the consideration of disorders without attributing to them an exclusive aetiological meaning: when intellectual capacity is restricted, due to a cerebral tissue with a poor genetic endowment, in addition to the possible difficulty of the parents mentioned above, there is a reduction in the capacity that the baby generally has for converting an unsatisfactory environmental adaptation into a good enough one. As a result, some psychoses are more common in mentally defective persons than in the normal population. On the other hand,

> [...] exceptional brain-tissue endowment may enable an infant to allow for a severe failure of adaptation to need, but in such a case there can be a prostitution of mental activity so that one finds clinically a hypertrophy of intellectual processes related to a potential schizophrenic breakdown. (1953a, p. 225)[30]

The possibility of deficit exists both in the case of poorly endowed cerebral tissue (which is a case of organic deficiency) and an exceptionally endowed one. *What counts is the mother's adaptive care of that singular baby*, for even when an individual's cerebral capacity is restricted (e.g., with an IQ of 80), if the special conditions of the facilitating environment are present, this individual may present a healthy emotional development and may even become an interesting and valuable person, "of good character and of reliable disposition, even capable of becoming a good marriage partner and parent" (1988, p. 13). On the other hand, if a child with an exceptional cerebral endowment (e.g., with an IQ of 140) suffers serious perturbations to his development, due to poorly satisfactory environmental care, he may become extremely ill, subject to psychotic crises, lacking a trustworthy character and with little chance of one day being able to take care of himself. Such children, instead of using their intelligence, frequently fall into a state of helpless confusion, or show difficulties that are ultimately diagnosed as mental deficiency (cf. 1954a).[31] The inherited potential is different in the two cases, but this is not what determines the person that the individual will be.

A few consequences emerge for the study of the maturational process: since the brain is the essential basis for the development by both the psyche and the mind of what is specific to them, this implies that in order to study the development of the psyche-soma, we must assume that lesions or primary physical illnesses are absent.[32] In order to study a developing person, it is necessary that he is physically healthy. It is only in the absence of primary body disease that such a complex study may be made. In this case, we examine the gradual integration of a person's body and psyche, allowing the formulation of certain basic principles (cf. 1988, p. 28).

In the case of the investigation of the mind, for example, we must be able to presume an intact cerebral tissue. We cannot learn anything, in terms of development, if the brain is damaged or mutilated by some lesion or physical illness. Supposing that the brain is intact, we cannot apply to the mind the same concepts that we attribute to the soma or to the psyche, in other words, we cannot say of the mind that in itself, it is healthy or ill. Mental functioning depends on the quality of brain tissue, but this can only be described in terms of better or worse, of a higher or lower IQ. The expression "mental health" makes no sense at all, says Winnicott and the same is obviously true of the expression "mental illness", since "in fact there is no direct link between the concepts of health and of intellect. In health the mind works at the level of brain functioning *because the emotional development of the individual is satisfactory*" (1988, p. 14; my italics).

The psyche may become ill, despite not having any brain problem, and it becomes ill if environmental insecurity does not allow it to dedicate itself to its task of imaginative elaboration, forcing it, on the contrary, to use its mental resources prematurely in order to remain on the lookout for the unexpected. In this case, the psyche becomes "mentalised". When this happens, says Winnicott, mental functioning becomes "a thing in itself" (cf. 1954a). This does not mean that the mind itself has become ill, but that it has started to work autonomously, being precociously hyper-activated, detached from what would be the experiences of the individual, which, in order to exist as such, should necessarily be psycho-somatic. There can be no experiences because the mind anticipates itself in state of alert, occupied with preventing any threat of environmental invasion. There is the emergence of a precocious consciousness (which is purely mental), a sort of premature me, a self that is not sufficiently developed for proper states of conscience. When this occurs, the psycho-somatic cohesion weakens, and may even be obstructed, establishing an opposition between soma and psyche, with the latter being dominated by the mind.

What is at stake from the perspective of development and of disorders relating to development is not, therefore, the physical or psychic *constitution*. A baby "is not what one may postulate by assessing that baby's potential. A baby is a complex phenomenon that includes the baby's potential *plus* the environment" (1970b, p. 253). In order to understand this, we need only observe a two-year-old child and perceive that she is no longer the same after the birth of a new baby in the family. In many cases, an illness is diagnosed which requires treatment. At the same time, Winnicott says:

> [...] the existence of illness patterns must not be allowed to obscure the reality that the child in question is a child *with a younger brother or sister*. With the same potential, this child would be different if he or she were the youngest child or the only child, or if a baby had been born but had died. (1970b, p. 253)

Whatever the inherited potential of the infant, the environmental care that he receives is a part of the process of his constitution as a person. If the adaptation to the needs is good enough, there is a chance that the individual will develop his hereditary potential almost to the maximum extent; in some cases, it will perhaps be necessary for the environment to compensate for and balance, as far as possible, the baby's tendency to illness or, even be able to cope with diseases that are already established.

In Winnicott's theory of maturational processes nothing is determined beforehand. There is only the virtuality of a tendency towards integration, which, in health, leads to the constitution of a unitary identity and the establishment of relations with the world and external objects. The individual may or may not fulfil his inheritance in the direction of integration, *depending* on what happens in the encounter with the facilitating environment. Furthermore, his form of fulfilling or of failing to fulfil it is entirely indeterminate and depends on imponderable elements, such as environmental care and to a large degree, on chance.[33] Existence is not based on any prior positivity that carries in itself causal determinations that the maturational process would only complete. There are no forces endowed with goals that are intrinsic to them, nor is there a pulsional conflict already at the beginning, which would set life in motion independently of the individual and of the circumstances in which this individual is launched. What drives the psyche is the very fact that the baby is alive and carries in himself the innate tendency towards integration. The integrating tendency is conceived not as the result of work done by the psyche, but is itself the foundation for the emergence of the psyche. The maturational process is the manifestation of the creative potential of human nature. It can only take place in a time and space of its own, which are not the linear time and space of natural processes in physical and biological terms.

Integration via personal experience

One of the basic thesis of Winnicott's theory of personal development is that for the individual to reach the point of feeling alive and become able to appropriate his inherited or congenital potentialities, all states of being must be experienced; otherwise, these states will remain unintegrated in the personality. This refers both to physical conformations and personality tendencies and to states and facts of life: birth, the continuity of being, the states of quietness or excitation, hits and misses, the aloneness of pre-dependence, the state of amorphousness of the beginning, unthinkable agonies, etc. Winnicott rejects the idea that elements belonging to an individual may be considered independently of his own experience of them.[34]

What does Winnicott understand by "experience"? The concept is not clearly defined in his work; it is one of those concepts, the meaning of which should become intelligible in itself, on the basis of the use which Winnicott makes of it throughout his work. First, experience varies according to the moment in the maturational process. We must hence differentiate the meaning of the term "experience" when it refers to these initial stages, from the one used when some experience of the unitary self and of the world is achieved, which will include a beginning of integration in time and space as well as the lodging of the psyche in the body. Second, gathering the several passages on the theme, we can affirm that "experience" and the "feeling of real" are mutually interwoven: only what is given in experience is real for the individual. But one can also say that something, a state of being, a fantasy, a dream or an event, is an experience only if it is felt as real. The "real" that is implied here has nothing to do with external reality, in the sense of a representable, perceptible reality that can be visualised and is sayable. Freud's so-called "reality principle", which in Winnicott's redefinition, "is the fact of the existence of the world whether the baby creates it or not" (1986h, p. 40) is, for Winnicott, the "arch-enemy of spontaneity, creativity and *the sense of Real*" (1984d, p. 236; my italics).

A man approximately forty years old, who suffers from a disbelief that corrodes any reality told me: "I was socialised before I had become a person. I know quite well what is expected from me and I fulfil my duties precisely, but nothing has ever made any sense. I don't feel real, I don't feel the world or the others as real. I don't have a history. I don't know why I live or go on living". This man does not have problems with the reality principle, but suffers from the lack of feeling of real.

One of the few references to the general character of what is experience is in a letter from 1952, to Money-Kyrle:

> Experience is a constant trafficking in illusion, a repeated reaching to the interplay between creativity and that which the world has to offer. Experience is an achievement of ego maturity to which the environment supplies an essential ingredient. It is not by any means always achieved. (1987b, p. 43)

It is the environment that early in life provides the indispensable ingredient for establishing the capacity for experience. This ingredient consists of the baby having the possibility to inhabit, for as long as necessary, a subjective world, which is ruled by the "illusion of omnipotence", with this being the only solid basis for the belief that will gradually be established in the reality of the self and of the world.[35] The limits of the subjective world are traced by the omnipotence scope of the baby. Everything that happens there becomes an experience of the infant, because, being dictated by the baby's rhythm and deriving from spontaneous gesture, it happens in such a way that it does not disrupt the personal sense of existence which, at this point, is the continuity of being. The capacity for experience is thus related to spontaneity and primary creativity and to the root of the true self, in short, to *being*.

In summary, according to Winnicott, the baby is already a human being since intra-uterine life, with this defined by his innate capacity for experiences. Despite being innate, this capacity must be exercised, made real and integrated into the personality and this will only happen if, during the initial stages, the baby is provided with facilitating care, otherwise the capacity will wither or be paralysed. The capacity for experience is hence an acquisition of development, which depends on an imponderable element: environmental facilitation. In this way it may not be achieved. For this reason, while:

> It is possible to seduce a baby into feeding and into the functioning of all the bodily processes, but *the baby does not feel these things as an experience* unless it is built on a quantity of *simple being* which is enough to establish the self that is eventually a person. (1987e, p. 12; my italics)

There are people who did not initially find a basis for being because they were not permitted the illusion of omnipotence; in them, the sense of real is so debilitated that no matter how many times they undergo certain situations, everything always falls apart and they must always start again as if nothing had happened. They record the fact in an archive of memories, but nothing in them was affected or changed. In general, it is said that these people do not learn with experience, but perhaps it would be even more accurate to say that they are incapable of having experiences. Instead of being there, in the present event, they are absent, defending themselves from some invasion, some kind of imprisonment, or preventing some distress which may arise; everything that occurs is hence external to them, in such a way that nothing lasts.

The irreplaceable value of experience seems to have been a conviction that permeated not only the theory but also Winnicott's own life. Having started to write his biography shortly before his death, the title of which was to be *Not Less than Everything*,[36] Winnicott wrote a prayer, in which he asked to God to be alive at the moment of his death, so that this would also be an experience, the last one.[37]

His well-known aversion to any kind of abstract theoretical construction detached from experience probably derives from this same conviction. It is as a function of this aversion that the term "experience" is not defined but simply used, so that it is understood not merely by the intellect, but by another type of precision, that of the specifically human context. Concepts must reach the reader in the field of experience, placing her directly in the situation. In order to indicate that maternal care happens through the identification of the mother with the baby and not via a deliberate mental act, Winnicott says: "we find that she does not have to make a sort of shopping list of things she must do tomorrow; she feels what is needed at the moment" (1965e, p. 71). Or also, while trying to show to mothers that they must not expect that babies will start to suckle as soon as they are born: "A period of time is needed for many babies before they begin to search, and when they find an object they do not necessarily want immediately to make a meal of it" (1968f, p. 64).

There are significant theoretical consequences deriving from the conceptions of experience, from the capacity of having experiences and from the fact that the baby, from the outset, is already a human being capable of having experiences. Certain difficulties presented by a specific infant, such as an expectation of persecution, instead of being attributed to heredity or to the unconscious of the species, may perfectly well be related to the birth process which was excessively slow or to other precocious experiences of environmental invasion. Researchers who so easily attribute some primitive manifestations in a baby to the heredity factor, do not take into account his pre-history and the fact that dependence is significant as soon as something such as a state of being initiates. It is very simple, says Winnicott, to affirm that paranoid babies have a hereditary tendency or are manifesting a constitutional factor, but what the argument of this line of reasoning does is to disregard and sidetrack "the very interesting and important phenomenon of the development of the individual, and the memory of personal experiences" (1988, p. 149).

It is true that since the body is always included, the biological hereditary factor (if it can clearly be isolated) is always present: while some newborn babies show an intense sensitivity to clarity and need shade; others have a thermal, tactile, or auditory sensitivity. Indeed, some are actually startled by noises, while others seem simply not to hear them. There are babies who are extraordinarily affected by the emotional atmosphere of the environment, while others are more isolated and meditative. Some are very quick or perhaps more sensitive to discomfort and pain and as soon as an impulse emerges, they are already screaming. There are others who are slow and need time to conclude an experience, resenting very much if the environmental rhythm is accelerated. There are babies whose sensitivity is more evenly distributed; in others a specific sensitivity is exacerbated. The fact is that there are babies of all kinds, and an accentuated sensitivity will probably predispose them to an extraordinary specific ability (sometimes responsible for genius) or to a disease: a baby with such sensitivity is highly susceptible to be affected and traumatised. Furthermore, as has already been mentioned, when considering these aspects, we must include the baby's pre-history and the fact that he has already had several experiences during intrauterine life.

A very sensitive child will certainly demand more of the mother. However, when we speak of active adaptation, we think precisely of the ability that leads the mother to adapt to a singular *certain baby*, and not of a technique for raising babies. Although, as already stated, genetics determines some individual patterns and characteristics, such as being taller or shorter, having more or less muscle mass, having better or worse brain tissue, more or less vitality or sensitivity, none of these are decisive in terms of development. When we attribute certain characteristics or disorders to the constitution of the individual, we are not paying due attention to the mother's adaptive technique.[38] The most important thing of all is that the baby has a mother who adapts to him and accompanies him as he is and can be, that is, developing his inherited potentialities in his maturational process in the best possible way. We must also include the factor of chance, contributing to the mother carrying out her function well: a fortunate conjunction, for example, would be the fact that a slow child has a mother who is also slow and not one that is too fast and who becomes bored by or impatient with the baby's slowness.

The fact is that, if we include the essential participation of the environment in the constitution of human psyche—a participation which precedes and is also a condition that makes the constitution of object relations possible—there is no escape: we have to scrutinise and take into account the extremely subtle details of the mother–baby relationship in the more primitive stages.

The state of unintegration of the primitive stages

If the entire maturational process moves towards integration, in what state is the baby when this process starts? Winnicott postulates that at the beginning and throughout all of the primitive stages, most of the time the baby lives in a state of unintegration:

> This bit of theory is needed if one is to reach to the place where infants live—a queer place—where *nothing has yet been separated out as not-me,* so there is *not yet a* ME. [...] rather that no mother, no object external to the self, is known; and even this statement is wrong because there is not yet a self. It could be said that the self of the infant at this very early stage is only potential. (1965c, p. 17)

Although there is a baby for the observer and for the mother, for the baby there is still no himself, no mother and no world. The baby is not yet a unit; the many aspects that will be integrated into the whole person that he will be are still disconnected. Before integration, it is as if the baby is spread out; "unorganized, a mere collection of sensory-motor phenomena, collected by the holding environment" (1965k, p. 148).

The unintegration, which is accompanied by a non-conscience (cf. 1988), is not a deficit. It is the baby's natural state of extreme immaturity and it means a lack of cohesion in a self, of integration in space and time, of psycho-somatic integration and ultimately of *wholeness*. The only temporality that the baby initially has, other than biological time, is the diffuse sensation of being able to go on being. The negative term, unintegration, has its raisons d'être: it refers to a *not-yet*, to a state prior to any integration and hence prior to the establishment of a me and of a psyche. This "negative" state has no pathological connotation, nor does it refer to what would be a state of chaos, since in the beginning, there is neither chaos nor order (cf. 1988). In addition, *unintegration* must be distinguished from *disintegration*, which has a defensive character and can only occur after some integration has been achieved.

When the infant is receiving good care, the unintegration

> [...] is the natural state and there is no one there to mind about it. Good care produces a state of affairs in which integration begins to become a fact, and a person starts to be there. In so far as this is true, so far does failure of care lead to disintegration instead of to a return to

> unintegration. Disintegration is felt to be a threat because (by definition) there is someone there to feel the threat. (1958d, p. 98)

The important point of the theory is as follows: *it is only from unintegration that the several forms of integration may be produced*. If integration were a given, human beings would not be the way they are, since health as well as difficulties and disorders, which are characteristic of human beings, are states relating to the success or failure in the integrative tasks of the initial stages, as achievements of development. On this point, Winnicott's position demonstrates a significant advance over the traditional theory, conceived on the basis of neuroses, which are disorders of a personality which is already integrated; this theory has no way of approaching the particular nature of these founding achievements and as such, does not allow us to assess the consequences of failure in these achievements.[39]

Starting from unintegration, small experiences of integration take place during states of excitation and immediately afterwards, the baby returns to the unintegrated state in order to rest. The state of integration gradually becomes more stable and consistent. However, it will never be a safe territory to which the individual has title of ownership. There will always be the risk of him losing himself, but for a healthy baby, this will increasingly depend on situations of extreme overload. The healthy individual is not constantly concerned with his psychic survival.

The mother–baby relation: absolute dependence

During the initial stages, the baby lives most of the time in a state of unintegration, a situation of absolute dependence, which is only possible by virtue of the adaptation of the mother, which is also absolute. While still in the uterus and during the first months after birth, dependence is so extreme that it is not possible to think about the new individual as a unit. "The unit is the *environment-individual set-up* of which unit the new individual is only a part" (1988, p. 131). This is the meaning of Winnicott's famous statement *"this thing such a baby does not exist"*. If this is so, there is no way of describing a baby, or a small child, without including the care that he is receiving in the description. It is only gradually that environmental care is incorporated as an aspect of the baby's self, at the same time as the facilitating environment gradually becomes something external and separate from the baby (cf. 1987c). The environment, initially the mother, or more precisely, the mother's way of being, *is a part of the baby and is indistinguishable from it*. We do not have two individuals, but a *sui generis* relation, which may be called *two-in-one*.[40]

The state of absolute dependence is not founded only on the fragility of the baby or on its inability to survive without help. Nor does it refer to what would be a massive influence from the environment that would "produce" the baby, from himself, as a *tabula rasa*. Nor even is it a question of affective dependence, since the baby is not mature enough to have feelings. The absolute dependence refers to the fact that the baby is entirely dependent on the mother in order to *be*—in the way that he *is* or *can be* at this initial moment—and in order to fulfil his innate tendency towards integration into a unit. The peculiar relationship with the mother during the initial stages of absolute dependence provides a pattern for the relations that the baby will develop with external reality. It is within this relationship that the illusion of contact with the external world is being built, as well as the trust that inter-human communication is possible and that life makes sense.

Although the word "dependence" implies the existence of another human being, this other is not yet an object in the classical sense of the term, since the baby is not sufficiently mature to have, to perceive or to desire objects. The mother is not an external object and nor an internal one, because the sense of externality, as well as that of inner world have not yet been constituted. From the baby's point of view, "there is, at this very early stage, no external factor; the mother is part of the child" (1965n, p. 61). Despite this, maternal care intrinsically participates in the gradual constitution of the self; with the baby being immediately affected by the kind of care that he receives.

The Winnicottian concept of initial "environment" must be understood in accordance with its two essential aspects: (a) it is neither external nor internal; (b) it is an instance which supports and responds to dependence: the baby is entirely dependent on another person *who is not yet another* separate or external to him.[41] We find here the embedded idea, the psychological and philosophical scope of which remains to be fully appreciated, that the reality of the self and that of the world are established during the development process, *within the mother–baby relation.* The constitution of the me, at the same time as the constitution of intrapsychic reality and external reality, only takes place within the relation with the other; the baby's self necessarily emerges from within the baby–mother unity. The "me" as an identity separate from the not-me is a surpassing of the primary identification that occurs within the initial fusional unity. This is the meaning of Winnicott's statement that the I AM status "[…] *means nothing unless I at the beginning am along with another human being who has not yet been differentiated off*" (1987e, p. 12; my italics). The ambit in which development takes place is not an intrapsychic space, but an inter-human one, something *in between* the mother and the baby.[42] This space is also pre-personal, since there are not yet two persons; each one is part of the other in the two-in-one unity. Despite this, it must be pointed out that, since the very outset, there is already a small detachment, a small gap between them, since "in the most intimate contact there is a lack of contact so that essentially each individual retains absolute isolation always and for ever" (1988, p. 157).[43] However, at the same time that this space already exists and will always exist, separating mother and infant and forever isolating the individual from the external world, *it does not yet exist* as such; achieving it is a conquest of development that will only start to be effective during the stage of transitionality.[44]

We can find something analogous to this fundamental isolation in biology: the "egg" is a guest in the mother's body and not a part of it. Throughout pregnancy it remains enveloped by substances that have been constituted to protect it, at the same time as they "separate" it from the mother. When the baby is born, this set of substances is lost; but neither the baby nor the mother loses anything of their own. From the viewpoint of the human person who is being constituted, this "space", which allows for the basic isolation, has always been and always will be there; at the same time, it will become, in due course, the first real distance between the mother and the baby, a distance that both separates and unites. The analogy of the "egg" hence evokes the essential aloneness, which is the original condition in which the baby finds himself at the most absolute beginning, when being emerges from non-being, an aloneness that will be preserved forever, no matter how communicative or well-related to external reality the individual may become. It is from this fundamental isolation that the basic illusion of contact will emerge and at a later stage, the potential space. In due course, this space will be filled with transitional phenomena and transitional objects that are simultaneously part of the baby and of the environment.

Additional characterisation of the facilitating environment: the good enough mother and the baby's father[45]

The facilitating environment is initially the "good enough mother". The expression "good enough" refers to the mother who is capable of acknowledging and responding to the infant's dependence, as a result of her identification with him, which enables her to know what his needs are at a given moment and to meet them. The "*enough*" goodness encompasses the mother's spontaneity and personal presence in her care of the baby, as well as her capacity for believing that the baby is an on-going maturational process and hence, it is not she (i.e., her care or control of the situation) that will give life to the baby. The mother merely facilitates a process which belongs to the baby. She is good enough because she attends to the baby to the precise extent of his needs, and not to her own, such as the need to be good or very good. What the baby needs is the concern and effective care of a real mother, who continues being herself consistently, fallible since human, but reliable precisely because she is fallible.[46]

From the outset, the good enough mother proceeds towards an absolute adaptation, and a little later, to a relative adaptation to the baby's needs. Winnicott insists that it is a question of "adaptation to *needs*" and not of satisfaction of desires. By so doing, he clearly characterises the specificity of the initial stages: the baby is not yet an individual with desires, but an immature being in a state of absolute dependence. With regard to this period, a source of misunderstandings

> [...] is the idea (that some analysts have) that the term "adaptation to need" in treatment of schizoid patients and in infant-care means meeting id-drives. In this setting it is not a question of meeting id-drives or of frustrating id-drives. There are more important things going on, and these are of the nature of giving ego-support to ego processes. (1965d, p. 241)

In a letter to Lili Peller of 1966, Winnicott mentioned that, having left paediatrics with a conscience alerted to child dependence, he found it exasperating that the only dependence which his psychoanalyst colleagues could consider was that related to instinctual needs. He then added: "In my more recent writings you have noticed that I have tried to enumerate the psychotic-type anxieties which cluster round the word need. These have nothing to do with instincts" (1987b, p. 156). In another text, he stated that in the most primitive initial stages,

> [...] the word "need" has significance here just as "drive" has significance in the area of satisfaction of instinct. The word "desire" is out of place as it belongs to sophistication that is not to be assumed at this stage of immaturity that is under consideration. (1970b, p. 256, note 7)

The environment adapts "to need arising out of being and arising out of the processes of maturation" (1965j, p. 183). That is, it is from the need to go on being that all the other needs emerge, and all of them largely prevail over any pleasure principle. That is the reason why the development of human instinctuality is thought by Winnicott within the more comprehensive line of the maturational processes.

The absolute adaptation of the mother to the baby's needs is temporary, but while it lasts it implies full involvement. A baby needs nothing less than a full person, that is, entirely surrendered or devoted to him, even if for a brief period of time at each day. This is generally possible because when the mother is healthy, she enters a state of "primary maternal preoccupation", which starts at the last months of pregnancy and lasts for some time after birth. This is a very special psychological condition, of heightened sensitivity that

> [...] could be compared with a withdrawn state, or a dissociated state, or a fugue, or even with a disturbance at a deeper level such as a schizoid episode in which some aspect of the personality takes over temporarily. (1958h, p. 302)

It is the baby and the totality of the baby's care that occupy the mother's life. By virtue of this state, which implies a partial regression, the mother becomes able to identify with the baby and know what he needs. At the same time, she retains her adult place, so that she is in a position not only to understand but also to take care of the infant effectively, providing what he needs. Being mature, the mother is not narcissistically wounded for having her personal life emptied in order to dedicate herself to caring for the baby. The good enough mother is devoted to the infant. The term "devotion", which implies the total involvement of the mother and her capacity for taking care of the baby, has nothing to do with sentimentality. Any kind of sentimentality, says the author, is worse than useless, for it contains an unconscious denial of hate and aggressiveness, which underlie all constructive effort, even when it is a question of raising a child.

Maternal care is frequently thought of in terms of indulgence, but the love or kindness of the good enough mother is not usually indulgent. If, as a result of some kind of deprivation, the infant presents a special period of need and the mother is capable of understanding the need that is thus communicated, she may become indulgent and "pamper" the child for a certain time, but this indulgence is actually a therapy that has become necessary by virtue of some failure of ordinary maternal care. "Therapy by the mother may cure, but this is not mother-love" (1958c, p. 128).

The adaptation of the mother to the child's need is not related to her intelligence, nor does it arise from knowledge that may be obtained from books or lectures. Her knowledge is of a nature that enables her to provide for the infant successfully, regardless of any intellectual appreciation of what is happening, nor of the need to understand everything. What orients her is her ability to identify with the infant. Such ability comes from her own experience of having been a baby and of having been taken care of; she retains bodily memories of comfort and safety as well as experiences of personal intimacy. Moreover, the mother knows what the baby's needs are, because she is alive and has an imagination. She is able to wait for the spontaneous gesture to emerge, because she "knows" of many subtle things such as, for example, that in order to be moved from one place to another, a baby needs to be prepared, and that the overall movement requires time. She also knows that it is more important to respect the baby's refusal to nurse, than to force him, due to discipline or fear of malnutrition, since in terms of development, "the basis of *feeding* is *not feeding*" (1968f, p. 64).[47]

Although primary maternal preoccupation is a state that arises naturally with maternity, there are women who fear it and resist the regression that it contains. They cling to their adult occupation and are unable or cannot bear to identify with the baby. This kind of mother will tend to take care of the baby mentally; her acts will be deliberate, governed by rules that are intellectually established. She may succeed in providing him with a few basic things, but she will not be capable of having the deep and silent communication which comes with intimacy. She will take care of the baby "as one is supposed to take care of babies", that is, providing impersonal care. This is typically the case of the mother who *does* but *is* not.[48] The good enough care required by a baby is not the care devised by thinking, which is deliberate or delivered mechanically; this care can only be provided by a human being, the mother or a substitute, who is alive and able to put herself in the place of another person, at the same time as she remains an adult and is continuously herself. It is surprising how babies seem to come endowed with a quality control of the communication we try to establish with them. When the mother, because of her identification and preoccupation with the baby, is alert in the sense of preventing and avoiding the occurrence of unpredictable events that may frighten or even traumatise the baby, such attention does not arise from an intellectual deliberation, but almost always occurs in her body. She is completely alert and this is reflected in her posture; her movements, her gaze are directed towards the baby and are naturally protective.

Even when she surrenders herself to the complete, psycho-somatic involvement with the baby, the mother, whose spontaneity is preserved, is able to be herself consistently. Starting from this, what has to be done takes place naturally, because "children always take the best from us."

For this reason,

> In order to be consistent, and so to be predictable for our children, we must be *ourselves*. If we are ourselves our children can get to know us. Certainly if we are acting a part we shall be found out when we get caught without our make-up. (1993b, p. 123)

With time, and according to the increasing maturational capability of the infant, the good-enough mother makes the adaptation progressively less absolute and in this way, she allows the baby to move gradually towards relative dependence and then towards independence. If the mother is healthy, de-adaptation occurs naturally, since it coincides with a moment when she is already tired of the demands that absolute adaptation requires. This passage is essential for the baby's development; if the mother is not able to abdicate from absolute dependence, it can generate serious difficulties for the child.

In describing the good-*enough* care of the *ordinary* devoted mother, Winnicott avoids any idealisation of the maternal or paternal figure.[49] Parents are not altruistic angels, nor is the world surrounding the baby a paradise. Children do not draw any benefit from mechanical perfection. If it were possible to make a choice, the author confesses, he would greatly prefer a mother who is capable of having doubts about her behaviour and of thinking that some things are going wrong due to something which she did or did not do, than a mother who "turned to an outside thing to explain everything", without assuming responsibility for anything (cf 1993d, p. 103). Moreover, if the mother is healthy, she will often hate her baby *much earlier than he has acquired the capacity to hate her.* Winnicott lists the good reasons that she has for so doing: the baby represented a danger to her body during pregnancy and birth; he interferes with her private life; he hurts her breast; she has to love him despite his excretions and everything else, even though he still shows his disappointment with her; his excited love is self-interested; he has no idea of what she does or sacrifices for him, etc. The mother naturally has to endure her own hate, without denying it to herself, but also without being able to do anything about it. She cannot manifest it directly towards the baby, except by means of songs or malicious expressions that she utters tenderly.[50] One of the most remarkable things in the ordinary mother is precisely, "her ability to be hurt so much by her baby and to hate so much without paying the child out" (1949f, p. 202).

There is yet another question: women who have just given birth are themselves necessarily in state of dependence.[51] It may even be said that mothers are as helpless with regard to the baby's helplessness as the baby is himself. In order to perform her task well, she needs to feel loved in the relationship with the child's father, and accepted both within the family circle and in the wider circles which constitute society (cf. 1958j). At this point, the father's role is extremely important, especially the function of protecting the mother and providing for the home. If adequately protected by her man, the mother is spared from having to concern herself with worldly things and to dedicate herself entirely to the inside of the circle formed by her own arms, at the centre of which is the baby. The father is also extremely necessary for helping the mother to feel well in her body and happy in spirit. Since, especially with regard to the first child, the mother tends to exaggerate her care, effectively wanting to become magical so as to guess the infant's need in advance, the father's help "makes human something in the mother, and draws away from her the element which otherwise becomes magical and potent and spoils the mother's motherliness" (1961a, p. 73). The effective presence and help of the baby's father provides moral support to the mother and a buttress for the order and security that she is trying to implant in the child's life. From a very early stage, children are sensitive to the atmosphere that is created in the home and to the stability that they feel in their parents, even when they still do not know that the parents exist as persons separate from them and with regard to each other.

At the same time, with regard to what refers directly to the baby that which is "paternal" necessarily comes after what is "maternal".[52] The father does not yet exist as a father, as the third party, since the baby does not even know of the existence of the mother and only establishes contact with the care that is offered to him. Since the baby does not yet even have a dual relationship, he is even less capable of having a triadic one. The father can nevertheless be very useful as a duplicator of the mother's care and, in this role, he has something of his own to add to the baby, as we shall see later.[53] Despite this, it is not good for the father to come onto the scene prematurely. The baby is not prepared for the inevitable differences in the ways of handling and holding. There are nevertheless cases of men who are more maternal than women and there are clinical reports of cases in which the father's aptitude for maternal care has minimised the environmental failure resulting from a pathology of the mother, saving the child from disorders that could have been much more severe than the ones that actually arose.[54]

If a little while later, the father begins to participate directly and actively, even if still in the maternal function, a certain paternal element is ultimately included in the constitution of the baby's self: from the child's perspective, the father is lived as an aspect of the mother "which is hard and strict and unrelenting, intransigent, indestructible" and who, when all goes well, gradually becomes the man who is transformed into a human being, "someone who can be feared, hated, loved and respected" (1986d, p. 131). This element contributes to a feeling of security of the home and to establishing the meaning of what a family is for a particular child (cf. idem).[55] Naturally, the way in which the child uses or does not use this father is determined by the way of being of the latter.

In a late text from 1969, reflecting on the innate tendency towards integration and the symbolism of this unitary status in monotheism, Winnicott adds another element to the participation of the father: regardless of whether or not the father has replaced the mother, at some point he appears to the baby as the first *glimpse of personal wholeness and totality* and in this way is used as a model for the baby's own integration. If the father is not present, the baby will somehow have to achieve integration, but this will be much harder to do, unless he can use another very stable relationship with a total person (cf. 1989i).

The paternal figure becomes especially significant when the baby reaches the stage at which, having achieved a unitary me, he is grappling with dealing the task of integrating instinctual life. At this stage of maturation, that of concern,[56] the child is conquering the capacity to take responsibility for the destructiveness inherent to primitive instinctual drives. Having started to appropriate the drives as belonging to the self, the child realises the harm that his instinctual impulsiveness does to the mother. He then begins to count on the father (his presence, firmness, ability to intervene and set limits) to protect the mother from his own drives. If the father does not play his part, the child will lose the freedom to move, act, and become excited, developing a self-control which paralyses his spontaneity and inhibits his instinctuality in general.[57]

As the baby achieves greater maturity, dependence slowly decreases. As a result of continuously adapting to the process of mutation and development of the child, the mother facilitates the gradual de-adaptation by progressively failing to adapt to the need, so as to help the child separate from her and to allow him to experience a relative dependence, so that he makes the transition that will lead to independence. The mother, then the father, and even later the family, the school, social groups, and increasingly wider circles provide the care relative to the needs of the new phase which is beginning.

The place of the parents implies *responsibility with their children.* It is up to the parents to keep the family and the home as a place of stability for the growth of the children, having to survive the various forms of destruction to which their children will expose them in order to grow up. This requires a few abdications. It is possible that the parents have kept themselves spontaneous and creative, which naturally is vital to them as persons and, to a certain extent, to their babies. When a child is present, however, they must be able to give up their place. The mother's spontaneity is highly necessary to the baby; being consistently herself is one of the sources which the infant needs to gain confidence. However, the adult mother does not expose the baby to her own drives. In addition, there are children who find themselves forced to live in an atmosphere of intense creativity, which nevertheless, belongs to the parents or the nanny and not to the child. "[…] this stifles them and they cease to be. Or they develop a technique of withdrawal" (1986h, p. 52). In order to raise children so that they may live in a world of real facts, remaining creative, "we do have to be uncreative and compliant and adaptive [...]" (idem). The same evidently holds for the analytical setting.

Winnicott's concepts of ego, self, and me

Since the terms "ego", "self", and "me" form part of the basic vocabulary of the theory of maturational processes and their meaning is far from being unambiguous, as may be proven by the diversity of meanings with which they are invested in different philosophical, theological, or psychological theories, it is appropriate to clarify their use in Winnicott's work.

In texts prior to 1962, Winnicott frequently used the terms "ego" and "self" indiscriminately, leading to conceptual inaccuracies. It was Fordham, a Jungian analyst and his personal friend, who made him recognise, probably at the start of the 1960s, that he

> was using the words "self" and "ego" as if they were synonymous, which of course they are not; they cannot be, since "self" is a word, and "ego" is a term to be used for convenience with an agreed meaning. (1964b, p. 490)

Winnicott realised that the two terms were not of the same semantic type. "Ego" is a theoretical term, the meaning of which is open to a consensual decision within a certain group of researchers, while the word "self" is a descriptive term in everyday language which "naturally knows more than we do; it uses us, and can command us" (1960a, p. 158).

The clearest statement by the author about the "ego" is in a text from 1962: "The term ego can be used to describe that part of the growing human personality that tends, under suitable conditions, to become integrated into a unit" (1965n, p. 56). The term "ego" is not used, as we can see, to designate an instance of the psychic apparatus, since Winnicott does not work with the heuristic concept of psychic apparatus, but to designate the tendency towards organisation and integration of the various psycho-somatic aspects which are not initially integrated and when everything goes well, gradually gather into a me. It does not have the same meaning as in traditional psychoanalysis; it was suggested to him by the psychology of the ego and by Edward Glover's concept of ego nuclei. In fact, in the traditional theory there is no concept equivalent to that of Winnicott's "ego", since neither in Freud, nor in Klein is there the conception of a tendency towards maturation. We must also bear in mind, in order to avoid the confusions which arise from this intricate terminological question, that the term "ego" is not one of Freud's: it was introduced into psychoanalytical literature by the English translation of Freudian works made by Strachey. When referring to the instance of the psychic apparatus which makes contact with reality, Freud spoke of the *Ich*, that is, "I" in German. It is most likely that Winnicott, in his readings of Freud, used Strachey's translation and when referring to this point in the Freudian theory, started to use the term "ego". In his own theory, he adopted the term "ego" in a modified sense, using "me" as well and giving different meanings to the two terms: one thing is the "ego", as a tendency towards maturation and another is the "me" (*I* from *I am*), as the result of the integrative task, the achievement of unitary identity.

In Freudian theory, at least in its initial formulation, the ego (*Ich*) emerges from the id, as a transformation, produced through the contact with the reality principle. The ego (*Ich*), says Freud, is that part of the id which was modified by the direct influence of the external world.[58] On the basis of this point, which is debatable even for Freudians, since it is difficult to understand how a given structure can give rise to another of a totally different nature, Winnicott welcomed the theoretical modifications introduced by E. Glover, based on his conception of nuclei or primitive unorganised ego structures, in order to formulate the primary state of unintegration, which is characteristic of the initial stages of development.[59]

Examples of the use of the concepts of ego and self may help to clarify the meaning of both terms. At a certain point, the author highlights that the ego is both weak and strong; all depends on the capacity of the mother to give ego support.

> [...] The infant's reinforced and therefore strong ego is able very early to organise defences, and to develop patterns that are personal [...]. It is this infant whose ego is strong *because of the mother's ego support* that early becomes himself or herself, really and truly. (1965c, p. 17)

In another text, Winnicott affirms that the baby's ego (its tendency towards integration):

> [...] is feeble in the extreme if there is no satisfactory facilitating environment. However, the mother or mother figure supplies the ego support, and if she does this well enough the infant's ego is very strong and has its own organization. (1989m, p. 101)

We should note the difference between the senses of "ego" and "self": the innate tendency towards maturation (integration) depends on the support provided by the environment. The ego support of the mother, or the mother's auxiliary ego, as Winnicott says in other texts, makes the baby's *ego* strong and facilitates integrative experiences, guiding the child more easily towards possessing his own organisation, towards *becoming himself*, that is, becoming a *self* integrated into a me. In terms of nomenclature, we should say that it is the *ego* which guides the integrative tendency towards a unitary *self*.[60] The self is the result of the integrative tendency, but it is necessary that the tendency is in operation. This is why Winnicott says "the ego offers itself for study long before the word self has relevance" (1965n, p. 56).

The term self was in turn used in two different ways as Winnicott's thought evolved. In the central and more general meaning, self refers to the unitary status achieved by the individual at the stage when the baby, if he could speak, would say I AM. If we adopt the term in this sense, the self is the result of a series of achievements of the integration process and is only established in a consistent manner in the stage when the infant achieves an identity, a unitary self. At this point, a healthy baby, operating on the basis of the true self, has already even integrated as an aspect of his personality an instrumental false self, which enables him to deal with social demands. As a synonym for the self, in this same sense, Winnicott also uses the term *"me"* or *"I"*. The "me" is therefore, the self that separates from the mother, achieving unitary identity and integrating into it both the true and the false self. When the term "self" is used in this sense of the integrated personality, Winnicott will say that prior to this achievement, there is no self.

This can be illustrated by an excerpt in which, describing the more primitive phases, he states that

> rather that no mother, no object external to the self, is known; and even this statement is wrong because there is not yet a self. It could be said that the self of the infant at this very early stage is only potential. (1965c, pp. 17–18)

At the same time, in *Human Nature*, there are passages in which he uses the term "self" for the *result of any* momentary *integrative experience* prior to reaching unitary integration into a me. For example, when mentioning the little moments of integration, in the excited states of the most primitive stage, he says that both the instinctual demand and the drive towards motility are preceded "by a gathering together of the whole self. Awareness becomes possible at such moments, because *there is a self* to be aware" (1988, p. 117; my italics).

This use of the term "self" for any integrative experience, even prior to the achievement of the unitary self, is corroborated later in his work, when he proposes a new formulation for his concepts of world and of subjective objects: in the excited encounter with the object (subjective), the baby is momentarily united and, through a *primary identification* with the object (the baby *is* the object) he lives the first experience of *being* as an *identity*. Using new terminology, which shall be clarified later in Chapter Three, Winnicott affirms that "when the girl element in the boy or girl baby or patient finds the breast it is the self that has been found" (1971i, p. 180). From then on, the author uses the term "self" increasingly frequently for any degree or form of integration, starting from unintegration, even when this integration is incipient and purely momentary.

Winnicott deals more explicitly with the concept of self and its difference with regard to the ego in an article from 1970, in which he states that,

> [...] the self, which is not the ego, is the person who is me, who is only me, who has a totality based on the operation of the maturational process. At the same time the self has parts, and in fact is constituted of these parts. These parts agglutinate from a direction interior-exterior in the course of the operation of the maturational process, aided as it must be (maximally at the beginning) by the human environment which holds and handles and in a live way facilitates. [...] It is the self and the life of the self that alone makes sense of action or of living from the point of view of the individual [...]. (1971d, p. 271)

J. B. Pontalis observed that in French psychoanalytical circles, Winnicott's concepts of being and self were received with hesitation and suspicion, as a result of them being wrongly approximated to Guntrip's notion of self. Aligned with a certain tradition in phenomenology, Guntrip had tried to introduce into psychoanalysis, together with the concept of self, the idea of a unified and unifying subject, who can recognise himself, who is unity and continuity, "whose being would be liable to escape from the *irreducibility* of conflict, the *otherness* of the unconscious, the *irreconcilability* of representations [...]" (Pontalis, 1981, p. 127). Pontalis is certainly right when he argues against Guntrip that "three quarters of a century of analytical experience undermines the illusion of a totally monadic subject, of a person totally sure of belonging to himself" (Pontalis, 1981, p. 127). It is nevertheless a mistake to pair Guntrip's self with that of Winnicott: the Winnicottian notion of tendency towards integration into a unitary self does not refer to the pulsional field, or to unconscious conflicts that would be overcome or annulled by it. It instead refers to all of the aspects of the individual, to his potentialities, which are initially unconscious, but not in the sense of the repressed unconscious: his body, his bodily memories, his temporality and spatiality, initially subjective and then, objective, the states of quietness and of excitation, instinctuality, fantasy, the externality of the world, etc., etc., etc., which, starting from unintegration will gradually integrate into a unity, being part of the whole person of the individual. According to Pontalis, this unitary status does not resemble the cohesion without fissures, or the self-possession intended by Guntrip. On the contrary, it is precisely because of the integration into a unity and the development of an internal psychic reality that the individual can then suffer unconscious conflicts.

Some philosophical and epistemological characteristics of the theory of maturational processes

The abandonment of causal determinism

The central question for the understanding and classification of psychic disorders is the establishment of the aetiology, a term which means, etymologically, a theory of the causes. This meaning was historically established from the conception of science, based on the principle of causality, and from the deterministic view regarding the nature of entities, which are object of scientific study. In view of what has been said before, Winnicott does not share that conception of human nature, nor does he defend a deterministic science. When describing the origin of the human being, he resorts to a series of expressions that do not admit a causalist interpretation: the passage from the potential baby to the actual one cannot be understood in a causal manner. This is not an updating of given properties already embedded in the individual and which would develop and manifest over time. To begin with, there are no intrinsic "determinations" in a baby, either somatic or psychic. With the sole exception of the tendency towards integration and of primary creativity, all possible characteristics of the baby still have to be created. Genetic determinations provide some organic limits, but not the orientation of what the person of the individual will be. The process of emergence of an individual, as a person with an identity, does not occur automatically, depending fundamentally on an imponderable internal factor, which is the baby's creativity, and on other equally imponderable factors, such as the psychic health of the mother and good fortune. In 1960, referring to the fact that the stages of development have a certain period for taking place, which varies from child to child, Winnicott affirms that *"even if they were known in advance* in the case of a given child, [these dates] could not be used in predicting the child's actual development because of the other factor, maternal care" (1960b, p. 43; my italics).

Although the inherited characteristics of the individual provide a pattern and a certain configuration of possibilities and limitations, the human being cannot be thought of as a predetermined product, either by his biological or psychic constitution, or by the external environment, which would mould him, as has been postulated by academic psychology. Once development has initiated, the human being is thrown into the indetermination of hits and misses which may happen, and it is these imponderable factors which determine how his potentialities will be realised. This is why Loparic, approximating Winnicott's conception to that of Heidegger, sees the "ongoing" of the human being in the personal growth described by Winnicott.

On the other hand, although depending fundamentally on environmental care, it is necessary to say that the environment, "does not make the infant grow, nor does it determine the direction of growth" (1963c, p. 223). When good enough, the environment does not determine the baby in a causal way; it merely supplies the facilitating conditions for the action of the maturational process. It is frequently thought, Winnicott affirms, that we make our children and that we teach them everything. The truth is precisely the opposite, since "we cannot even teach them to walk, but their innate tendency to walk at a certain age needs us as supporting figures" (1987b, p. 186).

The same holds for the emergence of psychic disorders. It is certain that the child's psychic health cannot be established without good enough environmental care. However, says Winnicott, "we also know that a corrective environmental experience does not cure the patient directly, more than a bad environment directly causes the structure of the illness" (cf. 1963a). The neurotic disorder, for example, is not caused by the parents.

Throughout Winnicott's work, we find many examples of non-causality. In a text dedicated to fathers, Winnicott discusses each person's responsibility regarding the choice of a marriage partner in terms of *anatomical and physiological* inheritance. In this text, he says that after the spermatozoid has penetrated the ovum, things start to operate by themselves, and what is necessary is the parents' shelter for the innate tendency towards maturation of the foetus so generated. It is very helpful for the parents to know that there is *nothing to be done* for a baby to be converted into a child, for a child to grow up, for the growing child to be good and clean, to grow up generous and for the generous child to know how to make a thoughtful choice of the appropriate presents for the appropriate people. "No-one has to make a child hungry, angry, happy, sad, affectionate, good or naughty. *These things just happen*" (1993b, p. 123; my italics). There are nevertheless many things that can be done indirectly: one of them being that "the mother often prevents schizophrenia by ordinary good management" (1987b, p. 45).

The origination of the human being or his maturation is not, therefore, an event that can be viewed as the effect of a cause. The power from which human existence emerges is not of the type that produces effects. It is rather permitting that *what does not yet exist comes into being,* that what is not present achieves presence, that the possibilities of being come to light, launched into the indeterminacy of life.[61] The non-causal character of Winnicott's theory is also revealed in the fact that there is not, despite the importance attributed to environmental care in the constitution of the individual, *any rule which may be stipulated* that the mother should follow, nor any legislation on maternal behaviour that guarantees that mothers will be successful in their task. On the contrary, any standardisation of how the "good-enough mother" should be would be the same as destroying her. The "knowledge" of the mother, which has been working well for thousands of years, does not admit to being categorised or taught; it is the fruit of an entirely personal understanding, which must be recreated with each new infant, even in the case of twins.

Here the question may emerge regarding the cognitive, and hence therapeutic gain, in distinguishing the non-causality of Winnicott's theory. A possible answer is as follows: a non-causal theory allows for the highlighting of the essential precariousness of human life and its fundamentally uncontrollable character. For Winnicott, it is essential to acknowledge this fact and remain close to something that can be called the "mystery" of the human being, although this should not lead us to any kind of mysticism. On the contrary, it is precisely due to the scientific task, to the rigour which characterises it, in the obedience to the specific nature of its object of study, that life's indeterminacy must be preserved as it is. We must not, and that is one of the methodological principles of the science of man practised by Winnicott, attempt to thematise man at the cost of distorting his nature. For this reason, it is often necessary to admit "obscurity to have a value that is superior to false clarification" (1989k, p. 240). This seems to be exactly the sense of the question raised by Winnicott in the letter to Anna Freud of 1954, already mentioned in the Introduction, when, after expressing his profound suspicion regarding the terms of metapsychology, he asks: "Is it because they can give the appearance of a common understanding when such understanding does not exist?" (1987b, p. 58).

A non-causal conception of human development may be considered as revolutionary not only to psychoanalysis, but for the philosophy of science itself. This is one of the points which fundamentally distinguishes Winnicott's thought from Freud's libidinal theory and from the Kleinian theory as well as from any other conception founded on the notion of forces, in which human development is understood according to laws governing natural entities.

Negativity

In Winnicott's conception of the human being, there is an intrinsic negativity, which cuts across all positivity of life and maintains a permanent tension between being and not being. This negativity is the furthest possible from the psychoanalytic conception of the death pulsion. What the study of babies and psychotics clearly reveals is that the human being has always been committed to being and not being. In other words, all *ability to be* starts from not being and *being* is never completely given to the human being. It is always a precarious achievement, which, as such, is not always achieved: "Some must spend all their lives not being, in a desperate effort to find a basis for being" (1984b, p. 112).

Because he conceives of human nature in this way, it seems entirely artificial and unnecessary to Winnicott to resort to speculative constructions of a naturalistic or energetic type, such as death pulsion. The concept of death pulsion or of destruction *enthrones evil as an entity operating in itself,* neglecting the full implication of human dependency, whether absolute or not, and hence, of the environmental factor, which can cause considerable damage.

What lies at the origin of man is not a positivity. The human being is not inferable from his genes, nor is he the result of a given constitution. "Genes are not enough", says Winnicott. Nor does he derive from the mother's desire.[62] To the question that Winnicott asks himself—"What is the state of the human individual as the being emerges out of not being?" he answers: "At the start, there is an essential aloneness". For the human being, he continues, "the emergence has been not from an inorganic state but from aloneness" (1988, p. 133). The "state prior to that of aloneness is one of unaliveness" (ibid., p. 132). Emerging from not-being, he is thrown in life and there is no discernible foundation for his existence. His only determination, which is structural and devoid of content, is being alive and the tendency towards maturation, towards integration into a unit. This tendency nevertheless depends on what happens, and may even fail. Moreover, the tendency towards integration carries in itself a negative "operator", and must always integrate not-being, which permanently crosses and accompanies its unfolding. Human life is conceived as an interval between two states of not-being-alive; the basis of human nature is a space between being and not-being. The fact that existence is open at its two extremities to nothingness provides the matrix for all manifestations of human life and of its possibilities: "In the development of the individual infant living arises and establishes itself out of not-living, and being becomes a fact that replaces not-being, as communication arises out of silence" (1965j, p. 191).

Health, in particular, may be viewed as the surpassing of the original state of not-being, and a slow appropriation of being, which, however, may always evade. As it is for Heidegger, also for Winnicott, life occurs as an appropriation that takes place against the background of the original negativity. Psychic illness, of which psychosis is the prototype, occurs if the tendency towards integration is *not* allowed to follow its course. That is, psychosis results from the fact that what *should have come to terms* in the beginning of the maturational processes—the baby's structural tendency towards integration and relation with all that is not-me—*did not happen*. This means, according to Winnicott, that life's positivity must be constituted so as to enclose the negativity of the origin, without denying it. It is on the original negativity that the fabric of presence is woven, thereby veiling the abyss of absence. It is only in this way that being and presence may occur: "*Only out of non-existence can existence start*" (1974, p. 95).

This is true for all achievements covered by the label of health, such as the ability to feed oneself and to communicate:

> The only real eating has as its basis *not* eating. It is out of not being creative, out of being isolated, that the creation of objects and of the world comes to have meaning. There is no enjoyment of company except as a development from essential isolation, the isolation that reappears as the individual dies. (1984b, p. 111)

Finally, all achievements are precarious and even what has been achieved may be lost. This is the reason why the "potential space" of playing and cultural life is identified as "the place where we live" (cf. 1971g). Playing is the experience of precariousness itself, of finitude, the area of illusion, which is only valid for a certain time, which opens and closes. This is why playing serves as a paradigm for creative life, the only one that is worth living. Precariousness means that the thread that ties man to life and to life's meaning may always break up, or may never be constituted:

> The link can be made, and usefully made between creative living and living itself, and the reasons can be studied why it is that creative living can be lost and why the individual's feeling that life is real or meaningful can disappear. (1971g, p. 93)

There is no possible *foundation* for this basic question in the metapsychologies that are available to us. The existence of the individual, her ability to be, is not at stake in traditional psychoanalysis. This is what Pontalis (1977) refers to when he states in the preface to his French translation of *Playing and Reality*:

> Even if Winnicott used classical concepts, it seems they were not quite adequate for what he wanted to clarify, it seems that the very idea of an unconscious, imposed on Freud by the psycho-neurotic functioning, does not appear to Winnicott to account for the dimension of *absence*, which he sees as a necessary void in the subject. I shall willingly suggest that if the Freudian topography of the agencies and the psychical places can describe the intrasubjective conflict, for Winnicott, this appears as secondary, as a construction where the self—the subject—is already mutilated. Our entire conception of psychic reality has been modified by this. (Pontalis, 1981, p. 152)

We have here the main reason why very early in his career as a psychoanalyst, Winnicott acknowledged the non-essential character of neuroses with regard to an understanding of human nature. In neuroses, engaging with life is not called into question. The *no* that concerns neuroses is one that occurs *within* life, being part of the individual's history. In psychoses, the *no* denies the possibility of being itself; it is not therefore part of a history, because a history is only constituted on the basis of being. The fundamental questions, of life or death, which afflict psychotics cannot even be formulated within the framework of traditional metapsychology:

> We seldom reach the point at which we can start to describe what life is like *apart from illness or absence of illness*. That is to say, we have yet to tackle the question of *what life itself is about*. Our psychotic patients force us to give attention to this sort of basic problem. (1967b, p. 133; my italics)[63]

Language and the descriptive categories of the theory of maturational processes

Winnicott usually starts the description of the process of emotional development with the later stages, those studied by traditional psychoanalysis, and then presents the more primitive ones, "into the unknown of the earliest moments at which the term human being can be applied to the foetus in the womb" (1988, p. 34). This is what he does, for example, in *Human Nature*.

The choice of this order of presentation is due to the fact that he knows that the vast majority of his presumed readers are psychoanalysts, used to thinking of the already established individual. They are also accustomed to the *language* of metapsychology, which does not refer to a "person", but to a "psychic apparatus", composed of forces, intensities of forces and mental mechanisms, intended to describe pulsional disorders and conflicts.

Since his conception of human nature and of the initial stages also substantially differs from that formulated by metapsychology and traditional psychoanalysis in general, Winnicott is especially careful with the language that he uses to express himself when approaching this theme, precisely in order to deal with the peculiarity of what is happening to the baby at the start of life. He repeatedly underlines that the description of each stage requires a new method of presentation and a specific language (cf. 1988). The language used for the description of human phenomena, he says, "grows up, so to speak, with the growing child" (1964e, p. 9), so that the language adequate for describing the achievements of a stage becomes "wrong" for another stage (1988, p. 34). In particular, it is wrong to describe the initial stages in the same terms as those used for the description of the oedipal phase, when it is assumed that personal identity and wholeness have been achieved; and when an internal life already exists with the presence of unconscious conflicts resulting from instinctual life and interpersonal relationships.

The insistence on changing language is far from being a caprice or an idiosyncrasy, as has been indicated in the Introduction. It reflects the demands imposed on theorisation by the initial phenomena of life themselves. Winnicott strives to communicate what happens, directly and without misrepresentations, in the "magic of intimacy", between the baby and the mother, and between the patient and the analyst in the clinical situation. He knows that in the experiential field, involving babies and psychotics, understanding does not occur in an exclusively intellectual or mental way but demands a type of proximity and communication with the patient, similar to the contact between mother and baby. To this language, essentially, belong silence, pre-verbal and pre-representational communication. In addressing the communication between mother and baby, Winnicott points out that the reader is being led "to a place where verbalization has no meaning" (1968d, p. 91). What connection can there possibly exist between all this and traditional psychoanalysis, which has based itself on the process of verbal interpretation of thoughts and verbalised ideas?

The theory of personal maturational processes not only opens the question of appropriately understanding the initial states, for which an entirely new language becomes necessary, but imposes new conditions on the descriptive language of the later stages. Although Winnicott's approach to the later stages retains a good deal of what is already configured by the classical literature on neurotic disorders, Winnicott indeed makes a *redescription* of phenomena relevant to the oedipal stage and, consequently, of the corresponding theory of neurosis. This redescription, carried out in its own terms, on the basis of the theory of maturational processes, has become necessary as a result of the new paradigm which underpins the whole of his theory.

Notes

1. The implications of the temporal character of human nature are central to the Winnicottian theory of psychoses.
2. In this text, Winnicott indicates that this tendency in his thought was already present, without him realising it, in articles of a decade earlier, that is, approximately from the end of the 1950s and the start of the 1960s. He cites as examples the title of his book *The Maturational Processes and the Facilitating Environment* and the article "Roots of aggression" (1964c), included as the only new chapter in *The Child, the Family, and the Outside World* and also published as an addendum to the article of 1939, "Aggression and its roots", in *Deprivation and Delinquency*.
3. The cited excerpts from Winnicott are in Winnicott, 1963d, p. 93.
4. On the essential split, cf. Winnicott, 1988, part four, Chapter Six.
5. The stages of development, with their respective tasks, will be detailed in Chapters Three and Four.
6. Cf. Chapter Three, section titled "The constitution of the primary self".
7. In many religions, this feature of human life is expressed through the metaphor of the pilgrim. On the wall of a thirteenth century convent in Toledo, Spain, one can read: "*Peregrino, no hay*

caminos, hay que caminar" [Pilgrim, there are no paths, you must walk]. The contemporary Italian composer Luigi Nono (1924–1990) used this line in one of his later compositions, dedicated to the film director A. Tarkovsky, in which the music has a slowness that is frequently unsustainable, almost subversive. Heidegger characterises this same feature by the term *Wanderer*, borrowed from the title of Hölderlin's poem.

8. It is only in Winnicott's book *Human Nature* that we find a sequential presentation of the stages of maturation; throughout Winnicott's work, we can nevertheless find several affirmations that allow us to corroborate this ordering.
9. In any case, achieving something and then losing it is entirely different from never having achieved it.
10. In this point resides one of Winnicott's central arguments for refusing, as inacceptable, Melanie Klein's theory of innate envy. It is not reasonable to attribute this kind of feeling to the infant as far as it presupposes an assessment of the external object in a moment when, given his extreme immaturity, he is not capable of knowing the existence of the external object, and even less, of its attributes. The feeling of envy can only be attributed to the individual who has already achieved the sense of externality.
11. In this same text, Winnicott introduces, *in his own terms*, what he considers to be Melanie Klein's most important contribution to psychoanalysis: the "depressive position". There he affirms: "the term 'depressive position' is a bad name for a normal process, but no one has been able to find a better" (1955c, p. 264). My suggestion is to call this stage, and its corresponding achievement, "concern". On this point, see footnote 31, Chapter Four of this book.
12. On the meaning of the expression "human animal" in Winnicott, cf. Loparic 2000b. In this article, clarifying an aspect of the paradigmatic shift of Winnicott's theory with regard to traditional psychoanalysis, Loparic observes that, while the latter neglected and even expurgated the body in favor of desire and other psychic manifestations, in Winnicott the body become *soma*, is permanently considered. "Freud", says the philosopher, "was not concerned with psychosomatic existence, but with gaps in consciousness, that is, in the psyche. [...] the body was at most included as a physical source of pulsions, regarded as its psychic representatives" (ibid., p. 393).
13. Loparic explains in the same previously mentioned article: "Essential to Winnicott, the term 'psyche' is not current in traditional psychoanalysis. In order to refer to the same domain of phenomena, it prefers the term 'soul', 'mind', 'psychic apparatus', 'subject', among others. Winnicott has never made explicit the reasons for his choice. It is due, at least partially, to etymology. In common Greek, *'psyche'* firstly means life, including animal life, and only secondarily does it mean immaterial or immortal soul, conscious self or the person as center of emotions, desires and feelings. In any case, according to Winnicott, in a certain sense and to a certain degree, the psyche is in the baby since the beginning of life. [...] Winnicott's use of the word *'psyche'* does not suggest anything that may be connected to the spirit, an entity that, according to the traditional interpretation, has the property of existing independently of the body. For the same reason, Winnicott excludes the word 'soul' from his vocabulary, except when designating 'a property of the psyche', which also depends, ultimately, on the brain's functioning and can be healthy or ill" (cf. Loparic, 2000b, p. 361).
14. A mere physical sensation becomes experience because the imaginative elaboration gives sense to it. In 1952, answering to a letter from Money-Kyrle, in which the latter mentioned the utility of drawing a distinction between ideas and sensations, Winnicott agrees but observes that "I would rather say the difference between ideas and experience" (1987b, p. 40).

15. On imaginative elaboration as creation of meaning, cf. Loparic, 2000b, section 7.
16. Cf. 1987b, letter 74. See also Chapter Four, footnote 4.
17. An illustrative example of how imaginative elaboration leads to the schematisation of the body is to be found in the book *Coordination Motrice et Psychomotrice du Tout Petit* (1992), by the experts in psychomotricity, M. M. Béziers and Y. Hunsinger. The proximity to Winnicott's theory was pointed out to me by Maria Emília Mendonça. In the item on changing clothes, the authors say that, when placed on the changer, the baby will push his feet against the person who is changing him. This pressure by the feet is important in many aspects, one of them being that "from the point of view of the static body, the entire extension of the back will be supported in this way by the changer. The baby stretches himself and opens the hip joints (extension) and presses with the feet, which provides him the *image of straightening up*, preparing the 'straightening up in the standing position'" (Béziers & Hunsinger, 1992, p. 49; my italics). There is reason to believe that this "image" is not a visual one, as if the baby saw himself in a standing position. It is rather a schematisation of how he feels to be totally stretched, erect and supported by the feet.
18. Cf. also Winnicott, 1969d.
19. Sometimes, as is the case in this quotation, Winnicott, when referring to any of the aspects of instinctual life, uses the classical terminology and speaks of "id" and "ego". This use has a communicative function, and the sense he gives to such terms in his own theory does not correspond to that attributed to them in traditional theory, ruled by other theoretical assumptions. Here, for example, "id" and "ego" are not instances of the psychic apparatus; the id is not constituted of pulsions. It is the general denomination, already recognised, for human instinctuality: "The instinctual life has to be considered both in terms of the bodily functions and of the imaginative elaboration of these functions. (By instinctual one means what Freud called sexual, i.e. the whole range of local and general excitements which are a feature of animal life; [...])" (1965h, p. 130). The term "ego ", in its turn, is used by Winnicott to designate the innate tendency towards development, in the sense of integration.
20. For a clarification of the use of the term "ego" in Freud and Winnicott, see section 10 of this chapter. Beyond the difference between the theories, regarding the "ego", the essential point in the question presented here is the fact that Winnicott conceives existence as psycho-somatic and constituted by experience, which is equally psycho-somatic, and not merely representational.
21. If, for centuries, medicine only considered the organic, psychoanalysis contributed to a perspective, which is nowadays widespread, in which everything is credited to the psychic aspect, with a complete disregard for the body autonomy, including the temporal one.
22. An interesting fact on the eternal discussion of the relations between body and psyche (or mind) is to be found in the item "psychoses" of the "*Enciclopedia de psiquiatria*" of Editorial "El Ateneo": the term "psychosis" was first used in a strictly psychiatric sense in the nineteenth century, by Ernst von Feuchtersleben (1806–1848), dean of the Medical Faculty of Vienna. "He used the terms psychoses and psychopathy indistinctly to mean mental illness, as a different thing from 'neurosis', or 'nerve infirmity'. According to Feuchtersleben, *the notion of infirmity does not derive from the mind, nor from the body, but from the relation of one to the other.* What is important is the interplay between both instances, and the way such process is configured, either as a unity or as 'body-soul' duality. The author limited himself to describing this situation and did not intend to explore its 'real complexity'" (Resnik, 1977 *apud* Vidal, Bleichmar, & Usandivaras (orgs.), 1977, p. 539; my italics).
23. In these cases, in general, it may occur that the imaginative elaboration gives a persecutory sense to the pain or distress.

24. For the detailing of the functions of child thinking, cf. Winnicott, 1989s.
25. "Rudimentary" here has nothing to do with the baby's mental capacity, which may even become exceptional if he is allowed to develop naturally.
26. According to Winnicott, this constitutes one of the important sources of headache as symptom.
27. Cf. Winnicott, 1954a.
28. It is important to mention here the distinction between hereditary and congenital factors. Heredity, in any of its meanings, relates to factors which existed before conception. The term "congenital" refers to two sets of disorders: those that include illnesses and deficiencies which existed prior to birth (during pregnancy) and those resulting from sequels of birth (cf. 1988, p. 38).
29. An eloquent example of how a child with a hereditary physical deformity may reach the sense of being a healthy self is offered in Winnicott, 1971d, pp. 262–265.
30. This picture configures one of the defensive organisations of schizophrenic type in which a split is present, designated by Winnicott as "split-off intellect".
31. States of mental confusion and serious learning difficulties have almost always been diagnosed, within a psychiatric context, as mental deficiency. Apart from cases of organic lesion, according to Winnicott, these are emotional disorders of the development process, related to environmental failure in the provision of care to these children. (Cf., for example, the case of Ashton, Chapter Twenty-five (1996c), by Winnicott, 1996a).
32. This category refers to those illnesses that are unquestionably physical, such aspolio and scurvy.
33. We can thus say that Winnicott conceives a non-causal theory of psychic disorders, which will be addressed below, in this same chapter. This is why Loparic calls the Winnicottian baby "ongoing", attributing to him the sense of being that Heidegger gives to *Dasein*.
34. This will hence be one of the central aspects of therapeutic work: to provide the conditions for the experiencing for the first time, under the special conditions of the analytical setting, of what has not been experienced.
35. The concepts of subjective world, area of illusion of omnipotence and capacity for illusion, central to Winnicott's thought, will be detailed in Chapter Three.
36. This is a line from T. S. Eliot's last "quartet".
37. Cf. Clare Winnicott, 1989.
38. The importance of the environment for the shaping of the individual's personality is not new. Already in 1946, the publication of Anna Freud's book *The ego and the mechanisms of defence* (1946/1968), provoked a reassessment of the role of maternity and environmental care in the primitive development of the infant. The works of Dorothy Burlingham and Anna Freud (1942), during the war, resulted in the development of the study about the external condition and its effects. Before the war, John Bowlby studied the backgrounds of disturbed children and, in a formal study of 150 children with various types of problems, discovered a direct link between theft and privation, with this later related in particular to separation from the mother during the early years of childhood (cf. Bowlby, 1951; Winnicott, 1951a). An important and detailed study on environment in Winnicott's work was developed by Serralha, C., 2007.
39. It is worth noting that in Winnicott, all achievements and capacities, that is, everything that the individual appropriates, starts from a non-capacity, an absence, a negative from which something emerges. This negativity, which is at the origin, is never entirely surpassed. It remains as the mark of precariousness of all life's achievements. Everything that comes into being may subsequently cease to be. This is one of the possible approximations of Winnicott's thought, without him knowing it, to M. Heidegger's ontology of finitude. This point will be resumed at the end of Chapter Four, in the section referring to death and the return to the beginning.

40. This expression was proposed for the first time, by Z. Loparic. Cf. Loparic, 1997a.
41. The conception of an environment that, at the outset, is not external to the baby, but a part of him, is entirely original not only to traditional psychoanalysis, but to psychology in general, and can only be understood in its peculiarity from the theory of personal development. This is the reason why, when we try to compare Melanie Klein and Winnicott, via the internal/external polarisation, we consider it a badly formulated question, and a fruitless debate, since when either of them mentions environment, they are not referring to the same thing.
42. In some passages of his work, as is the case in the following one, Winnicott asserts that, at the initial moment, what we find is "the complete merging of the individual in the environment, that which is implied in the words primary narcissism" (1988, p. 157). In the same work, he explains what he understands by primary narcissism: "Primary narcissism, or the state *prior to* the acceptance of the fact of an environment, is the only state out of which environment can be created" (1988, p. 130). In another text, referring to the immaturity and dependence that characterise this initial moment, we read: "I have never been satisfied with the use of the word 'narcissistic' in this connection, because the whole concept of narcissism leaves out the tremendous differences that result from the general attitude and behavior of the mother" (1972, p. 191).
43. This point of the theory will be explained in Chapter Four, section titled "The return to the origin".
44. The transitional stage and the phenomena of transitionality will be presented in Chapter Four, titled "Transitionality".
45. Psychoanalysts of Freudian and Kleinian orientation find it difficult to accept the idea that, initially, the relationship is exclusively with the mother, that is, purely dual, since this discards the conception of the Oedipus complex as structuring the individual.
46. The good-enough mother is the model of the analyst in Winnicottian clinical practice. Having preserved the differences, what is valid for the former is applicable for the latter. Regarding the mother's need to be "very good", I recall a young man who had been suffocated by such necessity in his mother. When entering the room in my practice for the first time, he said: "Why so many cushions? Do I have to use them all?"
47. This is another example of how Winnicott starts from negativity, from not-being-yet, in order for any achievement to make sense. In other passages, noting that the only real eating has not-eating as a basis, Winnicott observes that this point makes a formidable contribution to the issue of anorexia. Cf., for example, Winnicott, 1963d, p. 95 and 1965j, p. 182.
48. The distinction between "being" and "doing", between the breast that "is" and the breast that "does", will be examined in greater detail in Chapter Three, section titled "The constitution of the primary self".
49. In the preface of the book *Talking to Parents* (1993a), the editors mention that Winnicott, supported and stimulated by Isa Benzie during the long series of radio lectures for the BBC, reported that it was she, who, in his words, "pulled the phrase 'the ordinary devoted mother' out of what I had talked about [...]. This immediately became a peg to hang things on, and it suited my need to get away from both idealization and also from teaching and propaganda. I could get on with a description of child care as practised unselfconsciously everywhere" (1993a, p. xiv).
50. Winnicott points out again and again for the danger of sentimentality, which, according to him, is the denial of the natural hate from the part of the parents for being so affected by their children. Some lullabies are the expression of the parent's need to express their hate, preventing them from retaliating, which then would indeed be unbearable for the baby. One of these songs says:

"Rockabye baby, on the tree top,
When the wind blows the cradle will rock,
When the bough breaks the cradle will fall,
Down will come baby, cradle and all".

Some of the Brazilian lullabies also go in this direction:

"Boi, boi, boi
Boi da cara preta,
Pega esse menino
Que tem medo de careta".
[Bull, bull, bull,
Bull with a black face,
come and catch this boy
who's afraid of grimaces]

51. On the role of the father in environmental facilitation and possible paternal failures which hinder personal development, see the complex and exhaustive work of Claudia Dias Rosa, 2011.
52. Sometimes Winnicott is criticised for attributing an excessive responsibility to the mother and for the fact that this responsibility falls upon the mother and not the father. Feminists in general do not accept these ideas. Elisabeth Badinter, for example, cites Winnlcott's concept of the good-enough mother with extreme irony and equal incomprehension (1980). Winnicott however, describes and addresses the needs of the baby and not theories and/or ideologies. Regarding the fact that, in relation to the foundations of personality, the main responsibility lies with the mother, this duty does not seem to be excessive when we think that the period of absolute adaptation takes only a few months, two, three or four, and what the mother is doing is to avoid that her child is psychotic. Moreover, in the event that she was able to regress to the natural condition of primary maternal preoccupation, this will not be an overload but a need of the mother herself.
53. On this contribution by the father during the initial stages and on a few theoretical additions to this question, cf. Chapter Four, sub-section titled "The stage of concern".
54. Cf. the case of Sally, seventeen months, in Winnicott, 1996c, p. 207.
55. Winnicott reports the unprecedented case of a child who gave the name "Family" to his transitional object, noting how incredibly early this child tried to repair his parents' failure to provide a feeling of family cohesion. Thirty years later, this individual is still struggling with his incapacity for accepting his distance from his parents and the definitive disintegration of the family (cf. 1986d).
56. The stage of concern will be developed in Chapter Four.
57. This subject, as well as that of the place of the father in the Oedipus complex, will be addressed in Chapter Four, respectively in the description of the stage of concern and of the oedipal stage.
58. This conception naturally has theoretical consequences, one of which is the fact that the ego structuring is related to pulsional vicissitudes. On Winnicott's comment to this question, cf. Winnicott, 1964b.
59. Cf. Winnicott, 1989j.
60. In "Creativity and its origins" (1971g), Winnicott affirms that both schizoids and personalities of false self type ("extroverts") "have a sense that something is wrong and that there is a

dissociation in their personalities, and they would like to be helped to achieve unit status [...]" (1971g, p. 90).

61. Winnicott is not the only thinker, in the context of the theory of psychic disorders, to refuse the causal conception of man. Tellenbach, a psychiatrist influenced by phenomenology, also points to the difference between causality in the strict sense and of "having an origin". In his interpretation of the aetiology of melancholy, the causality principle is replaced by the principle of correlation. He resorts to analogy in order to express the difference: we cannot affirm, holds Tellenbach, that "trees blossom *because* it is spring". As regarding anything that flourishes from itself, we must say: "Trees blossom now that is spring even hibernation goes along with winter, and animal rut with autumn" (Tellenbach, 1980, p. 198).
62. It is quite common, and must be considered normal, the author says, that the child is the result of a little accident and "it is sentimental to put too much stress on the idea that the child was conceived in relation to any conscious wish" (1987c, p. 52).
63. There is also no way that we can find support for this question in philosophies of metaphysical type, in which the field of reflection is being as presence in its full positivity. We need Heidegger here. Rooted in non-being, there is, in the individual, an original split, essential and insurmountable. Juliano Pessanha, in his text on temporality in Freud and Heidegger, observes: "To break into the world, to give in to the temptation of existing, is to fall into scenes that distribute to each one a 'name', 'reality', 'duration', etc. This entry is a cut; a split between the strangeness of exile (*das Unheimliche*), the space of the night, where I am not yet, and the clear day of history (the house) which weaves me and speaks my name" (Pessanha, 1992, p. 82). Reaching life, endowing it with consistence and sense is an achievement. It is the work of forgetting, through the adhesion to the world's positivity, the primordial void that creeps in everywhere. Man, "thrown into the possibilities of the world, has already engaged in the fabric of meanings, having achieved a 'being' and a 'duration'. This duration is nevertheless always ultimately gnawed away, and marked by impossibility. To persist in the duration, to watch over the maintenance of the big factory of the world is to forget about the end, to escape, turning one's back on the great exile" (Pessanha, 1992, p. 82).

CHAPTER THREE

The primitive stages: absolute dependence

The prenatal stage: spontaneity and reactivity[1]

After presenting some general aspects of the theory of maturational processes, I shall now move on to the *description of the initial stages*, starting in this third chapter with the most primitive ones: intrauterine life, birth, the period immediately after birth, and the stage of the theoretical first feed, covering the entire period during which the baby lives in a state of absolute dependence on the mother.

When does the maturational process begin? In other words, at what point during gestation is it possible to consider that there is already a human being capable of having experiences? According to Winnicott, it is neither possible nor relevant to determine the exact point at which the foetus may start to be regarded as a human being who can be studied from a psychological viewpoint. Probably, he says that the only certain date is that of conception (cf. 1988, p. 29).

At some point after conception, a "first awakening" occurs, after which there is "a simple state of being, and a dawning awareness of the continuity of being and of the continuity of existence in time" (1988, p. 135). It is difficult, if not impossible, to observe this state directly: "It belongs to the infant and not to the observer" (1988, p.127).[2] Having reached the state of being, what the baby needs is *to go on being*. All other needs arise from the fact that the baby *is* and *has to go on being*. Throughout life until death, the continuity of being will remain as the fundamental problem; its preservation is equivalent to health.[3]

At a certain point during gestation, babies begin to move inside the uterus, and it is most likely that sensations begin during this phase. Clinical evidence allows us to assume that both the movement and the calm experienced in intrauterine life are meaningful to the babies and are somehow recorded. This is also due to the fact that cerebral development has reached a certain level, enabling the foetus to retain body memories. It is therefore likely that the storage of experience begins at that time, as does a central organisation of them, so that "body memories which *are personal* begin to gather in order to form a new human being" (1988, p. 21; my italics). This means that from a point before birth, nothing that a human being experiences is lost (cf. 1988, p. 127).

In terms of the personal maturation, the fundamental question, even at this initial stage, refers to the *opposition between spontaneity and reactivity*, an opposition that will be present in increasingly complex fashion throughout life. Searching for the appropriate language to describe this initial moment, Winnicott resorts to an analogy suggested to him by a patient:[4] the baby or the foetus is like a bubble. If outside pressure is adapted to internal pressure, the bubble can go on "existing". In the case of the human baby, we say that he goes on "being". If, on the other hand, pressure outside the bubble is bigger or smaller than inside, the bubble will react to the intrusion (impingement): it will be modified in reaction to a change in the environment, and not from an impulse of its own. For human beings, this means *an interruption of being, produced by a reaction to intrusion*. Once the intrusion ceases, the reaction also disappears, and the continuity of being may thence be re-established.

The decisive question is: where does the movement that generates contact start? Does the movement derive from demands arising from the baby's "aliveness", or is it a reaction to a change in the environment, a reaction that interrupts the continuity of being? In the former case, the baby is sleeping or quietly withdrawn and the mother preserves his isolation undisturbed, waiting for the moment when he will again make a movement, when he once again discovers the environment. The mother who follows this toing-and-froing of the baby from quietness to movement and vice-versa without interfering, based on the baby's needs, establishes a certain relationship pattern. In this case, the experiences and the body memories of the experiences *are personal*.

In the latter case, the initiative of movement arises from the environment. If it repeatedly anticipates the baby's movement, a pattern of relationship is established that may be called *intrusive*. During intrauterine life, the baby is more protected from invasive environmental movements, such as the oscillations in mood of an unstable mother. Even the conditions of intrauterine life are far from being the ideal ones, as is commonly assumed. There is growing empirical evidence that the foetus can feel sudden changes in the mother's cardiac rhythm, sharp movements or the effects of toxic or disorganised eating. Winnicott already knew that the mother's rigidity or inability to adapt, resulting from anxiety or from a depressive state, could affect the baby even before birth (cf. 1988). Environmental invasions force the baby to react and in this case, may establish a premature state of alertness, which has nothing to do with the perception of something, but with a certain tone of vigilance due to the potential threat of invasion (cf. 1974). The opposition between spontaneity and reactivity shows that "environmental influences can start at a very early age to determine whether a person will go out for experience or withdraw from the world when seeking reassurance that life is worth living" (1988, p. 128).

All of this becomes clearer after birth, when the baby must deal more directly with the mother's modes of being and with her emotional states. If she tends to act according to her own needs or anxiety and not to the changing needs of the baby, there is an intrusion, and the baby reacts. The reaction to invasion breaks the baby's *continuity of being*, since it bears no relationship to the vital process of that individual: "the infant that is disturbed by being forced to react is disturbed out of a state of 'being'. This state of 'being' can obtain only under certain conditions. *When reacting, an infant is not 'being'*" (1958f, p. 185; my italics).

If the contact is made on the basis of the spontaneous gesture of the baby, both the fact that he is alive and his own experience are felt as real and the accumulation of these personal experiences begins to integrate into personality; when, on the other hand, the reaction to the intrusion subtracts something from the sensation of true living, this may only be recovered by means of a return to isolation and quiet.

The experience of birth

Whatever the moment of the "first awakening", the fact is that at some point close to birth, the "great awakening" occurs, when "the baby, already alerted for the high dive" (1968d, p. 91). The effectiveness of the great awakening may be demonstrated by the perceptible difference that exists between a baby who is born prematurely and a post-term baby. The former is not yet ready for extra-uterine life, appearing poorly prepared for that condition, whereas the latter shows signs of having stayed too long in the uterus, being subjected to a sort of "state of frustration" for having been kept waiting when he was ready.[5]

The birth process is not traumatic in itself; it will only be so due to problems that may arise during birth.[6] Birth is considered normal when the foetus is able to cope with the reaction to the inevitable invasions on the occasion. The birth process evidently causes a discontinuity, even when everything goes well, although this can be tolerated, since the baby has already had several experiences of interruption of the continuity of being during intrauterine life, since he has not only accumulated body memories but has also organised defences against possible traumas.

The condition characterising normal birth is the baby being born at the right time, a full-term birth, that is, after nine months of life in the uterus, a deadline on which both physiology and psychology agree. For normal births, physiology coincides with "the readiness of the baby to abandon the uterus", so that he can feel the whole process as something natural, something which emerges from his own impulse. The birth process may nevertheless be traumatic and this will happen if, due to problems during birth, *delay* or *anticipation* occurs. These are the conditions, of a *temporal* nature, which characterise abnormal birth.[7] Difficulties and accidents of this type occur and are traumatic to various degrees, depending on the baby's capacity for tolerating intrusion, but they need not necessarily be decisive, unless a physical injury occurs. Apart from cases of physical injuries, which have their own psychological consequences, we may observe the differences which exist between the needs of a baby born in due time and those of the individual whose birth was traumatic as a result of being delayed or premature. It is precisely here that the "adaptation to the needs" of the good enough mother gains significance: it is up to her to understand and to adapt to the differences of the singular baby.

When everything goes well, birth constitutes an experience of great value for the future individual. The proof of this is the pleasure which almost all children and some adults extract from activities and games involving the dramatisation of one or another aspect of the birth process. This is why, if a baby is born by Caesarean section or is in a state of deep anaesthesia because the mother has been anaesthetised, he will have missed something very important, since from the baby's point of view, in the normal birth process "it was the infant's impulse that produced the changes and the physical progression, usually head first, towards an unknown and new position" (1988, p. 144). Hence, for the baby, the birth took place as a result of his own impulse; he was thus the one who made it happen.

At the same time, there is no reason to overestimate this experience. It is one of a series of factors, which are favourable for the development of reliability, stability, safety, etc. In cases in which everything went well during the birth process, it is unlikely that the birth experience will emerge as an important point in analysis. It is only when the complications of the birth process exceed the limits which the baby can tolerate, when unbearable degrees of invasion occur with their consequent reactions, that it becomes traumatic and a serious distortion may result, related to the premature and forced start of mental functioning. When this happens, the experience will be resumed several times in analysis, which is frequent in the treatment of psychotics.[8]

First moments of extra-uterine life

It is not as soon as the baby is born that he needs nourishment, or is completely ready to search for it. What he certainly needs is some time to recover from the discontinuities inherent to the birth process and to return to the feeling of continuity of being. This usually leads him into a state of quiescence. Crucially, he also needs the mother to establish contact with him. In addition to this, the development of the brain, combined with "the great awakening" and the experience of birth keep the baby busy with his new condition, at the same time as the primitive mind is cataloguing impressions and the series of small reactions to inevitable invasions of the new environmental situation.

In general, the newly born baby is extremely susceptible to all sensations relating to touch, temperature conditions, light, texture, etc., but, above all, there are two new facts with which he must deal: the start of breathing and the first experience of the action of gravity. We often assume that the inaugural experience of breathing is traumatic in itself. In Winnicott's view, however, what may be traumatic is not the start of breathing but a significant *delay* in it, associated with a prolonged birth. The start of breathing almost always occurs without major problems and is hardly significant (traumatic), except for inaugurating the sensation of something coming in and going out. At subsequent stages, difficulties involving breathing, such as asthma, will be linked to this first experience, which becomes a prototype for the "comes in and goes out". For babies who have suffered excessive invasions, "the to and fro of breathing is found to be intolerable", since the sensations related to breathing, which are "intolerably real", represent a total lack of defence and control over what moves in and out (cf. 1988). In addition to breathing, there is also the fact, unprecedented for the baby, of the action of gravity, which had not yet entered into play during intrauterine life. Accustomed to being contained all around, the baby now feels after birth that he is "pushed up from below". An alteration occurs, therefore, "from being loved from all directions to being loved from below only" (1988, p. 130).[9] This is why maternal care in physically "holding" the baby is not only that of holding, but of enveloping him from all sides.

The recovery of the continuity of being after delivery requires the reconnection with certain conditions which precede birth; in intrauterine life, the baby was used to feeling the mother's breathing, her abdominal movements, her body noises or her rhythmic changes of pressure, and it is likely that he needs to re-establish contact with these physiological functions of the mother. All of these experiences initiate communication with the mother, in addition to facilitating the constitution of time, a time that is necessarily primitive, subjective and pre-chronological. These are very subtle experiences, says Winnicott, which only human contact can provide.

A mother who is capable of identifying with the baby from the beginning will wait until he is ready for contact. Only in this way will contact not be felt as invasion, with the baby able to start having drives again and even to seek nourishment. If the mother is too anxious to play her part as provider, she will be incapable of letting the baby explore the breast with the mouth or with his little hands before feeding, or to hold it with his gums. Each baby has his own way of making his approach to the breast, and the mother knows that it will take time to understand the ways of her baby. What she needs is the opportunity to be natural and to find her own way with her baby (cf. 1988, p. 105). It is these aspects which appear to be simple but which involve highly complex issues that characterise the nature of the absolute dependence of the infant and the task incumbent on the mother.

The stage of the theoretical first feed: the fundamental tasks

In order to avoid the idea that the first concrete feed is the great inaugural moment of nursing, Winnicott uses the expression "theoretical first feed" to refer to the sequence of first concrete experiences in feeding. The stage that receives this name covers approximately the first three or four months of the infant's life. As its name states, during this period, the activity of breast-feeding is central, but this does not mean that feeding as satisfaction of hunger corresponds to what is essential. Nor does it mean that orality, in terms of libidinal contact, is the main aspect to be observed. Since the emphasis is on personal maturational processes and not on the development of sexual functions, the issue is not the configuration of the initial erogenous zones or the nature of the pulsional manifestation, but the beginning of contact with reality and of the constitution of a self which will gradually integrate into a unity. Instinctuality and erogeneity belong to and participate in the maturational processes, but do not constitute them. Alluding to the fact that traditional psychoanalysis has dealt almost entirely with instinctual needs (ego and id), neglecting the needs of the maturing being in a personal sense, Winnicott affirms:

> we are more concerned with the environmental provision which makes all the rest possible; that is to say, we are more concerned here and now with the mother *holding* the baby than with the mother *feeding* the baby. (1965k, pp. 147–148)

In Winnicott's theory, breastfeeding is the privileged situation during which, when everything goes well, the *beginnings of the relation to external reality are established*, of which the mother is the first representative. What is most important here is the quality of the human contact, the reality of the experiences that are being provided to the baby *through the act of breastfeeding*: the encounter with something which he does not know is an object, and the beginning of a very special communication with the mother, verbally unrepeatable and also the beginning of mutuality. This is why:

> [...] when the mother and the baby come to terms with each other in the feeding situation this is the initiation of a human relationship. This sets the pattern for the child's capacity for relating to objects and to the world. (1968f, p. 64)

The mother is thus the baby's first "object", with the following proviso: in this context, the term "object", as well as the expression "object relating" have a very peculiar condition; they should not be understood in the sense in which they are used both in traditional psychoanalysis and in common sense, presupposing the perception, from the start of something external to the baby, a capacity which, according to Winnicott, cannot be admitted at this point.[10]

At the stage of the theoretical first feed, the baby is involved in three tasks: (1) from the state of unintegration, carrying out the experiences of integration into space-time, that is, the temporalisation and spatialisation of the baby (*integration*); (2) the gradual indwelling of the psyche in the body (*personalisation*); (3) the beginning of object relations, which will later culminate in the creation and acknowledgement of the independent existence of objects and of an external world (*realization or having reality*), "that is, making real the infant's creative impulse" (1965s, p. 19). Winnicott refers to these fundamental tasks in numerous passages in his work, presenting them in varied orders. In *Human Nature*, he states that there is no obvious sequence that may determine the order of the description. However, in the 1962 text, "Ego integration in child development" (1965n), where central aspects of the theory of personal development are introduced, he states that the main tendency of the maturational processes is integration into space and time, beginning his description with this task, followed by that of the indwelling of the psyche in the body and finally by the beginning of contact with reality. In the article "Fear of breakdown" (1974), it is this same order that presides over the enumeration of the tasks: "In such a facilitating environment, the individual undergoes development which can be classified as *integrating*, to which is added *indwelling (or psycho-somatic collusion)* and then *object-relating*" (1974, p. 89). This is the order to which priority shall be given in this text.

The three basic tasks are mutually interdependent and none of them can be fully achieved without the others. Their discrimination has the function of clarifying a certain degree of specificity of these fundamental achievements. When all goes well, the baby faces these tasks more or less simultaneously, since, in order to initiate a sense of real and to be able to inhabit a real world, which is initially subjective, the baby must be gradually introduced into the order of time and space. Spatialisation begins with the gradual process of indwelling of the psyche in the body, making this body, which is held in the mother's arms, the first home. Dwelling in the body, the baby can start to occupy space, make presence concrete, establish distances and proximities and access the transitory nature of what ages and dies. Space and time are not objects to be found; they are, insofar as they are articulated with each other and constitute worlds, the condition for the possibility of finding any object. The three basic achievements form the foundations of an existence, which, because of the innate tendency towards development, moves towards integration into a unitary self.

As these tasks are being performed and the achievements are being organised with each other through the functioning of the ego, another task is being processed: *the constitution of the self as identity*. This fourth task was only mentioned together with the others after the mid-1960s.

It would only be made explicit in 1966, when, on finishing his theory of the subjective object, Winnicott introduced the concept of primary identification: during the excited experience of breastfeeding, the baby *becomes the object*, having his first experiences of identity.[11]

All these tasks are fundamental and express the basic needs of the baby, which stem from the primordial need to continue to be. They will have a certain degree of resolution concerning this initial stage; the establishment of the basis of personality and psychic health depends on that resolution. They nevertheless remain as tasks which, while growing in complexity in the subsequent stages, *will never be fully abandoned*.

In order for the basic tasks to be successfully accomplished, to become achievements of maturation, specific maternal care is required: integration in time and space corresponds to holding; the indwelling of the psyche in the body is facilitated by handling, which is a more specific aspect of holding, related to physical care; contact with objects is provided by object presenting. At the same time as the mother facilitates each of the baby's tasks in a specialised manner, the series of care actions by the mother constitutes the *total environment*, and the mode of being of the totality of care shapes a *world* for the baby. The first world that the baby inhabits is necessarily a *subjective world*, with the central characteristic of being reliable. Above all, environmental reliability means predictability: the mother prevents something unexpected from startling the baby, interrupting his continuity of being; the mother is reliable when, in the midst of the ever changing needs of the baby, who is sometimes quiet and sometimes excited, she maintains both herself and the environment constant and consistent so that, over time, the baby is gradually temporalised, becoming able, through the repetition of experiences, to recognise things and anticipate events.

I highlight here the distinction that Winnicott draws between world and objects. The world inhabited by the baby is one thing; the objects which may be encountered (created) within this world are another. *In order to encounter objects, a world, a context in which these objects may be found, must exist.* It is of great importance to note that besides being the object to be encountered (object-mother), the mother is initially also the context, the environment in which the encounter with the object may happen (environment-mother). Since she maintains the environment constant, regular, simple, monotonous, and predictable and since she allows the baby to create the object that he encounters, she provides him with the *illusion of omnipotence*, which, as we shall see, is the basis for *believing in* … This is not a question of believing in this or that, but about the capacity for "believing in …" Winnicott says: "I cling to this ugly, incomplete phrase, belief in …" (1963d, p. 94). The sentence tends to be completed, over time, with the belief that the world can be found and is reliable, that there is something somewhere which makes sense or someone who understands and responds to the need. The most important environmental care to be provided to the child in order to establish the capacity for "belief in …" is that he may "live for an adequate period in a subjective world in which the world of external reality does not impinge" (1989n, p. 286). The world that is initially constituted is the *subjective world*, that is, a reliable ambience, made of the totality of maternal provision.

Primary creativity

In order to accomplish the tasks of the initial stage, the baby relies on his *own* innate tendency towards maturation and on *primary creativity*. The baby nevertheless cannot create the world in a vacuum with only his own resources; a good enough provision of care is required so that he can realise his creative potential, making it real. Creativity is finite and must be exercised in order to stay alive.

Winnicott's concept of primary creativity is unprecedented in the context of psychoanalysis. Thoroughly altering the idea that the psyche, from its beginning, is constituted on the basis of mental mechanisms of projection and introjection[12] and that human creativity is a tributary of sublimated pulsions, Winnicott formulates the idea of a primary psychic creativity, which is inherent to human nature and is present from the onset: "The world is created anew by each human being, who starts on the task at least as early as at the time of birth and of the theoretical first feed" (1988, p. 110). It is the baby, says Winnicott, who "creates the breast, the mother and the world" (1989e, p. 457). Intimately related to basic spontaneity and opposed to reactivity, primary creativity participates in the constitution of what will be the unitary self, since "it is only in being creative that the individual discovers the self" (1971k, p. 73).

Both at this initial moment and during any subsequent phase, creativity is not about making something or an original or artistic output, but about how the individual relates to the sense of reality that characterises a given moment of the maturational processes; in time, the capacity to transit through the various senses of reality is added to this, without losing contact with the personal and imaginative world. Throughout life, and while developing, the healthy individual will go on exercising creativity in increasingly complex ways, but it is on the basis of *primary creativity* that any creative life can be constructed: creativity, then, "is the retention throughout life of something which belongs properly to the experience of the infant: the ability to create the world" (1986h, p. 40).

As is the case with other human potentialities, primary creativity, which creates the world and the various senses of real, must be exercised from the start of life; otherwise, it will wither away, and the individual will not become able to provide a personal meaning to the world. In order for the baby to be able to exercise it, the presentation of objects must initially be made in such a way that, at the same time as the infant establishes a relation with these objects, he is kept under the illusion of omnipotence, that is, he creates what he needs without any awareness of the assistance which makes this action possible. We shall see how this happens when all goes well.

On the occasion of the theoretical first feed, being endowed with primary creativity and provided with the necessary care, the baby already has "a personal contribution to make" (1988, p. 110). Supported by an instinctual tension (which he cannot yet acknowledge as emerging from himself), the baby reaches out with his hand or mouth towards an alleged object (he does not even suspect the existence of something). It is a "spontaneous gesture", since it arises from a "personal" need derived from the baby's aliveness. At this point, says Winnicott, "*the baby is ready to be creative*". His spontaneous gesture announces: *I need ..., I am searching for something ...* and, at this very moment, the facilitating mother places the breast in a position where it can be found, or turns the baby on the side, or provides what he needs to make him feel more comfortable. A feeling may then occur, which would be formulated as follows: *this is what I needed*. The baby will be able to complete the sentence "*I need ...*" with "*... a turn-over, a breast, a nipple etc*" (1968d, p. 100).

When the mother responds adaptively to the spontaneous gesture, the baby feels as if the nipple and the milk were the result of his own gesture: he experiences *creating what he encounters*. The mother knows that what the baby created in accordance with his need was actually found. She nevertheless has a commitment to the baby, consisting of never asking him whether he found or created the object. The paradox is inherent, says Winnicott; it is not there to be resolved, but to be sustained and endured. Through her absolute adaptation, the mother accomplishes what may be her most important task: to introduce the baby to *the illusion* that he is the one who creates the world that he needs. This is a necessary illusion since "each child must be enabled to create the world (the mother's adaptive technique enables this to feel to be a fact) else the world is to have no meaning" (1984b, p. 111).

We could consider, as in traditional theory, that the baby "hallucinates" the object; as this is the initial moment, however, this cannot be affirmed, since hallucination will only be possible shortly afterwards, when through repeated experience, mnemonic material exists which is sufficiently well installed to be used in hallucination, that is, in creation, now enriched with the details drawn from experiences. Initially, *the baby's condition is only that of creating the object*. The motive is "the personal need" (1988, p. 102).

For a baby who has never had a feed, hunger arises and, even though he is "ready to conceive of something" (1947b, p. 90), he does not know what to expect, since he has no previous experience. If at this point the mother places the breast where the baby reaches out for something and if he is given enough time to explore with his mouth, hands, and the sense of smell, "the baby 'creates' just what is there to be found" (idem). With the repetition of experiences, the baby forms "the illusion that this real breast is exactly the thing that was created out of need, greed, and the first impulses of primitive loving" (idem). Since every part of the experience is recorded somewhere, over time, the baby "may be creating something like the very breast that mother has to offer" (cf. 1947b, p. 90). Prior to weaning, on the thousands of occasions when the mother offers this peculiar experience of introduction to external reality to the baby and, since the breast is there to be created/found, the baby feels repeatedly that he creates what he needs. As a result, the hope and subsequently the belief will be established that "there is a live relationship between inner reality and external reality, between innate primary creativity and the world at large which is shared by all" (1947b, p. 90).

Providing the baby with the possibility of creating that which he encounters is an extremely delicate act of care, not contained in any specific action by the mother, but rather in "how" she presents the baby with the small samples of the world that he is apt to experience in the context of his omnipotence.[13] With regard to the constitution of the capacity for object relations, the baby depends entirely on *how* each fragment of the world is presented to him. It is these "modes of being" of the care, that is, the totality of the care making up the world created by the mother which, in a given way, update or also hinder the baby's tendency to be and his gradual integration into a unity. Firstly, the world must be presented to him in small doses, in a comprehensible way, which makes sense, that is, which does not surprise him. It is also necessary to avoid coincidences that would overburden the baby: the baby should not be moved to another room when he has chicken pox or earache, in order not to abuse his limited comprehension. Furthermore, if he is withdrawn into isolation or quietness, the mother understands that he *is not there to be found*; interacting with him on that occasion, imposing outside needs will interrupt his continuity of being at that moment, since when the creativity of the baby is absent, the samples of world that the mother presents him do not make sense. On the other hand, if the baby makes a gesture and the mother is absent, distracted, or self-absorbed, the gesture will be stalled in space, waiting for something that does not come.[14] In any of these cases, the result is not frustration, since there is not yet any desire, which is a highly sophisticated feeling characteristic of a unitary self, but breakdown in the continuity of being. If this is the pattern of the environmental attitude, then, annihilation may occur.

The paradox contained in the illusion of omnipotence lies in the fact that what the baby created was actually found by him (from the perspective of the observer) and was already there before he created it. However, *what the baby created is not exactly what the mother offered*, in the same way that *we never find in reality what we imagine*. This disparity will never be solved. It is inherent to human nature, and we will always have to deal with it throughout life.[15] Initially, however, the baby does not know anything about this, and it is vital not only for his psychic health but also for the richness of his personality, that the mother is able to allow the illusion to be established. Initiating the baby into the capacity for illusion is the essential task of the good-enough mother. She does this by keeping him for the adequate amount of time in a subjective world, presided over by the illusion of omnipotence: she protects his continuity of being, preventing an unpredictable outburst of a type of reality (which is external for the observer) that is not comprehensible to the baby during this primitive moment. Through the very paths of maturation, in his own time, the baby will have to create the externality of the world and achieve the capacity to relate to external reality without this representing a threat to his personal self; this capacity nevertheless depends on the fact that he was initially taken care of in such a way that the inaugural presentation of the world offered to him did not imply the loss of reality of the subjective world.

> For the lucky infant the world starts off behaving in such a way that it joins up with his/her imagination, and so the world is woven into the texture of the imagination, and the inner life of the baby is enriched with what is perceived in the external world. (1949a, pp. 73–74)

Excited states and quiet states

Before examining each of the fundamental tasks, we must distinguish between two states of the baby which are in permanent alternation with each other: excited and quiet. The two states and the delicate transition from one to the other represent something with which the individual will have to contend throughout his life; how he does this is determined by the way in which, with the help of the mother, this is initially done. What the baby needs at this point follows the guidelines described in the previously mentioned metaphor of the bubble and relates to the opposition between spontaneity and reactivity. While the quiet states are more clearly the occasion for tasks of integration in time and space, as well as the indwelling of the psyche in the body, the excited states are more directly related to the beginning of the establishment of contact with reality (when sucking and grasping objects), in addition to being the privileged moment for the observation of the roots of aggression.

The excited states

The emergence of an excited state in the baby may be described as follows: while he is in a quiet state, whether sleeping or simply resting, a drive emerges, almost always on the crest of an instinctual wave. A tension develops which quickly becomes urgency; the motor drive "hitches a lift" on it. The baby is filled with an indefinite expectation, since he knows nothing of his need or of what may be expected; in fact, the baby does not know of his own existence, or of the existence of objects, whether external or internal. The expectation, manifested through a spontaneous gesture, could be thus made explicit: the baby reaches out "to find something somewhere" (1988, p. 100).

The drives that lead the baby to excitement derive from two sources: instinctuality and motility. Both instinctual and motor drives are manifestations of the baby's "aliveness". Instinctuality is the field in which sexuality will develop as a significant aspect of the personal maturational process. Inherent to the instinctual impulsiveness of early life, in which sexuality takes root, is a destructiveness which also constitutes one of the roots of aggression. Another root of aggression is found in motility. Although these two types of drives, instinctual and motor, have their own specificity, it is to be expected that, in health, they merge into a global experience and, over time, act in an integrated way.

We shall initially examine the instinctual root of the drive and the excitement that derives from it. It is, however, important that we first clarify what Winnicott understands as instinctuality and how he sees it in the most primitive phases.

Winnicott uses the term "instinctual" to refer to the set of local and general excitations, which, for him, are an aspect of animal life. Instincts are "powerful biological drives which *come and go* in the life of the infant or child, and which *demand action*" (1988, p. 39; my italics). I highlight three aspects. First, as instincts *come and go*, they *do not constitute* the life of the baby, child or adult individual. When these return to a state of tranquillity, instincts also rest and, nevertheless, the continuity of being goes on. Second, with regard to what is strictly biological, the way instincts act on human beings does not differ from the way in which they act on animals. In general, instinctual excitation leads the child, the adult or any other animal to an expectation of satisfaction; a drive derives from this for acting and achieving a climax as well as a post-climax period. What is fundamentally different in human beings is that all bodily functions, including instinctual ones, go through imaginative elaboration and *it is to the imaginatively elaborated body that the individual relates.* For this reason, when speaking of instinctive excitation, it is always necessary to distinguish between the body itself and the ideas and feelings that the individual has of that body. From this perspective, there is no major difference either among the various types of instinctive demand. There is no reason for classifying instincts or for deciding whether there is only one instinct, if two or several of them exist.

Third, what characterises instincts is *the demand for action.* Since, however, in Winnicott's view, the core of the issue—even in the case of a biological drive—is the individual and not a pulsion, and since the meaning of the instinctual experience varies according to the stage of maturation, we must take into account the degree of immaturity of the baby: he knows nothing of the need that afflicts him or which type of action would effectively placate it; he does not even know of the existence of objects, and even less whether a certain object is the adequate one for the need which is affecting him. Making use of an object is also an achievement that can only be accomplished in due course. In this way, the action demanded by the instinctual drive is initially only a gesture with no definite goal, which does not focus on a particular object. For this reason, when referring to the instinctuality of the most primitive phase, Winnicott does not properly speak of instincts, but of *tensions or instinctual excitations*. He reserves the term "instinct", or "instinctual life", for when instinctuality is integrated and given a meaning by the individual as something that concerns him, which is lived as a personal experience with all its consequences; this achievement will only occur later, at the stage of concern. At this point, the baby will also be capable of *doing* something to the object, in an attempt to solve the instinctual urgency.

Initially, however, the baby is an immature, non-integrated being, who still does not inhabit the body, and has no knowledge of the fact that the instinctual tensions concern him. These are as "external" to him as the world is, with this also true of the anatomy of the body and of other biological functions. In reality, they are not even external, since the infant does not yet have the sense of internal or external. This does not mean that instinctual tensions are reduced to mere bodily sensations. Despite the fact that the infant does not yet have enough maturity to endow them with meaning, or to appropriate them as belonging to his or her own instinctual impulsivity, they are endowed with meaning since they are permanently elaborated imaginatively by the psyche. At the moment when the baby is hungry, he is stricken by something that hits, invades and threatens him—being hungry "is like being possessed by wolves" (1949d, p. 81)—but the baby does not know where the unease comes from, or how to distinguish the unease which emerges out of hunger from the unease resulting, for example, from a thunderstorm, a door slamming or from a sudden drop in temperature.

When the mother, who is identified with the baby, responds to him promptly, what she avoids is not yet a frustration, but an *interruption in the continuity of being*, since "instinctual demands can be fierce and frightening, and at first can seem to the infant like threats to existence" (idem). When the total environment provides global experiences, including mutuality and communication, and the mother gives ego support, the whole trajectory launched by instinctual tension becomes an experience that strengthens the ego and promotes the psycho-somatic cohesion of the child. Without this support, instead of being gradually integrated and personalised, instinctual tensions remain external and are felt as intrusions, and may even become persecutory, establishing a paranoid disposition.[16]

As integration becomes more consistent, the baby becomes increasingly capable of acknowledging instinctual drives as an aspect of the living self and not as environmental. When this development takes place, instinctual satisfaction will become an important reinforcing element of the self. Later still, after reaching unitary identity, the child will feel the instincts as his own; he will be startled and concerned with their manifestations and effects, both on him and on the mother. For the time being, however, the baby still knows nothing about this.

We can find all kinds of excitations in the baby, whether local or general. When the excitation is generalised, it may either be contributing to an experience of integration or may itself be the result of a greater integration along the path of maturation. If the excitation is local, we must consider the body function which is involved and which becomes the goal for imaginative elaboration. Some structures of excitation prove to be dominant in the successive stages of instinctual development (pre-genital, phallic and genital), both in terms of the functions involved and the imaginative elaboration of those functions. Excitation tends to occur in terms of the dominant instinct. According to Winnicott, the only pre-genital zone of excitation that is clearly prevalent during the primitive stages is the oral one. Although one may already find localised genital excitations in the baby, these should not be differentiated as such, since there are neither specific body functions nor the typical genital fantasy. This means that distinction between the sexes at this point is artificial and forced. The difference between male and female will only become significant in the phase of sexual development that Freud termed phallic. Winnicott considers this phase in his re-description of the sexual development as an aspect of the maturational processes, the most important one after the oral phase, taking place along this process, during the stage of concern.[17]

In the initial stages, instinctual excitation leads the child to prepare for the climax, for the satisfaction of instinctual tension, especially when the call reaches the peak of demand:

> If satisfaction can be provided at the climax of demand, then there is a reward of pleasure and also a temporary relief from instinct. Incomplete or ill-timed satisfaction results in incomplete relief, discomfort, and an absence of a much-needed resting period between waves of demand. (1988, p. 39)

This quotation shows that Winnicott distinguishes pleasure from satisfaction. Driven by instinctual urgency, what the individual seeks is to satisfy this urgency; but it is only when satisfaction takes place at the culminating moment of the demand, that is, when the mother is well synchronised with the baby, that the "reward of pleasure" arises. In terms of the need to go on being, however, satisfaction does not reduce to placating the instinct but requires a global experience, which implies being well held, being seen by the mother, engaging in communication with her, creating the object which he encounters and being able to exercise full motility during the instinctual experience. The previous citation also considers the two prerequisites which permit the period of rest, which is so necessary between two waves of demand: the first is that the child must have good experiences during the quiet states described below, so that he or she, for example, will not feel alarmed in the absence of excitation.[18] The second condition is that the instinctual satisfaction must form part of a wider experience, which includes communication and mutuality.

All of this leads us to the theme of the capacity for adaptation of the good-enough mother. At the beginning of psychoanalysis, the author notes, maternal adaptation merely meant satisfying the instinctual needs of the baby, regardless of the global context of safety and reliability, in which and from which instinctual drives "*whether satisfied or frustrated, become experiences of the individual*" (1965d, p. 241; my italics). In Winnicott, the prevalence of the reality of the experience as such over the pleasure or displeasure that resulted from it is clear. Firstly, it is necessary to guarantee the conditions for the experience to be real, by means of the environmental provision that makes everything else possible, so that afterwards, as the maturational process continues, this experience may come to be satisfactory or frustrating. Winnicott affirms that:

> [...] with good-enough mothering at the beginning the baby is not subjected to instinctual gratifications except in so far as there is ego-participation. In this respect it is not so much a

> question of giving the baby satisfaction as of letting the baby find and come to terms with the object (breast, bottle, milk, etc.). (1965n, pp. 59–60)

The surprising affirmation that *with good-enough care*, the baby is not "*subject to instinctual satisfactions*" means that if disconnected from a total experience, instinctual satisfaction may constitute a traumatic invasion:

> It is indeed possible to gratify an oral drive and by so doing to *violate* the infant's ego-function, or that which will later on be jealously guarded as the self, the core of the personality. A feeding satisfaction can be a seduction and can be traumatic if it comes to a baby without coverage by ego-functioning. (1965n, p. 57)[19]

From this perspective, it is easy to understand why Winnicott cannot accept that a libidinal connection to the breast or a search for satisfaction related to pulsional forces is seen in the breast-feeding situation. The needs of the baby are not dictated by the pleasure principle, but by the need to *be*, which includes reaching out and creating an object.[20] Satisfaction of instinctual tension is certainly necessary, but it only becomes an *experience* within a global experience of the encounter with the mother. Traditional psychoanalysis has accustomed us to think of the baby in terms of oral pulsions, but it is not adequate, saysWinnicott, "to refer to a first feed as an instinctual experience taking place and ending with no reference to the human being in whom the excitement is taking place" (1988, p. 113). Clearly, the baby must satisfy the instinctual urgency, but the main quality of the experiences of the theoretical first feed is not defined by the pleasure/displeasure polarity, but by the communication and intimacy that they provide and achieve, by the possibility of exercising primary creativity, since "a good object is no good to the infant unless created by the infant" (1965j, p. 181). Furthermore, if the mother understands that breastfeeding the baby consists solely of satisfying his hunger, without considering the needs of the ego, or in technical terms, if, for her, breastfeeding consists of an instinctual discharge, in the manner of the pleasure principle, there is a real risk of establishing a fear of satisfaction, since this becomes associated with the disappearance of the object. This risk can be avoided when we think in terms of a global situation: in addition to the object, there is an entire ambiance in which it is possible to let oneself be carried by the excited drive and to which one can return later for rest. The mother, in her function of total environment, remains there independent of her function as food provider.

Having said all this, it is almost superfluous to point out that Winnicott cannot accept that feeding is understood as a reflex act either. His insistence on this point results from his familiarity with common paediatric practice. He never lost an opportunity to address nurses who, thinking that they were doing their job well, picked up a baby wrapped in swaddling clothes, with trapped arms, pushing the breast into the baby's mouth and declaring their determination to force the baby to feed (cf. 1988, p. 104). In this case, he says, the best way to inhibit a baby from sucking the breast is to push the breast into the mouth "without giving any opportunity for the baby to be the creator of the object which is to be found" (1988, p. 104). Winnicott never tires of warning experts, whose work puts them in direct contact with women in labour and babies, that their main task is not to interfere with what the mother knows better than anyone else how to do, even when she is weak. The mother who has just given birth may be too weak even to lift the baby out of the cot without being helped, but she is still the only person actually suited to adapting to the needs of the infant, "needs which are indicated in ways that call specifically on the actual mother's subtlety of understanding" (ibid., p. 113). What she needs is physical help from doctors and nurses, but there is no reason for these professionals to take away from her the task which she is capable of doing better than anyone else: initiating the relationship with her baby.[21]

In addition to the instinctual tensions, the other source of drives for the excited states is *motility*, which, in Winnicott's theory, is one of the roots of aggression. Motility expresses itself even before birth, in the movements of the foetus, including the sudden and vigorous movements of the legs, leading some mothers to say that the baby is kicking. After birth, while moving and exercising the vitality of muscles and tissues, the child encounters something and in this way, the environment is constantly discovered and rediscovered. In this case, discovering the environment does not mean that the baby begins to "perceive" the existence of the environment and external things, but that through the repeated experiencing of the qualities of permanence, consistency, texture, etc., a growing "knowledge" gradually starts to accumulate in him, which is not mental and which is based on familiarity, a knowledge which is previous to the perceptive awareness of the external world.

Under favourable conditions, motility merges with instinctual tension, and the baby expends as much as possible of his primitive motor drive, or muscle eroticism, in instinctual experiences. Even so, there is always a surplus which has its specificity and which must be experienced as such. In this way, motility must find opposition, that is, "it needs something to push against, unless it is to remain unexperienced and a threat to well-being" (1958b, p. 212). This opposition, which exercises the baby's muscular strength, is necessary in order to give reality to the drive. Aggressive (i.e., spontaneous) drives, states the author, does not generate any satisfactory experience unless they encounter opposition (cf. ibid). Furthermore, what gradually changes the baby's vitality into a capacity for aggression is the contact with the object that resists and offers opposition; according to Winnicott, the so-called "aggressive potential" of a baby depends on the amount of opposition that he has encountered until that point.[22] It becomes clear here that in the first encounters, the baby not only needs a libidinal object, but also an external and consistent object: "*It is this impulsiveness, and the aggression that develops out of it, that makes the infant need an external object*, and not merely a satisfying object" (1958b, p. 217). The problem here is to provide the adequate amount of opposition, since excessive opposition inhibits the drive and prevents motility from merging with the instinctual experience.[23]

If, during the excited states, the mother allows the baby's aliveness to be expressed through both the instinctual voracity and the free movement accompanying excitation, motility gradually merges with the instinctual tension; this favours the imaginative elaboration of bodily functions and, as a consequence, the task of the indwelling of the psyche in the body is facilitated. Furthermore, when the mother allows the baby to explore and enjoy intimate contact with her body while he is feeding, she facilitates the acquisition of a feeling of ease with his own excited body and instinctual urgencies in the presence of the other. Winnicott says:

> In psychoanalysis, where there is time for a gathering together of all the early roots of the full-blown sexual experience of adults, the analyst gets very good evidence that in a satisfatory

> breast feed the actual fact of taking from part of the mother's body provides a "blue-print" for all types of experience in which instincts are involved. (1957c, pp. 53–54)

The sense of real, said Winnicott in 1950, originates in particular from the motor roots (and the corresponding sensorial ones), and when, in instinctual experiences, there is a weak infusion of the motor element, these experiences do not strengthen the sense of reality or the sense of existing. As a consequence, on many occasions, instinctual experiences are avoided precisely because they lead the person to a sensation of not existing.

As we have already seen, when the movement derives from the baby, the contact with the environment is an experience of the individual. However, if it is the environment that repeatedly has the initiative, instead of a series of individual experiences, a series of reactions to invasions occurs. In this event, motility is ultimately experienced only as a reaction to invasion. If this pattern remains in effect, an illness will arise. To a greater or lesser degree, the individual will then require opposition, not to give reality to his, but as a root of movement, and he will only be able to open the path to the important source of motility when something opposes him. In an extreme case, when *the drive is only experienced as a reaction to invasion*, the me is not established, since in the absence of personal impulsiveness, the primitive experiences of integration of the self, specific to the excited states, do not occur. In this situation, "the infant does indeed live, because of being seduced into erotic experience; but separately from the erotic life, which never feels real, is a purely aggressive reactive life, dependent on the experience of opposition" (1958b, p. 217). This unfavourable situation may be at the origin of one of the forms of paranoid disposition: the individual is always in search of the persecution which will trigger movement and only feels real when reacting to it. This represents a false mode of development, and he or she will need continuous persecution in order to feel alive.

These considerations lead to the question of the roots of aggression.[24] As early as 1939, in his first article devoted to the subject, Winnicott named the "aggressive" impulsiveness which some babies manifest as soon as they are breastfed, as "theoretical greed", "primary-love-appetite", stating that it originally forms part of the appetite and expresses itself in the act of eating and devouring. This impulsiveness, he says, may seem cruel, dangerous, but it is so only *by chance*. The term *greed*, the author continues, may express better than any other the idea of the original merging of love and aggression (cf. 1964c). Indeed, the instinctual tension generates a pressing need in the baby, a state of urgency which asks for immediate relief. With the participation of motility, in the nursing situation, vigorous activity of the gums may occur which could hurt the breast and cause cracks in the nipple. We cannot affirm, however, that the baby is trying to hurt, "because there is not enough baby there yet for aggression to mean anything" (1969b, p. 31). The term "aggression" only makes sense when an action is driven by a purpose, an intention, and the baby, at this point, is not yet in possession of reasons or intentionality. There is a great deal of confusion on that point, says Winnicott, because the term "aggression" is frequently used when what is meant is spontaneity. Aggression, in the beginning, is motility and part of the appetite, its manifestation resulting from the baby's aliveness. It is equally from his "aliveness" and from his absolute immaturity, particularly regarding time and the inability to wait, that his voracity derives. What would be called aggression is seen more as "evidence of life" (1965h, p. 127). The drive is part of the search for instinctual relief. The baby's goal "is gratification, peace of mind and body" (1964c, p. 88).

In the article "Aggression in relation to emotional development" (1958b), Winnicott admits the existence of a destruction that is inherent to the primitive love drive. This destructiveness must not be seen as a manifestation of aggression, since it is only incidental, forming part of the search for instinctual satisfaction. It must be studied completely separately from the aggressive reaction that results from the frustration caused by the non-satisfaction of instinctual needs or in face of the reality principle.[25]

At this point of the theory, Winnicott introduces a concept of maturation which is fundamental for understanding the aggressiveness and destructiveness contained in human nature: during the initial stages, the baby, unaware of the existence of the self and the environment, has no concern or compassion regarding the consequences of his excited love. The baby is a primitive *ruthless* self. It is thus convenient to say, Winnicott states, "that the primitive love impulse (id) has a destructive quality, though it is not the infant's aim to destroy since the impulse is experienced in the pre-ruth era" (1958b, p. 211).

This is one of the points for which it is possible to observe clearly the difference between Winnicott's conception of personal maturation and the theory of the development of sexual functions. For Winnicott, it is the individual who develops towards integration, and not the libido in terms of phases related to erogenous zones. So-called "aggressive" manifestations—eating, devouring, biting—are not successive results of sexual development, the progression of which is determined intra-psychically in accordance with the biological model. It is not a matter of saying that the oral zone is initially erotic and then sadistic or destructive. It is the baby, who, as he matures, becomes more potent and integrated into the body, increasingly needing to experience his strength and to deal with his growing capacity to recognise events and objects. Since the *baby is ruthless* during the initial stages, he continues to exercise his impulsivity at moments of excitation, without concern and with increasing strength and boldness.

There will be a long way to go before the ruthless baby gradually becomes concerned and compassionate, that is, he starts to feel responsible for the consequences of instinctual impulsiveness on the mother and on himself. All of this is nevertheless a work of growing integration, a gradual achievement which can only be effectively elaborated at the stage of concern, the moment when primitive "aggression"—which, in fact, is not yet aggression but incidental destructiveness belonging to the primitive love drive—will be integrated as part of the me and will then have a personal meaning. This nevertheless necessarily requires another achievement, described later in the text, even if in incipient form: the integration into a unitary self at the stage of the I AM, so that the baby becomes capable of relating as a whole person to a whole mother, and then, *because of being an I*, is able to feel concerned and worried about the effects of his own thoughts and actions on her.

The ruthless exercise of the instinctual drive, besides being the most primitive of the experiences of integration, is highly gratifying for the baby. The way it is received by the mother interferes crucially with the possibility and with the way in which aggression in increasing development will or will not be integrated to the total personality. With regard to the initial stages, what must not be forgotten is the situation of dependence. The baby depends entirely on how the mother receives the manifestations resulting from the fact that he is alive, has needs and completely occupies her; he depends on the way in which the mother responds to the spontaneous gesture. A mother who takes very good care of a baby in the quiet states may be startled and may react to him in the excited ones. She may become frightened or adopt a moralistic attitude or, perhaps, be of the type who resents the baby's attack as if it were one more of the attacks which life has inflicted on her. The mother's reaction may sometimes contain a kind of disapproval of what is alive or what appears to be aggressive precisely because it is alive. It may also be the case that she is emotionally ill. A mother's depression, for example, may traumatise the baby in a specialised way: full of vitality, the baby moves towards the breast and is dampened by the contact with a lifeless object. There is also the case of the mother who retreats, terrified of the pain, or of the supposed "aggression" of the baby; if vigorous and hungry, he will cling even more to the breast in order to hold it and keep it. In these cases, the baby is left with few alternatives, all of which are unfavourable: (1) to hide his impulses since the environment does not tolerate or accept "aggression" (spontaneity, vivacity); (2) to inhibit instinctual impulsiveness and develop a premature and defensive self-control; (3) to split the drives, which become then dissociated; and (4) to develop an anti-social tendency.

If instead of voracity, there is greediness, then this is no longer a manifestation of vitality. Greediness is a kind of imperative eagerness which is accompanied by suffering and which appears to be insatiable. In this case, we must assume that the child is suffering from some degree of deprivation. This type of deprivation results from the fact that some personal primordial need is not being acknowledged or met; in any of its variations, greediness means a compulsive search for a special care, one that we could call a "therapy", to be provided by the mother who caused the deprivation. If the mother can acknowledge the signal made by the child without becoming frightened and if she is willing to meet the need that is being communicated in this way, then in most cases, the compulsion will disappear (cf. 1958c). This greediness, which may manifest itself in various ways, including inhibition of appetite, dirtiness (abundant defaecation and urinating), or excessive destructiveness, is already a manifestation of the anti-social tendency and a precursor to theft. It can certainly be met and "cured" by the special, therapeutic adaptation of the mother, above all since, by being able to tolerate and understand the communication, she allows the baby's "hate" to be expressed at a moment when the deprivation complex is still close to the origin.

The deprivation that is revealed in greediness, even when related to nursing, does not concern instinctual needs, but the needs of the ego.[26] If the mother is "absent" while breastfeeding, or if nursing is carried out in an impersonal way, which is deficient in communication, intimacy, and mutuality, instinctual experiences become boring and, in this case, it may be "quite a relief to cry with anger and frustration, which at any rate can feel real and must involve the total personality" (1969b, p. 29).

In addition to instinctual motility and impulsiveness, Winnicott identifies a third root of aggression that was not perceived by traditional theory, since it did not consider the situation of dependence of the baby: it consists of the fact that the aggressive potential of certain children derives from the traumatic reactions provoked in them by environmental invasions. Traumas deriving from environmental failures, which frequently result from the mother's emotional state or psychiatric abnormalities,[27] inhibit the baby's spontaneity, prevent him from simply being, relaxing, living instinctual experiences; they leave a sort of alarm which is incorporated into him. Embedded in this is an anger, arising from the loss of being which results from those traumatic experiences. This feeling of anger, which is neither instinctual nor a development of motility towards aggression, cannot, however, be configured and felt as such at the original moment, on account of the baby's immaturity, which includes his total unawareness of the existence of an environment against which he must revolt.[28] When, at a later stage, the individual seeks therapeutic help and finds reliability (especially, in this case, when he finds a psychoanalyst capable of surviving what emerges), anger may start to manifest itself, in particular when the analyst fails and when, by acknowledging his own failure, this analyst provides the opportunity for the anger to be updated in the clinical context.[29]

This important root of aggression only became conceptually precise in the final phase of Winnicott's thought. It is presented very clearly in a written passage of 1969, added to the second version of the article "Transitional objects and transitional phenomena", of 1971. In this addendum, Winnicott states that there is a moment at the beginning of life when the baby is elaborating the capacity to keep people alive in his psychic reality, in the subjective world, and needs the concrete presence of the mother so that the memory and reality of presence as such do not fade away:

> Before the limit is reached, the mother is still alive; after this limit has been overstepped she is dead. In between is a precious moment of anger, but this is quickly lost, or perhaps never experienced, always potential and carrying fear of violence. (1953c, p. 29)

Anger is "lost or is never experienced" not because of a superego censorship, but as a consequence of the fact that the baby is not yet a me, does not know of the existence of the environment and that, for him, feeling has not yet sense or configuration. The identification of this important root of aggression led the author, who already disagreed with Freud on this theoretical point, to declare the insufficiency of the Freudian theory regarding the roots of aggression. Indeed, in Freud's view, unlike Winnicott's, the excited primitive love is not destructive in itself, and aggression is awakened in the individual by the anger provoked by frustration concerning the reality principle. Because it disregards dependence, says Winnicott, the Freudian theory of the roots of aggression,

> [...] becomes false because it avoids two vitally important sources of aggression: that which is inherent in the primitive love impulse (at the pre-ruth stage, apart from reaction to frustration) and that which belongs to the interruption of the continuity of being by impingement that enforces reaction. (1988, p. 133)

The quiet states

Since the quiet states of the baby have not been considered in traditional theory, Winnicott opens up an unusual field of reflection for the study of human nature and psychic disorders with the theoretical formulation of this theme. Where and how is the baby when he is not breastfeeding or reaching out for something, Winnicott asks. This is an invaluable area for investigation; first, because it focuses on the human need, which is never extinguished in the healthy individual, to abandon the world momentarily, withdrawing into solitude, remaining in quietness within the subjective world or protected from pragmatic objectivities within the potential space of art and culture. Second, because it shows that particularly in the initial stages, the *reality* of the excited *experience* in the encounter with the object depends on the fact that the drive that originated the search emerged from a state of rest, typical of non-integration. Third, because the difference between excited and quiet states provides the basis for the important distinction between two ambits which are generally confused: the *world* which the baby inhabits, and the *objects* that may be found (created) within this world.

During the quiet states of the theoretical first feed, the baby's need is to remain in the non-integrated state, in the relaxation characteristic of someone who feels well sustained. The baby surrenders himself to "contemplation", imaginatively elaborating the physiological states of digestion, or wrapped in the noises, smells, and movements of the environment. If the mother is holding him, he looks at her at length, she speaks to him or sings a song, he withdraws to a place where she has no access or he goes to sleep. The mother remains there, *sustaining the situation in time*, waiting for the baby to resume any search: when he wakes up and makes a gesture of communication, she is there, presenting him with a fragment of the world or handling which confirms to him that the world continues to be present and alive. It is the monotonous and regular repetition of this experience that gradually creates the capacity for trust in the baby. When this belief is established, which could be formulated as follows: "As soon as I need her, she will be there", the baby shifts very easily from the excited experience to the quiet one and vice-versa. The accumulation of such experiences becomes a pattern and forms the basis for the baby's expectations and for his capacity to "believe in …":

> The mother's capacity to meet the changing and developing needs of this one baby enables this one baby to have a line of life, relatively unbroken; and enables this baby to experience both unintegrated or relaxed states in confidence in the holding that is actual, along with oft-repeated phases of the integration that is part of the baby's inherited growth tendency. The baby goes easily to and fro from integration to the ease of relaxed unintegration and the accumulation of these experiences becomes a pattern, and forms a basis for what the baby expects. The baby comes to believe in a reliability in the inward processes leading to integration into a unit. (1968d, p. 97)

The isolation into which the baby withdraws to rest is not defensive; it is the natural place of quietness to which he surrenders, since he feels safe, relaxed, non-integrated, without taking any notice of the environment. This is the basis for the capacity of the child and of the healthy adult to withdraw from the world momentarily in order to rest, as well as the basis for the ability to be alone in someone else's presence, which will be acquired a little later. Furthermore, *it is only starting from the state of rest that any drive may be felt as real and may become a genuinely personal experience.* If this does not happen, the other alternative, which is not healthy, is the false life founded on reactions to external stimuli. There are babies who were never allowed, even in the initial stages of infancy, simply to lie down, to be left to their own ramblings or even to be taciturn. Their mothers make them jump up and down or smile permanently, or do any other thing that provides reassurance that they are still alive. These babies, says Winnicott, "lose a great deal and may altogether miss the feeling that they themselves want to live" (1949b, p. 28). If the child is given the opportunity of gradually discovering his own personal life, he becomes able "to flounder, to be in a state in which there is no orientation, to be able to exist for a time without being either a reactor to an external impingement or an active person with a direction of interest or movement" (1958g, p. 34).

When, instead of reliability, there is a pattern of invasions to which the baby must react, the sense of being is lost and can only be recovered by a return to isolation. Once this state of things is established, isolation no longer benefits the individual, since it increasingly becomes a defensive organisation and no longer a possibility of rest which arises from reliability. If invasions are excessive, there will not even be a place of rest for individual experience: in this event, the conditions permitting the individual to become an integrated unit in due course are lacking:

> The "individual" then develops as an extension of the shell rather than of the core, and as an extension of the impinging environment. What there is left of a core is hidden away and is difficult to find even in the most far-reaching analysis. The individual then *exists by not being found.* (1958b, p. 212)

This point is essential for the understanding of certain psychotic pathologies, since, according to the author, studying the material of the unexcited states brings us nearer to a study of psychosis (cf. 1965i, p. 27). A possible interpretation of this statement is that the basic difficulty in psychoses is contact with reality, and this is associated with failure in the task of initiating object relations, a task characteristic of the excited states. In order for the drive and the encounter with the object to be felt as real, however, they must arise from a state of rest. In other words, *the return to the relaxation of non-integration is the necessary condition for whatever happens in the excited states to be felt as real and may promote integration into a self that is also felt as real.* If what is established is an impossibility of rest, the gesture will be alienated already at the foundation.[30]

This is where the third point mentioned above comes in. As we have seen, the baby needs the mother to remain present and consistently herself, at the same time as she keeps the characteristics of the environment regular, by *holding in time* the passage from one state to the other. It is the mother, says Winnicott, who being capable of concerning herself with her task, "is able *to provide the setting* for the start of excited relationships" (1988, p. 100; my italics). Maternal concern opens up a context, a *medium* in which something may happen.[31] Constituted by the totality of the mother's care, this place is the world that the baby can inhabit, the place to which he withdraws to rest, the background for excited experiences. In it, a type of relationship occurs between the baby and the mother which differs from the one established with the object during the moments of excitation. The distinction between world and objects thus corresponds to a difference between two types of maternal care. In order to describe this "duality", Winnicott draws a difference between the "mother-object", which is the target of the excited drives, and the "mother-environment", which provides total environmental care, keeping the baby's world stable and reliable.[32]

This distinction is important in many senses. First, in order to examine the implications of dependence, bearing in mind the many attributions of the mother in her condition as facilitator of maturational processes. Second, in order to configure one of the baby's primary dissociations, which will only be "healed", that is, integrated into the personality, as he develops. The baby does not initially know that he is the same individual who is now quiet, with his world reassured by the mother and then, excited, grasping the breast excitedly; nor is he aware that the mother who lets herself be sucked voraciously, is the same person who takes care of him during his quiet states. The integration of the quiet and the excited states concerning the same baby, and of the "two" mothers into a single person will be an achievement of maturation that will take place in the stage of concern.

All of these conceptual elements relating to the gradual integration into a unity are decisive contributions of Winnicott's theory. If, as is the case with traditional theory, the constitution of the me and the capacity for perception of external objects are taken for granted, and if the mother has been regarded as an external object, or even an erotic object from the start then, there is no room for considering the constitution of reality, when it is precisely the constitution of the sense of reality of the world and of the very individual that may fail in the case of psychotics.

For the infant whose mother always left open the path of return to the quiet states of non-integration and kept his moments of quietness undisturbed, the capacity to absent himself and rest becomes a source of personal wealth, a place of protection where he can always return throughout his life, whenever he feels the need to rest from the world and momentarily release himself from the task of existing. This state of absence, disconnection or "introspective" isolation is not a sign of illness; on the contrary,

> a sign of health, that the child can use relationships in which there is maximal trust, and in such a relationship at times disintegrate, depersonalise and even for a moment abandon the almost fundamental urge to exist and to feel existent. (1971d, p. 261)

If, instead of this pattern, the quiet states do not have their own positive value, being no more than the negative of the excited states, it may be that a great anxiety develops in the individual with regard to tranquility and, over time, a permanent avoidance of quietness or even of the intervals in which there is absence of tension or excitation. The absence of tension appears to him or her to be stagnation, which resembles death.

As integration becomes more consistent, regression to non-integration as a natural primitive condition is no longer possible. If the maturational process continues and a further step is taken towards independence, *there is the definitive loss of the capacity for non-integration* (cf. 1988, p. 139). This experience may perhaps be repeated but very rarely and under very special conditions: a healthy individual may be capable of losing all references for a moment, entering a state of detachment from the world, comparable only to that sought by mystics. This state of non-integration may also occur under the specialised conditions provided by psychotherapy, and even physiotherapy.[33] For an individual who has achieved a certain stable degree of integration, however, the necessary rest shall be carried out by other, more complex means: he will know how to absent himself from the shared world, momentarily withdrawing into the subjective world, surrendering himself to an imaginative activity, to playful or artistic concentration and even to creative work.

From a certain degree of integration onwards, the opposite of this integration is no longer unintegration, but a state of "maddening" disintegration. When the person of the baby begins to emerge, "failure of care leads to disintegration instead of to a return to unintegration" (1958d, p. 98). Since transitions are gradual, however, there is an intermediate state in which a well cared for baby, in full development, may still relax in unintegration and tolerate, *but merely tolerate*, says Winnicott, feeling "mad" in the non-integrated state (cf. 1988, p. 118). If, however, the environment repeatedly fails to provide safety to the baby beyond his tolerance limit, the threat of disintegration becomes permanent, and the individual will carry with himself the feeling of an unnameable danger, which must be avoided at any cost. As a result of a withheld feeling of environmental insecurity, he may also establish an exaggerated form of self-care, a sort of automatic self-preservation, which is a defence against the disintegration which environmental failure, now turned into potential failure, threatens to provoke.[34]

The basic tasks

Integration in time and space

In the theory of maturational processes, the term "integration" is used both to designate the innate tendency towards development, which leads to the unitary status, and the various partial integrations which gradually take place along the journey, starting from the state of unintegration. The task of *integration in time and space* is the most basic and fundamental of the maturational tasks. In fact, there is no possible sense of reality, of body, of world or of self outside space or time; there is no individual if there is no memory of oneself, which maintains the identity amid the transformations; there is no encounter of objects if there is no *world* where objects may be found and if there is no *self* who can find them. The whole integrative process is based on the temporalisation and spatialisation of the baby, beginning at the start of life. For this reason, "the main trend in the maturational process can be gathered into the various meanings of the word *integration*. Integration in time becomes added to (what might be called) integration in space" (1965n, p. 59).

Temporalising and spatialising the baby does not mean inserting him into the time and space of the external world, since he is not mature enough for the sense of externality. The newborn lives in a sort of *continuum*, in a mere extended duration. Although a few small temporal markings have already been experienced in intrauterine life, such as the mother's breathing or the alternation of states of movement and quietness, his temporality is limited to his continuity of being. Since the baby initially inhabits a subjective world, initiating him into the sense of time and space means making sure that the time and space that rule this world are also subjective.

The first sense of time in the subjective world is that of the continuity of presence, established through the repeated experience of the mother's presence and permanence, of the continuity of the care which the world constantly presents to him. The baby does not know of the permanent existence of the mother, but feels the effects of her presence and slowly, while creating a memory of this presence, comes to count on it. In order to preserve the continuity of being and to keep alive the subjective world, the baby must be permanently reassured by this continuing presence, since

> [...] the innate creative impulse withers unless it is met by external reality ('realized'). Each infant must re-create the world, but this is only possible if, bit by bit, the world arrives at the moments of the infant's creative activity. The infant reaches out and the breast is there, and the breast is created. (1958j, p. 12)

The baby is consolidating the state of being which has emerged from non-being. The negativity of the origin is still very near, ready to emerge from each hole of mother's absence, which lasts long enough to erase the incipient memory of the presence, which is still unconscious. The mother who is capable of identifying with the baby is only absent for the time interval during which the baby can maintain the memory of her presence. The feeling that the mother exists lasts for "x" minutes. If the mother is away longer than "x" minutes, the image of her presence fades away. The baby is distressed, but if the mother returns within "x + y" minutes, the affliction is corrected. We can say that within "x + y" minutes, the continuity of being of the baby did not alter but, if the mother's absence lasts for "x + y + z" minutes, he is traumatised and the return of the mother no longer corrects his altered state. If the memory of the presence is erased, the sensation is that of annihilation, of madness. "Madness here simply means a *break-up* of whatever may exist at the time of *a personal continuity of existence*" (1967b, p. 131). After recovering from the trauma, the baby must *start everything again*, being permanently deprived of the root that could provide continuity with the personal beginning. The personal beginning, that is, the basis of existence, "implies the existence of a memory system and an organisation of memories" (idem). The erasing of the memory of the presence is one of the specific traumas that appear in the aetiology of psychotic pathologies. It is an unthinkable agony.[35] What prevents this agony from happening, in this specific case, the agony of losing all sense of real, is the fact that the mother weaves her presence permanently, continuously presenting herself and the world to the baby in small doses at the moment of the spontaneous gesture.

From the start of the maturational process, with the baby still in uterus, personal body memories start to come together to form a new human being. This means that having experiences and having memories of them is what marks the beginning of the human being. At the very outset, body memories are sparse but gather gradually and form a stock of experiences. From then on, expectations become increasingly more configured. If the baby feels that the continuity of being is guaranteed, that is, if he does not find himself forced to develop a state of alertness against potential environment invasions, he is in the condition, without being startled, of living the various experiences which are repeated according to a certain pattern. With time, he begins to have some "knowledge" of himself, of the environment and of what will happen, which is not mental but is based on increasing familiarity with the body sensations that are imaginatively elaborated and with the state of things surrounding him. This is the foundation of the baby's temporalisation, which is initially subjective: on the basis of present experiences, the baby begins to constitute a "past", a "place" to store experiences, from where he can anticipate the future, due to the fact that some things and some events have become predictable. A history begins. This is the basis for establishing the capacity for experience in an increasingly wider sense, since a real experience "is not so much a matter of a single happening as a build-up of memories of events" (1988, p. 100). Throughout this originary process of temporalisation, the psyche is working towards connecting together the past which has already been experienced, the present and the expectation of the future, providing the feeling of the me and justifying the perception that an individual exists inside that body (ibid., p. 46).

Together with the constitution of the sense of presence, a special type of *temporal marking* begins to occur, which, in health, comes necessarily prior to the perception of chronologies. This marking is made in natural and specifically human ways, of the intimacy with the mother's body (the rhythm of her breathing, her heartbeats); it is also ruled by the rhythms of the baby's body, to which the environment adapts: hunger, breastfeeding, excretion, sleep, waking up, sounds, light, and smells. The dating of time, therefore, is carried out by the maternal care which initially adjusts to the rhythm of physiological functioning, which has its own timing, and by the imaginative elaboration of this functioning and of bodily sensations. By so doing, the mother provides that the baby is initiated into the periodicity of time, having as matrix his own rhythm, the rhythm of the body. With the repetition of the experience, a sense of "future" begins to be constituted: the baby becomes *capable of anticipating what will come, based on his own needs*, made real through the mother's responses and attention. If the mother imposes a rhythm on the baby that is external to him, either a chronological one or one that follows her own needs instead of his, subjective temporality and psycho-somatic cohesion are impaired, if not prevented. In order to guarantee that external time does not interfere with the natural processes of subjective temporalisation, the baby's natural rhythm must prevail. Feeding must take place "exactly when the baby wants it, and ceases as he ceases to want it. This is the basis", says Winnicott (1945c, p. 33). The mother initially obeys the baby's rhythm and only gradually adjusts this rhythm to regular intervals which seem to be convenient and adequate to his needs, while also contemplating her needs as a woman and mother. Only then, can a baby, over time, compromise with the mother and *reach an agreement* regarding the regularity of breastfeeding. The baby may adjust to this interval and be hungry regularly every three hours, feeling this as his own need. This is the kind of "agreement" to which Winnicott refers when he states that it is only during the initial stages, when the baby does not yet know of the dependence, and when a creative relation to the object is permitted to him, that he can gradually learn to comply "without losing face" (1968d, p. 103). In other words, because of his primary creativity, the baby has a dignity even before he is a unitary me.

An interval of waiting that is too long, however, leads to distress; often "if the coming of the feed is delayed more than *X* minutes, then when it comes it is meaningless for the baby" (1984f, p. 58). The easiest way for the mother to regain the baby's trust is to breastfeed him as and when he demands for a while and then, only gradually, to resume the attempt to establish regularity. On many occasions, however, the mother who was taught to train her baby to acquire regular habits, starting with regular feeding at each three hours, "feels actually wicked if told to feed her baby just like a gipsy" (1945c, p. 33). The main difficulty with mothers allowing themselves to follow the rhythm of the babies stems from the fact that the responsibility of bringing up a child hangs over them and they readily accept the rules of scheduled feeding, the medical regulations and prescriptions that make life less risky, even if a little monotonous. A part of this difficulty must also be attributed to paediatric orientation. When the relation between mother and baby is developing naturally, says Winnicott, techniques, quantities and timetables may be left to nature's criterion.

There is no doubt that many difficulties in maternal adaptation are precisely related to time. One of them arises when mother and baby fail to establish or lose contact due to lack of synchronisation, since by temperament some babies are slower than their mothers, while others are more rapid. It may be particularly tedious for a quick mother to adapt to a slow baby, but it is not easy either if the opposite is the case. In any case, the mother must have the time and spend it on the task of caring for the infant. When she is good-enough, she knows that in order to lift him from the cradle and move him somewhere, he must be prepared for the movement: the baby must *receive a warning* and be lifted at the right time, with the mother holding all of the various parts of the body. In addition, the mother's act starts, continues, and ends, for the baby is being carried, from one place to another, for example, from the cot to the mother's shoulder (cf. 1988, p. 117). That is to say, the mother assists the baby in having *total experiences*. She must thus have *enough time to wait*, at the baby's pace, for him to go from the beginning to the end of the experience, with this experience having a beginning, a middle, and an end.[36] When we are in a hurry or worried, we cannot ensure total events and the baby is impoverished.

> Total happenings enable babies to catch hold of time. They do not start off knowing that when something is on it will finish. The middle of things can be enjoyed only if there is a strong sense of start and finish. (1949c, pp. 77–78)

The central aspect of adaptive care is related to time. Its basic characteristic is reliability and this means *predictability*. When we say that a child is well cared for, that means that his parents protect him from unexpected events, from being taken by surprise by something that he does not or cannot expect. Regular experiences, repeated thousands of times, create *a sense of predictability* in the infant. As the unitary self builds up, with environmental care being incorporated as a quality intrinsic to it, integration becomes an increasingly consistent state and the individual starts to be able to take care of him. In this way, dependence is gradually reduced. The development of the autonomy of the child in relation to the environment has to do with his growing capacity to make predictions (cf. 1987d, p. 95).

Although the purpose of this study is not to arrive at the *clinical implications* of Winnicott's theory of maturational processes and of psychoses, I believe it appropriate to mention that these very basic issues concerning the constitution of time serve as a guide for the analyst in her therapeutic task. The care in ensuring that one is guided by the needs of the baby or of the patient and in avoiding abrupt events calls into question the issue, for example, of the ending of each analytical session, which is relevant in any type of case, but especially with patients for whom the central aspect of personality is psychotic. Whatever problems we are dealing with, we cannot end the session abruptly by relying on the fact that the patient has an adult side and that the time schedule has been agreed. Often, especially during a phase of regression to dependence, the person is not in contact with objective time, nor is he sufficiently emotionally mature to benefit from a real manifestation of hate from the analyst, one of which consists of ending the session at the scheduled time,[37] which would be important in other types of disorders, It is necessary to help the patient, signalling with some kind of movement or gesture that the session is about to end. Sometimes, as in the case of babies, a few more minutes are enough for the patient to reach his own end and to prepare to leave. This care applies not only on this specific occasion, but also for reassuring the patient that we will ensure that nothing will happen abruptly. It is nevertheless possible that he will effectively need more time, longer sessions; for a certain period of time, we will have to extend the duration of the session on a regular basis, knowing in advance that the conclusion of the session, even if extended, will require equal care. It is only in this way, that the patient, like the baby, over time, will be able to comply "without losing face".

More time, however, is not always what a patient needs; it is not even certain that he will benefit from the fact that the ending of the session depends on his subjective time. Some patients are in therapy precisely in order to succeed in establishing a subjective time; at the originary moment, when this should have been established, there was only chaos in the environment, and these individuals had to cling rigidly to an objective time, serving as a reference for them and without which they immediately feel lost, in order not to succumb to complete disorganisation of personality. There are people who cannot tolerate any situation of an indefinite duration. I had a patient who had been seriously affected with regard to these basic achievements relating to temporality and spatiality. In addition to being born in an unstable and chaotic environment, his birth had been delayed and he had always felt imprisoned in any situation without a rigorously scheduled end. Winnicott says that among the typical characteristics of genuine birth memories is the feeling of being in the clutches of some external thing, causing the newborn to feel completely vulnerable and helpless. Inherent to this feeling of helplessness "is the intolerable nature of experiencing something without any knowledge whatever of when it will end" (1958f, p. 184). In addition to this, the patient had had no experience of personal communication and even though this was what he needed most, any proximity was felt as a potential invasion. At the start of the analysis, the session could sometimes be too long, and he stuck rigidly to the scheduled time. For this patient, the idea of a session without a predictable end or with an end that depended on a subjective time, which simply did not exist, was unbearable. There was yet another aspect: always attentive to the only compass that he had, his watch, he knew very well when the formal time of the session ended, but would wait for me to take the initiative. I noticed that both for him and for some other patients, the ability of the analyst to finish the session within the agreed time provides reassurance and the question here is not one of hate, since for this type of person, the fact that the analyst assumes the task of monitoring time means that the same analyst has adopted the position of the person providing care and who, by being undertaking to maintain contact with external reality, releases the patient to go on constituting his subjective world.

One of the characteristics of defensive organisations of a psychotic type is the impossibility that the individual presents of "having time", of being able "to rely on the duration of time", of allowing some time for the development of an event or an experience. In the face of an unexpected event, despair or lack of resources arises *immediately*. This gives the impression that this individual is always on the edge of an abyss. Subjective time has not been established and, consequently, the subsequent development of internal time which would enable a parenthesis for reflection and prevent him from being dragged by external requests, has not occurred either. This lack of time manifests itself in different ways. An adult patient reports how he eats: he does not have a meal, instead, he swallows the food. The feeling is one of being exposed to an urgency which he must rapidly bring to an end, because all of the food will be finished before he satisfies his hunger. During analysis, it was revealed that for his mother, breastfeeding or even at a later stage, feeding her children was a difficult task, from which she had to free herself as soon as possible. While she was breastfeeding, she was not there and had already moved on to her next task, seeking to rid herself of it as soon as possible.

Another example is that of a girl whose subjective world was rich and full of precious details, with a very peculiar personal time, entirely incompatible with external time, which was felt as unbearable and oppressive. She had had a fairly good start, when she had been able to commit herself to imaginative life. At a certain point, her mother became a widow and, overloaded with daily chores, which included financial management of the household and of life in general, could no longer adapt to the rhythm of her little daughter and frequently hurried her. The patient became an excellent professional in her area, which required creativity and imagination, but could not deliver her work without feeling oppressed by her deadlines and could not arrive at her appointments on time either. "Obedience" to shared time was an unbearable submission that offended her.

At the same time as the acquisition of the sense of time, the *spatialisation* of the baby is taking place, with both achievements intimately intertwined. This is a question of allowing the baby to gradually acquire the feeling, which is far from being innate or acquired automatically, of having *a place where he can dwell* and "feel at home", to which he can return to rest and which is "a basic place to operate from" (1986h, p. 39). The sense of dwelling is built on many levels but the baby must primarily dwell in his own body. It is no coincidence that the second basic task is termed "residence" or "indwelling of the psyche in the body".[38] Since his own body is the first dwelling, we should add that this body is not loose in space, but is being held and brought together within the mother's arms, or tucked up in the cradle; the mother's lap and the details of the environment, which initially are indistinguishable from the baby himself, are constituent parts of this dwelling and of the inaugural experience of dwelling. If the baby is left for a long time without being held, he loses contact with his own body, which remains unrealised and it is this that characterises the states of depersonalisation, which are at the root of psycho-somatic disorders.

Time and space are articulated in such a way that some temporal factors must be guarded for the baby's dwelling to be consistent and reliable; one of these is the regularity and predictability of the environmental conditions. It is not advisable, for example, to move the cradle constantly from place to place, since in a particular position, the baby becomes used to finding the ray of light that comes through the window and traces a luminous line on the bedroom wall. The baby's place must also be simple and protected from confusion, turmoil, and excesses: in the small "enclosure" opened and maintained by the mother, fragments of the world are presented to the infant in small doses and in a comprehensible way. In addition, when the mother lingers attentively and without haste on the details presented by the baby, she enables him to create and inhabit a niche made of *time and concentration*, within which something that belongs to the here and now may be experienced. This has important implications for clinical practice, especially with patients who are regressed to dependence. Winnicott says, for example, that "one of the main principles of the psycho-analytic technique is that a setting is provided in which the patient can deal with one thing at a time" for *"two or more factors spell confusion"* (1958f, p. 192).

The small circle protected by the patient attention of the mother gradually establishes the basis for the individual's capacity at a later stage to inhabit the incommensurable world of external reality, without losing the sense of being at home. When the safety of the small world is established, the maturing baby is "too glad to find mother behind the breast or bottle, and to find the room behind mother, and the world outside the room" (1945a, p. 22). The totality of maternal care enables the infant to live in a *subjective world*, populated by imaginative life with regard to body functions and the environmental atmosphere, the main characteristic of which is that of being protected from the invasion by any sample of external reality. This is the first world the infant inhabits and throughout his life will be his main refuge for resting. The chaotic mother repeatedly alters not only the emotional climate but also the concrete environmental conditions of the baby, so that he cannot build the "habit", familiarity and feeling of safety, which are characteristic of feeling at home. Instead of concentration, there will be dispersion and confusion. Even worse, there will always be the threat hanging over the baby that something incomprehensible may suddenly arise and drag everything with it. It should be noted that the term "invasion", which is used to designate the general character of the environmental failure, has a *spatial sense*. The invasion of the "sacred" territory suddenly pulls aside the curtain of the cloister and makes him glimpse the outward immensity prematurely. One characteristic of the state of panic is the fear of enormous open spaces without contours, as well as the feeling of losing all references. At several points in her diary, Renée, the schizophrenic girl treated by M. A. Sechehaye, mentions some elements of her feelings of unreality: she saw herself in an "illimitable vastness", or "the street became infinite" or "my eye encountered a field of wheat whose limits I could not see".[39] By contrast, Forrest Gump took his "house" with him wherever he went.[40]

At a later stage, after having lived for long enough in the subjective world, the baby will inhabit the potential space, the area of which will initially be filled with transitional phenomena and then, gradually and successively, with play and cultural and artistic activities, that is, with everything that is free from the judgment ruled by objectivity. When there is health, says Winnicott, this is the place where we live. One of the characteristics of play and of activities relevant to the potential space is the state of alienation, which can only occur if the feeling of safety has been incorporated, that there is someone taking care of the permanence of things out there, which is the basis for concentration in the older child and in the adult. If these first experiences of dwelling are guaranteed by the good-enough care, the individual will arrive at the external world with the foundation which, despite what is objectively immense, unfathomable and inhospitable, will allow him to create a niche where he can feel at home.

In the same way that integration in time and space is the most basic of tasks, *holding*, the specific maternal care which corresponds to it, is equally the prototype of all good-enough maternal care. This holding, which is simple and refers to the handling of the baby and all of the physical care related to his well-being, gradually extends as the baby grows up and his world becomes more complex. Encompassing care in general, including the atmosphere of calmness and regularity of the environment which the mother is able to sustain, "holding" extends to "holding a situation", which is a serene availability that remains, that slowly extends over time and *does not demand that anything happen*; she merely awaits the baby's movements and follows him in his innumerable comings and goings. When the baby is awake, the mother is there, offering the samples of the world according to the need which he expresses and she understands: breastfeeding, handling, a bath, a song or simply being together and looking at each other. The person who takes care of the regularity and vivacity of the place and holds the situation is the good-enough mother and, like her, the analyst or the therapist.[41]

As a consequence of this care, very basic pre-representational experiences are favoured, constituting the beginning of the baby's familiarity with certain aspects of the ambience, and which, in health, *must precede the perception of the same phenomena*. Because the mother maintains the regularity, simplicity, and monotony of the environment and the care, events are repeated and the baby becomes capable of some predictions: *if* there is this particular smell or noise, *then* that particular thing is going to happen. The baby is being temporalised, he is acquiring a sense of future in a subjective sense; this increases his ability to wait.

Integration into a self is never complete and neither relates to a state which is unequivocal or closed in itself; on the contrary, it is precisely the gradual integration into the globality of space-time what allows the experience of incompleteness. When the baby *is integrated in time* and begins to be dated, to have a present, a past, and a future, he starts to exist in a finite way, that of the essential human incompleteness: at the same time that *he is something*, part of this *being something* necessarily and simultaneously is also an already-not (past) and a not-yet (future). Because they have not been temporalised in the subjective sense, psychotics suffer precisely from immediacy and at the same time, from infinitude.

Dwelling of the psyche in the body: personalisation

For the task of the dwelling of the psyche in the body, Winnicott also uses the term "personalisation". This designation is due to the fact that the word "depersonalisation" is the term already consecrated in adult psychiatry for the various clinical states in which the patient complains about not having a relation with his own body or feeling that his body, or part of it, does not belong to him, etc. (cf. 1988, p. 145).

The task of the dwelling of the psyche in the body only makes sense if we accept the idea that initially, body and psyche are not yet united and will only constitute a unity *if everything goes well in the maturational process.* At the outset, *soma* and psyche are undifferentiated. Differentiation takes place gradually, at the same time as the tendency towards integration acts to gather them into a unit. This psycho-somatic partnership is not guaranteed however, nor should it be taken for granted. It is not self-evident that the baby's psyche and *soma* will operate as a unit in every case, in such a way that the baby will live in his body, which will function in accordance with the baby's use of it. This may or may not be achieved and once it is, it may be lost, even in health. Psycho-somatic cohesion is an achievement and may not be established unless there is the active participation of a human being who holds the baby and takes care of him, so that the baby is brought together in her arms and gaze. A baby who is not brought together by the mother feels spread: "In psychology it must be said that the infant falls to pieces unless held together, and physical care is psychological care at these stages" (1988, p. 117).[42]

Much has already been clarified regarding the task of personalisation in the section about the quiet and excited states. Feeling well held and brought together in the body, especially during excited experiences, the infant surrenders confidently to the care of the mother and under these conditions, the psyche may carry out its work of imaginative elaboration of the body functions and sensations. Gradually, the body becomes *soma* and an intimate connection of increasing complexity between *soma* and psyche is established, with the potentially psycho-somatic character of existence becoming real. The psyche begins to inhabit the body, making it its dwelling.

The gradual achievement of dwelling in the body is hence intimately connected to the process of spatialisation of the baby. For the entire time that psycho-somatic cohesion is in the process of being achieved, the mother's arms and the baby's body are one and the same thing, so that one may say that *the baby's first dwelling is his very body in the mother's lap.*[43]

The maternal care that corresponds to the task of dwelling of the psyche in the body is the handling. Handling is part of the holding, but refers specifically to physical holding. Handling-holding must include all of the necessary sensory experiences: being involved from all sides in a lively embrace which has temperature and rhythm and which makes the baby feel both the mother's body and his own; being tucked in his cradle in such a way that he will still be in contact with the covers and cushions instead of loose in space; the countless tactile sensations on being handled in every way during bathing, while being caressed, cuddled, smelt, etc.; subtle and graduated differences in luminosity, texture, and temperature; the necessary opposition for the baby to exercise movement; the active and concrete response to the excited states both with regard to reaching out for something and to instinctual and motor satisfaction. All these experiences enable the baby to inhabit the body, even if momentarily, facilitating a psycho-somatic association and contributing to the sense of "real"—of the reality of the self—as opposed to the "unreal": the fact of being alive and existing gradually gains consistency, weight, gravity. Through the growing connection that is established between psyche and *soma*, whatever experience the infant lives, the body functioning and the body sensations go together, being equally affected. Clumsy or hesitant holding acts against psycho-somatic union, prevents the development of muscular tonus and "coordination", and goes against the child's capacity for enjoying the experience of body functioning and of *being*. When there is safety, two things are taking place: at the same time as the mother facilitates the general tendency towards integration, especially the indwelling of the psyche in the body, she provides the conditions for the return to the relaxed rest of the non-integrated state.

In the initial stage, the mother's love is expressed through *physical care*, which ultimately is what the baby needs and what he is capable of integrating into the subjective world. To hold the infant properly and to handle him is a way of loving and, possibly, "the only way in which a mother can show the infant her love" (1960b, p. 49). The insistence on this point relates to the demystification of the intense network of mental mechanisms and feelings with which traditional psychoanalysis has endowed the baby in his relationship with the breast. Even when referring to later stages of development, Winnicott affirms that "children need more of their parents than to be loved; they need something that carries over when they are hated and even hateful" (1961b, p. 43). The mother, while she takes care of the body, knows that there is a person in this body. She takes care of its physical well-being, but in such a way that she addresses the *total person* of the baby, which he has not yet become, but will. She is the one who puts the baby together, not only in her arms but in her conception of the baby as a total human being. As Winnicott nevertheless observes, there are mothers who, although they have good natural conditions for physical care of babies, seem to ignore that there is a human being dwelling in the body which they bathe and feed. If this is the case, the baby cannot integrate into a whole and the foundations are laid for a psycho-somatic splitting. When maternal care promotes psycho-somatic cohesion, the personal me is felt as being contained within the boundaries given by the limits of the skin. At around six months, a baby already uses the circle or the sphere as a diagram of the self. The baby becomes used to occupying space, to having a visible presence, to being seen and recognised. In the absence of this, he will never achieve the reality of the self or an effective contact with external reality; he will never be able to perceive clearly what comes from within and what comes from without. Even in health, however, psycho-somatic cohesion cannot be considered to be fully established and not only at the beginning but throughout life, it will show its precariousness in situations of tiredness and in the passage between waking and sleep.

Babies are highly sensitive to differences in the way in which they are held. This is one of the main reasons why Winnicott insists that the good-enough care should be provided by the same person. When several people hold the baby (father, aunts, nannies), he is subjected to varied techniques, losing, at least in part, the familiarity that forms the basis of predictability. Even when only the mother takes care of the baby, he is sensitive to changes in her mood, which naturally have an impact on the body. Winnicott observed that during air raids in World War II, babies were not scared of the bombs that fell, but were immediately affected if their mothers panicked.

Provided that the mother spares the baby from outbursts dictated by emotional instability, it is good for him to feel her various moods, meaning that she is alive and is affected by events. It is a good thing that the mother is transparent and not opaque. At best, the opaque mother leads to an endless need to dismantle all toys and machines in order to find out how they operate. A patient of mine reports that her mother had always had an unalterable expression, eternally placid; she was never irritated or manifested any other type of emotion. She remembers peeking at her mother's face at a very early date, desperately trying to know what happened inside her. At about this time, she felt entirely lost and was gripped by the fear that her mother would die suddenly; she then thought, but did not have the courage to ask, that it would be a good thing if her mother left her a full list of everything that she should or could do, and everything that she could not. This girl developed a high degree of sensitivity to and a sense of being threatened by any type of alteration in people's physiognomy or in her environment.

Babies also feel the difference between tense holding, which is uncomfortable for the mother, and relaxed holding which is a natural part of her tasks and which costs her nothing. The same patient once told me that she was now aware that she had never sat fully on her buttocks; her mother could not bear physical contact, and since a very young age she had always felt that she was a burden on her mother, with this being excessively painful. In moments of anxiety, she would go to the bathroom to smell the towel that her mother had used and this would calm her.

From the sensitivity of babies in relation to the mother's moods emerges the issue of the mother's consistency, of her capacity to be herself. The baby feels the difference between studied gestures, in which the soul is not present, and other, spontaneous ones, which indicate that the mother is really there: all of her and not just her mind. It is often the case that the mother is suffering from anxiety or is excessively controlling due to her fear of dropping the baby, or has warm skin and a fast heartbeat due to anxiety and in these cases, the baby cannot allow himself the luxury of relaxing, which will only take place as a result of pure exhaustion. When, after the experience of integration, returning to rest is made systematically difficult, the situation may become more serious than we would normally expect, since it is only from the non-integrated state that the experience of integration may be felt as real. If the mother acknowledges her own difficulties and wants to preserve the baby carefully, she places him in the cradle, which is a very welcome alternative, or asks for the help of a good nanny. In fact, the baby needs both experiences. Even mothers who feel confident and enjoy holding their babies, may sometimes feel drowsy or may be experiencing a period of depression. If they are good-enough, they will put the baby in the cradle, because they know "that your sleeping state is not alive enough to keep going the infant's idea of a space around" (1957e, p. 20). When the act of holding the baby is adequate, however, he gains confidence, returning to non-integration *while he is being held*. This, according to Winnicott, is the richest experience.

The beginning of the contact with reality: object relations

At the beginning of life, the baby is not sufficiently mature to know of the existence of external reality, to perceive the objects that belong to it, and even less to relate to them effectively. He still has not developed a sense of externality or the capacity for perception, characteristic of relations to objects that are perceived objectively. Separating the self from objects (which is a very sophisticated achievement and depends on other previous achievements) will only begin later, from the stage of object use onwards, when the baby himself creates the sense of reality that is specific to externality. After this, he will still have to complete the achievement, separating the self from the total environment, which will only take place at the I AM stage.[44]

As soon as the baby is born, he has neither the sense of externality nor any other sense of reality. In order for some sense of reality to be initiated, the baby must be provided with the only one that is possible for him at this point of development: *the reality of the subjective world*. Without establishing a subjective reality, the baby cannot proceed with the gradual achievements of maturation, which include the sense of real that is specific to transitionality and then the sense of external and shared reality. As Loparic has showed (1995a), the different senses of reality correspond to different "worlds", which differ according to a space and a time that are peculiar to each one. In each of these worlds, objects may be found, the mode of presence (or "reality") of which differs from the others in spatio-temporal terms; the mode of presence of the subjective object, for example, is not the same as that of transitional objects and is radically different from that of objects which are objectively perceived that belong to external reality.[45] The relation of the human individual to subjective objects is characterised by the fact that it excludes any separation between subject and object, since this sense of reality "is prior to action and to representation, conditions of life under the aegis of the principle of reality, to be understood as: of the external reality which characterises the objects of the external world" (Loparic, 1995a, p. 52). It is also important to note that the reality of the subjective world not only leaves nothing to be desired in terms of the feeling of real, to the reality of the objective world, which will follow it later but, in some cases, will continue, throughout life, to be always more real than objective reality itself.[46]

The main characteristic of subjective objects is that of being reliable.[47] The character of reliability was clarified earlier when the excited states of the baby were being examined: it refers to the fact that the good-enough mother provides the baby with the experience of creating what he encounters and also protects him from the irruption of anything unpredictable that may interrupt his continuity of being. Encountering a subjective object thus means that the baby finds, that is, creates what he needs at the moment when he needs it. The object comes to the baby at the *exact moment* when the need arises, and it is of the exact size of the baby's possibility of receiving and assimilating it *as part of him at that precise moment*. Subjective objects "exist as immediate, unconditioned presences" (Loparic, 1995a, p. 54). Their nature is such that the baby is not confronted with something that he cannot embrace in experience; they do not surprise or startle him, that is, they are not untimely, in the sense of being unpredictable. Their form of presence is of a kind that does not denounce the external character of their existence and in this way, does not extrapolate the scope of the baby's subjective experience. For all these reasons, the subjective object is reliable and, in this sense, real.

The beginning of the object relation (with subjective objects) takes place during the baby's moments of excitation. The maternal provision which is specific to this task is that of object-presenting. The baby nevertheless only creates from what he finds. For the subjective world to stay alive and for the infant to go on creating the objects that he needs, someone must make a continuous effort to present samples of the world to him in a way that is comprehensible and appropriate to the maturational capacity of the moment. An insufficient presentation of objects blocks the child's path towards feeling real and relating to the real world of objects and phenomena (cf. 1965c). There are environments that simply abandon the baby to his own resources and provide no material for creation:

> But someone has to be there if that which is created is to be realised, actual. If no one is there to do this, then, in the extreme, the child is autistic—creative into space—and boringly compliant in relationships (childhood schizophrenia). (1986h, p. 49)

The sense of the real of subjective reality, which will be the foundation for all others, rests on reliability, as has been already said.[48] It is this which actually constitutes the subjective world and it is only because the baby inhabits a subjective world that he can find subjective objects. In this world, the baby experiences total control over objects. This is thus a magical world in which the demands of the objective world have not been registered. The breast appears when hunger emerges, and disappears when the tension ceases. The absolute adaptation of the mother maintains the baby in the area of the illusion of omnipotence; and only there can he begin to be.

Sustaining the illusion of omnipotence and preserving the subjective world entails ensuring that the baby is not surprised with a sense of reality for which he is not yet prepared. If the mother insists on breastfeeding the baby or on exciting him when he has already gone to rest, and if, instead of corresponding to the baby's gesture, the mother replaces it with her own, the existence of something outside the infant's sphere of omnipotence emerges before he is prepared for such reality. An intrusion then occurs. This nevertheless does not mean that the baby perceives the object confronting him; he does not perceive it, because he is not capable of perception. He feels, nevertheless, the presence of something strange and incomprehensible, which falls upon him, so to say, and which he cannot embrace in the scope of his experience.

In due time, the baby will have to accept the fact of the external existence of the world, over which he will have no control; however, if he is initially provided with a creative and subjective relation to the world, he will gradually be able to submit himself to the evidence of this other reality "without losing face" (cf. Winnicott, 1968d, p. 103). According to Winnicott, it is entirely wrong to think that the sense of reality of a child depends on the mother's insistence on the external and objective nature of the things of the world. It is only starting from the illusion that a child can be expected to become able gradually to accept the independent existence of the external world and to assimilate disillusions: "Adaptation to the reality principle arises naturally out of the experience of omnipotence, within the area, that is, of a relationship to subjective objects" (1965j, p. 180).

When illusion is well installed, there gradually emerges "an intellectual understanding of the fact of the world's existence prior to the individual's, but feeling remains that the world is personally created" (1988, p. 111). Winnicott speaks of *intellectual* understanding. This means that after the capacity for illusion has been installed, the child *learns*, over time, of the separate existence of external reality, now understanding that the world has always been there, independently of the individual. The feeling that the world is created and will continue to be created personally nevertheless does not disappear. If the individual stays alive, his personal root is set in the imaginative world, and it is only from this place that the acceptance of the external world does not equal annihilation.

Throughout life, the central problem of the relation to reality remains the same: the world which is objectively real and shared has a lot to offer as long as its acceptance does not mean the loss of the reality of the personal imaginative world (cf. 1949m, p. 70). We can never be too careful when the preservation of the bonds which link external reality to subjective reality is at stake. If an older child, who is three or four years old and lives simultaneously in the shared world and in his own imaginative world, tells us that he wants to fly, we must not hit him head-on with the weight of objective reality, answering that children do not fly. On the contrary, we must pick him up and make him swirl high up the room, so that he really feels that he is flying like a bird.

> Only too soon the child will find that flying cannot be done magically. Probably in dreams magical floating through the air may be retained to some extent, or at any rate there will be a dream about taking rather long steps. [...] At ten years or so child will be practicing long-jump and high-jump, trying to jump farther and higher than the other. That will be all that remains, except dreams, of the tremendously acute sensations associated with the idea of flying that came naturally at the age of three. (1949m, p. 70)

The constitution of the primary self

The considerations of the previous section refer to the beginning of access to the senses of reality (through the reality of the subjective world) and to object relations with subjective objects.

According to Winnicott, however, the baby does not exist as a unitary individual yet, as a me. *Who* is it then, who, being in a world, encounters objects?

The unitary self is the result of the integrative tendency and reaches a more consistent and stable state at the stage when the individual, if he could talk, would say: I AM. We know, however, that integration does not occur all at once, or once and for all. *From the state of unintegration*, brief moments or periods of integration take place, and it is only gradually that the general state of integration is established on a stable basis. These moments of vivacity and of excitation are preceded by "a gathering together of the whole self" (1988, p. 117); this experience of being gathered together into a unitary self, even if momentarily, but from the creative drive, is felt as real. The encounter with the object "gives reality" to being alive, and also to the need, not only in the sense of satisfaction, but in the sense of *giving reality* to the need, the drive, the gesture which "reaches out ..." and the something that is found. What the immature self of a very young baby feels as real is this self-expression of the self (cf. 1993e, p. 25). We may well affirm, briefly, that in Winnicott, emotional health is related to the preservation of the creative drive throughout life: the experience initiated on the basis of it is integrative and is felt as real; it is the accumulation and integration of those experiences which gradually constitute the primary self in the direction of a unitary identity. Shortly after finishing breastfeeding, the baby's self falls apart, and he returns, at rest, to the state of non-integration.

In a later formulation of this same issue (cf. 1971i), Winnicott would say that the experiences of integration, which take place during the theoretical first feed, are the first and inaugural *experiences of the self*, of being as *identity*. That is, on encountering the subjective object, the baby has an experience of *primary identification* with the object, the baby *becomes the object: he is the breast*. This constitutes an experience of *being*, which has a new sense beyond that of the continuity of being: that of *being as identity*. Winnicott names this experience of being, which is present in men and women, the "pure female element". While the pure female element concerns *being*, the "pure male element" relates to *doing*. This distinction between being and doing is a new way of formulating the difference between subjective object and object objectively perceived:

> In this relatedness of pure female element to "breast" is a practical application of the idea of the subjective object, and the experience of this paves the way for the objective subject—that is, the idea of a self, and the feeling of real that springs from the sense of having an identity. (1971i, p. 177)[49]

What interests us here is the relation between the constitution of the initial self and the experience of the "pure female element". Winnicott says: "When the girl element in the boy or girl baby or patient finds the breast it is the self that has been found" (1971i, p. 180). *Being* is the most simple of all experiences and perhaps because of this, the most difficult to be conceived by means of reflection. Besides being the most simple, it is also the most important of all experiences, the basis for all subsequent ones, including the subsequent experiences of identification. For this reason,

> complex the psychology of the sense of self and of the establishment of an identity eventually becomes, as a baby grows, no sense of self emerges except on the basis of this relating in the sense of BEING. (1971i, p. 177)

Since Winnicott uses the term "breast", as we shall see, to designate the totality of the maternal care, we must say that in the primary experience of integration, the baby becomes identical to the care that he receives: he *is* that care, more precisely: the baby becomes the reliability of that care. Indeed, through the regular repetition of the experience, he will incorporate this environmental care as a part of the self. Although this question of identity is only completely formulated in the text of 1966, already in 1963, Winnicott writes that since the baby is merged with the mother, not having separated yet the "me" from the "not-me", "what is adaptive or 'good' in the environment is building up in the infant's storehouse of experience as a self quality, indistinguishable at first (by the infant) from the infant's own healthy functioning" (1963d, p. 97).

It is this sense of being that makes the baby feel not only real, but also integrated into an incipient identity, which is the primary self. In order to achieve this, however, it is essential that the drive emerges from a state of rest, in non-integration, and that it is hence personal, creative: the searching comes from the baby; it is not the environment that imposes something. If, as has already been mentioned, the initiative comes from the environment, what is left for the baby is to react and not to be. Furthermore, the baby must encounter a breast that "is", the breast of a mother who is capable of being, and not a breast that "does". The breast that "does" is a breast of the "pure male element", which is not satisfactory for the initial experience of identity.[50] During the time when the baby and the mother are a unity, if the mother has a breast that *is* then the baby can also be. The adaptation of the mother allows the baby, as he creates the breast, to create himself as someone who is. If the mother is not capable of making this contribution, the baby must develop without the capacity for being, or with a weakened capacity for being. In this case, "Instead of 'being like', this baby has to 'do like'" (1971i, p. 179).[51] When the mother is of the type that does, and imposes her mode of functioning on the baby, if she *makes him nurse,* instead of *allowing him to be, as he nurses* (thus, becoming the breast), an alert and a reaction occurs. The reaction breaks the continuity of being and exacerbates the split between spontaneity and reactivity or submission. If this is the environmental pattern, the baby will still build an identity, but this will be false and artificial, since it will be built defensively, aiming at protecting the true and spontaneous self; this self is isolated in order not to be traumatised. When spontaneity is isolated, however, being deprived in this way of opportunities for real experiences, the creative impulse is inhibited and the *true self loses expression and the opportunity to become a reality that is alive.* Without the ballast of being, the false identity must be permanently doing something, endlessly and uselessly trying to find being in doing.

Two other points must be noted here. First, the difference between being and doing must not be understood in terms of active and passive. The basis for everything is being, with the dichotomy between active and passive making sense only in relation to doing, which should only emerge from being. Second, we must bear in mind that the sense of "*being* the subjective object" of primary identity, precedes the idea of being-with-something or with someone. Two separate persons, Winnicott says, may *feel* that they are one, but in the question that is being examined here, "the baby and the object *are* one" (1971i, p. 177). In this latter case, therefore, there is no actual object relation, but a relation of "being". The relation with objects, the basis of which is *to have been the object*, will take place later, if everything goes well, and if the baby can, in due time, create the externality of the world and begin to relate to objects objectively perceived. In order for a relation to exist, there must be two individuals. There is a curious relation here that cannot rigorously be called a relation, because there are not yet two, but *two-in-one*. This is why, having already formulated the final version of his theory of the primary identity, Winnicott affirms: "it is axiomatic that there is no relating to a subjective object" (1989n, p. 187).

With regard to the term "breast", Winnicott uses it in a different sense from that of traditional psychoanalysis, especially in Kleinian psychoanalysis: "This language involving 'the breast' is jargon" he says (1969d, p. 225). It misleads us into thinking that the baby can make contact with an object which, even if understood as a partial one, is external to him (from the baby's own perspective), in that the immature baby still has not established a sense either of the external or of the internal. The word "breast" does not therefore refer to any object either external or internal, not only because there is not yet an individual capable of perceiving objects, but also because from the baby's perspective, no object is detached from the total environment.

Taking into account the totality of his thought, we can say that in Winnicott, the term "breast" has two fundamental meanings. Firstly, the breast is a *subjective object*; it is the first subjective object that the baby encounters, on the plane of *object relations*, the special character of which has just been mentioned. The mother who is there, available as breast, is the object-mother, that is, the mother who is the target of the baby's excited love and who provides the breast in such a way as to allow him to have the experience of creating the object. The experience of object relation, in the specifically Winnicottian sense, is nevertheless only possible against the background of a subjective world, which is permanently reassured by maternal reliability. In a second sense, "breast" is the name given by Winnicott to the *totality of care* with which the environment-mother provides the baby, a totality that includes the care relative to the three basic tasks.[52] Considering that the central characteristic of the care is reliability, when the baby encounters the breast, he encounters not the care itself, but the *way of being* of the care, that is, the environmental reliability. In other words, he encounters the *subjective object* (breast-object) in a *subjective world*, made of the totality of the care (breast-environment). We are now able to complete both the concept of subjective object and the full meaning of dependence. An object is subjective when, on encountering the object (which is presented by the mother in such a way that it does not detach from her, being external only to the observer), this object is created by the baby, and at the same time that he creates the object, he creates himself as identity, becoming, in this experience of primary identification, the object itself. At this precise point, the deep character of dependence emerges clearly. The mother supports the baby in three fundamental ways through the care that she offers. First, by preserving the area of illusion of omnipotence, as environment-mother, she opens and maintains a reliable subjective *world* (space and time) in which an encounter with an object may occur, and to which the baby can return to rest. Second, she enables him to reach the self, promoting an experience of *identity*, in which he becomes the object. That is to say, the mother aids in establishing "who" encounters objects. Finally, she is herself the object (subjective), the breast, the warmth, the milk, etc., which is encountered (mother-object).[53]

The mother does all of this because of her identification with the baby; because she accepts and is willing to respond to his immaturity and dependence. Her knowledge of the baby's needs is not intellectual, in the same way that the care is not really deliberate. If she is good enough, her understanding comes "from a deeper level and not necessarily from that part of the mind which has words for everything" (1968f, p. 61). Her communication with the baby, which takes place from a deep understanding, is silent: "The main things that a mother does with the baby cannot be done through words" (idem). Winnicott affirms:

> Acts of human reliability make a communication long before speech means anything—the way the mother fits in when rocking the child, the sound and tone of her voice, all communicate long before speech is understood. (1968b, p. 147)

The mother may or may not speak to the baby. This, however, is not the main issue, since when it comes to human communication, "the language is not important" (1968d, p. 95). What matters is that *through the experience of effective care*, the mother is always telling the baby that she is reliable, not because she is a machine, but because she knows, at each moment, what he needs. The baby, says Winnicott, "does not know about the communication except from the effects of *failure* of reliability" (ibid., p. 98). Either communication is silent and reliability is guaranteed, or it is traumatic, causing the experience of an unthinkable or primitive agony (cf. 1970b, p. 201).[54] If the mother needs to show her reliability and to guarantee the baby's acknowledgement of it, she will fail precisely there, since she will be imposing her external existence on him and calling for an understanding for which he is still too immature. In this case, this mother lacks confidence in the baby's maturational process in progress.

An essential aspect of this silent communication, within the strange form of "relation" which provides the baby with the primary identity is the mother's gaze.[55] Often, while nursing, the baby looks around and it is probable that he does not look at the breast, but at the mother's face. What does the baby see when he looks at the mother's face? He sees himself, affirms Winnicott; not as an *image*, since he is not yet capable of perception. What emerges in the mother's gaze is her own vision of the baby and the satisfaction that it contains. In other words, the mother is looking at the baby, and her face and gaze reflect what she sees, that is, *her vision of the baby*. To be seen by the mother's gaze is one of the fundamental bases of the feeling of existing: "When I look I am seen, so I exist" (1967a, p. 154). There is, however, the case of the baby, whose mother has an opaque gaze, herself trapped in her own interior; in this case, it is not the baby who is reflected there, but her own mood, or even worse, the rigidity of her defences. In this case, what does the baby see? There are babies, says the author, who have already become used to not receiving what they are seeking. They look and they do not see themselves. This has consequences:

> First, their own creative capacity begins to atrophy [...]. Second, the baby gets settled in to the idea that when he or she looks, what is seen is the mother's face. The mother's face is not then a mirror. So perception takes the place of apperception. (1967a, p. 151)

Winnicott uses the term "apperception" as opposed to "perception". It refers to the creative gaze, characteristic of the subjective world. It is linked to the word "to create", in the sense of "to bring into existence", to the fact that someone is able to go on "seeing everything afresh all the time" (1986h, p. 41). When there is health, this ability to look creatively at the world does not disappear. Even later, when the individual is able to relate to the world of objectively perceived objects, this gaze will never be entirely subject, as perception is by definition, to the objective outlines of external reality. If the mother's gaze does not reflect the baby, but what he sees is the mother's own face, then a fact from external reality violates the baby's legitimate experience of omnipotence.

When the mother protects the area of illusion of omnipotence at the same time that, in small doses, she presents the world to the baby, he makes the experience of creating the world and himself continuously and of having a place to inhabit. In this way, the mother provides her own person as raw material for the child to create, so that eventually the subjective mother is very similar to the mother who is objectively perceived. For Winnicott,

> In the course of time the individual becomes able to forgo the *actual* presence of a mother or mother-figure. This has been referred to in such terms as the establishment of an 'internal environment'. It is more primitive than the phenomenon which deserves the term "introjected mother". (1958g, p. 34)[56]

Establishing an "internal environment" does not mean *to introject* imagos or maternal functions, but to incorporate maternal care and the sense of reliability.[57] The baby is not a dynamics in search of content, he does not relate yet to objects and possesses neither an inside nor an outside for a mechanism such as introjection to make sense. When primary creativity is considered, it is not necessary to postulate that the human being, as a baby, becomes an individual and has a world only because he is able to project what has been previously introjected; that is, "excreting what has been incorporated" (1988, p. 110). On the basis of the Winnicottian conception of the human being, it is not difficult to understand why human psychic life cannot be seen in the terms of body symbolism. There is no way of reconciling the concepts of creativity on one side, and those of introjection and projection on the other. The author is keen to emphasise "the concept of primary creativity, and of absolute originality, as against the projection of previously introjected (digested and worked over)" (1988, p. 112).

Notes

1. The book *Human Nature* is taken as the basis for the analysis presented in this section.
2. With this sentence, Winnicott highlights the fact that essential things happen to the baby, which are inaccessible to the observer. It follows from this that the study of severe pathologies of schizophrenic type, which originate in the most primitive phases, is especially fruitful if carried out by observing and treating older children and adults who regress to dependence and not through observing babies. He says: "My experiences have led me to recognise that dependent or deeply regressed patients can teach the analyst more about early infancy than can be learned from direct observation of infants [...]" (1965m, p. 141).
3. On this point, Loparic says: "As in Heidegger, the inner difficulty of life does not come from its finitude, from having-to-die, but rather from *having to go on being*. According to Winnicott, it is from this having-to-be that all other human needs originate" (Loparic, 2000b, p. 359).
4. Cf. Winnicott, 1958f, p. 182.
5. Winnicott uses the word "frustration" here in the common and not in the technical sense, since for him, "such words as *frustration* begin to have meaning in the sense that the infant is able to hold in his mind the idea that something was expected but the expectation was not completely

fulfilled" (1987c, p. 54; my italics). This condition evidently cannot be affirmed at such a primitive moment, with a long maturation process being required before frustration may exist, that is, before it may be experienced as such.

6. Winnicott emphasises the need to distinguish birth experience from birth trauma (cf. 1958f). Like Freud, he considers Otto Rank's thesis that birth would be traumatic in itself because it causes a dramatic separation from the mother, to be entirely unfounded. The newly born baby is not sufficiently mature even to feel connected to the mother; he merely feels either security and continuity or insecurity and discontinuity; he thus cannot experience any separation (cf. 1958f).
7. Cf. Winnicott, 1958f. Trauma at this point is related to delivery and birth. I highlight its temporal character since, according to Winnicott, this is the specific character of traumas which form the basis of psychotic pathologies. The question will be developed in a future book on schizophrenic psychoses in Winnicott's work.
8. On birth and trauma experience, and on the importance of this issue in the analysis of psychotics, cf. Winnicott, 1958f.
9. We should note the meaning that Winnicott gives to the word "love" at this beginning of life. He associates it with contact and physical care, which are the only manifestations of love that the baby is capable of receiving.
10. I shall clarify the sense in which Winnicott uses the term "object" when referring to the mother later in the text.
11. Winnicott clarifies the concept of primary identification, which forms the basis of the experience of primary identity, by distinguishing being from doing, one of the most complex points of Winnicott's theory, which shall be addressed later.
12. In reviewing the book *Psychoanalytical Studies of the Personality* (1952), by Fairbairn, Winnicott criticises the fact that the former does not take primary creativity into account and says: "In his theory, primary psychic creativity is not a human property; an infinite series of introjections and projections form the infant's psychic experience. Fairbairn's theory here lines up with the theory given us by Melanie Klein, which also allows no tribute to be paid to the idea of primary psychic creativity" (1953b, p. 420).
13. The word "omnipotence", used for this primitive stage, describes a special characteristic of dependence and means that the baby does not know anything about his own existence or that of the external world. We must not confuse this specific meaning of the *experience of omnipotence*, in the area of illusion, characteristic of the subjective world, with the *feeling of omnipotence*, which relates to a power which knows no limits and precisely "belongs to hopelessness about dependence" (1971h, p. 40).
14. This configures the trauma of the non-event, which will be retained, not in the repressed unconscious, which already presumes a high degree of maturation, with an already established internal psychic reality, but in the not-happened unconscious, which is the negative form of the Winnicottian originary unconscious. To name a type of unconscious that does not consist of repressed material (Freudian unconscious), but the very primitive one, proceeding the advent of representations, which retains the lost memory of the breakdown, I will use the expression "not happened unconscious", coined by Zeljko Loparic for this purpose. This "not happened" unconscious is merely the negative side, so to speak, of the primary unconscious, the content of which can only be reached in dreams and "contributes fundamentally to all significant experiences of human individual" (1963c, p. 218).

    The phrase was inspired by a phrase by Winnicott in the 1974 text, "Fear of breakdown". Referring to the breakdown which occurs when environmental intrusion is of the type leaves the baby's gesture without a response, Winnicott says, "To understand this it is necessary to think not of trauma [in the sense of something imposed] but of nothing happening when something might profitably have happened" (1974, p. 93).

What "did not happen" was the experience which, from rest or motivated by an impulse, would have been completed and would have provided continuity to the maturation process due to the environment adapting to the needs and rhythm of the baby and which was lost due to lack of environmental favour: the environment did not respond, was hasty or intervened in the baby's gesture. His reaction to this environmental failure interrupts his continuity of being, which constitutes a breakdown. While it occurs, the breakdown is not actually experienced, since the baby is not yet a unitary person able to experience and record what exceeds his area of omnipotence; even so, he suffers the consequences of this "disaster" which occurs to him, even before an "I" has been established.

15. The issue of illusion and, initially, the illusion of omnipotence is one of Winnicott's basic contributions to the theme of the constitution of the self and of the senses of reality. It is an issue of utmost complexity and a central theme in philosophy. Within the context of psychoanalysis, Winnicott is one of the only thinkers to attach due weight and status to it. This contribution, central to an understanding of his thought, has nevertheless been the target of distortions and/or improper assimilations by/to psychoanalytical tradition. For example, Michael Jacobs (1995), after stating that Winnicott is undoubtedly an original thinker, primarily because of the concepts which are clearly "his output", such as the transitional object and the squiggle game [sic], notes that there is a second sense in which Winnicott may be considered original: the "ability to adapt and adopt the concepts and aspects of clinical practice which others invented". Here, Jacobs continues, "we may cite the significant change which he made in Freud's concept of illusion, which in Winnicott became a means of perceiving [*sic*] the present, more than as an indication, as in Freud, of the child's desire" (Jacobs, 1995, p. 27).
16. Depending on its moment of origin, some cases of denial or inhibition of the instinctual source may be understood not in terms of censorship of undesirable content, but as retreat as a reaction to intrusion. The instinctual tension is intrusive and interrupts the continuity of being if there is not an active facilitation by the mother. Before the indwelling of the psyche in the body, the body is as foreign to the baby as the things in the external world, so that instinctual tensions are as intrusive as anything intrusive deriving from the environment.
17. Cf. Chapter Four, section titled "The stage of concern".
18. In a text from 1957, Winnicott states that the lack of instinctual tension may generate anxiety, but if there is integration of the sense of time within the personality, this will enable the baby to wait for the natural return of instinctual demand (cf. 1958g, p. 33). For a more extensive development of this question, cf. Winnicott 1958b and 1958g. See also the case described in Winnicott 1986a, in addition to the introduction to the same book by Masud Khan.
19. It should be noted that this quotation offers a good example of the Winnicottian use of the terms "ego" and "self". Oral satisfaction may be traumatic if it violates the "ego function", that is, what is already integrated in the baby and exists as an incipient self. The trauma affects the person of the baby, whatever is the existing degree of integration and affects the maturational process.
20. The idea that the baby is not driven mainly by the principle of pleasure/displeasure, but by the search for the object had already been proposed by Fairbairn. Despite the fact that Fairbairn developed this point in a different direction from that of Winnicott, the latter affirmed in a text of 1969: "I am obviously near to Fairbairn's statement made in 1944 that psycho-analytic theory was emphasizing drive-satisfaction at the expense of what Fairbairn called 'object-seeking'. And

Fairbairn was working, as I am here, on the ways in which psycho-analytic theory needed to be developed or modified if the analyst could hope to become able to cope with schizoid phenomena in the treatment of patients" (1970b, p. 256).

21. Winnicott cites Merrill Middlemore who, in the book *The Nursing Couple* (1941), describes how immensely careful she had to be in order not to interfere with this extremely delicate situation of the mother and the baby at the beginning of the relationship. "She took care", says Winnicott, "not be expecting successes or afraid of failure. There must be very few who are equipped to make this type of observation of intimacy" (1988, p. 105).
22. In their fine book *Le bébé et la coordination motrice* [The baby and motor coordination] (1994), the experts on psychomotricity, M. –M. Béziers and Y. Hunzinger, affirm that one of the caring actions which can promote well-being and safety in the baby, facilitating motor coordination, consists of the mother ensuring, while handling or breastfeeding the baby, that his feet are supported, so that they can exert pressure against the armrest of the armchair, the mother's hands or against her body.
23. The experts cited in the previous note remind the reader that for the baby, life is movement and that since the beginning, we must be careful to "avoid any obstacle to the expression of his or her movement" (Béziers & Hunzinger, 1994, p. 32).
24. Winnicott dedicated much of his theoretical effort to elucidating the aggressiveness and destructivity inherent to human nature. It should be noted that the two concepts, aggressiveness and destructivity, are necessary for distinguishing two forms of "aggression" that are radically different. This will become clearer throughout this book, especially in Chapter Four, in the sections referring to the stages of use of an object and of concern. This question runs through the whole of Winnicott's work and his formulations change as his thought evolves. It took him a long time to arrive at a more finished formulation, which only occurred, according to him, in one of the latest and more important articles, "The use of an object", of November 1968. In *Human Nature*, in a footnote added in 1970, he points out that with regard to the lack of a satisfactory formulation for the roots of aggression "this is the reason why I could not publish this book" (1988, p. 79).
25. It is not difficult to perceive that Winnicott's conception of the roots of aggression is completely at odds with the theories of Freud and Klein. With regard to Freud, the central point of discord is the fact that he conceives of aggression as a reaction to frustrations in contact with the reality principle, assuming a high degree of development in the baby, which is inconceivable during the initial moments. With regard to Melanie Klein, the motives are well known: in order to explain aggression, especially in the primitive stages, she invokes a constitutional destructiveness in the individual. In relation to both them there is another objection: the two theories fail to consider the baby's dependence and the fact that he reacts to the kind of care he receives.
26. On this question cf. Winnicott, 1965n and 1965r.
27. The theme of the invasive and traumatic environmental pattern deriving from psychiatric abnormalities of the mother, will be developed in another study, which aims to clarify Winnicott's theory of psychoses.
28. The existence of this non-instinctual anger, actually related to the loss of being became clear to me as a finding of clinical practice. Guided by this phenomenon, I searched for some observations by Winnicott which would provide a basis for it. As in other cases, I found a number of extremely interesting affirmations scattered throughout his work. It is the results of this search which are presented here.
29. For a more extensive study of the therapeutic use of failure by the analyst, see Dias, 2011b, text 3.
30. This theme is of great importance for the configuration of schizoid pathologies.

31. In the clinical case presented in the article "Withdrawal and regression", Winnicott points out to the patient who withdraws and snoozes during the session that his withdrawal at that moment is an escape from the painful experience of being precisely between the states of waking and sleeping, or between speaking to the analyst and withdrawing. The patient then says that although he remained lying on the couch, he had had the idea of being curled up. At this point, Winnicott made a highly significant interpretation: "In speaking of yourself as curled up and moving round, you are at the same time implying something which naturally you are not describing since you are not aware of it; you imply the *existence of a medium.*" The patient showed he had grasped the idea of a medium that provided him with *holding,* saying: "Like the oil in which wheels move" (1955a, p. 257). It is this medium that may be called *the mother's lap.*
32. By proposing the terms "object-mother" and "environment-mother" in order to distinguish two aspects of maternal care, Winnicott proceeds with great caution, afraid that these terms may become empty *slogans* and "develop a rigidity and an obstructive quality" (1963b, p. 102).
33. In her book *Ginástica holística: história e desenvolvimento de um método de cuidados corporais* [*Holistic gymnastics: history and development of a method of bodily care*] (2000), Maria Emília Mendonça, who sought in Winnicott a greater understanding of certain phenomena occurring in her clinical practice, discusses the subtle details of her method of bodily care and reflects upon the importance of the teacher–student relationship. She states that she always noticed that in group classes, some students "disconnected" from the class for a few moments; perhaps due to the silence, or perhaps because they were rocked by the teacher's voice; these students reached a state of quietness, departing from the objective action that was taking place. She intuitively perceived the importance of not interfering in an abrupt manner with these states which, according to her, were not a manifestation of disinterest, but, on the contrary, of trust. After a while, the student would return with an enhanced sensation of presence in class. It is only from this moment on, the author observes, that class may effectively start for that student (Mendonça, 2000, p. 205).
34. Fear of disintegration is one of the central aspects of psychotic pathologies of a schizophrenic type.
35. The unthinkable agonies constitute the core concept of psychotic pathologies in Winnicott's work. They will be studied in detail in a forthcoming book.
36. An important example of total experience, on the occasion of the activities of excretion of the infant, is found in Winnicott, 1949e.
37. Cf. Winnicott, 1949f.
38. The theme of the dwelling in the body will be developed next, when the task specific to it is described: the indwelling of the psyche in the body.
39. M. Sechehaye, 1994, respectively pp. 22; 30; 22.
40. Forrest Gump is the name of the character and the title of the film by director Robert Zemeckis (1994).
41. Referring to the care to the patient that regresses to dependence, Winnicott says that "'holding', like the task of the mother in infant-care, acknowledges tacitly the tendency of the patient to disintegrate, to cease to exist, to fall for ever" (1965d, p. 241). Hence, the need to sustain the presence and vivacity of the world.
42. The already cited M. –M. Béziers and Y. Husinger corroborate this point and show that the position of well-being, for the baby, is the one in which he is "rolled up". When feeling safe, the baby naturally adopts this rolling up position. Under pathological conditions or "if the baby is suffering from some discomfort, this 'rolling up' will not occur on being taken in the mother's arms. On the contrary", the authors state, "what we will observe is the reverse position 'in extension':

head and arms pulled back, the back arched and the extensor muscles pulled taut" (Béziers & Hunsinger, 1994, p. 20).

43. I recommend to the reader the excellent work by Vera Regina F. de Laurentiis (2016) regarding the process of indwelling of the psyche in the body, starting from the initial moments and through every stage of maturation.
44. On the distinction between separating objects and separating the environment from the self, Winnicott, 1964d.
45. For Winnicott, an essential aspect of the issue of the access to reality is that there is not a single sense of reality, but several. Human development can be seen as the process by means of which the many senses of reality with their different types of object are gradually established, along with the constitution of various possibilities of object relation of the human individual. In traditional psychoanalysis, there is only one sense of reality. For a development of this issue, cf. Loparic, 1995a.
46. This is true above all in the cases of schizoid pathologies.
47. We should note here that the expression "subjective object" is not the most fortunate. First, because the very etymology of the term "object" leads us to think of an object of perception (*ob-jectum*), which is not specifically the case at this point. Second, because the term "subjective" can easily lead us to think about the subject/object polarity, which belongs to a certain lineage of Western thought, in which the subject is above all a thinking being, endowed with consciousness and filled with representations and feelings. In addition to the fact that Winnicott's thought does not belong to this lineage, at this point of maturation, the baby is not a self-conscious being and does not yet have objects of mental representation. We must thus bear in mind the specific sense which Winnicott attributed in his theory to the expression "subjective".
48. Winnicott uses the term "reliability" to name the central characteristic of the faciliting environment. In Webster's Encyclopedic Unabriged Dictionary (1996), the verb "rely", deriving from the Latin *religare,* means "to depend confidently, put trust in". The adjective "reliable" means "that may be relied on, trustworth […] that can be dependent upon with confident certainty". Winnicott could have used "trustworthness", which also contemplates the idea, in the sense of confidence, of dependability, but predominantly used reliability. It is likely that he preferred this term, since it was used more in common language, or also, as it seems to me, since the term includes, due to its etymological root, the sense of linkage, contact, recontact, reconnection, referring not only to the initial contact of mother and baby, which is what causes the engagement of the baby with life, but also due to the idea that what is reliable is the thing with which one can always restore links, to which one can always reconnect. This question is of such importance in Winnicott, that the breakdown of reliability during the initial stages constitutes a traumatic experience and results in disorders of a schizophrenic type. In Winnicott's classification of traumas according to the moment of maturation, the breakdown of reliability is described as the first sense of trauma. Cf. Winnicott, 1989d. On environment reliability as participating in the constitution of the self, cf. Dias, 2011b, text 1.
49. In a text dating from 1968–1969, which is a response to comments on his 1966 article "The split-off male and female elements to be found in men and women", Winnicott affirms that as a result of the clinical work described in this article, he saw himself in condition to compare *being* and *doing*. "I discovered myself looking at an essential conflict of human beings, one which must be operative at a very early date; that between being the object which also has the property of being, and by contrast a confrontation with the object which involves activity and object-relating that is

backed by instinct or drive. This turned out to be a new statement of what I have tried to describe before in terms of the subjective object and the object that is objectively perceived" (1972, p. 191).

50. In Winnicott's proposition, "being" and "doing" are two forms of object relation, with the difference between them to be understood on the basis of the line of maturation. While the first one is based on the need to be, the second already presupposes a separation between me and not-me and is based on instinctual drives. This last question, already related to doing, will be implicitly examined in sections "The stage of concern" and "The oedipal stage" of Chapter Four.
51. This point has important implications for the understanding of psychotic defences and for clinical work with schizophrenic patients who regress to dependence and whose central problem lies in an absence of the experience of *being*, which was replaced by a defensive organisation supported by *doing*.
52. In the article "Transitional objects and transitional phenomena", referring to the repeated creation by the baby of the mother's breast as a "subjective phenomenon", Winnicott introduces a note, in which he states that the term "breast" includes "the whole technique of mothering. When it is said that the first object is the breast, the word 'breast' is used, I believe, to stand for the technique of mothering as well as for the actual flesh" (1953c, p. 15, note 3). In another article, he notes that he has made it very clear that "the word *breast* and the idea of breast-feeding is an expression that carries with it the whole technique of being a mother to a baby" (1969b, p. 26). He also points out in another text: "The part-object is a whole object from the infant's point [...]" (1989g, p. 431).
53. Maternal failures only become traumatic when they establish a pattern of failure. With regard to this pattern, the mother may fail in the totality of the care, which includes these three modes of favouring, or she may fail in a more specific way, being able to provide certain aspect of the care, but failing in another. Without taking into account other factors that may play a role, such as the presence of an aunt or nanny, it can be said that the difficulties or disorders of the individual will assume different configurations according to the nature of maternal failure.
54. On unthinkable agonies, central for the understanding of psychotic pathologies, cf. Winnicott, 1968d; 1974, and 1989q. The issue will be examined in detail in another study in the process of conclusion.
55. Cf. Winnicott, 1967a.
56. In this citation, we note the distinction, emphasised by Winnicott, between "internal environment", which is no object, but rather the reliable (or unreliable) modes of being of the mother and the total environment, and the Kleinian expression "introjected mother", which supposes an inside, with the mother as an internal object. Emphasising the difference between his theory and Melaine Klein's, Winnicott notes that the expression "internal object" is a mental concept (cf. 1953c). He also says: "'The good mother' and 'the bad mother' of the Kleinian jargon are internal objects and are nothing to do with real women" (1987b, p. 38).
57. On the difference between incorporation and introjection in Winnicott, see Dias' study, 2011b, text 7.

CHAPTER FOUR

The stages of relative dependence and independence

The stage of disillusion, weaning, and beginning of mental functions

The stages in which the baby gradually moves from absolute to relative dependence on the mother's care still form part of the early phases of development; since they precede the structuring of the me as a unity, if a pattern of environmental failure is established, there is still risk of psychosis. During this period, the tasks of integration in time and space, of indwelling of the psyche in the body and of contact with reality (still subjective), parallel to the constitution of the primary self, which began during the stage of the theoretical first feed, continue along the maturational process, requiring new resolutions, which will constitute new tasks. Throughout life, these tasks will set the individual before new challenges to be faced and experienced. The description provided here does not cover the features assumed by these initial tasks in the later stages of life, being limited to the aspects concerning the initial stages.

What characterises this stage, during which disillusion begins, as well as the subsequent ones, is the fact that, unlike the stages described in the previous chapter, a gradual de-adaptation of the mother is initiated regarding the needs of the baby. If healthy, the mother emerges naturally from the state of "primary maternal preoccupation", already tired of the limitation of her world and of the extreme demands imposed by the baby's absolute dependence. Small failures begin to occur, which, because they occur as the baby progressively matures, still form part of the adaptation agenda. This coincides with the baby's need to continue with the maturational process; the mother's de-adaptation is vital for initiating the break up of the undifferentiated mother–baby unit, in order to set in motion the long and slow process of separation which will lead the little individual to the integration into a unitary and separated me, capable of establishing relations with the not-me or the external world.

The mother's de-adaptation triggers the process of disillusion of the baby. But disillusion, with its own acquisitions, *can only take place on the basis of a well-founded capacity for illusion*. It is often thought that in Winnicott's theory, as is the case in common sense, disillusion is a merely negative process of breaking an illusion, but this is not entirely correct. According to the author, what the baby leaves behind as he matures *is not the basic illusion*, which will remain if the baby is healthy, but rather the illusion of *omnipotence*. Over time, the child will progressively understand that he is not the one who effectively creates the world; that its existence is prior to and independent from him. The child will learn that the world has always been there and will continue to be there after his death. However, the *feeling* that the world was created personally and may continue to be created does not disappear. Despite an intellectual understanding, the individual retains the capacity for illusion, exercising creativity naturally, which is, as we have already seen, "the retention throughout life of something that belongs properly to infant experience: the ability to create the world" (1986h, p. 40).

Among the various aspects of the total process of disillusion, weaning is a particularly significant achievement. When the baby himself does not promote it, it is the mother who must carry it out; for this purpose, she needs her aggressiveness, she must count on some capacity for hating, whether actively or passively, which may be triggered when necessary. If, however, the mother is depressed, she will fear her hate, which may not be within reach of her consciousness; in this way, she will not be in a condition to fulfil her role in the disillusionment process, of which weaning is an aspect. In addition to being able to hate the overload which the baby represents, she must also be capable of facing the baby's wrath or hate, caused by the de-adaptation.[1] In other words, the mother who is healthy can face ambivalence in object relating and use it appropriately (cf. 1989d, p. 146). As Edna Vilete puts it, the mother must be able to

> [...] acknowledge and endure the child's hate, as well as accept that, for sometime, she will become the mean mother for him. Accepting means surviving as the strong mother, who is able to take care without the resources of omnipotence with which she was invested by the child until then. (Vilete, 2000, p. 158)

It is during this period that mental functioning and intellectual processes begin to be exercised specifically, helping the baby to deal with the gap existing between the complete and the incomplete adaptation. It is the flaws in maternal care that drive forward the use of the mind; it is by means of the incipient intellectual understanding that environment failures start to be taken into account, becoming understandable, bearable, and even predictable (cf. Winnicott, 1953a). If, until then, everything went well and the baby was spared a precocious and defensive mind functioning due to the good-enough adaptation, he is already capable, at this point, of using a type of knowledge *which is not mental* but stems from the *growing familiarity* with the bodily sensations and things of the environment. The baby already recognises rhythms, sounds, smells, emotional moods on a pre-intellectual plane and is already in possession of a certain pre-representational "if ... then" scheme.[2] When the baby is healthy, it is on this basis of a non–mental understanding that intellectual functioning begins to operate, without being a pathological defence aimed at controlling potential intrusions. From that moment onwards, the baby starts to use his intellect to know that the noises in the kitchen indicate that food is about to turn up. The "if … then" scheme becomes more refined and can now be properly thought out; instead of simply becoming more excited and impatient with the noises, the baby uses these new resources to be able to wait. Furthermore, in this phase of de-adaptation, there is a first glimpse of dependence: the infant learns, *in his mind*, that the mother is necessary. This, naturally, leaves him very exposed and no care is enough to avoid hurting the baby's dignity.

There are two general environment attitudes which are especially important in facilitating the individual's natural tendency towards maturation. They must be present at all stages, those prior and those subsequent to this one, but are particularly significant at the point when the baby is moving towards relative dependence: on one hand, the continuous existence of the conditions for a high degree of dependence, which may be again necessary, depending on the circumstances; on the other, the provision of opportunity for the individual to separate gradually from the mother and connect to the family, and from the family to the social unit closest to it and so on in ever wider circles. In this last sense, the mother's love, or the therapist's, means not only meeting the needs of dependence, but giving the opportunity which, at the appropriate time, will allow the child or the patient to move gradually from dependence to autonomy. As infants grow and develop, they acquire an increasing capacity to signal their needs; there are mothers who, because they have become excessively good and skilled in the technique of taking care of their children, do not always pay attention to the countless signs of communication and continue to guess and meet their needs as if they were still merged in with the environment. In this way, very often,

> […] the mother, by being a seemingly good mother, does something worse than castrate the infant. The latter is left with two alternatives: either being in a permanent state of regression and of being merged with the mother, or else staging a total rejection of the mother, even of the seemingly good mother. (1960b, p. 51)

On the other hand, the process of separation must be gradual. The child must break free from the mother's arms and lap, "but not to go into space"; the child moves away to a wider area, albeit still under control, "something that is symbolical of the lap from which the child has broken away" (1965p, p. 90). This movement of going away and releasing oneself, which will effectively start at the stage of transitionality, will remain real throughout life. Life, says the author, "is a long series of coming out of enclosures and taking new risks and meeting new and exciting challenges" (1965q, p. 115). In a text on the importance of the family as the thing which gives continuity to the mother's lap, which one must leave, Winnicott notes that each individual must walk the long path from being merged with the mother to being separate yet still related to her, and then, to mother and father together; the journey continues through the larger group known as the family, with the father and the mother as the main features. The family has its own growth […]. The family protects the child from the world, but gradually the world finds its way in via the aunts and uncles, the neighbours, the earliest schoolmates. "This gradual environmental seeping-in is the way by which a child can best come to terms with the wider world, and follows exactly the pattern of the infant's introduction to external reality by the mother" (1961b, p. 40).

Despite often being a burden and a hindrance, the family never ceases to be important throughout the individual's life. It is responsible for many of our journeys, since we escape, emigrate, change address because of the need to break away; then, we return periodically because we need to renew contacts with family (cf. 1961b).

In order for the explorations outside the fence to continue to be challenging and exciting it is necessary, however, that above all at the beginning, the path of return to the more primitive stages, of regression to dependence, is always open, since "coming out of the enclosure is very exciting and very frightening; and that once out, its awful for the child not being able to get back" (1965q, p. 115).

A central aspect of environment reliability consists in *always keeping the possibility of return open, a need that lasts forever*. The older child, the adolescent, the healthy young person and adult have various immaturities to fall back upon either for fun or during a period of need, whether in secret auto-erotic experiences or in dreaming (cf. 1965p). These immaturities indicate health, being "the residues of the healthy states of dependence that are characteristic of all the earlier phases of growth" (1954b, p. 181). Healthy individuals have this ability because the foundation was given to them at the initial stages, through the experience of countless returns to unintegration and, during the period described here, through the mother's capacity for allowing the baby to return to dependence and to the subjective world, whenever this proved necessary.

The stage of transitionality

The description of the phenomena of transitionality was undoubtedly the most rapidly accepted of Winnicott's contributions and was the reason why he became known and famous. Indeed, for a long time, the majority of the articles and comments on his work were predominantly devoted to this theme. The indisputable originality of the phenomenon, which had never been conceptualised before by traditional psychoanalysis, made it easy to assimilate into the already established body of theory, without further questions regarding the conceptual appropriateness of such assimilation. In addition to the fact that its particular place in the maturational process was ignored by analyses of the issue, the apparent simplicity of the phenomenon lent itself to such popularisation, that Winnicott felt obliged, in *Playing and Reality*, to re-issue a slightly modified version of the original article "Transitional objects and transitional phenomena", in which he tried to correct some distortions in the interpretation. He pointed out, for example, that what interested him was "not so much the object used as the use of the object" (1971e, p. xvi). That is, what is important for the psychoanalytical knowledge is not the description of new objects (internal, external, bizarre, *petit a*, etc.) but rather, the modes of being and relating of the human being.

From the perspective of the totality of Winnicott's work, the transitional phenomena are fundamental for the human maturational process, since they inaugurate one of the stages, and one of the achievements of maturation, leading the individual to a new sense of reality which, in the healthy individual, will establish a specific area of experience. The capacity for what is specific to transitionality, however, depends on the successful resolution of the tasks of the previous stages, since the experiences that take place within the transitional area and the new sense of reality which results from them are necessarily rooted in the subjective world of the baby. It is the reality based and experienced in his subjective world that provides a foundation for this transitional sense of reality. If the subjective sense of real has not been established, the transitional phenomena will not have meaning and the individual will not be able to enjoy their rewards. A baby who has not been provided with a sense of safety which is incorporated as a belief cannot "absent himself", being distracted with the transitional object; on the contrary, he can only remain alert, preventing possible invasions.

Transitional phenomena do not belong to the instinctual line, but to the ego line, of the maturational process; they are in the direct line of the achievement of the task of establishing contact with external reality, which began with the theoretical first feed. At the outset, the task of contact with reality is facilitated by the fact that the mother presents the world to the baby in such a way that, initially, the infant does not have to know that the object was found instead of being created by him. The baby thus begins to relate to reality, which is external from the perspective of the observer, via creativity and not via submission. At a subsequent moment in development, the I AM stage, he will have to start dealing with the fact of the separate existence of the world, and the great challenge will be to relate to the objectivity of the external world without the loss of personal spontaneity and primary creativity. Transitional phenomena are precisely halfway, as an intermediary and facilitating passage, in this "long journey", which goes from reality conceived subjectively to reality perceived objectively.[3] The "third area of experience" must therefore be preserved at every stage of the maturational process and in any sector of life, so that external, naked, and raw reality has a personal meaning. Over time, it must also be exercised on its own terrain, the arts and culture in general. But even when the individual has already accessed the shared world and even when, through talent, he becomes capable of artistic creation, creativity continues to be primarily a phenomenon of life; it has to do with the way in which the person becomes capable of relating to external reality, *without the loss of the personal sense of existence.*

Transitional phenomena emerge from the area of the illusion of omnipotence, within which the reality of the subjective world has been constructed. When they start to occur, at around eight to ten months, the process of disillusion has already started. They are responsible for giving continuity to the illusion, with gradual changes to omnipotence. They are characterised by the clinging to the transitional object and constitute the beginning of the capacity for symbolisation; they subsequently develop into the capacity for play and, as development continues, extend themselves to the entire cultural field. Transitional objects and then play are the precursors of the adult's capacity for using the field of culture, religion, and art for the necessary and salutary rest from the eternal task of separating facts from fantasy. What lies at the beginning of everything, however, is the illusion, since the child needs to start living "in a subjective state, being the creator of all" (1986c, p. 16).

How do transitional objects come about and in what way do they promote the passage to the reality of objects that are perceived objectively? It is an observable fact that, shortly after birth, babies suck their fingers and wrists, adopt some technique of touching their face or mutter sounds. These activities, which are normally seen as an oral autoerotic exercise are in part already transitional, being precursors of the subsequent adoption of a beloved object by the baby: the teddy bear, the edge of a blanket or a nappy. In order for the pre-transitional sense of these activities to become explicit, we must be able to see more than excitation and oral satisfaction in these primitive phenomena; we must acknowledge the baby's drive to reach an object, his capacity for creating, inventing, originating an object, his increasing ability to recognise a not-me object, the beginning of an affectionate type of object relation, etc. (cf. 1953c).[4]

In due time, as a result of the baby's increasing maturity, during the mother's de-adaptation, this phenomenon occurs, which had not yet received attention from analytical research but which had been noticed by mothers: the attachment of the baby to certain objects which he, so to speak, elects.[5] Invested with a very special importance, transitional objects are treated with great affection by the baby, but also with brutality, requiring them to be durable. For quite some time, they become indispensable, irreplaceable, particularly during moments of tension, unease, and anxiety such as the passage from wakefulness to sleep or during prolonged absences of the mother, who knows that the object cannot be replaced, not even by an equivalent one and that it must not be washed, however dirty it may be, since this would introduce a break in the continuity of the baby's experience, and that it must be taken on the family travels. If the baby is permitted this experience then over time, the object will lose the meaning that it had at that time, being "not so much forgotten as relegated to limbo" (1953c, p. 7).

During the period of absolute adaptation of the mother, object presenting, that is, the provision of raw material for the creation of subjective objects, was carried out in such a way that the external reality of the object did not confront the reality of the subjective world. The nature of object relation was that of primary identification with the object: the baby *is* the object. As integration becomes more consistent, maturation demands that something of the external world gradually interferes in the area of omnipotence of the infant. Being able to adopt a transitional object already announces that this process is underway and, from then on, some changes are introduced. A small break occurs in the omnipotence. With the transitional object, some characteristics of external reality start to enter into experience: the transitional object adapts itself but not as absolutely as the mother does. From *being* the object, the baby changes to *possessing* the object and, by means of this possession, he postpones the abandonment of magical control over the world, prolonging for some time the omnipotence which was originally satisfied by the mother's adaptation (cf. 1988). During the phase ruled by transitionality, the baby will abandon the omnipotent magical control which characterises the relation to subjective objects, gradually assuming control via manipulation, involving the pleasure of muscular exercise and coordination. Shortly afterwards, another achievement will be made, when the baby can already know that a particular object was given to him and he is be able to say "ta", "thereby acknowledging a limitation of magical control and acknowledging dependence on the goodwill of people in the external world" (1988, p. 107).

Many other acquisitions are occurring while the baby uses transitional objects; some of them show the intimate connection between the functioning of the body and personal maturation. In parallel with the development of coordination, a gradual enrichment of bodily sensitivity takes place, with the sharpening of the senses and corresponding imaginative elaboration of sensory experiences. The sense of smell, for example, reaches a peak which perhaps is never repeated with this intensity, except in psychotic episodes; texture and temperature, dryness and humidity have a tremendous meaning; palate becomes much more refined and one frequently observes the baby drooling. It is also possible to observe, during this phase, the beginning of the capacity for feelings of affection. Since all of this adds up to the voracious appetite which emerges with hunger, the baby reminds us, Winnicott jokes, of the lion in its cage, with tender feelings for the bone which is about to be destroyed.

At the beginning of the passage from absolute to relative adaptation, transitional objects play an indispensable supporting role, since they replace the mother who is de-adapting and hence disillusioning the baby. Transitionality marks the beginning of the distinction, of the breaking of the mother–baby unit. The infant, who is a creator of worlds, creates the first region, the first distance, the inaugural area of separation between him and the mother: the potential space.[6] Gradually, from the *two-in-one* fusional unit, two individuals will emerge, permitting the initiation of what is properly called a relationship, the bases of which are provided by the *sui generis* experience with the subjective object.[7] The transitional object enters the precise space between mother and baby, which is both separation and the symbol of the union with what is being separated; it represents the mother or the breast, or even the child's self, as it exists at this point of maturation. The symbolic activity which starts here brings a great breadth of experience, since "the symbol of union gives wider scope for human experience than union itself" (1986d, p. 135). I believe that this is the meaning of Winnicott's polemical assertion that over time, the transitional object becomes as indispensable or more indispensable than the mother herself.

It may occur that the same concrete object—the teddy bear, the blanket, the dummy—which initially is subjective, becomes transitional. It is thus not a question of one particular object being subjective and another one transitional. What changes is not the object, but its *sense of reality*, and it is to this that Winnicott refers when he affirms that this phenomenon enables us to observe something of the *nature of the object* (cf. 1953c), that is, of the change in the nature of object relation within the maturational process, specifically because

> it is not the object, of course, that is transitional. The object represents the infant's transition from a state of being merged with the mother to a state of being in relation to the mother as something outside and separate. (1953c, pp. 19–20)

In order for this transition to take place, for transitionality to be configured as such, the baby must gradually create a new space, a new "world". What maturation promotes is the capacity, inherent to every human being, to create worlds and transit between them. At this point, the potential space is being created, the third area of experience, the place where, if we are healthy, we may live (cf. 1971g), temporarily spared from the task of separating facts from fantasy. If the baby enjoys the satisfactory environmental conditions which enable him to create this new world, in which the continuity of the basic illusion is preserved, this area will be available for the creation and exercise of the capacity for symbolising and playing, extending itself over the course of life to the arts and to culture in general. Everything that subsequently happens in the potential space maintains the characteristics of the original transitional phenomena: it is neither inside nor outside; it belongs neither to the "internal" personal psychic reality, nor to external and shared reality; it is neither delirium, nor objectivity. In this way, transitional objects and phenomena initiate human beings into what will always be most important to them: "a neutral area of experience which will not be challenged" (1953c, p. 17).

But where is this space? What is the nature of this space and of playing? In an article on the various senses of reality in Winnicott's work, Loparic notes that:

> [...] more primitive than use and representation, while subsequent to the experience of contact, is play. This type of access to reality is a way of being of the baby, which can only be realised in its own *space*, termed potential. This space differes from that of representation by an essential characteristic: it is not exterior, internal or external, but is a component of the baby's being. The baby is not "inside" potential space, in the way that we say that a tree is in a garden, it *is* this space. (Loparic, 1995a, p. 53)

The baby hence does not transit from one object to another, but from one world to another. More precisely: since he is himself this space, we should say that he transits from one sense of reality to another within himself, as modes of his being, and that he may inhabit the different worlds which he creates, in which new objects may emerge. The baby can only accomplish this, however, if he has inhabited a subjective world for a sufficient period of time and continues to inhabit this world, the reality of which is not doubted. Winnicott asserts that where there is trust and reliability, there will also be a potential space "that can become an infinite area of separation", which may be creatively filled with play by babies, children, adolescents and adults, which in time becomes enjoyment of cultural heritage. "The special feature of this place where play and cultural experience have a position is that it *depends for its existence on living experiences*, not on inherited tendencies" (1971j, p. 146).

The passage from the subjective world, which is never lost, to the transitional world only occurs in time and takes time to establish itself as an achievement. Even if the process of separation and symbolic activity have been initiated, this does not guarantee that the image and meaning of the transitional object are kept alive, unless concrete maternal care continues to sustain the process. That is, the baby may use the transitional object to serve as mother, *while the subjective object is alive, real, good-enough and not very persecutory*. This subjective object, in turn depends, with regard to its qualities and duration, on the existence, vitality and behaviour of the external object, that is, on the concrete care of the real mother:

> Failure of the latter in some essential function indirectly leads to deadness or to a persecutory quality of the internal object. After a persistence of inadequacy of the external object the internal object fails to have meaning to the infant, and then, and then only, does the transitional object become meaningless too. (1953c, p. 13)

Before going any further, I would like to clarify the use of the expression "internal object" cited above. At the time when this article was written (1951), Winnicott had not yet formulated the concept of subjective object, which he only did in 1962. Although this text was revised for the publication of *Playing and Reality* (1971), and Winnicott did not make alterations regarding this point, I understand that in it, "internal object" refers to the "subjective object". The arguments are as follows: first, from the perspective of the theory of maturational processes, it is only possible to speak of an internal object when we refer to a point of maturation at which there is already an internal world or reality, and this achievement only occurs after the baby has reached a unitary identity in the I AM stage, with transitionality prior to this. In 1963 (1965j), referring to the more primitive versions of what Klein denominated "internal", Winnicott stated that when we refer to the beginning of life,

> [...] the word internal cannot be used in the Klein sense since the infant has not yet properly established an ego boundary and has not yet become master of the mental mechanisms of projection and introjection. At this early stage 'inner' only means personal, and personal in so far as the individual is a person with a self in process of becoming evolved. (1965j, p. 185)

Second, Winnicott maintains the expression "internal object" in order to emphasise the point which really interests him, namely, that "the transitional object is *not an internal object* (which is a mental concept)" (1953c, p. 13); it does not therefore have a life of its own and depends for its survival on the relation, communication, and ultimately on the maintenance of continuity of environmental care. In Winnicott's theory, the constitution of the internal world supposes that the separation me/not-me has occurred, with the existence of a system of fantasies, including everything resulting from the repressed unconscious; as soon as the internal world already exists, the real experiences, satisfactory and unsatisfactory—and this refers to the reality of the global experience and not only to the pleasure principle—lead respectively to the existence of things felt as good or as bad in the child's internal reality. Although the objects and conflicts of the internal world are influenced by the relationships occurring in real life, internal life has a certain autonomy which allows it to be examined as something in itself. None of this is already established in the transitionality phase.

We must hence point out that the reality and symbolic character of the transitional object depend on the vivacity and reliability of the subjective object, which in turn depends on the permanence and vitality of the external object. The loss of the subjective object is "a great catastrophe", something that belongs to the order of things which Winnicott's theory terms unthinkable agonies. If the child "loses" the mother, if the mother disappears for too long a period, "the subjective object dies" and the symbolic capacity of the transitional object dissipates. For this reason, despite the importance of the symbolic character of the transitional object, Winnicott pointed out that what is initially important is not so much its symbolic value, but *its reality*.

What happens if a pattern of environmental failure is established during this phase, and the baby starts to lose reliability? When deprivation is not excessive, a compulsive use of the transitional object itself may occur, such as a dummy, with this use being a communication of the same sort as greediness. If the deprivation is serious and prolonged, the baby loses the capacity for sucking. At this stage, when the baby has just started to differentiate from the mother, the loss is not only of the object, but of a part of himself, for example, the mouth. Indeed, the very capacity for play, sucking the tip of the blanket, playing with the mouth or the fists, tickling the nose, loses meaning.[8] If the baby loses the transitional object, which is sustained by the corresponding subjective ones, he loses the mouth and the breast at the same time, creativity and the path to objective perception.

Contact with reality depends fundamentally on creativity, without which no reality, not even the external one—and perhaps above all the external one—can be reached or have meaning. The reality with which we are concerned here is not that of the reality principle, as formulated by

Freud, but rather that of the feeling of real that is founded on an illusion. It is only by means of this feeling of real that the sense of external reality is reached.[9] However, the transitional object "is one of the bridges that make contact possible between the individual psyche and external reality" (1965k, p. 192). Losing the transitional object as a consequence of the mother's failure to keep the subjective world alive results in disbelief and hopelessness regarding the capacity for relating to objects: interest in the object fades, with the baby knowing nothing about what has happened. He only feels that something very important has been lost, that something has died even though this something may be there, now devoid of meaning.[10]

Creativity is thus in the service of the contact with reality; it relates to being alive and to feeling real, it refers to the way in which the individual allows reality to emerge, to the way he welcomes events, that is, the way in which any person, whether a baby, a child, an adult, or an elderly person, looks at or accomplishes something. No special talent is required for this creativity. Creativity is also originary and is not a sublimation of the pulsional conflict.[11]

The potential space, as third area of experience, maintains open the permanent, insuperable tension between creating and discovering. Due to this tension, there is an excitement that is particular to the transitional phenomena and hence to playing, albeit which is not of an instinctual character; it refers essentially to the ego organisation, being a question here of a

> [...] part of the ego that is not a body-ego, that is not founded on the pattern of body *functioning* but is founded on body *experiences*. These experiences belong to object-relating of a non-orgiastic kind, or to what can be called ego-relatedness. (1967b, pp. 135–136)

Playing is exciting in itself, especially because of the precariousness that is inherent to it. Its territory is the interplay between personal psychic reality and the experience of controlling real objects. Because of spontaneity, because of what it lacks of form, because of the absence of rules, (which makes Winnicott insist on the difference between game and play), playing provides a limited experience of the emergence of something frightening, because it is unpredictable. It is easy to see how much the author differs from the Kleinian theory, on the basis of the new paradigm in which he is moving. In the former, the importance of playing lies not in itself but in the fact that by means of playing, unconscious and repressed phantasms come to light; for Klein, therefore, playing has the function of a masturbatory discharge, of controlling anxiety or fulfilling desire. In Winnicott's theory, on the other hand, the importance of playing lies not in the content, but in playing itself, in the type of concentration which characterises it, in the fact that the child is able to "lose himself" there, being plunged into a state of virtual detachment, which is related to the concentration in older children or in adults.

The stage of the use of an object

The topic of the development of capacity for using objects is entirely original in psychoanalytic literature. While much has been said about object relations based on mechanisms of projection and introjection, the ability to *use an object* and the requirements needed for this have never been considered. The formulation of this achievement derives naturally from the theory of maturational processes and is considered by the author to be one of the most complex and difficult points of his thought.

Any consideration regarding the capacity for using objects requires that we start from the conception that this capacity initially does not exist. In the maturation process, this achievement, as well as that of transitionality, continues that initiated at the stage of the theoretical first feed, which concerns the establishment of relations with external reality; it is only at this stage, however, that objects may start to be perceived and used as external ones. In order to achieve this, the mother must have been able, from the outset, to present the world to the baby in small doses and in a comprehensible manner, so that he has had the opportunity, through primary identification, to *be* the object (subjective). Subsequent to this, already during the de-adaptation period, the "mixed" reality of transitional objects (part of the baby and part of the world) leads the infant to *possess* the object. During the transitional phase, he continues to live in a subjective world, but the omnipotence characterising the basic illusion is shattered, and some small aspects of external reality are included in experiences. From a certain point onwards, these two senses of reality no longer suffice and the tendency towards maturation pushes the baby towards another sense of reality: that of external and shared reality, in which he can use objects, which are now seen from the perspective of objectivity.

Even during the primitive stages, while living in an entirely subjective world, the baby is being provided with experiences of contact with objects which, since they arrive as subjective objects, are small samples of external reality (from the observer's perspective). Repeated experiences with these objects, not only become part of the baby through primary identification, but also gradually render the object meaningful, even though he does not yet know of his separate existence.[12] This will emerge with full clarity when the baby elects and attaches himself to the transitional object. Until this point is reached, we are still in the field of what is termed "object relating", although at this stage, the expression is inaccurate, since there is no actual relation with subjective objects as there are not yet two entities. From this point onwards, if all goes well, the baby can move from *relating to the object* to *using the object*. In order for this to occur, there must be a change for the baby regarding the "*nature of the object*", that is, a change in the sense of reality of that object, which implies the creation of a world other than the subjective one or the potential space. According to Winnicott, this change is one of the most difficult and significant achievements of maturation, in addition to constituting, when it fails to be accomplished, "the most irksome of all the early failures that come for mending" (1969d, p. 222).

What exactly is the point to which Winnicott draws attention when he distinguishes "object relating" from "object usage"? In terms of the maturational processes, object relating is prior to and the basis for the development of the capacity for using objects. While *object relating* is a kind of experience that allows us to think the individual as an isolated being, living in a world which consists of a bundle of projections[13] and communicating with subjective objects within the context of the illusion of omnipotence, *object usage* may only be described, in the same way that the capacity for *using objects* itself can only be effected, if the independent external reality of the object is considered. Since psychoanalysis has always preferred to eliminate all environmental factors, unless these could be considered in terms of projective mechanisms, it is much easier for analysts to examine object relating than object usage. When examining usage, however, there is no other way: the analyst "must take into account the nature of the object, not as a projection, but as a thing in itself" (1969d, p. 221).

This change in the *sense of reality of the object*, from object relating to object usage, does not occur with the mere passage of time. In order to use an object, the baby must develop the *capacity* for using objects, which implies him beginning to consider the object as a "thing in itself", external and separate from himself, in its property of having always been and continuing to be there independently of him and hence, outside his omnipotent control. In order for the object to be used, it "... must necessarily be real in the sense of being part of shared reality, not a bundle of projections" (1969d, p. 221). In this way,

> [...] between relating and use is the subject's placing of the object outside the area of the subject's omnipotent control; that is, the subject's perception of the object as an external phenomenon, not as a projective entity, in fact recognition of it as an entity in its own right. (1969d, p. 222)

It should be noted, from the quotation, that it is the infant who gives the object an external character. He does so by expelling the (subjective) object to outside the ambit of omnipotence: something (someone) which is part of the self or of the subjective world is detached or expelled, in order to be examined and/or attacked. Winnicott terms this operation of expulsion of the object as something that no longer belongs to the subjective world the "*destruction*" of the object. *The object which is destroyed by the baby is the subjective object.* In other words, it is the subjective character of the object that is being destroyed. The destructiveness that is implied here is not of an instinctual character, although it is supported by the experiences of primitive instinctual impulsiveness, which, at this point, has not yet been integrated as part of the self, and does not derive either from anger stemming from frustration. It is a destructiveness *without anger*, which refers to the individual's need, characteristic of maturation, to begin to inhabit a world which is not his projection and in which there are objects which, having their own existence, may be used. If the capacity for relation and communication of the little individual is restricted to the communication with subjective objects, which was indispensable during the stages of absolute dependence, over time, it becomes a dead end (cf. 1965j, p. 184).

How does the destructiveness which leads to the capacity for using objects manifest itself? In many different forms, which naturally come mixed with aggression of another nature such as the instinctual one. The baby who by now is physically stronger, begins, for example, to kick the mother or to effectively bite the breast; or makes an effort to wear it out; or even to reject it while observing the mother's reaction; or simply to stop needing it.[14] However a particular baby begins to destroy the object, which is still subjective, what characterises the phenomenon is that being neither hungry nor angry, the baby *needs to destroy* the object. That is to say, there is a *real drive to destroy* which must be experienced.

Winnicott's thesis is hence that there is a destruction, which is prior to the functioning of the reality principle, a destruction that *has a particular role in the creation of reality*, with the baby placing the object outside of the self, that is, outside the subjective world. What the individual is creating at this stage is not properly an object, but a new sense of reality, that of externality. "It is the destructive drive that creates the quality of externality" (1969d, p. 226). The destructive urgency has, therefore, a vital positive function, that of objectifying the object.[15] In 1970, the author wrote that we would not get anywhere with the study of aggression if we were to think of it as irrevocably connected to jealousy, to envy, to anger from frustration or to the instinctual functioning habitually termed as sadistic. (cf. 1989n, p. 287). For him, human aggressiveness and destructiveness are phenomena related to the issue of the constitution of reality: "More nearly basic is the concept of aggression as part of the exercise *that can lead to the discovery of objects that are external*" (1989n, p. 287).[16]

What must be highlighted here is that the conquest which is being achieved by *the experience of destruction depends on the survival of the object.*[17] Surviving, in this context, means not retaliating, not changing attitude, remaining reliably the same. The word "destruction" is required, affirms Winnicott, not so much because of the baby's drive to destroy, "but because of the object's liability not to survive, which also means to suffer change in quality, in attitude" (1969d, p. 225). The baby's drive to destroy is real, and he must experience it but can only do so if there is safety, that is, if there is no risk that the object will succumb. *In the event that the object survives,* the drive changes into the *capacity* for using the object which has survived. At the same time as it releases the baby to continue exercising the destructive drive, which is real, the survival of the object releases him to destroy objects in the unconscious fantasy. In other words, the survival of the object leads to the usage of the object, and the usage leads to the separation of two phenomena: the destruction in the unconscious fantasy and the placing of the object outside the area of projection. Winnicott illustrates how events would unfold and what the baby would tell the object in the circumstance of the destruction:

> "I destroyed you", and the object is there to receive the communication. From now on the subject says: "I destroyed you". "I love you". "You have value for me because of your survival of my destruction of you". "While I am loving you I am all the time destroying you in (unconscious) *fantasy*". (1969d, p. 222)

It should be noted that it is only from this moment onwards that fantasy starts for the individual,[18] inasmuch as it is here that the separation between fact (survival of the object) and fantasy (the destruction of the object in unconscious fantasy) takes place. After this achievement of maturation is accomplished, the subjective object will always be destroyed in the unconscious fantasy.

This accomplishment, the creation of the sense of external reality and the achievement of the capacity for using objects and for unconscious fantasy is so important for maturation and so difficult to describe conceptually that before we go any further, it is worth examining some differences and additions which were made to the theory as Winnicott's thought evolved. Even before 1968, when he arrived at the most complete formulation of this type of aggression, as destructiveness which leads to the creation of externality and to the capacity for using objects, Winnicott already stated that human aggression "is always linked in this way with the establishment of a clear distinction between what is the self and what is not the self" (1964c, p. 94). In this text of 1964, he still related aggression to the primitive instinctual drive and made no reference to the value of object survival. Aggression is exercised by the child, he observed, in the form of a magical destruction, which is hence of the same nature as magical creation, albeit in the opposite direction. Through this child's magic, the world can be annihilated in the twinkling of an eye and recreated through new eyes. The primitive or magical destruction of all objects is necessary for the object to cease to be part of the "me" and become "not-me", *"from being subjective phenomena to being perceived objectively"* (1964c, p. 98, emphasis added). Allowing time for the maturational process, the child "becomes able to be destructive and becomes able to hate and to kick and to scream instead of magically annihilating that world" (1964c, p. 98). In this formulation, the beginning of the achievement takes place with the child carrying out a magical destruction (that is hence not effective) which changes, over time, and with the development of the capacity for accepting that hate and love live together in human nature, into the real possibility for aggression. In this way, the author asserts, *"actual aggression is seen to be an achievement*. As compared with magical destruction, aggressive ideas and behaviour take on a positive value, and hate becomes a sign of civilization" (1964c, pp. 98–99).

What is new in the 1968 formulation is that this achievement starts with a *real drive* to destroy. That is, the baby, who is still ruthless, has by now a new muscular power and improved motor coordination and in order to continue with development, must expel the subjective objects from within the ambit of omnipotence. In order to achieve this, it effectively bites its mother, throws objects forcefully and is prepared to treat the transitional object brutally. All of this, which the mother must be capable of surviving, is accompanied by the still remorseless idea of having destroyed the object. If the object survives, meaning that it has an independent existence, the baby discovers that it may continue to destroy objects, albeit now within the realm of unconscious fantasy, because the object that it needs to use remains unscathed, which may thus be used.

The assumption underlying the concept of the destructiveness that creates the externality "goes right to the base of the existence of the human individual, and to the most fundamental aspect of object-relating". The axiom, postulates the author, is "[...] *what is good is always being destroyed*" (1986e, p. 262). In terms of the maturational process, what is the meaning of the need to destroy what is good? An answer to this question, says Winnicott, must point to the *actual qualities* of the good thing, that is, to the fact that the good thing *can survive because of its own real qualities.* That is, the object survives by itself and not because it is protected from destruction by the baby, since, after surviving destruction, the good thing will be loved, valued, and almost adored in a new way. This, notes the author, "has come through the test of being ruthlessly used and of having been the object, unprotected by us, of our most primitive impulses and ideas" (1986e, p. 263). If the baby has to protect the object due to its fragility, he will not make the necessary experience of destruction and will not come to relate to the external object, will not be able to use it, or to love or hate it. While initially referring to the mother, this will subsequently extend to the father and at a later stage, to all objects that are loved and cherished.[19]

In the theory of maturational processes, the capacity for love only emerges after destruction, the survival of the object and the advent of the capacity for destroying in the unconscious fantasy. It is true that Winnicott also speaks of primitive *love*, referring to the baby's excited states, charged with instinctual tension, but this "love" consists of needs and knows nothing of the external existence of the other. Love for the object that survives destruction is something completely different and is now the feeling of a me who, while incipient is whole and separate, directed at another individual, who is whole and separate. The prerequisite for this love is the same as for the exercise of mature genitality, not just a solitary exercise; in this case as well, the object must be perceived as external and separate from the individual. That is, love is also constituted within the maturational process.[20]

It follows from this that both objective reality and love depend on the fact that there is always destruction. This becomes the unconscious backdrop for the love for a real object, situated outside the area of omnipotent control of the subject. In order to demonstrate the fundamental character of this destructiveness which creates the externality and leads to the achievement of the relation to external reality, Winnicott reflects on the place of the Monarchy among British people, since they realise that "it is in the personal inner psychic reality that the thing is destroyed" (1986e, p. 263). It becomes clear that things survive due to their own properties independently of our dreams of destruction. This brings a great sense of relief into waking life and a new sense of confidence; "the world now begins to exist as a place in its own right; a place to live in, not as a place to fear or to be complied with or to be lost in [...]" (1986e, pp. 263–264).

The capacity for using an object, which includes its destruction as a subjective object, is perhaps the most difficult and painful achievement of the maturational process. If the mother succumbs to the destruction, the child will not be able to complete this passage. If she survives, assisting the child in the difficulties specific to that stage, the child will have the necessary time to acquire ways for dealing with the shock of realising the existence of a world situated outside of the child's control. In general, the passage from the subjective to the objective takes place through subtle gradations which accompany the changes characteristic of development, but without the participation of the mother, these changes occur abruptly and in ways that are unpredictable to the child (cf. 1964c, p. 98).[21] Instead of the child being the one who creates the world's externality, this bursts into his world. In this way, whilst the process of objectification of reality is taking place, the good enough mother will spare the child external changes. Thus protected, he will be free to play and experience everything within his personal psychic reality, both destructiveness and love; he will dream and in these dreams, there will be destruction and murder. Such dream activity, accompanied to some degree of bodily excitation, will constitute a concrete experience and not just an intellectual exercise. Destructiveness thus has a positive value, which is the paradoxical fact of being related to the creation of the externality of the world. Something is nevertheless lost; some subjective object has to be sacrificed as subjective, even though its subjective meaning does not disappear. Those who were nevertheless fortunate enough to succeed in creating a rich subjective world will always have a wealth of subjective objects which may be destroyed in favour of the shared reality which enriches experience.

In order to illustrate what happens when children cannot make the experience of destruction, Winnicott uses Jung's account of his early childhood in an autobiographical book.[22] Everything suggests, the author maintains, that Jung had no contact with his basic destructiveness. At the age of four, a framework of child schizophrenia was already installed: around a pathological split between the true and the false self, a defensive organisation was built against the danger of disintegration of the falsely integrated personality. At the basis of this split was a precocious external factor, his mother's depression, which was apparently compensated by his father's maternal attitude. When Jung was three years old, he suffered a psychotic breakdown relating to his parents' separation. The point emphasised by Winnicott, however, arises from Jung's account of the way in which he used to play; his play consisted of concrete and constant construction and destruction, with the building up of an edifice always followed by an earthquake that would destroy it. What does not appear in the material is the imaginative destruction followed by a feeling of guilt and then by construction. In other words, Jung does not describe himself playing constructively in relation to the fact of his *having destroyed* in his unconscious fantasy. This is understandable, observes Winnicott, since it is indeed extremely difficult for a child to achieve primitive destructiveness if he is cared for by a clinically depressed mother.[23] Since this had been his situation,

> [Jung] spent his life looking for a place to keep his inner psychic reality, although the task was indeed an impossible one. By the age of 4 he had adopted the sophisticated theory of the underground of the dream [...]. He went down under and found subjective life. At the same time he became a withdrawn person, with what was wrongly thought at the time to be a clinical depression. (1964b, p. 488)

In other words, the issue for Jung was not depression related to guilt or to responsibility for the aggression contained in instinctual impulsiveness, which is characteristic of the stage of concern as we shall see below. The question was a more primitive and basic one: the origin of Jung's difficulty is located, in terms of maturational processes, in the incapacity for the *destructiveness which creates externality*, which concomitantly establishes the self as a me separated from the not-me. The capacity for this destruction depends on the feeling of confidence that the object will survive. Jung could not destroy the mother in his fantasy, or expel her from his omnipotent control in order to constitute her as a separate person, in exteriority, since she had no chance of surviving. This difficulty undoubtedly gives rise to a depressive disorder, albeit of a nature which does not refer to the problems typical of the stage of concern, but which is linked to the despair, typical of personalities of the false self type, of achieving a personal reality which permits the establishment of real relations with the world and external objects.

Despite having demonstrated the need for the destruction of the good object in order to continue with the process which leads to the capacity for establishing relations with the reality objectively perceived, Winnicott did not make clear what it is, in terms of human nature, which requires that the good object, precisely the one created by the individual, is always destroyed.[24] I believe that this question refers to a fundamental problem, glimpsed but not developed by the author, the examination of which would require the assistance of a philosopher, a poet or, maybe, a schizoid in the Winnicottian sense.[25] We may perhaps believe that the good must be destroyed because what is important is creating and not the object that is created. The object, even the good one, must be destroyed, because after having been created, it becomes something of the world, an engagement, an attachment, something to which the identity remains linked or even imprisoned. The good must be destroyed to avoid the objectification of the human being, even with regard to his creations. What matters, what is vital and what makes life worth living is to be able to continue creating *ex nihilo*, from the essential aloneness, from primary creativity, as always.

The stage of I AM

It is at this stage, appropriately termed I AM, that the achievement of unity in an integrated *me* takes place. While it is not possible to determine the exact ages for the maturational achievements, the author suggests that around the age of eighteen months, children begin to establish the integration of the personality. This integration only achieves greater stability around the ages of two or three years. In any case, there is a well-defined point in the life of any child when he realises that he is a unitary existence, with some kind of established identity. If the child could talk, he would say: I AM.

The me which is achieved at this point is the result of a long process of integration which began with the primitive non-integrated self: throughout the initial stages, the various aspects of the personality were gradually integrated, including the instrumental false self, meaning that the me of unitary identity includes the true and the false self. Now, after having repeated experiences of expelling the mother from the ambit of omnipotence, during the previous stage, that is, after having objectified the mother and hence separated from her, at this stage of I AM, the child can separate from the total environment.

The unitary status of the me is not a cohesive whole, without fractures or free of conflicts, but a state of spatial-temporal integration, where "there is one self containing everything instead of dissociated elements that exist in compartments, or are scattered around and left lying about" (1971g, p. 90). With this achievement, we reach an end and a beginning, since the state of I AM, the feeling of being real and of existing as identity "is not an end in itself, it is a position from which life can be lived" (1989h, p. 435).

At this point, the child inhabits the body more firmly; he perceives himself as having a contour, with a limiting membrane, the skin, which separates him from everything that is not-me. Any not-me is repudiated as external; at the same time, the child now has an inside, a personal psychic reality, where memories from experiences may be collected and related, including all the formations of the repressed unconscious, which, added to the originary unconscious that is not repressed, but simply forgotten, enrich the infinitely complex structure belonging to the human being (cf. 1965k, p. 191; 1965q, p. 112).

The integration of the personality in a one-year-old child points to a remarkable change in the sense of independence. This is evidently not always true, but, at certain moments and in some relationships, it can be said that he already has an established identity. The child is already able to keep alive both the feeling of the presence of the mother and by incorporation, the memory of the care to which he is accustomed for far longer than the few months which was previously the case. With regard to personalisation, for most of the time, he remains firmly rooted in the body; when this is the case, not only does the use of the body reinforce the development of the unitary personality, but reinforces bodily functioning as well, promoting muscular tone, coordination, adaptation to temperature changes, etc. Integration is never a guaranteed state, however, either in a healthy adult or even less in a recently integrated baby. Everything is extremely variable at this age; not just from one child to another, but in the same child at different moments. It may well occur that in a healthy child the psyche loses contact with the body and there are circumstances in which it is not easy to restore this. If he is awakened and taken from the cradle in a moment when he is immersed in deep sleep, he will be startled and scared because of the abrupt change in body position at a moment when the psyche was absent from it.

In addition to the questions involving the daily routine of a one-year-old child, there are those related to the scope of integration itself. The moment when a sense of integration begins is an extremely difficult and vulnerable one. The baby sees the world and itself from a new position, the me. The daring of being a self, which now has boundaries marking a territory necessarily includes the repudiation of the not-me. The integration into a self is thus an act of hostility towards the not-me and brings along the expectation of an attack. The new individual feels himself to be "infinitely exposed" and will only be able to face and endure the struggles of this achievement at this point, "if someone has her arms round the infant at this time" (1965k, p. 148). This is the meaning of the affirmation that:

> [...] the most aggressive and therefore the most dangerous words in the languages of the world are to be found in the assertion I AM. It has to be admitted, however, that only those who have reached a stage at which they can make this assertion are really qualified as adult members of society. (1986d, p. 141)

For a certain amount of time, the experiences related to the achievement of unitary identity generate a state that could be called paranoid, and which constitutes one of the roots of the tendency towards paranoia.[26] In this situation, the protection provided by the mother is essential, since it lies "between the repudiated external world and the newly integrated individual" (1988, p. 121). The paranoid state, when refering to this achievement, is smaller when integration occurs at the original time specific to the achievement and potentially greater when the individual reaches integration at a late stage, as for example, in the case of an adult patient who is retracing the maturational path in psychoanalysis. Furthermore, since integration depends both on environmental provision and personal factors such as the pattern of personal impulsivity, of motility, sensibility, intelligence, etc, it may be favoured more by one of the factors involved than by another. Ultimately, the expectation of persecution is more frequent if integration occurs with the support, above all, of personal factors, some of which are hereditary. When the baby achieves integration basically due to environmental care, so that one could say that the self was somehow impelled to agglutinate, then a relative absence of expectation of persecution may occur and unlike in the previous alternative, there is a basis here for naïvety, for a certain incapacity to expect persecution and for an almost irrevocable dependence on good environmental provision (cf. 1988, p. 124).

In order to express the precarious situation of the recently integrated I AM, Winnicott alluded to the figure of Humpty Dumpty, the short round character of the traditional English song, the personification of an egg which falls from the wall, breaking itself into pieces. Winnicott says, the wall on which Humpty Dumpty is precariously perched, is like the mother who has ceased to offer her lap. The child needs time to explore this changeover stage thouroughly. He advances in certain directions but often needs to return and regress to situations which already appeared to have been overcome. He must be given the opportunity to experience several types of object relations during the same day and at times, simultaneously. A child may be entertained by playing with an aunt or a dog at the same time as he has some objective perceptions and makes creative discoveries. The next moment, he may merge into the cradle or the mother or with familiar smells and re-establish himself in a subjective environment. Throughout life, it is these familiar patterns of the child, those of the subjective world which, more than anything else, nourish him for all other types of relations with reality so that "when the child discovers the world there is always the return journey that makes sense" (1986d, p. 135).

Advancing towards the future and independence is also a "return journey", to one's origins. In the healthy individual, regardless of the degree of objectivity that he has been able to achieve, the subjective world remains the source of personal wealth and inalienable singularity. Despite the fact that the subjective and the objective never coincide, *it is possible to keep bridges open which allow for a transit between the various senses of reality*. The mature adult is capable of objectivity without losing touch with the personal imaginative world. He makes concessions to society via an instrumental false self without losing the thread which connects him to himself, that is, without the loss of primary spontaneity and creativity.

The maturational tasks continue. Achieving I AM status does not yet make the baby a whole person. It is nevertheless the platform, the position from where life may be lived. More specifically, it is the condition of possibility for the next stage, that of concern, in which the baby begins to feel concern regarding his instinctual impulsiveness and to worry about the results of the primitive love drive on itself and on others.

The stage of concern

Having achieved the status of a unitary me to some degree, the child is now capable of accomplishing the task of integrating instinctual life. When this integration is achieved more consistently, the child will become a whole person, capable of relating to whole persons. At the beginning of this stage, drives, which until now have been external to the person of the baby and invasive if the baby was not assisted in dealing with them, begin to be integrated, to have meaning and to be accessed with regard to their consequences. From ruthless, the baby now starts to feel *concerned* with the impulsiveness which dominates him during the excited moments, as if saying: "This has to do with me, this concerns me, this is my business"; the baby also becomes *anxious* since he begins to perceive that this impulsiveness affects and may hurt the other; he thus realises that he is the one who, with his own hands, makes "a hole, where previously there was a full body of richness" (1955c, p. 268) in the mother. The anxieties characteristic of this period are extremely complex, since concern relates not only to the effects of the voracious impulsiveness towards the object of excited love, but also to the consequences on the self of the experience of excitation (cf. 1988, p. 79). From then on, a feeling of guilt and of responsibility arises with regard to the destructiveness inherent to instinctual impulsiveness.

One of the most important things which occurs during this stage is that the child begins to perceive that not only is he one and the same person, whether he is excited or quiet, but also that the mother who takes care of him, changing and pampering him during the quiet states is the same person whom he vigorously attacks during the excited states. The mother has been and for some time will continue to be environment-mother and object-mother simultaneously; while the former was and continues to be tenderly loved and caressed, the latter is repeatedly damaged and destroyed. During the time when the child is combining the environment-mother and the object-mother into one person, the real mother must continue to play two roles, in each one playing her part in the task of caring for the baby. The mother is responsible for maintaining the environment safe and reliable and offering herself as the object to be used, consciously sucked, destroyed and a cause for concern:

> The object-mother has to be found to survive the instinct-driven episodes, which have now acquired the full force of fantasies of oral sadism and other results of fusion. Also, the environment-mother has a special function, which is to continue to be herself, to be empathic towards her infant, to be there to receive the spontaneous gesture, and to be pleased. (1963b, p. 76)

Up to this point, an enormous growth has taken place: from the mother–baby unit to the relation of a me to an external and separate not-me; from pre-ambivalence to ambivalence, from primary dissociation between quiet and excited states to a discrimination between these two states and an integration of both into the self. Even now, however, the baby can only relate to *one* other: the mother. All of the elaboration of the capacity for concern, guilt and responsibility for the damage provoked by instinctual impulsiveness occurs in an exclusively dual plane, within the relation of the baby to the mother, who only gradually becomes one only person to the child.

The task of integrating instinctuality, with all of its inherent aggressiveness, requires time and an on-going personal environment; in the lack of understanding on the part of the environment, of what is happening and of a certain type of care, this achievement cannot be made. Winnicott's argument is as follows: the human baby cannot cope with the weight of the guilt and fear resulting from the full realisation that the "aggressive" ideas and acts contained in the primitive ruthless love drive are directed towards the same person who takes care of him and on whom he continues to depend, now in a relative form. Since all this takes place within the dual relation and is elaborated with regard to the mother, the child must face these issues alone, since he "is not yet advanced enough to make use of the idea of a father intervening, and by intervening making the instinctual ideas safe" (1988, p. 70).

The tendency of the child who begins to face the fact that aggression is part of his nature is to project this aggression outwards, onto the world, which becomes populated with threats, establishing a vague and magical feeling of fear which spreads everywhere. It is the mother's receptive and protective availability that neutralises the retaliatory and magical character of these fears:

> As each infant begins to collect a vast experience of going on being in his or her own sweet way and to feel that a self exists, a self that could be independent of the mother, then fears begin to dominate the scene. These fears are primitive in nature, and are based on the infant's expectation of crude retaliations. The infant gets excited, with aggressive or destructive impulses or ideas, showing as screaming or wanting to bite, and immediately the world feels to be full of biting mouths and hostile teeth and claws and all kinds of threats. In this way the infant's world would be a terrifying place were it not for the mother's general protective role which hides these very great fears that belong to the infant's early experience of living. The mother (and I'm not forgetting the father) alters the quality of the small child's fears by being a human

> being. Gradually she becomes recognized, by the infant, as a human being. So instead of a world of magical retaliations the infant acquires a mother who understands, and who reacts to the infant's impulses. But the mother can be hurt or become angry. When I put it this way, you will see immediately that it makes an immense difference to the infant if the retaliatory forces become humanised. (1993c, pp. 105–106)

The resolution of this crucial difficulty, which consists of accepting that destructiveness is personal and coexists with love, depends on the child developing the capacity for repairing or, mending, to use the preferred expression of the author. The child has an urgent need to know that the damage may be fixed and repaired, that the hole can be mended, that even destructive ideas and actions may be balanced with some gifts. Only then will he feel free and safe to continue to exercise his own impulsiveness. This capacity will nevertheless only be developed

> [...] *if the mother holds the situation*, day by day, then the infant has time to sort out the rich imaginative results of instinctual experience, and to rescue something that is felt to be "good", supportive, acceptable, unhurting, and with this imaginatively to repair the damage done to the mother. (1988, p. 70; my italics)

The essential element here is the continuous presence of the mother, her survival for the entire period when the baby or the child is integrating the destructiveness which is a part of his own nature. First, for holding the situation: the mother remains there, alive and available, that is, accessible both physically and in the sense of not being preoccupied by something else during the necessary interval of time between the baby's aggressive attack, the advent of guilt and the gesture of repairing or mending. Second, for her survival value, which means not retaliating, not changing her attitude, not withdrawing because of feeling personally offended by any cannibalism of the baby, not adopting a moralistic attitude aiming at providing precocious education or training of the baby in civility. Surviving is not remaining indifferent or immune to what is happening; it does not mean permissiveness. The child now knows that he is hurting or wounding someone when he is excited; he knows and needs the mother to know it as well. The latter does not pretend that "it was nothing"; she does not play the martyr who endures the attack because, after all, this is her place as mother. No. If she is alive, she feels and defends herself: without tension, without fears regarding the cruel nature of the son, without reviving old stories of violence suffered. Surviving thus means that the mother does not renounce her role in the disillusionment process: she *can bear being hated*.[27]

The fact is the child must exercise his impulsiveness and faces the fear that the damage is irreversible. When the mother provides the opportunity for the "benign circle" of "hurting-made-good" to repeat itself countless times, the baby gradually comes to believe in the possibility of a remedy, in the constructive effort, and if good conditions for enduring the guilt are provided, he has more freedom for instinctual love.

> The result of a day-after-day reinforcement of the benign circle is that the infant becomes able to tolerate the hole (result of instinct love) Here then is the beginning of *guilt* feeling. This is the only true guilt, since implanted guilt is false to the self. (1955c, p. 270)

If several and alternating people take care of the baby, as in the case of an institution, the child loses the opportunity for mending (which must be done to the same person who was hurt) and the benign circle cannot be established. Nor are there conditions for these dynamics to take place when, even if they derive from the mother, care is impersonal and mechanical.

It is during the achievement of the capacity for concern that the child's temporalisation is established more consistently. His new awareness regarding the damage that he causes during moments of excitation is both retroactive and is projected into the future: he not only comes to know that he is now the one who, in the excitement of the moment, sucks, devours, wears out, in brief, causes damage to the mother, but also knows that he *has always done so, will continue to do so*. There is no remedy, the drive to live implies grasping, using, and devouring whatever is needed to stay alive. If, due to growing confidence in the act of repair, the child feels free to exercise his impulsiveness and, shortly afterwards, having felt guilty, makes the gesture: a smile, a caress, a cuddle, signaling that he has mended the mother's body, then the day's work is completed. When the benign circle fits entirely into a single day, "tomorrow's instincts can be awaited with limited fear. Sufficient unto the day is the evil thereof" (1988, p. 72). The achievement of the capacity for concern is thus followed by a more complete sense of time, since it is at this point that present, past, and future articulate themselves (cf. 1988, p. 34). Integration at the level of the whole person means responsibility, conscience, "the collection of memories, and by the bringing of the past, present and future into a relationship, it almost means the beginning of human psychology" (ibid., p. 119).

It should be noted that it is only at this point that a psychic life inhabited by internal conflicts begins: the child now has an inside and an outside; a personal and complex internal world, with fantasies and anxieties in opposition to the external world. The life that takes place in this internal world, in the manner of a soap opera, with plots and characters, is endowed with such autonomy that the growing complexity and richness of this internal world may be an object of consideration in itself; a terrible dispute takes place there between the destructive and the constructive tendencies of the personality, in addition to a special type of anxiety, the feeling of guilt derived from the idea that the destructive drive emerges precisely when love is operating. In this way, what is "good" is constantly threatened by what is "bad".[28] It is nevertheless this anxiety which, under favourable conditions, leads the child to constructive or actively loving behaviour, resurrecting the object and repairing what was damaged. It is this which later will form the foundation of every personal initiative or constructive work. The task of the good enough mother is to remain there, available to *acknowledge and receive the repairing gesture*. The baby's capacity for repair is very limited and he depends on someone acknowledging his "symbolic gift". If the child realises the damage and "no person can be found to accept a gift or to acknowledge effort to repair" (1958b, p. 207) then he will despair. In this event, the change from ruthlessness to concern and guilt is undone and aggressiveness reappears, sometimes implacably.

The child's tolerance of his own destructive drives, a tolerance constituted by the experience of the survival of the mother, results in the ability to enjoy ideas (even destructive ones) and the bodily excitement corresponding to them. Such development makes room "for the experience of concern, which is the basis for everything constructive" (1984c, p. 87). Without destructiveness, says Winnicott, there is no true love. For a long period of time,

> [...] the small child needs someone who is not only loved but who will accept potency (whether it be boy or girl) in terms of reparative and restitutive giving. In other words the small child must go on having a chance to give in relation to guilt belonging to instinctual experience, because this is the way of growth. There is dependence here of a high order, but not the absolute dependence of earliest phases. (1955c, p. 271)

In Winnicott's theory, it is in this way that the foundation of a *personal* morality is established, which is not imposed from outside or taught, which is not merely intellectual and apprehended, but which emerges naturally from the experience of the "original goodness", that is, of environmental reliability (cf. 1963d, p. 94). It is this experience that, by sustaining personal growth, leads to the awareness of the existence of the other and to the capacity for cross-identification, of putting oneself in another's place.[29] Living with the construction and destruction inherent to human nature is also the foundation for the capacity for play and later, for working and finding joy and fulfilment in work. It is also with regard to this achievement, where there is failure, that disorders may arise which may be covered by the term active depression or a certain type of paranoia and sometimes, the anti-social tendency.[30]

We should note that, in Winnicott, morality is established in a non-oedipal context and does not refer to a law or prohibition; what is essential to it is not defined in terms of adequacy or transgression, except secondarily, for the individual who is already socialised, but in terms of ensuring that the child can be him so that he also acquires the capacity of letting the other be as a self. Winnicott regarded morality as innate, in the sense that a tendency exists in every human being to develop a feeling of responsibility for one's own actions, although this achievement remains to be integrated into the personality via personal experience. As with all other aspects of human nature, the tendency is only realised if the environment facilitates it, initially providing the baby with the experience of original goodness, of being the object of understanding, concern, and respect.[31]

The elaboration of the capacity for concern is a long process. It is difficult to determine a starting date, other than the requirement of already possessing some degree of integration into a me, which will assume the blame. As a result of this, Winnicott does not agree that the task and achievements of this stage can be dated to the early days, weeks, or months of life, as Melaine Klein did in her theory of the "depressive position", since achieving this capacity requires "the development of a sense of time, on an appreciation of the difference between fact and fantasy, and above all on the fact of the integration of the individual" (1955c, p. 274). Since, however, between the initial condition of ruthlessness and the subsequent capacity for feeling concern and responsibility there is an entire period during which this capacity is in the process of being established, it is possible to find scattered signs of guilt around the age of six months[32] or before one year. With regard to the task specific to the stage, however, the process reaches its peak of elaboration around the age of two and a half, albeit without ever establishing itself consistently before the age of five. The difficulties at the beginning of the stage are evidently different from those arising at the end of it.

One of these differences consists of the fact that at some point starting from the second half of the elaboration of concern, the father enters the picture in the role of father, that is, as the third person and his existence and real presence become extremely important. At the start of the maturational process, the father existed only as a duplication of the maternal role. As we have already seen, even in this role, something of him was added, an aspect "which is hard and strict and unrelenting, intransigent, indestructible" (1986d, p. 131), which was experienced by the baby as an aspect of the mother. As the child accedes to the mother's separate and external existence, this aspect differentiates itself and becomes part of the father, who then becomes significant as a man, "who turns out to be a human being, someone who can be feared and hated and loved and respected" (1986d, p. 131).[33]

When the child realises that the father is a person other than the mother and glimpses the family triangle, he begins to see or imagine the exciting relationship which exists between the parents. This is crucial for his security, since the stability of the parental relationship, expressed by the parents' interest in each other, allows the child to begin to dream of taking the place of one of them, without the risk that this might actually become true. At a certain point, there is a shift in the way the child perceives the triangle: now it is he who is the third person. Winnicott terms this discovery—the perception of the triangle with the child at its vertex—the "primal scene".[34] If healthy, the child is capable of dealing with the anger resulting from this new awareness and to use it for masturbation, taking responsibility for the conscious and unconscious fantasies that accompany it.

It is with the father in this position, in relation to the mother, but in a situation which is still prior to the oedipal one, that a sense of family begins to be shaped for the child. It is the mother and the father together and the relationship between them plus the atmosphere that they both imprint on their home that provides the basis for the first circle beyond the mother's arms. This circle gradually widens to include grandparents, aunts and uncles, old friends, and even neighbours, but the central characteristics continue to bear the mark of the parents, some of which they bring from their own families. This sense of family includes that of a family history to which the small individual child very slowly comes to belong. This belonging to the family group provides the individual with the feeling of having roots, a lineage and provides the foundation for customs and traditions to be preserved. Family consistency and continuity also provide a second chance for the grown-up individual, when a return is needed: for the adolescent who, for example, needs to re-enact his primitive experiences, or even for a young person who goes out into the world, becoming increasingly independent, "though retaining the hole for creeping back into" (1989n, p. 288). In any such case, however, Winnicott says: "the precondition is clear. The precondition has to do with the mother, and with two parents together, and the family, and the extended family and the local social setting including the school, and so on" (1989n, p. 286).

Again with regard to the child's discovery of the place that he occupies in family life, we should point out that the capacity for dealing with the feelings generated by the primal scene leads to the establishment of another achievement of the utmost importance: the capacity for being alone. There are several studies in the psychoanalytic literature on the fear of being alone, or on the desire to be alone, but little has been said about the capacity for being alone. Although this capacity is only established in a consistent manner after the experience of the primal scene,[35] *"this experience is that of being alone, as an infant and small child, in the presence of mother"* (1958g, p. 30). That is to say, while still very young and before knowing of the existence of the environment, the baby could be alone, in quietness or close to essential aloneness, due to the reliability on the mother's continuous presence and care. "In the course of time the individual introjects the ego-supportive mother and in this way becomes able to be alone without frequent reference to the mother or mother symbol" (1958g, p. 32).

The child now begins to *count on the father* to do his part, consisting of protecting the mother from the attacks of the child himself during the moments of the excited drive. It is here that the intransigent and indestructible element of the father helps the child to release himself to instinctual life and its consequences. The presence of a strong, intervening father, who provides this type of security makes the instinctual ideas and actions safer, allowing the child to run the risk of moving, acting, and getting excited, since the father is present, ready to remedy the damages or, with his strength, to prevent them from happening (cf. 1989l, p. 184). The father becomes the necessary support in the search for instinctual satisfaction without much danger. If this kind of assistance cannot be provided due to the father's absence or to the mother's depression, the child will become inhibited and will lose the capacity for excited love. He will have to adopt a precocious self-control of drives, before he is capable of doing so on the basis of a paternal strength that would have been gradually incorporated as his. In these cases, there is inhibition of the spontaneity and of the drive, in addition to a permanent fear that some aspects of the destructiveness escape control. The result may be depression or one form of anti-social tendency.

What is more, without the experience of counting on the father to place limits on the instinctual drive, the child is later unable, at the oedipal stage, to rival the father, to have the experience of a confrontation which is highly necessary for his development. The child's need, specific to this stage, is to count on the availability and survival of the mother and on the firmness of the father. This becomes especially clear in the study of anti-social tendencies, when it is possible to distinguish two types of deprivation:

> One is in terms of loss of object and the other is in terms of loss of frames, loss of controls. In a sense you could say loss of mother and loss of father—the paternal father, not the standing-in-for-mother father. The thing is the frame, the strength—the deprivation in terms of that. (1989f, p. 578)

The lack of frame for containing the picture and the resulting non-incorporation of limits becomes evident in cases of fully developed delinquency, especially when it involves theft and destruction. What stands out in these cases, says the author, "is the child's acute need for the strict father, who will protect mother when she is found. The strict father that the child evokes may also be loving, but he must first be strict and strong" (1946, p. 116).[36]

Throughout the whole of the stage of concern, while the child is trying to deal with the aggression contained in instinctual life, instinctuality is being integrated, along with a growing sense of the parts of the body, thus strengthening personalisation and spatialisation. It is approximately at this point that an important aspect of sexual development occurs. Excitations become increasingly localised. Both phallic erection and clitoral excitation begin to take on an importance of their own. Until then these excitations were possible, but did not have the sexual and gender character that they now acquire; prior to now, they were associated with the excitation of food or the thought of food and, shortly afterwards, with the activities of excretion. As has been already indicated, in these pre-genital phases, despite the emergence in the baby of all sorts of excitation, including those of a genital character, there was still insufficient maturity for the imaginative elaboration of the genital function.

At some point during the elaboration of the stage of concern, probably around the age of two, the child enters what Winnicott termed the exhibitionist or ostentatious phase, approximately the same as the one denominated by Freud as the phallic phase. This is the moment, in terms of the maturational process—and in terms of the development of gender and sexual identity as aspects of this process, in which the distinction between boys and girls starts to become meaningful. The central feature of the exhibitionist or phallic phase, relates to the obvious quality of the male organ, as opposed to the hidden quality of the female organ. Male genitals are thus central and sightly, with their erections and periodic sensitisations, whereas "the female state is a negative matter". The existence of this stage "marks the parting of the ways between the boy and girl infant" (1988, p. 41).[37] At the beginning of this phase, erection is the most important element. Both erection and the sensitisation of the clitoris arise in direct relation to a person who is actively loved or through ideas of rivalry with the loved person as background. Later, in the second phallic phase, there will be "a more open aim of penetration and impregnation, and here a real person is likely to be the object of love" (1988, p. 44). Since the excited experience is one of the ways through which the child inhabits his or her own body and relates to others, children who experience erections or vaginal contractions in relation to other people or to bodily functions are in a diferent and healthier position than boys and girls who do not have these integrative experiences (cf. 1986g, p. 145).

From the phallic phase onwards, along with the distinction of gender, we must also consider the fact of bisexuality: there is always a boy inside a girl and a girl inside a boy and this is especially undeniable in the case of girls. At this point, the evidence emerges that boys have something that girls do not; in addition to erection, they can, for example, urinate in a way that girls cannot. To varying degrees, they may feel inferior or mutilated and, in this case, "penis envy is a fact" (ibid., p. 186). The trauma that this may represent nevertheless varies, affirms Winnicott, and depends very much on external factors, such as the atitude and expectations of the parents, the nature and the position of the brothers in the family, etc. The frequent phenomenon of delusion among girls that there was a penis in them which no longer exists or that they have one which has yet to develop; the delusion among boys that girls have a penis, aiming to avoid the castration anxiety; in brief, the denial of the diference between being a male and being a female during the phallic stage is; for the author, a universal phenomenon, which belongs to this stage and which requires a good deal of healthy growth in order to be achieved as such. If the individual carries the burden of previous stages, such things may undoubtedly cause psychic disorders of varying degrees of severity, such as perversions or sadomasochist configurations.[38] In any case, experiences relating to gender difference, characteristic of this phase, are complex and difficulties arise both in health and in illness. The difference is that when there is a disorder, fantasy or play, which could help with the self-expression and integration of these aspects into the structure of personality, are prevented due to repression, which is a sophisticated defence mechanism for those who already have an inner life and instinctual conflicts connected to interpersonal relations. The difficulties of the phallic phase only assume an exaggerated importance, however, for those who on reaching it have already suffered previous deprivations of another nature.[39]

The examination of the tasks of this stage, in light of personal development, is especially important in order to relativise the seriousness of the difficulties of this period, as is supposed in traditional theory. Freud probably attributed the origin of psychoses to the threat of castration, which belongs to this period, due to the fact that, there was no place in his theory for the consideration of the previous stages in which the constitution of reality is processed. In order to account for psychoses, which he understood as a loss of reality or a disruption of the connection to reality, assuming that this was established, he chose the reality of castration as the paradigm of reality to be avoided.[40]

The oedipal stage

If the child truly achieves the capacity for experiencing the anxieties of the oedipal situation, this means that he is already established as a unitary identity. Being firmly integrated and having become a whole person as a result of having integrated the instincts and taken responsibility for the effects of instinctual impulsiveness, it may be said that he is no longer subject to the risk of psychosis.[41] He has now sufficient psychic health to be able to experience the difficulties inherent to instinctual life within the frame of triangular and interpersonal relations. In clear and explicit opposition to the Kleinian theory, Winnicott states that it only makes sense to speak of triangular relations or of the Oedipus complex when referring to the whole person:

> I cannot see value in the use of the term Oedipus Complex where one or more of the trio is a part object. In the Oedipus Complex, for me at least, each of the three of the triangle is a whole person, not only for the observer but also and especially for the child. (1988, p. 49)

Difficulties relating to the oedipal stage do not result from environmental failures or negligence, although these may complicate the resolution of the phase, but from difficulties of life and interpersonal relations and cannot be prevented by means of adequate care. During this period of life, even the healthiest child may present various neurotic symptoms: despite being vitally active, he suddenly looks pale and withered; he is sweet and affectionate but may suddenly be filled with rage, behaving cruelly towards animals or anything else; he has nightmares and drives away the mother who comes to console him; is very daring and, at the same time, manifests all kinds of fears; from time to time, he is suspicious of the food served to him, refusing to eat at home, but devouring anything at his grandparents' or neighbour's house. There is now an *internal world*, in which a whole life of intense and violent fantasies and feelings develop; instincts and bodily excitation are present in play, and identification occurs with either of the parents.

Mixed with the feelings which have been recently integrated and have become meaningful, it is the moments of excitation clearly determined by instinctuality which are most important; much of what is occurring between one excitation and the next relates either to the preparation for instinctual satisfaction or to the attempt to keep instincts under control or also, to the task of keeping them alive indirectly through play, through healthy masturbation (which is not compulsive) or through the dramatisation of a fantasy (cf. 1988, p. 54). When the child is healthy, he is in acute state of attraction towards the parent of the opposite sex, with tensions regarding the parental figure of the same gender, due to the ambivalence, that is to say, to the coexistence of love and hate. A major part of the child's emotional life remains unconscious and even in the most satisfactory of environments, the child has drives, ideas, fantasies, and dreams in which the unbearable conflict between love and hate unfolds, between the desire to preserve and that of destroying and in a more complex way, between the heterosexual and homosexual positions with regard to the identifications with the parents.[42] All of this indicates that the child is alive and elaborating the difficulties inherent to life.

Through the birth of another baby, for example, the child may nevertheless need to regress to patterns which have already been overcome, and even to dependence. If the child had a good start and his personality is structured, he loses nothing of his previous achievements. He may even exhibit regressed behaviour, but these are defences against anxiety arising from instinctual conflict. The main defence is repression, since, by now, a special type of unconscious has already been developed: *the repressed unconscious.* Maintaining repressed contents under control requires a huge amount of energy, due to the tendency they have to reappear in dreams, fantasies or to be projected onto external phenomena. A particular result of repression is the inhibition of instincts: there is loss of a part of the instinctive drive in the object relation and this may result in a serious impoverishment of the child's vital experience (cf. 1989p, p. 69).

If, on reacting to the arrival of his little brother, a child loses the phallic and genital characteristics of fantasy and of excited playing to the point even of losing achievements of integration such as psycho-somatic cohesion and the capacity for object relations, then this is no longer neurosis and an accurate observation will reveal that the child's development has in some sense been forced, having left important immaturities which now reveal themselves by means of a regression.[43] There are cases in which the child does not achieve any oedipal complex whatsoever; his development has been paralysed at a previous stage, so that "the true and full-blooded triangular relationships never became a fact" (1963c, p. 219). While they are not frequent, it is also possible to find cases in which a mixture occurs, of normality, insofar as the child is capable of experiencing the Oedipus complex, and psychosis, in the sense of immaturity, which remains restricted to a particular aspect (cf. 1963c, p. 219).

After the perception of the family triangle, the child begins to have *loyalty* problems. He is still inexperienced with feelings, especially those involving the triangular relationship, and needs a situation in which there is tolerance regarding what may seem disloyal, but which is merely an experiment forming part of his development (cf. 1986d, p. 138). He begins, for example, to establish a relationship with the father and in so doing, gains a new perspective; he comes to see things from the point of view of the father, thus developing a new attitude with regard to the mother:

> Not only can the mother be seen objectively from where the father is, but also the child develops an in-love type of relationship to the father which involves hate of the mother and fear of the mother. It is dangerous to go back to the mother from this position. There has been a

> gradual build-up, however, and the child returns to the mother and in this familiar orientation sees father objectively and the feelings of the child contain hate and fear. (1986d, p. 138)

If the father does not ensure this other perspective for the child, the child will have to deal with the need to move away from the mother on his own; he will have to exercise self-control and will experience considerable difficulty in elaborating the oedipal situation. A good example of this situation is found in a clinical note by Winnicott (1989o), regarding a patient whose problems, at the time described in the analysis, related to his sexual identity, which had been considerably hindered as a result of the type of relationship established with him by his mother during the initial stage and the absence of an effective father who would play his part. In addition to this difficulty mentioned above, the result for this young man of the primary relations was *complete inexperience regarding a certain position with regard to the father*, in other words, his ability to see the mother from the father's perspective. In analysis, this manifested itself in his impossibility to place and use the analyst in this position. As we shall see, this obstacle was particularly acute for the oedipal question. In the relevant passage, Winnicott states:

> [...] the whole hour was a muddle and no interpretation of mine was of any use. The patient was exasperated. What eventually did do some good was my interpreting that the analysis has continued in his relationship to his wife but here now, whatever it may have been at other times, he was working out his exasperation with his mother and his absolute hopelessness about dealing with her [...]. Eventually he felt that I had really met the situation when I said the home relationship is so much like your relationship to your mother that there is no man and therefore you cannot come to me because it is no use, there is no man to come to. There is no question of there being a father on whose knee you could sit looking at your mother, etc. (1989o, p. 186)

This toing and froing of the child must take place within the context of the mother–father relationship, although it is not necessarily restricted to it: it may also occur with the child going to the nanny and coming back to the mother, or going to the grandmother, aunt or older sister. These possibilities may be experienced within the family and the child may gradually be reconciled with the fears associated with them. These fears include instinctuality and the child may enjoy excitation in relation to these conflicts, provided that it is permitted and contained by the adults and may be elaborated in play. Perhaps, Winnicott observes, "the tremendous interest that children have in playing fathers and mothers derives from a gradual widening out of the experiencing of the experimentation with disloyalties" (1986d, p. 138).

What is the role of the environment at this stage? The more we advance in maturation, the less important the environment becomes for the structuring of personality. It nevertheless continues to be important in another way: the child needs a stable domestic environment in which he feels safe, in order to play and dream and elaborate his internal life, which is convulsed by the coexistence of love and hate, without having to worry about the stability of home. For this purpose, the family structure must remain solid and survive the constant tests caused by internal turbulence. It is within the family that the child can move forward step by step, from the relationship between three people to other, ever more complex circles. The author nevertheless points out "it is the simple triangle that presents the difficulties, and the full richness of human experience" (1988, p. 39).

The nature and behaviour of the parents, the place of the child within the family, among other factors, affect the classic picture known as the Oedipus complex. If, for example, the father is at the table during breakfast, the child will feel safe to dream that he will be run over by a car or that someone's husband is shot during a robbery. If, however, the father is absent, the dream will be terrifying, causing feelings of guilt or a state of depression (cf. 1989p, p. 68). There is a huge difference in the nature of the difficulties of a child according to the history of his development and the type of problem which must be confronted at this point. A father who is weak or incapable of playing his part is one thing; the collapse of the family due to discord or even the separation of the parents is another. When the family proves to be solid and enduring, it functions as a frame of reference which gives the child the feeling that it is safe to have feelings and even aggressive actions. This allows the child to explore crudely destructive activities which are related to movement in general and more specifically those activities which take place within the fantasy formed around hate. On this couse, due to environment safety, with the mother supported by father, etc., the child becomes capable of doing something very complex, namely, of integrating his destructive and love drives; with the result that the child acknowledges

> the reality of the destructive ideas inherent to living and to loving, and finds a way of protecting himself and the people and the objects that he loves. [...]. In order to achieve this in his development, the child *absolutely requires an environment that is indestructible in essential respects.* (1968e, p. 94)

When there is deprivation, for example, in terms of breakdown of the family, something very serious happens to the psychic organisation of the child. He becomes insecure about his ideas and aggressive impulses. Immediately,

> [...] the child takes over the control that has been lost and becomes identified with the framework, the result being that he loses his own impulsiveness and spontaneity. There is much too much anxiety now for experimentation which could result in his coming to terms with his own aggression. (1968e, pp. 94–95)

To an ever increasing degree, we must be able to deal with the fact that nowadays, families break up more easily than when Winnicott formulated his theory. The theory of maturational processes nevertheless remains essential for parents who, while they dissolve their marital life, want to maintain the emotional stability and development of their children. It is no certainty that children will suffer more from the concrete, emotional, and geographical separation of their parents than they do when the parents stay under the same roof without having an emotional relationship or real communication. Since the parents have a perfect right to seek what they feel to be better for themselves, it is in any case important that each one of them continues to perform his role with regard to the child. They may need to be even more present and not neglect the care and orientation required by their children, for whom some form of explanation of what happened, accessible at their level of maturity, is vital, and that the parents, no matter how disappointed and angry, do not begin to denigrate each other's parental image.

The child's sexual life now reaches the primacy of genitality. When this is achieved, fantasy is already enriched with the typical masculine and feminine acts of penetrating and being penetrated or impregnating and being impregnated (cf. 1988, p. 41). The important fact continues to be erection as a part of a relationship, but it is now associated with the idea of provoking irreversible changes to the body of the beloved person.[44] The child is capable of genital sexual experiences with all of the fantasies and excitation which accompany it and this constitutes a new potency, even if physical immaturity obliges him or her to postpone the capacity to proceed with the genital act which potentially leads to procreation until puberty. When, at a much later stage, puberty arrives bringing with it another level of potency, the experiences and fantasies realised during childhood will be of immense help to the new condition.

Any study on instinctuality which requires action, that is, an act of doing, especially with regard to the genital phase, is more adequate for the description of the male than of the female.[45] On the male side, it is possible to distinguish accurately between the fantasy of the phallic experience and that of the genital experience, both in the boy and in the boy-in-the-girl. Whereas during the phallic phase, the boy's performance is in line with his fantasy, in the genital phase, his performance is deficient with regard to his fantasy; this gap calls the boy's potency into question and as we shall see, this will have a meaning in the oedipal situation, as is redescribed by Winnicott. Furthermore, differently from the girl, the boy is "complete" in the phallic phase, whereas, in the genital phase, he *depends on the female in order to complete himself.*

Even if it is not as evident as in the male, feminine genitality cannot be defined only in negative terms: the woman is not a castrated male. The penis envy experienced during the phallic phase does not necessarily establish itself as the determinant of feminine sexuality, unless there is already a split masculine component in the girl, triggered previously. When in an adult woman, this split pure masculine element[46] has been potentialised by a painful experience of penis envy, in the exhibitionist phase, a defensive organisation is established which may be regimented and put at the service of the ideological aspect of a social struggle such as the feminist movement. A significant example of this situation is found in a letter by the Bulgarian psychoanalyst and linguist Julia Kristeva to the French essayist Catherine Clément.[47] Writen while her son was in a Paris hospital for a surgical operation, Julia wrote to Catherine that a popular saying kept running through her head: "Nothing is more sacred for a woman, than the life of her child" (p. 56). After commenting that this sentence constitutes one of those banal pieces of popular wisdom that has always held true and which may lend itself to mockeries such as "what a shame that women stick to children, don't you find?", she writes:

> The great, subtle pediatrician, the English psychoanalyst Winnicott has a curious idea I like, namely, that the mother's primordial connection to her child stems from "being", and is distinguished from "doing", which occur only later, with the drive, desire, and acts. Like you, it occurred to me that the "serenity of Being" imagined by Heidegger may be rooted in these zones of experience, if one chooses to see such things with an anthropologist's eye. *She is* simply *there*, the mother, with a part of her that is already an *other*. *Being there with*: the dawn of difference. Peace, recognition, devotion. It is not that she "does" nothing, but the eagerness

> for action is suspended in a capable tenderness. Seduction, affect, drive, desires—the assets of the lover she was, barely nine months earlier, are not destroyed but deferred, "inhibited regarding the goal" (as my colleagues, the female psychoanalysts who have read their Freud, would say). I distrust that suggestion of inhibition; I prefer to speak of waiting. The serenity of maternal love is a deferred eros, desired in waiting. [...] It is truly at the dawn of the mother's connection to the child that a miraculous alchemy occurs: the "object" of erotic satisfaction, the father (or some relationship, profession or gratification) is slowly resored into a loved, and only loved, "other". Love-tenderness takes the place of erotic love: the "object" of satisfaction is transformed into an "other"—to care for—to nourish. (Clément & Kristeva, 2001, pp. 56–57)

Despite being infused by the traditional psychoanalytic perspective, the above citation demonstrates that Kristeva-as-mother understands well the distinctive character of maternal love and the distinction between "being" and "doing" proposed by Winnicott, in addition to drawing an interesting connection to the issue of the serenity of the second Heidegger, referring it to this peculiar region of human experience. This serene maternal love, which is typically feminine, anything but phallic and is constituted by the identification with the mother herself and to the women's lineage, nevertheless seems to stifle her, since later in the letter she herself states:

> [...] it is here that I take my distance somewhat from the kindly Winnicott. Even though I find that serenity of the mother–baby being seductive, I only half-believe in it. Per female narcissism, that "other me" of the child is a "me me" all the same: the mother is never short on the tendency to annex the cherished other, to project herself onto it, to monopolize it, to dominate it, to suffocate it. [...] Moreover, the mother also remains a woman, with her desires and her erotic or professional "doing", and that tension of existence (that bisexuality, if you prefer) is continually interfering with her serenity and her connection to the child. A warm, conflictual connection, laden with all the noise of the world. And fortunately so! Without that pulsating, active, phallic share of maternal love, where would the call of language come from, the thrill of breaking free, that erection (yes, I say the word and insist upon it), which allow the mother and baby to stand up, to move beyond each other toward third parties? (Clément & Kristeva, 2001, pp. 57–58)

This citation not only demonstrates a vigorous reassertion of femininity constituted in the masculine line of penis envy, but also a suspicion about the possibility of a woman entirely surrendering herself to maternity, even if only temporarily and also, of being able to let the child be.[48]

For Winnicott, however, the imaginative elaboration of genital functions shows that genitality incorporates much of what is pre-genital, with this being truer for the feminine side of human nature. There is a basic feminine fantasy and sexuality which have their origins in the earliest childhood, founded on the girl's identification with the feminine side of human nature: identification with the mother and through her with the female lineage. This means that the elements pertaining to girls participate more in the category of *woman* than do those of the boys in the category of *man*. The fantasies relating to complete genitality, being penetrated, pregnancy, breastfeeding etc., which are still concretely remote, appear associated, in games and in dreams, with the girl's capacity to identify herself with the mother and the woman. In girls, ideas about genitality:

> [...] find fullest expression through identification with mother or with older girls who are able to experience and to conceive. The little girl's play, in so far as she is *truly female*, is of type that shows a mothering tendency [...]. (1988, p. 46; my italics)

The identification of the girl with what could be termed a "feminine lineage" is a recurrent theme in Winnicott's work. According to him, even if we can see that the vagina of a little baby becomes active and excitable on the occasion of breastfeeding and anal experiences, in fact, "the true female genital functioning tends to be hidden, if not actually secret" (1988, p. 46). When, at a later stage, genital eroticism is intensified and appears, for example, in compulsive masturbation, normally, "the type of fantasy is of collecting and of secrecy and of hiding" (1988, p. 46). That is why any description of feminine sexuality must include the girl's fantasies regarding her insides and those of her mother. Unlike boys, girls are led to think and to feel the inside of the body very early and throughout their lives. The ability to keep a secret, for example, is a characteristic which typically belongs to the feminine side of human nature; if a girl cannot keep a secret she will not become pregnant. From the masculine side, the tendency is to fight and to push things into holes. If the boy cannot develop this aggressive aspect of his nature, he will subsequently be incapable of deliberate impregnation of a woman.

Winnicott's central thesis that every woman has always belonged to the female lineage means that, unlike men, who are one and become increasingly more unified, the woman is always a trio. It is this trio that is often represented in the famous figuration, the painting of the Three Graces. There are always three women in every woman: girl baby, woman female/mother, and mother's mother (cf. 1986g, p. 192). Or, in another formulation: female infant, veiled bride, and old woman (cf. 1988, p. 47). They are always all three from the start: when the mother takes care of the little baby, she does so in accordance with the care that she has received, that is, by the hand of her own mother, so that something of the grandmother becomes part of the girl; when, shortly afterwards, the girl plays and generally does so by taking care of a doll, putting a little house in order, cooking, etc., this is the mother herself and the grandmother. During adolescence and in youth, the woman blossoms as a female and, there is a lot of the fragile cuddly girl in her as well as of the seductive woman who attracts the male both for sexual relations and to make her a mother. In the elderly woman, as the female withers away, the little baby increasingly installs herself, requiring care from the grown up children, at the same time as she continues to be the mother who now takes care of the grandchildren.

> Whether a woman has babies or not, she is in this infinite series; she is baby, mother and grandmother [...]. This enables her to be very deceitful. She can be a sweet little thing to catch her man, and then become a dominating wife–mother, and later gracious grandmother. It's all the same because she starts off three, while man starts off with a tremendous urge to be one. One is one and all alone, and ever more shall be so. (1986g, p. 192)

In any case, with regard to the constitution of sexual identity, we must also consider bisexuality, especially in the context of fantasy and in relation to the capacity for identification with any of the parents. Leaving aside other aspects which may intervene in this particular case, the main factor which determines this identity is the gender of the person with whom the child is in love at the critical age, that is, between weaning and the latency period (cf. 1988, p. 48). Although it is easier and more convenient for the individual to develop in a way that is largely congruent with the characteristics of his or her physical constitution, "society gains much if it can tolerate the homosexual as well as the heterosexual in the emotional development of children" (1988, p. 48). If the development of the boy's personality is going well from other perspectives, a strong identification with the mother, including effeminate behaviour, may be valuable for exploring many potentialities. In girls, a certain masculinity is not only tolerated, but also expected and valued.

In healthy instinctual and emotional development, in addition to these identifications, girls effectively pass through a moment when they feel inferior because they do not have a penis, so that the male-in-the-female is always present and is always important, albeit not necessarily decisive. Penis envy must not be ignored as a source of powerful motivations in girls and in women, with this becoming clear, above all, in the analysis of neuroses in women. Conversely, femininity in the boy, to the same extent as his masculinity, is fundamental, albeit variable, as a function of several hereditary characteristics, environmental influences, identification with parents and wider cultural patterns. With regard to the boy's identification with his mother, we must distinguish between his capacity to identify with the woman in terms of her female genitality and his identification with her in her role as mother. This latter is more accepted within the culture and less problematic for the male genitality of the boy, since it is more closely related to the type of fantasy than to the localisation and the imaginative elaboration of bodily functions.

With regard to girls, however, even when they develop their femininity including some element of penis envy, which belongs to the masculine aspect of the development of sexual identity, correcting the "defect" is not as in Freud, in having a son by the father, but by acknowledging the dependence on the other. Winnicott describes the sequence through which, under normal conditions, the envy of the penis is overcome. In order to face the superiority of boys, the girl imagines having a penis growing in her. She then thinks that she already had one, which was taken from her as a punishment for excitation. This is then followed by the idea that since she does not have a penis, she may use one by proxy, that is, some male may act on her behalf. She will then say something like: "I shall let the male use me. In this way I get a deficiency made up but acknowledge a dependence on the male for completeness" (1988, p. 45). This, says Winnicott, is how the girl discovers "the true female genital" (1988, p. 45).

It should be noted that, while the "true genital" refers to the female, to the wreathed and veiled bride of the trio of women, in the strict line of elaboration belonging to the phallic phase of sexual development, true femininity, including genitality, belongs to the line of personal maturation and necessarily combines the female-woman with the potential mother through the girl's identification with the mother and the female lineage. This means that although the male-in-the-female is always present and penis envy is a fact at a certain point of the development of sexuality, this kind of resolution fails to account for true feminine sexuality and if the sexual identity of the woman is built on the problem of penis envy, the path will be precarious.

The constitution of sexual identity, as well as gender differences, are elaborated by Winnicott within a theory of sexuality belonging to the theory of instinctuality, which is in turn a part of the maturational process. At a later stage in his thought, more precisely in 1966, and driven by his clinical work, the author was led to perceive another aspect of bisexuality and to formulate the concepts of "pure female element" and "pure male element", both present in girls and boys, men and women.[49] I understand that the term "pure" specifically seeks to mean that while refering to the bisexuality present in the human individual and in each case, interfering with the constitution of the sexual identity, the pure female and male elements are not in themselves of an instinctual or sexual character, nor do they relate to the individual's biological gender. Furthermore, due to their nature, they are not repressed and, instead, it may occur that they are split off from the total personality.

These elements constitute a new way of formulating the two modes of object relation: the relation with subjective objects (pure female element) and the relation with objects perceived objectively (pure male element). The "pure female element" relates to *being*, to the experience of primary identity, in which one *is* the same as the other (the baby *is* the object), an experience that takes place within the context of the illusion of omnipotence, with subjective objects. In normal development, the pure female elemento presides over the relation of both girls and boys with their mother. The "pure male element", which occurs only later in the maturational process, relates to *doing*; it is based on instinctual drive and already presupposes the establishment of a me, as an integrated identity, separated from the not-me and the world, as external reality. If everything goes well, *doing* only arises at the point when instinctuality is being integrated as part of personality. In brief, while the female element *is*, the male element *does*. *Doing*, says Winnicott, must come after and on top of *being*.

It is only in terms of the pure male element that the distinction between active and passive makes sense, that is to say, between an active relationship (doing something with the object), or a passive allowing oneself to relate to (allowing to be done to oneself), with each of these atitudes being supported by the instinctual drive. It nevertheless must be noted that, while based on instinct, which demands action, the *doing* of the pure male element is not instinctual in itself.

According to the author, this new approach greatly enriched his understanding both of bisexuality and of the constitution of identity, including sexual identity, since it led him to clarify an essential dilemma of the human being, which must operate at a very early date, namely the conflict "between being the object which also has the property of being, and by contrast a confrontation with the object which involves activity and object-relating that is backed by instinct or drive" (1972, p. 191).

The insight which led Winnicott to this new level of theoretical understanding, by the realisation of the phenomenon consisting of the presence, both in men and women, of a pure female or male element, of the other sex, which is not biological, split off from the total personality, occured to him during the analysis of a middle-aged man, who was married, had a family, and was professionally successful (the patient FM)[50]. This man had already undergone a long analysis following a traditional line, but continued seeking help, since he felt that something very important had not been achieved. At a moment prior to the stage of analysis at which he was able to formulate the question in terms of a split-off pure feminine element, Winnicott already knew, because of the patient's frequent compulsive fantasies about being a woman, that a complete exploration regarding the feminine self which inhabited him would be necessary. The previous analysis of this patient had also required regression to a state in which "at the centre there is nothing" (cf. 1989r, p. 51). On this occasion, it was found that his entire life had been built as reactions to invasions which he, so to speak, collected, since this was how he managed to feel active and potent in different areas and at different levels. While in regression, he had to set aside many things, including his potency, since this proved to be entirely reactive. After achieving and managing to remain as nothing for a few sessions, the only tolerable state after acknowledging that it was the only real one in his life, the patient began to reveal himself in a positive manner. At the end of one session in which the theme was thouroughly elaborated, he spoke of the sensation of being tightly wrapped between the legs and the effect that this had on his genital organs and on his ability to urinate. In view of the material that he already had, Winnicott interpreted that while he was a baby, his mother had probably arranged his nappies in way that would be appropriate for a girl; with the possible result that he had never been free to urinate as a boy, pointing out that it would have been very different had he been born in a cabin in the forest and lived freely with nature. The patient immediately captured the meaning of what it would be to urinate freely. In a subsequent session, the patient told him that from what he could remember, that was the first time he felt that his penis was his own. "It looks", said Winnicott, "as if this is the beginning of his potency which he has never had although in fact he has a family" (1989r, p. 52).

The way in which the case unfolded and in which Winnicott dealt with the trasference enabled him to formulate a new aspect of the same problem: the-girl-in-the-boy, or the feminine self, in that man, could be seen as a *split-off pure female element*, which, despite being part of his sexual identity, was not properly sexual and had been dissociated from personality at a very primitive stage. This condition, the author pointed out, had nothing to do with homosexuality. The basis of this split-off pure female element, as we have seen, resided in the fact that when he was a baby, the patient had been the object of a delirious cross-identification: his mother had seen a girl in him and had treated him physically as such, making him ajust to the mother's idea that her baby was a girl. The point here is not so much how the mother saw him or whether she had wished for a girl, but the fact that she had translated this conception into a type of care that suited a girl and not a boy. The imaginative elaboration of the sensation did the rest.

The analytical situation which made possible the new understanding was that, at a certain point after the elaboration mentioned above, the man started to mention something that could be understood as penis envy (cf. 1971i, p. 170). Winnicott told him:

> I am listening to a girl. I know perfectly well that you are a man but I am listening to a girl, and I am talking to a girl. I am telling this girl: 'You are talking about penis envy'. (1971i, p. 170)

After a break, the patient said: "If I were to tell someone about this girl I would be called mad" (ibid.). The issue could have ended there, but Winnicott decided to take it further and made the observation which surprised himself and which, with regard to transference, touched the core of the problem. Winnicott observed: "It was not that *you* told this to anyone; it is *I* who see a girl and hear a girl talking, when actually there is a man on my couch. The mad person is *myself*" (1971i, p. 171). It was not necessary to elaborate it, the author wrote, because he hit the target.

The patient then said that now he felt sane in a mad environment. That is, he had been released from his dilemma. Winnicott observed: "This madness which was mine [when he took on the madness of the mother who saw a girl where there was a boy] enabled him to see himself as a girl *from my position*. He knows himself to be a man, and never doubts that he is a man" (1971i, p. 171). The patient said later: "I myself could never say (knowing myself to be a man) 'I am a girl'. I am not mad that way. But you said it, and you have spoken to both parts of me" (1971i, p. 171).

In a case such as this one, the analyst must be able to accompany, tolerate, and even provide the patient with the full experience of delirious identification. "It could be said", says the author, "that the patient was in search of the right kind of mad analyst and that in order to meet his needs I had to assume that role" (1971i, p. 189). With regard to this new understanding, he noted that

> [...] Here was no new theoretical concept, here was no new principle of technique. In fact, I and my patient had been over this ground before. Yet we had here something new, new in my own attitude and new in his capacity to make use of my interpretative work. [...] I found myself with a new edge to an old weapon. (1971i, pp. 172–173)

Returning to the more general questions concerning the oedipal stage, it must be said that although the child is capable of having genital experiences, he must wait until puberty in order to be capable to realise his fantasy, which means that at the genital phase the child's ego is able to deal with a tremendous quantity of frustration (cf. 1988, p. 44). The focal point here, and this is one of the aspects presiding over Winnicott's redescription of oedipal themes and the anxiety of castration, is that the child *must deal with impotency*. As a result, from this perspective, the presence of an intervenor father brings great relief; "fear of castration by the rival father becomes welcome as an alternative to the agony of impotence" (1988, p. 44).

Assuming there was a good start, it is possible to examine the different defences used by the child to deal with the anxieties resulting from the Oedipus complex. In the triangular relation, the child "is overtaken by instinct and loves. This love involves physical and fantasy changes and is violent. It leads to hate. The child hates the third person" (1988, p. 54). The boy may be in love with the mother and, as we have already seen, the existence of the intervening father provides relief for the agony of real impotence. This is nevertheless only one side of the story. The other one is that he lives the painful conflict of ambivalence in which he perceives himself to hate, wishing to castrate or kill the father and fearing retaliation regarding fear of castration by the father whom he loves and trusts, because he is in love with his wife.

If the child is healthy and the foundations of the home are solid, anxiety stemming from this situation can be tolerated and he eventually recovers from the moments of high instinctual tension. The fact is that hate may now appear freely, since "[...] what is hated is a person, one who can defend himself, and one who is already loved"; and someone "[...] who can survive and punish and forgive" (1988, p. 54). If this is actually experienced, as a result of the father doing his part, then he begins to be used as "prototype of conscience". Incorporating the father whom he knows, the boy reaches an agreement with him: on one side, he loses something of his instinctual potential capacity, renouncing part of what he had been claiming; on the other side, he shifts the love object to a sister, aunt, nanny, that is, someone who is less involved with the father. At best,

> [...] the boy enters into a homosexual pact with the father, so that his potency becomes not entirely individual but instead (through identification) a new expression of the father's potency that has been taken in and adopted. [...] By identification with the father or father-figure the boy gets a potency by proxy, and a postponed potency of his own, which can be recovered at puberty. (1988, p. 55)

If, due to absence or incapacity, the father does not intervene during the oedipal phase, this is perceived by the boy as a non-acknowledgement and a non-legitimation of his potency and also deprives him of the experience of rivalry. The central issue in the oedipal situation described by Winnicott is not just the threat of castration but, due to the establishment of rivalry, the legitimation of the child's potency. In other words, there are more and other ambivalences in the oedipal situation than those indicated by traditional theory. The rivalry between the boy and the father, regarding the oedipal question, does not necessarily include deadly hatred and the boy, who needs the experience of rivalry, under reliable conditions does not necessarily want to kill the father.[51] Child aggression in the traditional psychoanalytical lexicon has assimilated with destruction, hatred, hostility, anger, and a similar confusion, resulting from the use of these terms as synonyms, led to no few consequences with regard to the analytical work.

There are cases in which the difficulties of the oedipal phase already derive from the stage of concern, with the child having had to inhibit his instinctual drives since he could not depend on the active presence of a father who would protect the mother from his impulsiveness. This was the case of patient B, the protagonist of the book *Holding and Interpretation* (1986a). His main issue during the second period of his analysis, related to the problems of the stage of concern (cf. 1986a, p. 21), in addition to him showing a split in the mind with regard to the psyche-*soma*. The achievements relating to the capacity for concern had been made difficult not only due to the difficult relationship established with the mother, but also as a result of the fact that his father had been more maternal than paternal, and could not play his role when the boy needed him to do so.[52] At a certain point, when patient B embarked on an intellectual digression on the prohibition of incest, Winnicott told him:

> You are using society's prohibition of incest between son and mother because you cannot find the man who will get in between you and your mother, which means that father did not play his part here, and so you have no hate and no fear of man and you are back in the old position of either being frustrated by the woman or else developing an internal inhibition. (1986a, p. 82)

On another occasion, while mentioning a dream, the patient said: "To sum up, my own problem is how to find a struggle that never was. In the dream it was the struggle that was missing". Winnicott answered: "You were not able to get the relief that the triangular situation brings when a child is in a clash with father; relief from the struggle with mother alone" (1986a, p. 165).

In addition to the difficulties arising from the impossibility for the father to play his part, this young man could not develop the necessary homosexual relation with the father during the phallic phase and could not identify with him. At a certain moment in analysis, when it became clear that his affective and sexual choices had always been directed towards "the girl with the penis of adolescent dreams" the patient observed: "I might be looking for a man, which would be a kind of homosexuality, which would imply that I'm an effeminate type of man". Winnicott replied:

> No, I don't think so. The fact is you are looking for father, the man who prohibits intercourse with mother. Remember the dream in which the girl friend originally appeared and this was about a man, one who was ill. (1986a, p. 77)

The patient noted:

> This would account for my lack of grief or of feeling when my father died. He had not met me as a rival and so left me with the awful burden of making the prohibitions myself. (Ibid)

The analyst observed:

> Yes, on the one hand he never did you the honour of recognizing your maturity by banning intercourse with mother, but also he deprived you of the enjoyment of rivalry and of the friendship that comes out of rivalry with men. So you had to develop a general inhibition, and you could not mourn a father you have never "killed". (Ibid)

Instinctual tension, which is characteristic of this period, reaches its peak at some point between the ages of three and five or six, when it is either resolved or shelved, also on account of the endocrinological phenomenon of suspension of instinctual tension during the latency period. During this period, when the child is healthy, the child experiments with play, dreams, and fantasies, deriving a benefit from the identification with the parents and other adults. The immature pre-genital and genital experiences, which are within the child's reach, include the body and bodily pleasures which do not depend on the help of others. If there is reliable family support, if someone remains present and calm, the child begins to realise that the passage of time, sometimes hours or perhaps minutes, brings relief for practically everything, however intolerable it might seem. Child sexuality, says Winnicott, is something very real. It may or may not be mature by the time the transformations of latency appear, bringing relief. If sexuality is "immature or distorted or inhibited at the end of this first period of interpersonal relationships, so will it reappear as immature or distorted or inhibited at puberty" (1988, pp. 57–58).

Puberty and adolescence

If, at the age of puberty, sexuality is not mature, the individual will not be able to face the important and difficult physical changes associated with this phase and personal maturation itself, which emerges during adolescence. Even for the healthy youngster, there is no escape from the anxieties which result from this passage; however, the way the individual will deal with them depends essentially on the pattern, which was previously established, during childhood. The child who was well cared for is able to tolerate, to a certain extent, the new feelings and strangeness which arise from body changes and which do not depend on him, as well as to avoid, refuse, or defend himself from situations involving unbearable anxiety. Of this acquired pattern, which is largely unconscious, also make part residues of some inevitable early failures. On the other hand, it is of great help for the individual when puberty provides a potential for male potency, and its equivalent for girls, that is, when full genitality has already become a characteristic since it has been achieved in the reality of playing during the phase preceeding the latency period. However,

> boys and girls at puberty are not deceived into thinking that instinctual drives are all, and in fact they are essentially concerned with being, with being somewhere, with feeling real, and with achieving a degree of object constancy. (1971f, p. 25)

Yet nothing ensures the absence of problems. There is no cure for puberty or adolescence and the only thing to do is give time and survive the turbulence, which may even be greater, the better the start, since the sense of freedom and of personal richness do not make things any simpler.

During puberty, to the important alterations resulting from physical growth and the development of sexuality are added the physical capacity for genital experience and for actually killing (cf. 1965c). In other words, an overwhelming and frightening potency arises, since what once belonged to the realm of fantasy can now become concrete reality: the power to destroy and even to kill, the possibility of prostituting oneself, being impregnated, going mad on drugs, commiting suicide.

Another point to be mentioned—and in that, the psychology of the adolescent may greatly help to understand the nature of psychotic suffering—are the typical anxieties of adolescence, which repeat those of the primitive stages: the adolescent, like the baby, is essentially isolated. Furthermore, like the baby, it is only from this isolation that he may launch himself and come to establish some relation which is felt as real. The group phenomenon in adolescence is that of a collection of isolated individuals who attempt to form an aggregation around some common interest or preoccupation, albeit with the personal self receded and protected. Isolation is also associated with a feature of sexuality, more precisely, with sexual indefinition: the child does not know yet if he will be heterosexual or homosexual, unless environmental patterns force definition. There is a long period of uncertainty during which, in general, an unstoppable masturbatory activity occurs, which should be understood not so much as sexual activity, but rather as a way of *getting rid of sex*. The same may occur to heterosexual or homosexual experiences which, far from being a form of union between complete human beings, are rather a way of discharging tension. When there is immaturity in instinctual life, "then there is danger of ill health in the individual, in personality or character or behaviour" (1971f, p. 26). In this case, we must remember "that sex can operate as a part–function so that, although sex may seem to be working well, potency and its female equivalent can be found to deplete, instead of enrich, the individual" (1971f, p. 26).

What indicates that the adolescence repeats the patterns of the primitive stages is the fact that the child suffers from the feeling of irreality, with the main struggle relating to feeling real. There exists in the adolescent a rigid morality not in terms of what was socially established as good and bad, which is precisely what he despises and rebels against, but in terms of what is felt as real and what is felt as false: the adolescent does not accept false solutions. What is worst, what is intolerable is to betray oneself. Like the psychotic, the adolescent cannot compromise. Some acquiescence, which is a part of health and necessary for conviviality, becomes a threat of personal extinction (cf. 1962). This is a particularly difficult period for the individual who, having not had a good start, bears with him the threat of disintegration, since adolescence drags him close to collapse. On the contrary, for the individual who had a good start, time will take care of many things, in case the family environment survives and remains reliable. In anyway, throughout adolescence, there will certainly be acute management problems and the need for firm support and reliability, since growing up means occupying the place of the genitor: "In the unconscious fantasy, growing up is inherently an aggressive act [...]. If the child is to become adult, then this move is achieved over the dead body of an adult" (1969a, pp. 169–170).

Adult age

Having emerged relatively unscathed from adolescence, it is possible to discriminate at least four tasks, which, interdependent of each other, await the individual in adult life. Even for those who had a good start, the first task is to continue to develop and staying alive, even in old age, until death. Naturally, this depends on the preservation of primary creativity, on the capacity to allow oneself to be hit by events and to continue to surprise oneself:[53] "Each member of the adult community is growing, and continues to grow, we hope, throughout life" (1961b, p. 44). At the same time, if the individual was able to experience omnipotence at the appropriate time, with maturity, he gives up being the steering wheel and adopts a more comfortable position of being a piece in the gear, even because, at this point, it is not the place that he has in society which tells him who he is. If, however, he did not have the opportunity to begin life with the small experience of being omnipotent, he may become someone who needs to exacerbate omnipotence, creativity, and control; something like "trying to sell unwanted shares in a bogus company" (1986h, p. 50). The mature adult, on the contrary, is capable of creativity without losing contact with the richness of the subjective world; the adult can make concessions without feeling robbed of spontaneity. Health is related to condescendence and imposture and when maturation elapses favourably,

> the individual becomes able to deceive, to lie, to compromise, to accept conflict as a fact and to abandon the extreme ideas of perfection and an opposite to perfection that make existence intolerable. Capacity for compromise is not a characteristic of the insane. (1988, pp. 137–138)

The second, more specific task would be the fact that, once personal maturity is achieved, which includes the idea of value and that there are people and things which deserve to be preserved, there gradually emerges social maturity and what booms and flourishes with it is the capacity for valuing and promoting, when possible, the democratic way of life (cf. 1950a,

p. 243, note 3). Democracy is one of the most important achievements and, simultaneously, a remarkable contribution of the healthy adult to society, but it can only become possible with the existence of a good proportion of individuals who have been successful in their personal maturational process. Winnicott resumes this point several times in his work: society depends essentially on its healthy members, since it is precisely those individuals who have achieved maturity who are capable of establishing and ensuring the "[…] *innate tendency towards the creation and re-creation and maintenance of the democratic machinery*" (1950a, p. 243). Viewed from this perspective, it necessarily involves having to ensure the family institution: "In this way, democracy (in one meaning of the word) is an indication of health because it airses naturally out of the family, which is in itself a construct for which healthy individuals are responsible" (1971f, p. 38).

> Society depends on the integration of family units, but I think it is important to remember that these family units in turn depend on the integration which takes place in the growth of each individual member. In other words, in a healthy society, one in which democracy can flourish, a proportion of the individuals must have achieved a satisfactory integration *in their own personality development*. The idea of democracy and the democratic way of life arises out of the healthy and the natural growth of the individual, and can be maintained in no way except by the integration of the individual personality, multiplied of course many times according to the number of healthy or relatively healthy individuals […] to carry the unintegrated personalities who cannot contribute in, otherwise society degenerates from democracy. (1961b, p. 47)

The same position is corroborated in *Human Nature*:

> In a community in which there is a sufficiently high proportion of mature individuals there is a state of affairs which provides the basis for what is called democracy. If the proportion of mature individuals is below a certain number, democracy is not something which can become a political fact since affairs will be swayed by the immature, that is to say, by those who by identification with the community lose their own individuality or by those who never achieve more than the attitude of the individual dependent upon society. (1988, p. 152)[54]

We shall see now the third task, which consists of the acceptance of impotence and of imperfection. People, the author observes, have to

> […] accept what they are and the history of their personal development along with the local environmental attitudes and influences, and they have to get on with life and living, attempting to interweave with society in such a way that there is a cross-contribution. (1986g, p. 188)

Having to face imperfections of the me and of the world, as they are, often causes depression. When it is not mutilating, or linked to psychotic disorders, however, depression is a state of spirit proper of truly responsible people, of those who are really valuable. They get depressed precisely because they are able to see and to accept the precariousness of human condition and the fact that the world is never the way we imagine it; and also because they clearly realise that their capacity for loving and for constructing coexists with their own hate, wickedness, and destructiveness. Depression is thus inherent to life and to maturity. This may be terrible, but not being able to doubt or to suffer perturbations is a condition which is even worse (cf. 1965o, p. 52). "The fact is that the sense of *doubt* is very close to its opposite which is *belief*, and to a sense of values, and to the feeling that *there are things worth preserving*" (1965o, p. 52). Most likely, the greatest suffering in the human universe is the suffering of the normal, healthy, or mature person: "Unhappy is a you or a me who, over a phase, is conscious of the lack of what is essential to the human being, much more important than eating or than physical survival" (1986h, p. 44).

All this is linked to the fourth, and perhaps, most important and difficult task of adulthood: to be able to age and to die. At this point, the fact that integration can never be fully achieved emerges thoroughly. What always lacks, to man is his own end. In October of 1970, shortly before his death in January 1971, while addressing an association of social workers for maladjusted children, Winnicott mentioned a type of growth "to becoming smaller": "If I live long enough I hope I may dwindle and become small enough to get through the little hole called dying" (1984g, p. 220). Learning to die, however, is only possible for someone who has lived and has had experiences. It is only possible to have lived and to continue to live having achieved the unitary status which makes it possible to say I AM. Only from this condition is it possible both to live and to die. "There is no death", says Winnicott, "except of a totality" (1984f, p. 61). When there is a sense of wholeness in personal integration, this brings with it

> […] the *possibility* and indeed the *certainty of death*; and with the acceptance of death there can come a great relief, relief from fear of the alternatives, such as disintegration, or ghosts—that is the lingering on of spirit phenomena after the death of the somatic half of the psycho-somatic partnership. (1984h, pp. 61–62)[55]

Fearsome is the internal death. Even when healthy, no one is safe from losing that which links them to life and to the meaning of life. The question always remains: why is it that creative living can be lost and why the individual's feeling that life is real or meaningful can disappear? (cf. 1971g, p. 93). Grateful to one of his patients for the expression "phenomenal death", Winnicott affirms: "many men and woman spend their lives wondering whether to find a solution by suicide, that is, sending the body to death which has already happened to the psyche" (1974, p. 93).

The return to the origin

The maturational process begins with "the first awakening". We can now ask: where and how does it end?

In *Human Nature*, Winnicott tries to bring together these two extreme moments of human existence. Refering to the beginning of maturation, he asks:

> What is the state of the human individual as the being emerges out of not being? […] What is the fundamental state to which every individual, however old and with whatever experiences, can return in order to start again? (1988, p. 131)

His answer is as simple as it is unexpected: *if the individual were to re-start, he or she would have to return to the state of essential aloneness.* Since, "at the start is an essential aloneness" (1988, p. 132).

Perhaps we should understand that human life constitutes an attempt to forget this aloneness. An attempt that is always frustrated, since the essential aloneness remains throughout life as an occult backdrop, untouchable and unspeakable, shadow of nothingness, inscribed in the very bosom of the origin and with which "there is no communication with the not-me world either way" (1965j, p. 189). Winnicott does not tire from emphasising the need which we have [...]

> to recognize this aspect of health: the non-communicating central self, for ever immune from the reality principle, and for ever silent. Here communication is not non-verbal; it is, like the music of the spheres, absolutely personal. It belongs to being alive. And in health, it is out of this that communication naturally arises. (1965j, p. 192)

Astonishing affirmation, which points to a dimension of isolation, elusive for any mundane event, yet inherent to being alive. Winnicott also says that,

> Except at the start there is never exactly reproduced this fundamental and inherent aloneness. Nevertheless throughout the life of an individual there continues a fundamental unalterable and inherent aloneness, along with which goes unawareness of the conditions that are essential to the state of aloneness. (1988, p. 132)

What can we understand from this? The sentence "[...] except at the start [...]" refers to the affirmation that "at the start is an essential aloneness". The essential aloneness of the beginning will be, therefore, overcome, transposed, in some sense, since "there is never exactly reproduced this fundamental and inherent aloneness" (1988, p. 132). At the same time, however, that the inherent state of aloneness is altered, *something of it remains and there continues to be a fundamental aloneness*. It is thus, a split, a basic split which lies at the very root of human existence and remains "uncurable": while something remains as an untouchable background, forever lonely, another part of the individual is launched into the light of the world, in order to inhabit it, so that life, which includes living close to things and with the other, may establish itself and happen.

The individual only "knows" of essential aloneness when, through the experience of the "first awakening", life enters the extreme quieteness of the beginning: "The experience of the first awakening gives the human individual the idea that there is a peaceful state of unaliveness that can be peacefully reached by an extreme of regression" (1988, p. 132). Although the baby or the foetus has no capacity to worry about death, "there must be, however, a capacity in every infant for concern about the aloneness of pre-dependence since this has been experienced [.... .]" (1988, p. 133).

What does all this have to do with the final moment of the maturational process? Winnicott has another surprising answer: it is the same as the initial state. "Most of what is commonly said and felt about death is about this first state *before aliveness*, where aloneness is a fact and long before dependence is encountered" (1988, p. 132).

Winnicott identifies the end of the maturational process with the initial moment. In this way, maturation as a whole is characterised as a process of return to the origin, as a *circular* movement which goes back to the place where it started. He leaves no doubts: the state prior to the essential aloneness is a state of not-being-alive. It is to this state, which T. S. Eliot called "pure simplicity, costing not less than everything", that the human individual necessarily returns: "The life of an individual is an interval between two states of unaliveness. The first of these, out of which aliveness arises, colours ideas people have about the second death" (Winnicott, 1988, p. 132).

Second death? The first one is prior to the beginning, whence being emerges from not-being and, from there on, the path is a journey towards the second one. There is a nothingness prior to the start and a nothingness after the end. Life consists of the interval between these two nothingnesses. Life does not rule absolutely, however, as an event immune to these two nothingnesses. They traverse it from end to end. It is by means of this fundamental link that "there is no enjoyment of company except as a development from essential isolation, the isolation that reappears as the individual dies" (1984b, p. 111).

In death, which is the great return, the essential aloneness will close onto itself, completing the life cycle. While the individual is still alive, it will remain as a background, as a non-configurable reserve which delivers man to the task of existing as unprecedented and personal history, without the support of any determination, sustained only by the illusion of the power to create. It will also remain as a matrix for all possibilities of return, of retreat by the individual who, when healthy, needs to rest from the task of existing and of permanently having to separate fantasy from reality, of what is perceived subjectively from what is perceived objectively. Essential aloneness is the only true and unknowingly desired quietness, which comes closest to the condition of pure simplicity that costs nothing less than everything.

On the inside cover of the notebook where Winnicott started to write his autobiography, which would be entitled *Not Less Than All*, there is a fragment from T. S. Eliot's *Four Quartets:*

> What we call the beginning is often the end
> And to make an end is to make a beginning
> The end is where we start from. (Eliot, 1980, pp. 144–145)

Brief comparison of the theory of maturational processes with the traditional psychoanalytic theory of the development of sexual functions

Elaborated from the author's experience of babies and psychotics, Winnicottian psychoanalysis is based on the theory of maturational processes, meaning a process of integration starting from a state of unintegration, which gives special emphasis to the primitive tasks of constitution of the self and access to the senses of reality. The issue here is the baby in the mother's lap. Traditional psychoanalysis, developed from the study and treatment of neurosis, is based on the theory of the development of sexuality in terms of object relations oriented by the pleasure principle, which privileges the Oedipus complex, that is, the child in the mother's bed.[56] There are fundamental differences between these two theoretical frameworks of psychoanalysis. With regard to the theoretical premises, some of these differences were cited at the end of Chapter One. I shall point out here some differences between the Winnicottian theory of maturational processes and the traditional theory of the development of sexual functions.

According to Winnicott, the theory of the development of sexual functions ignores the initial stages of maturation, taking for granted certain acquisitions regarding the structuring of personality: the constitution of the reality of the self and of the external world. These initial achievements should on no account be presumed or regarded as an automatic result of growth. It is the experience of dealing with these tasks of maturation and their successful resolution which constitute the foundations of psychic health. Psychosis is precisely the failure to achieve them and in this case, there will not even be an individual there, who, answering for a me, may become entangled in intrapsychic conflicts to the point of suffering from the vicissitudes characteristic of instinctual life and interpersonal relationships.

Another distinction between Winnicott's maturational paradigm and the oedipal paradigm of traditional psychoanalysis lies in the fact that at the basis of Freud's understanding of neuroses is the psychic conflict, the theoretical foundation of which is pulsional duality. Freud could not change this concept, since he ran the risk of losing the entire theoretical construction of psychoanalysis.[57] For Winnicott, however, moving along another theoretical horizon, there is no need to conceive of pulsional forces in conflict in order to set life in motion and provide theoretical support for the difficulties, impasses, and disorders, even the most primitive ones. What drives life and the psyche is the very fact that the baby is alive and carries within him the innate tendency towards integration; it is from this that the tasks and vital needs derive. Having to go on being and to develop already places the individual in the face of enough challenges and difficulties, bearing in mind, in particular, his situation of extreme dependence on environmental care, which may humanly fail at any time. It is thus not necessary to postulate instinctual and affective conflicts in order to explain the baby's primitive anxieties.

Freudian theory conceives of development in terms of the development of *sexual functions*. This derives from Freud's central thesis that neuroses are disorders which relate to a sexual conflict. The central theme of the conflict is the Oedipus complex, and it is within the resolution of the complex that the constitution of the subject occurs. Even when Freud becomes interested in psychoses, in attempting to respond to the theoretical impasses created by his theory of narcissism, the questions that he formulates derive from the same field configured for the understanding of neuroses. The inadequacy of his theory of psychoses is already established in his premises: Lacking the means to accept a domain of problems, which falls outside the pulsional conflict, Freud must fit psychotic pathologies into this domain. According to Winnicott, however, maturation does not refer to isolated functions, but specifically to integration into a wholeness and to the tendency to live as a unit. Even though personal maturation includes the gradual integration of instinctuality and the development of sexuality, it is not within this domain that the individual is constituted. There are people who, because their development was interrupted during primitive phases, will never attain sufficient maturity to suffer from problems inherent to the oedipal situation. In Winnicott's theory, there must be first an individual so that something like human sexuality may occur.

These are some of the reasons why Winnicott affirms that although it is much easier to describe the maturational processes with regard to instinctual functions than in terms of the ego and its complex evolution, this latter alternative can no longer be avoided. We may illustrate how, in the theory of maturational processes, Winnicott makes the achievements of the ego prevail over sexual functions, as well as how these achievements are considered as a condition for the possibility of instinctual life. Returning to an aspect of the development of instinctuality within the maturational process, that of the progression of instinctual dominance in accordance with the functions involved and the imaginative elaboration of these functions, Winnicott lists the pre-genital, phallic, and genital phases as the only important ones to be considered; in his view, the subdivision of phases, proposed by K. Abraham (erotic oral, sadistic oral; erotic anal, sadistic anal, etc.), are essentially unsatisfactory, since it consists of the application to the primitive stages, of the model of progression, ranging from the pre-genital to the genital and implying seeing the infant from what we already know about the child who walks, instead of seeing the baby in his immaturity.

Winnicott's central objection, however, is the fact that it is not the fantasy of oral activity that is initially erotic, that is, non-sadistic, pre-ambivalent, and only then, sadistic, destructive, and ambivalent. "It's better to say that is the infant who changes, starting ruthless and then becoming concerned" (1988, p. 42). The establishment of ambivalence is related to maturational changes of the self and not to the development of instinctual functions. Regardless of the phase of the process, the character of personal development remains. In the oedipal stage, for example, instinctual life, coupled with the achieving of genitality, will cause sexuality to gain prominence. This position, however, is not structural, but characteristic of this stage. Neurotic disorders are, as Freud described them, of a sexual character, but because the individual orbits the oedipal question and is stricken by the instinctual turbulence which accompanies it, he does not become an eminently instinctual or sexual being. His issues as a person remain as issues and, just as before, sexuality does not define or constitute him. In the clinical situation, the therapist must keep in mind the question of knowing whether someone is already there, a me who is there to be found, who feels alive and capable of giving meaning to instinctual life and sexuality, or whether, regardless of the content with which the individual cloaks his immaturity, for example, a false family soap opera, this therapist must be alert to the conditions which facilitate the constitution of the primary self.

Unlike in traditional psychoanalysis, the achievements of maturation do not occur automatically. The human baby depends, even in order to reach the point of being a baby, on the concrete and continuous presence of a facilitating environment. The process is not initially intrapsychic, but interpersonal, albeit, in the beginning, in a very peculiar sense. The dynamics of development, since they are taking place within a relationship of absolute dependence of the baby with regard to the environment, does not exclusively or mainly result from internal or constitutional factors, but from environmental facilitation. Furthermore, the primary relation with the environment mother is not initially object related. The baby is not yet a unitary me, who already has an internal world, within which the conflict between good and bad internal objects occurs; he is neither aware of the existence of an external world or of external objects. At the very outset, the "relation" with the mother is not even dual and must be described as a baby–mother unit of two-in-one. It is within this *sui generis* relationship, the reality of which is subjective, that the contact with external reality begins, albeit without the baby realising that is external. Since it is not even dual, the relationship is even less triangular. Nor can it be said to be erotic, since the baby is not governed by the pleasure principle, but by the need to be, to feel real, and to achieve existence in a real world. For this purpose, what he needs is the mother's reliability, personal communication with her, intimacy, and the opportunity to create the world.

With regard to the roots of aggression, it is easy to perceive Winnicott's disagreement with Freudian theory. For Freud, in the first topic, human aggression begins as a reaction to frustrations in the contact with the reality principle. In Winnicott's view, this theory fails to cover these roots, since "this anger at frustration does not go early enough" (1988, p. 79). That is to say, the baby is not mature enough to have desires, or to be frustrated or to feel angry about something that is external to him, since he does not have a sense of externality. Precisely because it did not examine the questions governing the initial stages of maturation, Freudian theory ignores two significant roots of aggression: the destructiveness inherent to the primitive instinctual drive (as early as 1939, Winnicott said that the babies "bite chiefly when they are excited, and not chiefly when frustrated" (cf. 1957b, p. 87) and the reactions to environmental invasions which interrupt the continuity of being.

In Freud's view, the mental mechanisms of projection and introjection are active from the outset and drive the psyche. According to Winnicott, the foundations of psychic health do not rest on mental mechanisms, nor do the initial tasks and their resolutions refer to mental processes. Many achievements are required before these processes enter into action. On the contrary, if mental processes were led to operate precociously, before some psycho-somatic integration is established and prior to the establishment of some "knowledge" of an experiential and non-mental nature, this will have a pathological defensive character and will lead to the establishment of a disorder of a schizophrenic type.

Furthermore, mental mechanisms are conceived by traditional theory according to a bodily model of incorporation and excretion. Winnicott's conception of primary creativity excludes the idea of a human psyche built on the basis of the projection of objects previously introjected, that is to say, digested, reprocessed, and expelled. An important theoretical element at the basis of this difference lies in the fact that for Freud and, to an exaggerated degree, for Melanie Klein, the judgment of attribution (good and bad) precedes that of existence. It follows that the constitution of the *Lust-Ich*, the originary pleasure-ego, may be thought of in terms of the projection of what is bad (not pleasurable) and the introjection of what is good (pleasurable), which also means that an inside and an outside would precede the existence of an individual. In Winnicott, the existence, the sense of real (subjective), necessarily precedes any judgment of attribution, which assumes the perception of the existence of the object. Furthermore, at the beginning, the "good" and the "bad" are articulated precisely with the existence, or non-existence, of something real in the subjective sense. Good is the experience which is real, even when it is frustrating; bad is the false experience, in which something seems to happen but does not.

Nor can Winnicott accept the recourse to phylogeny, on which Freud drew so extensively when, discovering the error in his first theory of seduction, he had to account for the effectiveness of fantasies of seduction. From then on, protofantasies (*Urphantasien*) were introduced into the theory, which consisted of typical phantasmatic structures, such as the originary scene, castration, seduction, which would organise psychic life, whatever the personal experiences of the individuals. Freud legitimated them through the argument that they constituted a phylogenetically transmitted inheritance. In Winnicott's view, only what the individual experiences may be considered as belonging to him; otherwise, it remains external.

Finally, for traditional psychoanalysis, culture, sociability, morality, and art are products which derive from the pulsional conflict via sublimation. Pulsions form their foundation, that is to say, transformed instincts. According to Winnicott, however, instincts are instincts, biological drives, and in this, there are no differences between human beings and animals, except insofar as in human beings, all bodily functioning is imaginatively elaborated, which does not occur even to the most interesting of animals. Moreover, if the individual begins by introjecting objects and then by projecting them, as the traditional theory states, then he is made of the world and there is no room for primary creativity. All creativity, including artistic creativity in general, is understood in terms of the sublimation of the libido. This is why the phenomenon of transitionality could not be conceived within traditional psychoanalysis. Winnicott sees the individual as creative not because he sublimates: he is creative because he is human. Creativity is primary and refers to the capacity which all human beings have for recreating the world.

This point may be illustrated by the difference between Freud and Winnicott in their approaches to artistic production and to art in general. According to the latter, the attempts by Freudian psychoanalysis to analyse artwork loses sight of the essentials. It may be possible to relate the work of artists to their childhood or to link themes in their work to their sexual inclinations, as, for example, was done for Leonardo da Vinci. Besides irritating artists and creative people in general, these studies circumvent the central question of creativity, giving the impression that it is possible to explain and determine the reasons why a particular person is capable of artistic realisation. The question which moves Winnicott on this point becomes even clearer if we examine the difference between his concept of play and that of Melanie Klein. When she observes children's play, she asks herself the question: which fantasies are expressed in this play? In Klein's view, play demonstrates the inhibitions and performs many *functions*: the fulfilling of desires, control of anxiety, masturbatory discharge, etc. Klein is not interested in play itself, but only in the symbolic *use* which the child makes of it; that is, the purposes served by play are more important than play itself. For Winniccott, this perspective not only ignores the essential aspect of play, but causes it to lose something of its clinical meaning: play is therapeutic, not because it expresses unconscious conflicts, but because it is a natural form of life and creativity in itself.

Many of the points cited above relate both to Freud and to Melanie Klein. More specifically with regard to Klein, the differences, on the one hand, are more complex and on the other, simpler. They are more complex because, while both Winnicott and Klein were seeking answers for the same primitive period, the differentiating line is more delicate and simpler because the foundations of Klein's theory are so clearly antagonistic to Winnicott's that in a sense, it is easier to trace their frontiers. I shall limit myself to point out the following differences:[58]

1. In order to explain certain primitive phenomena (such as precocious paranoia), Melanie Klein resorts to the constitutional factor, in this way putting an end to any discussion on the role of the environment. That is to say, she disregards the fact of dependence and the nature of the care that the baby receives. If we accept the initial situation of absolute dependence, however, a phenomenon such as precocious paranoia need not be attributed to heredity; we do not need to assume the existence of an evil entity operating in isolation; we can see in it a reaction of the baby to a pattern of environmental intrusions or to some sort of failure which leads to privation.
2. In Klein's view, what goes on with the baby is intrapsychic; she does not take into account the real interpersonal experience, which takes place in the subjective plane, except in terms of fantasy.

3. Klein's theory takes for granted that the baby is capable of establishing relations with *external* objects at the very start of life. Since, in Winnicott's view, this capacity is an achievement of the maturational process, which, in the event of failure, is specifically responsible for psychoses, this means that, from the author's perspective, the Kleinian assumptions in principle eliminate any possibility of an effective consideration by Kleinian theory of the initial stages of development and, as a consequence, of psychoses, particularly of those of a schizophrenic character.
4. According to Klein, these primary object relations occur with objects that are still partial, but in her view, the subject of the relation is already present; there is an *initial unit of the mind* which may be actively split by the destructive action of the death pulsion. This changes the whole perspective of research on the initial stages which could be considered as acceptable to Winnicott.[59]
5. In describing the phenomena of the primitive stages as pre-oedipal, Klein intended to elucidate psychoses by pushing back the same elements present in the theory of neuroses: she postulates the precocious Oedipus and introduces the father's penis into the dual baby/breast relationship, reconfiguring the triangle. For Winnicott, what happens in the primitive stages is not pre-oedipal, but non-oedipal; the tasks of the constitution of the self and of access to reality do not refer to pulsional issues, but to the baby's need to go on existing and take place in an exclusively dual plane. Furthermore, for Winnicott, it is not possible to speak of Oedipus, except with regard to whole persons and on no account to partial objects.
6. The type of disruption which Melanie Klein studies, concerning the depressive position, refers to the handling of weaning which, according to Winnicott, takes place approximately between the ages of nine and eighteen months. For him, however, *prior to weaning, there is the wider question of disillusion*. It is the mother who performs the role of disillusioning the baby. This can only be accomplished, however, on the basis of a previous stage in which the mother, because of her special adaptation, provides the baby with the illusion of omnipotence. It is only on the basis of illusion that disillusion may occur.

   "Weaning", says Winnicott, "implies successful feeding and disillusionment implies the successful provision of opportunity for illusion" (1953a, p. 221). Failures relating to weaning cannot cover schizophrenic phenomena, which are related to more primitive stages, the tasks of which are of a primordially different nature from those belonging to this moment of maturation. In order to arrive at psychoses of schizophrenic type it is indispensable to refer to the stages in which dependence is absolute:

   > To make progress towards a workable theory of psychosis, analysts must abandon the whole idea of schizophrenia and paranoia as seen in terms of regression from the Oedipus Complex. The aetiology of these disorders takes us *inevitably* to stages that precede the three-body relationship. The strange corollary is that there is at the root of psychosis an *external factor*. It is difficult for psychoanalysts to admit this after all the work they have done drawing attention to the internal factors in examining the aetiology of psycho-neurosis. (1989i, p. 246)

7. According to Winnicott, death does not make sense until the capacity for hating is achieved, implying the perception of the other as a complete human person; in addition to the others,

this is one of the reasons why the so-called death pulsion, or destruction, is unacceptable in the description of the basis of destructiveness.

8. In Klein's view, the psyche is constructed on the basis of bodily models of incorporation and expulsion; introjection and projection. This presupposes an inside and an outside which are already constituted, which, in Winnicott's view, is not possible for the baby in a state of non-integration.

In summary, these are Winnicott's reasons for affirming that the theory of libidinal development does not explain or provide treatment for the type of disorder affecting psychotics. Consequently, it cannot understand the basic problems of human nature revealed by psychosis.

Notes

1. If the mother is healthy and manages to be aware of her feelings, she will certainly hate the baby circumstantially and, as we saw in Chapter Two, she will do something such as complain under her breath, albeit without taking any revenge on the baby. The mother's *unconscious* hate, is something completely different, for which two different situations should be distinguished, which affect the baby differently: if the mother is depressive or depressed, on the whole, she does not have conscious access to her hate since she fears this feeling which would put her in contact with her destructiveness. In this event, the unconscious hate may occasionally fall on the baby, but, here, it is not his existence with all the discomforts accompanying it that is at the basis of her impossibility of being destructive but rather the fact that she had not sufficiently integrated this aspect of her personality at the time. The mother may nevertheless harbour an unconscious hatred for the baby, which does not refer to a depression in the mother, but to *the very fact that the baby exists*, to the interference that he causes in her life. This unconscious hate leads to massive reactive formations constituting, according to Winnicott, one of the basis for the establishment of an autistic pathology in the child. This phenomenon will be addressed in another study, which is being prepared.
2. I believe that it is to this phenomenon of a pre-representational and without a doubt, pre-linguistic knowledge that Gilberto Safra draws attention in his article "A vassoura e o divã" [The broom and the couch] (1996). Safra approximates this phenomenon to Suzanne Langer's concept of "presentational symbols", which she created in order to distinguish a semantics of sensoriality from a semantics of discursive forms. Since Suzanne Langer belongs to a line of thought which, together with Cassirer, approaches human phenomena from the point of view of a philosophy of representation, I believe that it is more useful to approximate this phenomenon to what Heidegger names "pre-understanding". Winnicott heads in this direction when he describes the pre-verbal, pre-symbolic and pre-representational nature not only of the communication between mother and baby, but also of the growing non-mental knowledge that the latter acquires because of the repeated experiences of environmental reliability. Cf. Winnicott, 1968d, and in the current study, Chapter Three, heading "Integration in time and space".
3. According to the theory of maturational processes, inhabiting a subjective world and relating to subjective objects are prerequisites for achieving transitionality, an *intermediary* passage to relating to the shared world and to objects perceived objectively. Cf., for example, the article where, enumerating the tasks that preside over the beginning of life, Winnicott refers to "the

baby's initial steps in object-relating, which lead to the ability to adopt symbolic objects and to the existence of an area in between the baby and persons in which play is meaningful" (1996c, p. 216).

4. In a text from 1945, in which Winnicott sketches out ideas on transitional phenomena, which eventually came to light in 1951, he alludes to the universal practice of thumb sucking or sucking a dummy, assuming that all agree that the finger is sucked not only for pleasure, but as a consolation. As he developed the subject and in a still rudimentary formulation of it, he mentions that having no doubts that these phenomena, such as normal finger sucking, are "an attempt to localize the object (breast, etc.), to hold it half-way between in and out. This is either a defence against loss of object in the external world or in the inside of the body, that is to say, against loss of control over the object" (1945d, p. 156). This "half-way between in and out" was a "between" and was what he would eventually call potential space in a 1951 article.
5. An allusion to these objects had already been made, in the analytical literature, by M. Wulff, in terms of fetish objects. For Winnicott, this approach is unsatisfactory and leads to misunderstandings: first, because he does not accept that these objects primarily have the nature of fetish, except in pathology; second, because he does not agree with the traditional interpretation of fetish, followed by Wulff, who transforms a phenomenon which is universal, the attribution of a penis to the mother, into pathology. For a thorough discussion of the theme, cf. Gurfinkel, 1996.
6. As we have seen in chapter III, this space already exists potentially, on the basis of the fundamental isolation of the individual. Cf., also, chapter II, section 8.
7. It should be pointed out that at this moment, the expression "internal object" may not yet be used. The baby still does not have an "inside" in which he can store images, representations, a territory where the fight between the constructive and destructive aspects of human nature takes place (cf. 1986d, p. 133]. This fight with his inner objects can only take place after the baby reaches the I AM unitary status and begins to feel concerned with his destructive drives.
8. Cf. Winnicott, 1993e.
9. Winnicott goes so far as to assert that the illusion with which the bridges between subjective and objective reality are built "may be the essential basis for all true objectivity" (1951b, p. 391).
10. The fear of losing the capacity for relating to objects, the origin of which may be located in the loss of the subjective object, is one of the traumatic experiences, unthinkable agonies, which form the basis of psychotic pathologies.
11. Winnicott's concept of creativity is not easy to grasp, maybe as a result of trivialisation by the media, or because it usually refers to artistic and/or original creation, or even because psychoanalysis understands it in the sense of sublimation. Pontalis himself, who, in many articles, strongly criticised the misunderstandings derived from Winnicott's theory of creativity, replies a question by Anne Clancier (1987) on the notion of creativity as follows: "I don't care for the word, still less for its promotion, here there and everywhere. Trying to get everybody to believe that there is a treasure inside him is a false scent. To say, as Winnicott does, even with humour, that one can be as creative in frying eggs as Schumann composing a sonata, don't you find that rather excessive?" (Pontalis, in Clancier: 1987, p. 143). It appears that Pontalis did not understand Winnicott's concept of creativity accurately, since the feeling of being able to create and of creating, which is closely related to spontaneity, does not depend on the output that is created. Creativity relates to the phenomena of life, to the reality of the experience, and not merely to bold creation or to artistic creation; creativity should be acknowledged, says Winnicott, but not so much by the originality in the production "as by the individual's sense of the reality of the experience" (1988, p. 109). Cf., also in the same text, p. 109.

12. It is known that during moments of pain or anxiety, the baby only accepts the mother's lap and knows how to discriminate this lap from all others, including the father's, even when he frequently plays the mother's part.
13. When referring to the initial stages, Winnicott often uses the term "projection" to designate a creation, by the baby, of the object or the world. In a text from 1960, for example, he notes that the baby can only receive what comes from the external world if theses things are included in "the infant's omnipotence and sensed as projections". At this point, he adds the following footnote: "I am using the term 'projections' here in its descriptive and dynamic and not in its full metapsychological sense" (1960b, p. 46, note 2).
14. Refering to this theme, in a text written in 1963, and hence before his complete formulation of the question in 1969, Winnicott affirms, alluding to the clinical work, that there is an intermediate state in normal development, in the passage between what is subjectively and what is objectively perceived, when "the patient's most important experience in relation to the good or potentially satisfying object is the refusal of it. The refusal of it is part of the process of creating it" (1965j, p. 182). I would add: it is part of its creation as external reality, inasmuch as this type of aggression as refusal and the ideas linked to it "lends itself to the process of placing the object, to placing the object separate from the self, in so far as the self has begun to emerge as an entity" (1965j, p. 181).
15. It would be interesting to distinguish between two possible meanings of the term "objectify", with the first being the one described above, and a second meaning in which "objectify" means treating what belongs to personal relations as relating to objects.
16. The destructiveness which creates the sense of externality is, according to the author, one of his most difficult concepts. After reading the article on object usage at the New York Society of Psychoanalysis, in 1968, his work was subject to considerable criticism. At a later stage, he made comments on that criticism, which resulted in some addenda gathered afterwards in Chapter Thirty-four of *Psychoanalytical Explorations*. The theme certainly caused perplexity in the psychoanalytical milieu: if in traditional psychoanalysis, reality is given and not created during the maturational process; if destructiveness is always related to envy or sadism, or to anger deriving from frustration, which comes precisely from the reality principle, then, what kind of destructiveness is it that is non-instinctual and *without anger*?
17. This is the meaning of the affirmation that we cannot describe the usage of the object without considering the nature of the object, in this case, the external one or, in other words, we cannot characterise a given relation without taking into account the features and the behaviour of the object.
18. Although in previous texts, the word "fantasy" sometimes appears as a synonym for imaginative elaboration, which has thus occurred since the beginning of life, it should be noted that, according to Winnicott's last writings, fantasy as something pertaining to the inner world only begins for the individual when he achieves object usage, that is, when he achieves a sense of external reality. Cf. Winnicott, 1969d, especially pp. 222–223.
19. In adult relationships, the destruction of the object in its subjective character takes the form of a sudden estrangement with regard to someone who is so close, intimate, and familiar that he or she was not seen for him- or herself and in some cases had never been seen in his or her exteriority.
20. This is why it is so important to know how to detect the emotional age of the individual in clinical practice, since for people who regress to dependence, we must account for the fact that in many cases, the word "love" may not yet make any sense.

21. On aggressiveness and destructiveness in Winnicott, see also the study by Dias E. 2011b, text 4. I also refer the reader to two other studies, in the same book, on object usage (text 5) and on Theodore Kaczynski, the Unanomber terrorist (text 10).
22. Cf. Jung, 1963. Cf., also, the review by Winnicott of this book (1964b).
23. Cf. Winnicott, 1964b, p. 490. For these statements, Winnicott based himself on Fordham's book on the work by Jung. Cf. M. Fordham, 1962, Lecture number 119.
24. In an article dedicated to Winnicott, Marion Milner (1987) recounts that after her first reading of "The use of an object", she telephoned Winnicott with the following question: "Yes, but just why does the good object have to be destroyed?" Winnicott took some time before answering: Because it is necessary (Milner, 1987, p. 284).
25. The peculiar sense that Winnicott gives to the schizoid personality will be examined in the next book on Winnicott's theory of psychoses, which is in preparation.
26. Shortly after having made this statement, Winnicott adds, without doubt referring to the Kleinian hypothesis of the innate paranoid disposition: paranoid tendency "very early yet not inherited or truly constitutional" (1988, p. 124). It should also be noted that the tendency to feel persecuted, related to the achievement of the unity in an I AM, is entirely different from the paranoid disposition resulting from a pattern of environmental invasions or from the one, the origin of which is the discovery of personal destructiveness.
27. On the value of the mother's survival and that of the analyst, cf. Dias, E. 2011b, text 6.
28. Good and bad are placed in inverted commas, since although they are in common use, as a general rule, their meaning in psychoanalytical literature is interpreted on the basis of Kleinian theory. I believe that this is also the reason why in a text on the depressive position, Winnicott added a footnote referring to these terms, in which he stated that "The words good and bad are an inheritance from the dim past; they are also suitable words for description of the extremes that every infant feels about inside matters—whether these be forces, objects, sounds or smells. I am not referring here to the use of the terms good or bad by parents and nurses who wish to implant morality on the infant" (1988, p. 71).
29. A detailed consideration of Winnicott's concept of "cross-identification", that is to say his redescription of the mechanisms of projection and introjection, lies outside the scope of this study. In rough terms, this is the ability to put oneself in the place of another and to allow for the reverse; "to enter imaginatively and yet accurately into the thoughts and feelings and hopes and fears of another person" (1986f, p. 117). While this capacity, which is a sign of health, belongs to a rather advanced maturational stage, its basis is established in the originary experience of having had someone identify with your needs, which were incommunicable at a verbal level.
30. Winnicoot's approach to the achievement of the capacity for concern is largely based on Melanie Klein's theory of the depressive position, considered by him as the greatest of her contributions to the psychoanalytical thought. A few differences should nevertheless be highlighted. Winnicott cannot agree, for example, with the conception of aggressiveness which is involved in the phenomenon, or with the precocity with which these achievements take place, according to Klein; nor does he agree with the pre-conditions or causes of "depression": he cannot see Oedipus in the baby's attack on the mother's breast. In addition, the expression "depressive position" is not entirely adequate for him, since despite the fact that Klein has described the phenomenon as an achievement of normal maturation, her term suggests that when normal babies reach this stage, they fall into a state of clinical depression.
31. For a more detailed analysis of the origin and nature of morality in Winnicott, cf. Loparic, 2000a.

32. If, as a result of conditions of environmental unreliability, a precocious me emerges, therefore immature for states of awareness and "perception" of external objects, this "precocious me" will have a premature awareness of its existence, dependence, and impulsiveness and may be stricken by guilt and responsibility, which, due to the basic immaturity, cannot be integrated into the personality. In these cases, guilt is devastating.
33. An in-depth investigation, in Winnicott's view, on the role of the father in the child's maturational process and the possible failures which interfere with it is to be found in Rosa, 2011.
34. Winnicott considered that if a child is exposed to the sight of his parents having sexual relations, which is the last thing he needs in emotional terms with regard to them, he will experience a maximum tension, which may be traumatic (cf. Winnicott, 1988, p. 59).
35. Cf. Winnicott, 1958g, p. 33.
36. The distinction between the two types of deprivation is extremely important in the diagnosis and treatment of the several types of anti-social tendency. With regard to this distinction and father failures in general, I refer the reader to the meticulous work of Claudia Dias Rosa, 2011.
37. It is worth noting the moment and sense in which gender distinction becomes significant for Winnicott, in order to highlight conceptual differences relative to Freudian psychoanalysis, particularly for the theory of psychosis, cf. Freud, 1924b, 1924e, and 1925h.
38. Perversions may be seen, for example, as an "elaborate attempt to bring about some kind of sex union in spite of the delusion that the girl has a penis" (1986g, p. 187). In this same generalised delirium that there is a penis in the woman, both in men and in women, Winnicott finds one of the roots of feminism. At one extreme, he says, "it is woman's protest against a male society dominated by phallic-phase male swank; and at the other extreme it is a woman's denial of her true inferiority *at one phase* of physical development" (1986g, p. 188).
39. Freud insisted until the end of his life on the importance of the effect of the inferiority trauma of women, derived from the phallic phase (Cf. Freud 1925j, 1931b, and 1933a). According to Winnicott, this insistence was understandable, since it was on the denial of the lack of a penis in girls that he based the etiology of psychoses, a denial which aimed to prevent the anxiety of castration.
40. Cf. Freud, 1924b, 1924e, and 1925h.
41. It is clear that even if individuals begin well, they may subsequently develop a psychosis, if they are exposed to traumatic situations beyond their capacity for tolerance at that time or which exceed their capacity for tolerance over time. For example, Winnicott mentions the case of prisoners, who are victims of cruel political persecution, etc. (cf. 1971g, p. 91). In any case, this psychosis will differ from one established during the more primitive stages as a result of traumatic environment failures, notably because a failure of maturation is one thing and its achievement and subsequent loss another. It may also happen that in situations of overload, or because the child did not elaborate the conflict between love and hate adequately, regression to previous stages occurs, with the loss of past achievements. The extent of this regression will depend on the consistency of achievements preceding the oedipical complex (cf. 1988, end of Chapter Two, Part II and 1989p, p. 68).
42. It should be noted that in order to refer to the identifications made by children with the parent of the same gender, Winnicott uses the term "homosexual". This identification and proximity constitute a necessary phase of maturation.
43. To illustrate this situation, see the case of the little Piggle in Winnicott, 1977/1987.
44. Traditional psychoanalysis dealt predominantly with the satisfaction of desire and not with the genital capacity and act in themselves. It did not develop the issues relating to the body

strictly speaking. For the same reason, the issue of the initial genitality is ultimately linked to the consequences deriving from the prohibition on touching forbidden fruit and not, as Winnicott states, to the fear of provoking irreversible changes in the other person's body. For Winnicott, the question of loving is personal and takes into account the imaginative elaboration of the result of the impulse in the body of the loved person.

45. This issue in Winnicott's work became clearer in a subsequent formulation of 1966, in which sexual identity is was conceived by Winnicott in non-instinctual terms, as we shall see later.
46. The Winnicottian concepts of "pure female element" and "pure male element" will be made explicit later in this same chapter.
47. This letter is in the book *The Feminine and the Sacred* (2001) with the collected correspondence between Julia Kristeva and Catherine Clément from November 1996 to September 1997.
48. Kristeva's position is closely in line with that of Lacan. According to the French psychoanalyst, the mother never wants the baby for himself; what satisfies her in the baby is what he represents, the phallus. According to Lacan, the child is not merely the child, since he is also the phallus (cf. Lacan, 1956–1957, p. 57). In another passage of the same seminar, Lacan also notes that the woman only achieves satisfaction with her baby because the baby contains something which calms her, since it fulfils her need for a phallus.
49. This new formulation was already made explicit in Chapter Three of this study, since it is also the most complete with regard to the issue in question, the constitution of identity as such; it serves here to clarify the issue of bisexuality in non-sexual terms.
50. In order to refer to Winnicott's clinical cases without having to describe them each time, I shall use an acronym to make them recognisable. I shall refer to this case as FM, since it is the clinical example which illustrates pure female and male elements (1971i).
51. The article by Ricardo Rodulfo was originally a lecture delivered at the IV Winnicott Coloquium, promoted by PUC-SP, in 1999, and not yet published.
52. This patient was in analysis for two periods, with some of the sessions being clinically reported by Winnicott. From the first period of analysis, we have only the introduction to his clinical annotations, inserted by Khan in the Introduction to the book *Holding and Interpretation* (1986a). From the second period, there are two groups of annotations: the first dates from 1954 (1955a) and is composed of annotations referring to six episodes of analysis; the second one comprises the book *Holding and Interpretation*, which encompasses six months of the second period of analysis. Refering to the first period of analysis, Winnicott says that the young man, at the time "a schizoid case", had looked for him saying that "he could not talk freely, that he had no small talk or imaginative or play capacity, and that he could not make a spontaneous gesture or get excited" (1986a, p. 20).
53. For this purpose, it is necessary to preserve sensitivity. Winnicott tells that when he worked as a paediatrician at the ambulatory of the Paddington Green Hospital, he was promoted to task of taking care of beds, which meant *status*. He said that not knowing quite well the reason, he did not accept it. He managed to get a permission to use beds when necessary, but passed on the interned patients to his assistant. He subsequently understood why he did that: "[...] the distress of babies and small children in a hospital ward, even a very nice one, adds up to something terrific. Going into the ward disturbs me very much. If I become an in-patient doctor I shall develop the capacity not to be disturbed by the distress of the children, otherwise I shall not be able to be an effective doctor. I will therefore concentrate on my O. P. work and avoid becoming callous in order to be efficient" (1987b, p. 168).

54. Regarding the relation between maturity and democratic machinery, I refer the reader to Roseana Moraes Garcia's excellent work on aggression in Winnicott's work (2009).
55. Winnicott did not have children and, at the end of his life, knowing that he was very ill and had very few time left, "he then goes to discuss the difficulty that a man has dying without a son to imaginatively kill and to survive him—to provide the only continuity that men know" (*apud* Clare Winnicott, 1989, p. 4).
56. The "baby in the mother's lap" and the "child in the mother's bed" are expressions created by Z. Loparic in order to define the paradigmatic exemplars of the Winnicottian and the Freudian theories respectively (cf. Loparic, 1997a).
57. On pulsional duality and the dynamic viewpoint in Freud, cf. Loparic, 2001b and 2006. See also Simanque, 1994, Chapter Three.
58. Details of the differences between Winnicott and Klein are provided in the following texts by Winnicott: 1965g; 1988, Part II, Chapter One; 1989c, and 1989e.
59. In the attempt to establish a dialogue with the Kleinians, by various means, Winnicott wrote a letter to Joan Rivière in 1956: "My trouble when I start to speak to Melanie about her statement of early infancy is that I feel as if I were talking about colour to the colour-blind. She simply says that she has not forgotten the mother and the part the mother plays, but in fact I find that she has shown no evidence of understanding the part the mother plays at the very beginning" (1987b, pp. 95–96). In the same letter, commenting on the essay "A study of envy and gratitude", presented by Klein to the British Society of Psychoanalysis (cf. Klein, 1984), he distinguised three themes contained in the essay, stating that, with regard to the third one, namely, "[…] the interesting attempt Melanie is making all the time to state the psychology of the earliest stages" (1987b, p. 94), he felt that "she has let herself down badly by making a statement which it is very easy to pull to pieces, and which can easily hold up the study of the development of Ego stability and the researches which are going on in various parts the world into the treatment of psychosis" (1987b, p. 95).

FINAL CONSIDERATIONS

The aim of this book has been to present the conceptual assumptions of the theory of maturational processes, in an articulate and unified manner, describing the various stages of the process with their different tasks and achievements.

Its primary motivation was the central position occupied by this theory in Winnicott's *opus* and also because it constitutes the necessary theoretical horizon from which Winnicott's theory of the psychic disorders can be explained, although this is a topic for a future book which will deal with psychoses in particular. Third, observing that to date and as far as I am aware, Winnicott's work has not been the focus of an analysis that would clarify its internal unity, there was a need to emphasise the central place of the theory of maturational processes and its status as the frame of reference for the study of human phenomena, demonstrating not only the conceptual articulations of his thought as a whole, but the important theoretical and clinical developments resulting from the connection between the stages of maturation and the various types of psychic disorder. Fourth, this study was motivated by the acknowledgement of the richness, relevance, and efficiency of Winnicott's contribution to the therapeutic task, reflected in the author's own clinical cases and illustrations, which are confirmed both in my own experience and by that of other analysts who have permitted themselves to be oriented by this perspective.

Carrying out the plan for this research project as it was conceived, soon proved to be a rather solitary task. In addition to finding poor bibliographic support in the secondary literature, this author encountered a series of difficulties since the conceptual and descriptive elements underlying the basic assumptions of the theory of maturational processes, as well as the characterisation of the various stages, are scattered throughout Winnicott's work. By applying the methodological principle of reading the parts starting from the whole and understanding the whole from the parts, all of Winnicott's work was carefully deployed with regard to the theme of maturation against the background of psychoses, in other words, of the problems relating to the continuity or discontinuity of maturational process and to success or failure in constituting the unitary identity. Having also considered the author's own suggestion that both psychoanalysis in general and his own work should be read from a historical perspective, this author was obliged to follow the evolution of each concept. This aspect of the research also revealed the remarkable progress which occurred throughout Winnicott's scientific career, particularly during the 1960s. This latter task, which permeated the whole of the work, has been given a special emphasis in Chapter One.

In order to open and sustain the course of the research, this author was obliged to consider objections to this sort of project, entailing the questioning of various established ideas about Winnicott himself. I shall point out two of them: first, the idea that a conceptual organisation of Winnicott's work would be contrary to its spirit, the unsystematic nature or alleged lack of theoretical unity of which supposedly constitutes the principal characteristic to be preserved; second, the idea that the articulation of Winnicott's thought and the demonstration of its unity would kill its inherent poetry. Even though I consider the fear upon which these objections are partly based, of creating an orthodoxy, of petrifying his thought, to be a valid one, I nevertheless believe that I have succeeded in showing that the key to averting this danger derives from the careful and organised study of his theory, since Winnicott the theorist knew how to protect the various dimensions of the human in his conceptions, emphasising and securing, without mystification, the many and varied aspects of human existence, including creativity, wherever it may be exercised, on the basis of tradition. Regarding the risk of destroying its poetry, I start from the position that the poetic aspect of Winnicott's work results not from its lack of a systematic character but from the fact that he knew how to preserve the specific nature of human phenomena by using different languages, appropriate to each stage of development. This was his precise procedure when he illuminated the poetic and almost unutterable character of the phenomena characterising the initial stages, such as the subtlety of the pre-verbal relation and communication between mother and baby, at the initial moment of his life, describing them in a language which does not injure their essential nature, which, after all, is a poet's approach. The complexity and internal articulation of Winnicott's thesis nevertheless clearly demonstrates that his writing, whether addressed to mothers or to psychoanalysts and to the scientific public in general, far from being restricted to poetic evocations, offers an impressive body of concepts which, even if they do not constitute a closed "system", may legitimately be characterised as "theoretical", a status which Winnicott himself reserved for his contribution.

I thus believe that I can affirm that the main challenges to the set task have been overcome. In the light of historical-hermeneutic analysis, it proved possible to reconstitute the central theme of Winnicottian psychoanalysis, the theory of personal maturational processes, briefly showing that this theory:

a. is based on a set of assumptions and recurrent ideas in Winnicott's work which, with the evolution of his thought, were endowed with increasing depth and cohesion;
b. is founded, in particular, on a theory of human nature, characterised as a mode of temporalisation which, at each stage, represents a certain form of integration of the human person;

c. is the horizon from which the psychic phenomena of health and sickness in general may be accessed;
d. presupposes various philosophical theses which are not commonly found in theories of the human sciences in general.

The characterisation of the theory of maturational processes in this book also demonstrates that in order to set forth his theoretical viewpoint and the new phenomena illuminated by his theory, Winnicott abandoned abstractions or speculations of a metaphysical character. In describing the various stages of maturation, he used terms of ordinary language as frequently as he could, linked to lived experience, which were sometimes raised to the category of technical terms. Throughout his work, he highlighted that the terms intended to describe one stage would be incorrect for describing another.

In addition to demonstrating, in this way, the breadth of Winnicott's contribution, in the last section of Chapter Four, I have also listed some basic differences between Winnicott's theory of maturational processes and traditional psychoanalytic theory regarding the development of the sexual functions. This comparison not only served to highlight the innovation of Winnicott's conceptions, but also to raise another issue, namely, deciding on the precise nature of the change in psychoanalytic theory caused by Winnicott's work. Since this latter question is essentially epistemological in nature, despite permeating the whole of the study, it was only indicated, but not developed, since it falls outside the scope of this study.

Since the theory of maturational processes is the theoretical horizon from which it is possible to explain the nature of the various psychic disorders, a study of this theory allows us to glimpse what will be studied in detail in my next work. Broadly speaking, it may be said in advance that according to Winnicott, *psychoses* are related to the environmental failure in facilitating the tasks of the initial stages, which start at some point during intrauterine life and last until the stage of I AM. If the environment fails repeatedly, in the form of an established pattern, to adapt to the needs of the baby during the stage of absolute and even relative dependence, the process of personal maturation will be interrupted (at this primitive moment, in which the foundations of personality are being constituted) giving rise to a psychotic disorder. There will evidently be different types of psychotic disorders depending on the point, within the initial stages, at which the baby was traumatised by environmental failures.

If everything goes well until the achievement of the unitary identity (at the milestone in the maturation process represented by the I AM stage), the child, who is now one or two years old, will then have to confront the integration of the instinctual drives during the stage of concern. If the environment does not favour this achievement, there will be the risk of *depression*, the central problem of which consists of the difficulty in accepting and integrating the destructiveness relating to human nature, arising precisely with regard to the loved object.

In favourable cases when this achievement is also realised, the child, who may be said to have seeded the bases of personality (in this sense being whole and healthy), will have to grapple with the anxieties resulting from interpersonal relations, now possible because of the maturity that has been reached; in particular, with the situation in which the Oedipus complex may be effectively experienced, that is, between whole persons. All this mobilises anxieties relating to instinctuality, to feelings and to the fantasy taking place in the internal psychic reality. Here, the facilitation of the environment does not have the same importance as during the previous stages, although it should remain consistent enough for the small individual to deal with his personal internal problematic and to avoid succumbing to *neurosis*.

Psychosis, depression, and neurosis are the main diagnostic categories of Winnicott's classification of psychic disorders, with their different natures defined in terms of their aetiologies, that is, their point of origin in the line of maturation, according to the task with which the baby was involved at the time of the trauma and to the nature of this trauma. In addition to these disorders cited above, there are three others which do not constitute diagnostic categories in themselves, since they always appear in conjunction with the previous ones. These are: the anti-social tendency, psycho-somatic disorders, and paranoias. These disorders are also characterised according to their point of origin; the last two have multiple meanings which vary according to this same criterion.

Winnicott always emphasised the existence of gaps in his understanding of the maturational processes, particularly with regard to the initial stages, encouraging analysts to observe and describe their analytical experiences, in order to develop the theory further. There is also still much to be done in order to understand the results already achieved by Winnicott in his study and theory. This account is also far from representing a complete analysis of what already exists. Each aspect discussed in a section could constitute a theme for future research in itself. This is true both of the initial stages and of all the subsequent ones.

Several points relating to the main theme presented here have only been outlined and also require additional treatment. The most important of these consists of the relevance of the results obtained here to psychoanalytic practice. Indeed, this study will only achieve its full psychoanalytic meaning when the clinical implications deriving from this new understanding of the primitive stages of maturation and the role of the environment in the facilitation of the innate tendency towards maturation become clear, with this meaning, for the initial stage, the participation of environmental care in the constitution of the self and personal identity. This will imply a new vision of the therapeutic task, in the light of Winnicott's theory of human nature and of the mishaps of its circular temporalisation.

REFERENCES

Abram, J. (1996). *The Language of Winnicott: A Dictionary of Winnicott's use of Words*. London: Karnac.
Abram, J. (2013). *Donald Winnicott Today*. London: Routledge.
Amado, G. (1979). *De l'enfant à l'adulte*. Paris: Press Universitaires de France.
Aubin, H. (1975). *Les psychoses de l'enfant*. Paris: P. U. F.
Badinter, E. (1980). *L'amour en plus*. Paris: Flammarion.
Béziers, M. -M. & Hunzinger, Y. (1994). *O bebê e a coordenação motora*. São Paulo: Summus.
Bogomoletz, D. (2001). Resenha de Jan Abram 2000: A linguagem de Winnicott: dicionário das palavras e expressões utilizadas por Donald W. Winnicott. *Natureza Humana, 3(1)*: 177–186.
Bowlby, J. (1951). *Maternal Care and Mental Health*. Geneva: W. H. O.
Burlingham, D., & Freud, A. (1942). *Young Children in Wartime: A Year's Work in a Residencial War Nursery*. London: Allen & Unwin.
Chaslin, Ph. (1912). *Eléments de sémiologie et clinique mentales*. Paris: Asselin et Houzeau.
Clancier, A., & Kalmanovitch, J. (1987). *Winnicott and Paradox: From Birth to Creation*. London: Tavistock.
Clément, C., & Kristeva, J. (2001). *The Feminine and the Sacred*. New York, NY: Columbia University Press.
Davis, M., & Wallbridge, D. (1981). *Boundary and Space: An Introduction to The Work of D. W. Winnicott*. London: Mark Paterson.
Dias, E. O. (2001). Resenha de Jan Abram: A linguagem de Winnicott: dicionário das palavras e expressões utilizadas por Donald W. Winnicott. *Psychê, 5*: 163–169.
Dias, E. O. (2003). *A teoria do amadurecimento de D. W. Winnicott*. São Paulo: Imago.
Dias, E. O. (2011b). *Sobre a confiabilidade e outros estudos*. São Paulo: DWW editorial.
Dias, E. O. (2014a). *A teoria do amadurecimento de D. W. Winnicott* (3ª ed.). São Paulo: DWW editorial.
Eliot, T. S. (1980). *The Complete Poems and Plays 1909–1950*. New York, NY: Harcourt Brace & Company.
Fairbairn, W. R. D. (1952). *Psychoanalytic Studies of the Personality*. London: Routledge, 1994.

Fordham, M. (1962). An evaluation of Jung's work. *Guild of Pastoral Psychology*, Conference 119.
Freud, A. (1966). *The Ego and the Mechanisms of Defense*. London: Karnac.
Freud, S. (1915e). The unconscious. In: J. Strachey (Ed.), *The Standard Edition of the Complete Works of Sigmund Freud* (vol 14, pp. 153–213). London: Hogarth and the Institute of Psychoanalysis, 1989.
Freud, S. (1923b). The ego and the id. In: J. Strachey (Ed.), *The Standard Edition of the Complete Works of Sigmund Freud* (vol 19, pp. 1–66). London: Hogarth and the Institute of Psychoanalysis, 1989.
Freud, S. (1924b). Neurosis and psychosis. In: J. Strachey (Ed.), *The Standard Edition of the Complete Works of Sigmund Freud* (vol 19, pp. 151–159). London: Hogarth and the Institute of Psychoanalysis, 1989.
Freud, S. (1924e). The loss of reality in neurosis and psychosis. In: J. Strachey (Ed.), *The Standard Edition of the Complete Works of Sigmund Freud* (vol 19, pp. 189–197). London: Hogarth and the Institute of Psychoanalysis, 1989.
Freud, S. (1925h). Negation. In: J. Strachey (Ed.), *The Standard Edition of the Complete Works of Sigmund Freud* (vol 19, pp. 249–257). London: Hogarth and the Institute of Psychoanalysis, 1989.
Freud, S. (1925j). Some psychical consequences of the anatomical distinction between the sexes. In: J. Strachey (Ed.), *The Standard Edition of the Complete Works of Sigmund Freud* (vol 19, pp. 259–276). London: Hogarth and the Institute of Psychoanalysis, 1989.
Freud, S. (1931b). Female sexuality. In: J. Strachey (Ed.), *The Standard Edition of the Complete Works of Sigmund Freud* (vol 21, pp. 223–244). London: Hogarth and the Institute of Psychoanalysis, 1989.
Freud, S. (1933a). New introductory lectures on psycho-analysis. 33ª lecture: Feminity. In: J. Strachey (Ed.), *The Standard Edition of the Complete Works of Sigmund Freud* (vol 22, pp. 104–125). London: Hogarth and the Institute of Psychoanalysis, 1989.
Freud, S. (1937c). Analysis terminable and interminable. In: J. Strachey (Ed.), *The Standard Edition of the Complete Works of Sigmund Freud* (vol 23, pp. 211–254). London: Hogarth and the Institute of Psychoanalysis, 1989.
Freud, S. (1940b). Some elementary lessons in psycho-analysis. In: J. Strachey (Ed.), *The Standard Edition of the Complete Works of Sigmund Freud* (vol 23, pp. 279–288). London: Hogarth and the Institute of Psychoanalysis, 1989.
Gadamer, H.-G. (1976). *Verité et méthode*. Paris: Éditions du Seuil.
Garcia, R. M. (2009). *A agressividade na psicanálise winnicottiana*. São Paulo: Tese de Doutorado em Psicologia Clínica, Pontifícia Universidade Católica.
Geets, C. (1981). *Winnicott*. Paris: Jean-Pierre Delarge.
Glover, E. (1932). *On The Early Development of Mind*. London: Imago, 1956.
Graña, R. B. (1997). Apresentação à edição brasileira. In: D. W. Winnicott, *Pensando sobre crianças* (pp. xi–xii). Porto Alegre: Artes Médicas.
Green, A. (1976). The borderline concept. In: *On Private Madness*. London: Karnac, 1997.
Green, A. (1977). La royauté appartient à l'enfant. *L'Arc, 69*: 4–12.
Greenberg, J. R., & Mitchell, S. A. (1983). *Object Relations and Psychoanalytic Theory*. Cambridge: Harvard University Press.
Grolnick, S. (1990). *The Work & Play of Winnicott*. London/NewYork: Jason Aronson.
Gurfinkel, D. (1996). O carretel e o cordão. *Percurso, 9*: 56–68.
Hartmann, H. (1958). *Ego Psychology and the Problem of Adaptation*. New York, NY: International Universities Press.
Heidegger, M. (1974). *El ser y el tiempo*. México: Fondo de Cultura Econômica.
Heidegger, M. (1987). *Zollikon Seminar*. USA: Northwestern University Press, 2001.
Home, H. J. (1966). The concept of mind. *International Journal of Psychoanalysis, 47*: 42–49.

Jacobs, M. (1995). *D. W. Winnicott*. London: Sage.

Jaspers, K. (1959). *General Psychopathology (vol. 1)*. London: Johns Hopkins Paperbacks, 1997.

Jung, C. G. (1963). *Memories, Dreams, Reflections*. New York, NY: Pantheon.

Kanner, L. (1935). *Child Psychiatry*. USA: Charles C Thomas, 1972.

Khan, M. (1975). Introduction. In: D. W. Winnicott. *Through Paediatrics to Psychoanalysis* (pp. xi–1). London: Karnac, 1992.

Klein, M. (1946). Notes on some schizoid mechanisms. In: *Envy and Gratitude and Other Works 1946–1963*. London: Virago, 1988.

Klein, M. (1957). Envy and Gratitude. In: *Envy and Gratitude and Other Works 1946–1963*. London: Virago, 1988.

Knobloch, F. (Org.). (1991). *O inconsciente: várias leituras*. São Paulo: Escuta.

Kuhn, T. S. (1970). *The Structure of Scientific Revolutions*. Chicago, IL: The University of Chicago Press.

Lacan, J. (1956–1957). *La relation d'object—Le séminaire, livre IV*. Paris: Éditions du Seuil, 1994.

Laplanche, J., & Pontalis, J. -B. (1967). *Vocabulaire de la psychanalyse*. Paris: Presses Universitaires de France.

Laurentiis, V. R. F. (2016). *Corpo e psicossomática em Winnicott*. São Paulo: DWW editorial.

Lins, M. I. A. (1997). História e vida na obra de Winnicott. In: A. Podkameni & M. A. Guimarães (Orgs.), *Winnicott 100 anos de um analista criativo* (pp. 13–22). Rio de Janeiro: Nau.

Loparic, Z. (1983). Heurística kantiana. *Cadernos de história e filosofia da ciência, 5*: 73–89.

Loparic, Z. (1985). Resistências à psicanálise. *Cadernos de história e filosofia da ciência, 8*: 29–49.

Loparic, Z. (1995a). Winnicott e Heidegger: afinidades. *Boletim de novidades, 69*: 53–60.

Loparic, Z. (1995b). Winnicott e o pensamento pós-metafísico. *Psicologia USP, 6*: 39–61.

Loparic, Z. (1997a). Winnicott: uma psicanálise não-edipiana. *Percurso, 9*: 41–47.

Loparic, Z. (1997b). A máquina no homem. *Psicanálise e Universidade, 7*: 97–113.

Loparic, Z. (1998). Psicanálise: uma leitura heideggeriana. *Veritas, 43(1)*: 25–41.

Loparic, Z. (1999a). O conceito de *Trieb* na psicanálise e na filosofia. In: J. Machado (Org.), *Filosofia e psicanálise: um diálogo* (pp. 97–157). Porto Alegre: Edipuc.

Loparic, Z. (1999b). Heidegger and Winnicott. *Natureza humana, 1(1)*: 103–135.

Loparic, Z. (1999c). É dizível o inconsciente? *Natureza humana, 1*: 323–385.

Loparic, Z. (2000a). A moralidade e o amadurecimento. *Anais do IX Encontro Latinamericano sobre o pensamento de D. W. Winnicott* (pp. 300–316).

Loparic, Z. (2000b). O "animal humano". *Natureza humana, 2*: 351–397.

Loparic, Z. (2000c). A semântica transcendental de Kant. Campinas: UNICAMP, CLE.

Loparic, Z. (2001a). Além do inconsciente. *Natureza humana, 3(1)*: 91–140.

Loparic, Z. (2001b). Esboço do paradigma winnicottiano. *Cadernos de história e filosofia da ciência, 11*: pp. 7–58.

Loparic, Z. (2005). Elementos da teoria winnicottiana da sexualidade. *Natureza humana, 7*: 311–358.

Loparic, Z. (2006/2011). De Freud a Winnicott: Aspectos de uma mudança paradigmática. In E. Dias & Z. Loparic, (Orgs.), *Winnicott na Escola de São Paulo* (pp. 29–58). São Paulo: DWW editorial, 2011.

Loparic, Z. (2013). From Freud to Winnicott. In: J. Abram (Ed.), *Winnicott Today* (pp. 113–156). London: Routledge, 2013.

Luz, R. (1989). O espaço potencial: Winnicott. *Percurso, 2*: 25–32.

Machado, J. A. T. (Org.). (1999). *Filosofia e psicanálise: um diálogo*. Porto Alegre: Edipuc.

Mello Filho, J. (1989). *O ser e o viver*. Porto Alegre: Artes Médicas.

Mendonça, M. E. (2000). *Ginástica holística: história e desenvolvimento de um método de cuidados corporais*. São Paulo: Summus.

Meyer, L. (1994). O que faz fracassar uma formação? *Percurso, 12*: 83–88.

Middlemore, M. P. (1941). *The Nursing Couple*. London: Hamish Hamilton.

Milner, M. (1987). Winnicott and overlapping circles. In: *The Suppressed Madness of Sane Men* (pp. 279–286). London and New York: Routledge.

Misès, R. (1969). Origines et évolution du concept de psychose chez l'énfant. *Revue Confrontations Psychiatriques—Psychoses de L'Enfant*, *3*: 9–29.

Outeiral, J. O. (1991). A tendência antissocial. In: J. Outeiral & R. Graña (Orgs.), *Donald W. Winnicott: estudos* (pp. 129–135). Porto Alegre: Artes Médicas.

Outeiral, J. O. (1994). Apresentação à edição brasileira. In: D. Winnicott, *Explorações psicanalíticas* (pp. vii–xv). Porto Alegre: Artes Médicas.

Outeiral, J. O. (1997). Sobre a concepção de pai na obra de D. W. Winnicott. In: I. F. Catafesta (Org.), *A clínica e a pesquisa no final do século: Winnicott e a universidade* (pp. 91–104). São Paulo: Instituto de Psicologia da USP.

Outeiral, J. O., & Graña, R. (Orgs.). (1991). *Donald W. Winnicott: estudos*. Porto Alegre: Artes Médicas.

Pessanha, J. G. (1992). O ponto K: Heidegger e Freud. *IDE—Revista da Sociedade Brasileira de Psicanálise, 22*: 80–89.

Phillips, A. (1988). *Winnicott*. London: Fontana.

Podkameni, A., & Guimarães, M. A. (Orgs.). (1997). *Winnicott 100 anos de um analista criativo*. Rio de Janeiro: Nau.

Pontalis, J. -B. (1981). *Frontiers in Psychoanalysis: Between the Dream and Psychic Pain*. London: Hogarth.

Rodman, R. (1987). Introduction. In: D. Winnicott, *The Spontaneous Gesture: Selected Letters of D. W. Winnicott* (pp. xiii–xxxiii). London: Karnac, 1999.

Rosa, C. D. (2011). *As falhas paternas em Winnicott*. São Paulo: Tese de Doutorado em Psicologia Clínica, Pontifícia Universidade Católica.

Rycroft, C. (1985). *Psychoanalysis and Beyond*. London: Chatto and Windus.

Safra, G. (1996). A vassoura e o divã. *Percurso, 17*: 69–74.

Sechehaye, M. A. (1947). *Autobiography of a Schizophrenic Girl: The True Story of "Renée"*. London: Penguin, 1994.

Serralha, C. A. (2007) . *Uma abordagem teórica e clínica do ambiente a partir de Winnicott*. São Paulo: Tese de doutorado em Psicologia Clínica, Pontifícia Universidade Católica.

Shepherd, R., Johns, J., & Robinson, H. T. (1997). Introduction. In: D. Winnicott, *Thinking about Children* (pp. xix–xxxii). London: Karnac, 1996.

Simanke, R. T. (1994). *A formação da teoria freudiana das psicose*. Rio de Janeiro: Editora 34.

Tellenbach, H. (1961). *Melancholy: History of the Problem, Endogeneity, Typology, Pathogenesis, Clinical Considerations*. Pittsburgh: Duquesne University Press, 1980.

Vidal, G., Bleichmar, H., & Usandivaras, R. J. (Orgs.). (1977). *Enciclopedia de psiquiatria*. Buenos Aires: El Ateneo.

Vilete, E. P. (2000). Sobre "O homem morto que caminha". *Natureza humana, 2(1)*: 149–164.

Webster's Encyclopedic Unabridged Dictionary of the English Language (1996). New York/Avenel: Gramercy Books.

Winnicott, C. (1984). Introduction. In: *D. Winnicott, Deprivation and Delinquency* (pp. 1–5). London: Routledge, 1994.

Winnicott, C. (1989). D. W. Winnicott: a reflection. In: *D. Winnicott, Psychoanalytic Explorations* (pp. 1–18). London: Karnac, 1989.

Winnicott, C., Shepherd, R., & Davis, M. (1984). Introduction, parts 1 (pp. 9–12), 2 (pp. 81–83), 3 (pp. 161–162), 4 (p. 231). In: *D. Winnicott, Deprivation and Delinquency*. London: Routledge, 1994.

Winnicott, D. W. (1931a). Fidgetiness. In: *Collected Papers: Through Paediatrics to Psychoanalysis* (pp. 22–30). London: Karnac, 1992.

Winnicott, D. W. (1931b). A note on normality and anxiety. In: *Collected Papers: Through Paediatrics to Psychoanalysis* (pp. 3–21). London: Karnac, 1992.

Winnicott, D. W. (1941). The observation of infants in a set situation. In: *Collected Papers: Through Paediatrics to Psychoanalysis* (pp. 52–69). London: Karnac, 1992.

Winnicott, D. W. (1945a). Getting to know your baby. In: *The Child, the Family and the Outside World* (pp. 19–24). London: Penguin, 1985.

Winnicott, D. W. (1945b). Towards an objective study of human nature. In: *Thinking about Children* (pp. 3–12). London: Karnac, 1996.

Winnicott, D. W. (1945c). Infant feeding. In: *The Child, the Family and the Outside World* (pp. 30–34). London: Penguin, 1985.

Winnicott, D. W. (1945d). Primitive emotional development. In: *Collected Papers: Through Paediatrics to Psychoanalysis* (pp. 145–156). London: Karnac, 1992.

Winnicott, D. W. (1946). Some psychological aspects of juvenile delinquency. In: *Deprivation and Delinquency* (pp. 113–119). London: Routledge, 1994.

Winnicott, D. W. (1947a). The child and sex. In: *The Child, the Family and the Outside World* (pp. 147–160). London: Penguin, 1985.

Winnicott, D. W. (1947b). Further thoughts on babies as persons. In: *The Child, the Family and the Outside World* (pp. 85–92). London: Penguin, 1985.

Winnicott, D. W. (1948). Paediatrics and psychiatry. In: *Collected Papers: Through Paediatrics to Psychoanalysis* (pp. 157–173). London: Karnac, 1992.

Winnicott, D. W. (1949a). The world in small doses. In: *The Child, the Family and the Outside World* (pp. 69–74). London: Penguin, 1985.

Winnicott, D. W. (1949b). The baby as a going concern. In: *The Child, the Family and the Outside World* (pp. 25–29). London: Penguin, 1985.

Winnicott, D. W. (1949c). The baby as a person. In: *The Child, the Family and the Outside World* (pp. 75–79). London: Penguin, 1985.

Winnicott, D. W. (1949d). Weaning. In: *The Child, the Family and the Outside World* (pp. 80–84). London: Penguin, 1985.

Winnicott, D. W. (1949e). The end of the digestive process. In: *The Child, the Family and the Outside World* (pp. 40–44). London: Penguin, 1985.

Winnicott, D. W. (1949f). Hate in the countertransference. In: *Collected Papers: Through Paediatrics to Psychoanalysis* (pp. 194–203). London: Karnac, 1992.

Winnicott, D. W. (1951a). The foundation of mental health. In: *Deprivation and Delinquency* (pp. 168–171). London: Routledge, 1994.

Winnicott, D. W. (1951b). Critical notice of *On Not Being Able to Paint* (Marion Milner). In: *Psychoanalytic Explorations* (pp. 390–392). London: Karnac, 1989.

Winnicott, D. W. (1953a). Psychoses and child care. In: *Collected Papers: Through Paediatrics to Psychoanalysis* (pp. 219–228). London: Karnac, 1992.

Winnicott, D. W. (1953b). Review of psychoanalytic studies of the personality (W. R. D. Fairbairn). In: *Psychoanalytic Explorations* (pp. 413–422). London: Karnac, 1989.

Winnicott, D. W. (1953c). Transitional objects and transitional phenomena. In: *Playing and Reality* (pp. 1–34). London: Routledge, 2005.

Winnicott, D. W. (1954a). Mind and its relation to the psyche-soma. In: *Collected Papers: Through Paediatrics to Psychoanalysis* (pp. 243–254). London: Karnac, 1992.

Winnicott, D. W. (1954b). Needs of the under-fives. In: *The Child, the Family and the Outside World* (pp. 179–188). London: Penguin, 1985.

Winnicott, D. W. (1954c). Two adopted children. In: *Thinking about Children* (pp. 113–127). London: Karnac, 1996.

Winnicott, D. W. (1955a). Withdrawal and regression. In: *Collected Papers: Through Paediatrics to Psychoanalysis* (pp. 255–261). London: Karnac, 1992.

Winnicott, D. W. (1955b). Metapsychological and clinical aspects of regression within the psycho-analytical set-up. In: *Collected Papers: Through Paediatrics to Psychoanalysis* (pp. 278–294). London: Karnac, 1992.

Winnicott, D. W. (1955c). The depressive position in normal emotional development. In: *Collected Papers: Through Paediatrics to Psychoanalysis* (pp. 262–277). London: Karnac, 1992.

Winnicott, D. W. (1957a). The mother's contribution to society. In: *Home is Where We Start From* (pp. 123–127). London: Penguin, 1990.

Winnicott, D. W. (1957b). Aggression and its roots. In: *Deprivation and Delinquency* (pp. 84–99). London: Routledge, 1994.

Winnicott, D. W. (1957c). Breast feeding. In: *The Child, the Family and the Outside World* (pp. 50–57). London: Penguin, 1985.

Winnicott, D. W. (1957d). The contribution of psycho-analysis to midwifery. In: *The Family and Individual Development* (pp. 106–113). London: Routledge, 1995.

Winnicott, D. W. (1957e). Knowing and learning. In: *Babies and Their Mothers* (pp. 15–22). London: Free Association, 1988.

Winnicott, D. W. (1958a). *Collected Papers: Through Paediatrics to Psychoanalysis*. London: Karnac, 1992.

Winnicott, D. W. (1958b). Aggression in relation to emotional development. In: *Collected Papers: Through Paediatrics to Psychoanalysis* (pp. 204–218). London: Karnac, 1992.

Winnicott, D. W. (1958c). The antisocial tendency. In: *Deprivation and Delinquency* (pp. 120–131). London: Routledge, 1994.

Winnicott, D. W. (1958d). Anxiety associated with insecurity. In: *Collected Papers: Through Paediatrics to Psychoanalysis* (pp. 97–100). London: Karnac, 1992.

Winnicott, D. W. (1958e). Psycho-analysis and the sense of guilt. In: *The Maturational Processes and the Facilitating Environment* (pp. 15–28). London: Karnac, 1990.

Winnicott, D. W. (1958f). Birth memories, birth trauma, and anxiety. In: *Collected Papers: Through Paediatrics to Psychoanalysis* (pp. 174–193). London: Karnac, 1992.

Winnicott, D. W. (1958g). The capacity to be alone. In: *The Maturational Processes and the Facilitating Environment* (pp. 29–36). London: Karnac, 1990.

Winnicott, D. W. (1958h). Primary maternal preoccupation. In: *Collected Papers: Through Paediatrics to Psychoanalysis* (pp. 300–305). London: Karnac, 1992.

Winnicott, D. W. (1958i). On the contribution of direct child observation to psycho-analysis. In: *The Maturational Processes and the Facilitating Environment* (pp. 109–114). London: Karnac, 1990.

Winnicott, D. W. (1958j). The first year of life: Modern views on the emotional development. In: *The Family and Individual Development* (pp. 3–14). London: Routledge, 1995.

Winnicott, D. W. (1958k). Paediatrics and childhood neurosis. In: *Collected Papers: Through Paediatrics to Psychoanalysis* (pp. 316–321). London: Karnac, 1992.

Winnicott, D. W. (1960a). Counter-transference. In: *The Maturational Processes and the Facilitating Environment* (pp. 158–165). London: Karnac.

Winnicott, D. W. (1960b). The theory of the parent-infant relationship. In: *The Maturational Processes and the Facilitating Environment* (pp. 37–55). London: Karnac, 1990.

Winnicott, D. W. (1961a). The effect of psychotic parents on the emotional development of the child. In: *The Family and Individual Development*. (pp. 69–78). London: Routledge, 1995.

Winnicott, D. W. (1961b). Integrative and disruptive factors in family life. In: *The Family and Individual Development* (pp. 40–49). London: Routledge, 1995.

Winnicott, D. W. (1962). Struggling through the doldrums. In: *Deprivation and Delinquency* (pp. 145–155). London: Routledge, 1994.

Winnicott, D. W. (1963a). Dependence in infant-care, in child-care, and in the psycho-analytic setting. In: *The Maturational Processes and the Facilitating Environment* (pp. 249–259). London: Karnac, 1990.

Winnicott, D. W. (1963b). The development of the capacity for concern. In: *The Maturational Processes and the Facilitating Environment* (pp. 73–82). London: Karnac, 1990.

Winnicott, D. W. (1963c). The mentally ill in your caseload. In: *The Maturational Processes and the Facilitating Environment* (pp. 217–229). London: Karnac, 1990.

Winnicott, D. W. (1963d). Morals and education. In: *The Maturational Processes and the Facilitating Environment* (pp. 93–105). London: Karnac, 1990.

Winnicott, D. W. (1963e). Review of *Childhood Schizophrenia* (William Gooldfarb), part of three reviews of books on autism. In: *Thinking about Children* (pp. 193–194). London: Karnac, 1996.

Winnicott, D. W. (1964a). *The Child, the Family and the Outside World*. London: Penguin, 1985.

Winnicott, D. W. (1964b). Review of *Memories, Dreams, Reflections* (C. J. Jung). In: *Psychoanalytic Explorations* (pp. 482–492). London: Karnac, 1989.

Winnicott, D. W. (1964c). Roots of aggression, part of aggression and its roots. In: *Deprivation and Delinquency* (pp. 92–99). London: Routledge, 1994.

Winnicott, D. W. (1964d). The value of depression. In: *Home is Where We Start From* (pp. 71–79). London: Penguin, 1990.

Winnicott, D. W. (1964e). Introduction. In: *The Child, the Family and the Outside World* (pp. 9–11). London: Penguin, 1985.

Winnicott, D. W. (1965a). *The Family and Individual Development*. London: Routledge, 1995.

Winnicott, D. W. (1965b). *The Maturational Processes and the Facilitating Environment*. London: Karnac, 1990.

Winnicott, D. W. (1965c). The relationship of a mother to her baby at the beginning. In: *The Family and Individual Development* (pp. 15–20). London: Routledge, 1995.

Winnicott, D. W. (1965d). Psychiatric disorder in terms of infantile maturational processes. In: *The Maturational Processes and the Facilitating Environment* (pp. 230–241). London: Karnac, 1990.

Winnicott, D. W. (1965e). Providing for the child in health and crisis. In: *The Maturational Processes and the Facilitating Environment* (pp. 64–72). London: Karnac, 1990.

Winnicott, D. W. (1965f). The price of disregarding psychoanalytic research. In: *Home is Where We Start From* (pp. 172–182). London: Penguin, 1990.

Winnicott, D. W. (1965g). A personal view of the kleinian contribution. In: *The Maturational Processes and the Facilitating Environment* (pp. 171–178). London: Karnac, 1990.

Winnicott, D. W. (1965h). Classification: Is there a psycho-analytic contribution to psychiatric classification? In: *The Maturational Processes and the Facilitating Environment* (pp. 124–139). London: Karnac, 1990.

Winnicott, D. W. (1965i). Growth and development in immaturity. In: *The Family and Individual Development* (pp. 21–29). London: Routledge, 1995.

Winnicott, D. W. (1965j). Communicating and not communicating leading to a study of certain opposites. In: *The Maturational Processes and the Facilitating Environment* (pp. 179–192). London: Karnac, 1990.

Winnicott, D. W. (1965k). Group influences and the maladjusted child: The school aspect. In: *The Family and Individual Development* (pp. 146–154). London: Routledge, 1995.

Winnicott, D. W. (1965l). The effect of psychosis on family life. In: *The Family and Individual Development* (pp. 61–68). London: Routledge, 1995.

Winnicott, D. W. (1965m). Ego distortion in terms of true and false self. In: *The Maturational Processes and the Facilitating Environment* (pp. 140–152). London: Karnac, 1990.

Winnicott, D. W. (1965n). Ego integration in child development. In: *The Maturational Processes and the Facilitating Environment* (pp. 56–63). London: Karnac, 1990.

Winnicott, D. W. (1965o). The family affected by depressive illness in one or both parents. In: *The Family and Individual Development* (pp. 50–60). London: Routledge, 1995.

Winnicott, D. W. (1965p). The family and emotional maturity. In: *The Family and Individual Development* (pp. 88–94). London: Routledge, 1995.

Winnicott, D. W. (1965q). Now they are five. In: *Talking to Parents* (pp. 111–120). Cambridge/ Massachusetts: Perseus, 1993.

Winnicott, D. W. (1965r). From dependence towards independence in the development of the individual. In: *The Maturational Processes and the Facilitating Environment* (pp. 83–92). London: Karnac, 1990.

Winnicott, D. W. (1965s). The relationship of a mother to her baby at the beginning. In: *The Family and Individual Development* (pp. 15–20). London: Routledge, 1995.

Winnicott, D. W. (1966). Psycho-somatic illness in its positive and negative aspects. In: *Psychoanalytic Explorations* (pp. 103–114). London: Karnac, 1989.

Winnicott, D. W. (1967a). Mirror-role of mother and family in child development. In: *Playing and Reality* (pp. 149–159). London: Routledge, 2005.

Winnicott, D. W. (1967b). The location of cultural experience. In: *Playing and Reality* (pp. 128–139). London: Routledge, 2005.

Winnicott, D. W. (1968a). The aetiology of infantile schizophrenia in terms of adaptive failure. In: *Thinking about Children* (pp. 218–223). London: Karnac, 1996.

Winnicott, D. W. (1968b). Children learning. In: *Home is Where We Start From* (pp. 142–149). London: Penguin, 1990.

Winnicott, D. W. (1968c). The concept of clinical regression compared with that of defence organization. In: *Psychoanalytic Explorations* (pp. 193–199). London: Karnac, 1989.

Winnicott, D. W. (1968d). Communication between infant and mother, and mother and infant, compared and contrasted. In: *Babies and Their Mothers* (pp. 89–103). London: Free Association, 1988.

Winnicott, D. W. (1968e). Delinquency as a sign of hope. In: *Home is Where we Start From* (pp. 90–100). London: Penguin, 1990.

Winnicott, D. W. (1968f). Environmental health in infancy. In: *Babies and Their Mothers* (pp. 59–68). London: Free Association, 1988.

Winnicott, D. W. (1969a). Death and murder in the adolescent process. Part of contemporary concepts of adolescent development and their implications for higher education. In: *Playing and Reality* (pp. 169–176). London: Routledge, 2005.

Winnicott, D. W. (1969b). Breast-feeding as communication. In: *Babies and Their Mothers* (pp. 23–34). London: Free Association, 1988.

Winnicott, D. W. (1969c). Contemporary concepts of adolescent development and their implications for higher education. In: *Playing and Reality* (pp. 186–203). London: Routledge, 2005.

Winnicott D. W. (1969d). The use of an object and relating through indentifications. In: *Psychoanalytic Explorations* (pp. 218–227). London: Karnac, 1989.

Winnicott, D. W. (1969e). Physiotherapy and human relations. In: *Psychoanalytic Explorations* (pp. 561–568). London: Karnac, 1989.

Winnicott, D. W. (1969f). A link between paediatrics and child psychology: Clinical observations. In: *Thinking about Children* (pp. 255–276). London: Karnac, 1996.

Winnicott, D. W. (1970a). Dependence in child care. In: *Babies and Their Mothers* (pp. 83–88). London: Free Association, 1988.

Winnicott, D. W. (1970b). The mother–infant experience of mutuality. In: *Psychoanalytic Explorations* (pp. 251–260). London: Karnac, 1989.

Winnicott, D. W. (1971a). *Playing and Reality.* London: Routledge, 2005.

Winnicott, D. W. (1971b). *Therapeutic Consultations in Child Psychiatry.* London: Karnac, 1996.

Winnicott, D. W. (1971c). Introduction (part one). In: *Therapeutic Consultations in Child Psychiatry* (pp. 1–11). London: Karnac, 1996.

Winnicott, D. W. (1971d). Basis for self in body. In: *Psychoanalytic Explorations* (pp. 261–271). London: Karnac, 1989.

Winnicott, D. W. (1971e). Introduction. In: *Playing and Reality* (pp. xv–xviii). London: Routledge, 2005.

Winnicott, D. W. (1971f). The concept of a healthy individual. In: *Home is Where we Start From* (pp. 21–34). London: Penguin, 1990.

Winnicott, D. W. (1971g). Creativity and its origins. In: *Playing and Reality* (pp. 87–114). London: Routledge, 2005.

Winnicott, D. W. (1971h). Dreaming, fantasying and living: a case-history describing a primary dissociation. In: *Playing and Reality* (pp. 35–50). London: Routledge, 2005.

Winnicott, D. W. (1971i). The split-off male and female elements to be found in men and women. In: *Psychoanalytic Explorations* (pp. 169–182). London: Karnac, 1989.

Winnicott, D. W. (1971j). The place where we live. In: *Playing and Reality* (pp. 140–148). London: Routledge, 2005.

Winnicott, D. W. (1971k). Playing: Creative activity and the search for the self. In: *Playing and Reality* (pp. 71–86). London: Routledge, 2005.

Winnicott, D. W. (1972). Answer to comments (part III of Chapter Twenty-eight). In: *Psychoanalytic Explorations* (pp. 189–192). London: Karnac, 1989.

Winnicott, D. W. (1974). Fear of breakdown. In: *Psychoanalytic Explorations* (pp. 87–95). London: Karnac, 1989.

Winnicott, D. W. (1977). *The Piggle: An Account of the Psycho-Analytic Treatment of a Little Girl.* London: Penguin, 1991.

Winnicott, D. W. (1984a). *Deprivation and Delinquency*. London: Routledge, 1994.

Winnicott, D. W. (1984b). The absence of a sense of guilt. In: *Deprivation and Delinquency* (pp. 106–112). London: Routledge, 1994.

Winnicott, D. W. (1984c). Aggression, guilt and reparation. In: *Home is Where We Start From* (pp. 80–89). London: Penguin, 1990.

Winnicott, D. W. (1984d). Varieties of psychotherapy. In: *Deprivation and Delinquency* (pp. 232–240). London: Routledge, 1994.

Winnicott, D. W. (1984e). Freedom. In: *Home is Where We Start From* (pp. 228–238). London: Penguin, 1990.
Winnicott, D. W. (1984f). *Sum*, I am. In: *Home is Where We Start From* (pp. 55–64). London: Penguin, 1990.
Winnicott, D. W. (1984g). Residential care as therapy. In: *Deprivation and Delinquency* (pp. 220–228). London: Routledge, 1994.
Winnicott, D. W. (1986a). *Holding and Interpretation. Fragment of an Analysis*. New York, NY: Grove, 1986.
Winnicott, D. W. (1986b). *Home is Where We Start From*. London: Norton, 1990.
Winnicott, D. W. (1986c). Psychoanalysis and science: Friends or relations? In: *Home is Where We Start From* (pp. 13–18). London: Penguin, 1990.
Winnicott, D. W. (1986d). The child in the family group. In: *Home is Where We Start From* (pp. 128–141). London: Penguin, 1990.
Winnicott, D. W. (1986e). The place of the monarchy. In: *Home is Where We Start From* (pp. 260–268). London: Penguin, 1990.
Winnicott, D. W. (1986f). Cure. In: *Home is Where We Start From* (pp. 112–120) London: Penguin, 1990.
Winnicott, D. W. (1986g). This feminism. In: *Home is Where We Start From* (pp. 183–194). London: Penguin, 1990.
Winnicott, D. W. (1986h). Living creatively. In: *Home is Where We Start From* (pp. 35–54). London: Penguin, 1990.
Winnicott, D. W. (1986i). The pill and the moon. In: *Home is Where We Start From* (pp. 195–209). London: Penguin, 1990.
Winnicott, D. W. (1987a). *Babies and Their Mothers*. London: Free Association, 1988.
Winnicott, D. W. (1987b). *The Spontaneous Gesture: Selected Letters of D. W. Winnicott*. London: Karnac, 1999.
Winnicott, D. W. (1987c). The beginning of the individual. In: *Babies and Their Mothers* (pp. 51–58). London: Free Association, 1988.
Winnicott, D. W. (1987d). Preliminary notes for "Communication between infant and mother, mother and infant, compared and contrasted". In: *Babies and Their Mothers* (pp. 107–109). London: Free Association, 1988.
Winnicott, D. W. (1987e). The ordinary devoted mother. In: *Babies and Their Mothers* (pp. 1–14). London: Free Association, 1988.
Winnicott, D. W. (1988). *Human Nature*. London: Free Association, 1992.
Winnicott, D. W. (1989a). *Psychoanalytic Explorations*. London: Karnac, 1989.
Winnicott, D. W. (1989b). Roots of aggression (part of Chapter Fifty-three). In: *Psychoanalytic Explorations* (pp. 458–461). London: Karnac, 1989.
Winnicott, D. W. (1989c). Contribution to a symposium on envy and jealousy. In: *Psychoanalytic Explorations* (pp. 462–464). London: Karnac, 1989.
Winnicott, D. W. (1989d). The concept of trauma in relation to the development of the individual within the family. In: *Psychoanalytic Explorations* (pp. 130–148). London: Karnac, 1989.
Winnicott, D. W. (1989e). The beginnings of a formulation of an appreciation and criticism of Klein's envy statement. In: *Psychoanalytic Explorations* (pp. 447–457). London: Karnac, 1989.
Winnicott, D. W. (1989f). D. W. W. on D. W. W. In: *Psychoanalytic Explorations* (pp. 569–582). London: Karnac, 1989.
Winnicott, D. W. (1989g). Discussion of "Grief and mourning in infancy" (John Bowlby). In: *Psychoanalytic Explorations* (pp. 426–432). London: Karnac, 1989.

Winnicott, D. W. (1989h). Character types: the foolhardy and the cautions (Michael Balint). In: *Psychoanalytic Explorations* (pp. 433–437). London: Karnac, 1989.
Winnicott, D. W. (1989i). The use of an object in the context of "Moses and Monotheism". In: *Psychoanalytic Explorations* (pp. 240–246). London: Karnac, 1989.
Winnicott, D. W. (1989j). Fragments concerning varieties of clinical confusion. In: *Psychoanalytic Explorations* (pp. 30–33). London: Karnac, 1989.
Winnicott, D. W. (1989k). Comments on my paper "The use of an object". In: *Psychoanalytic Explorations* (pp. 238–239). London: Karnac, 1989.
Winnicott, D. W. (1989l). Clinical illustration of "The use of an object". In: *Psychoanalytic Explorations* (pp. 235–237). London: Karnac, 1989.
Winnicott, D. W. (1989m). The importance of the setting in meeting regression in psycho-analysis. In: *Psychoanalytic Explorations* (pp. 96–102). London: Karnac, 1989.
Winnicott, D. W. (1989n). Individuation. In: *Psychoanalytic Explorations* (pp. 284–288). London: Karnac, 1989.
Winnicott, D. W. (1989o). Clinical material (part II of Chapter Twenty-eight). In: *Psychoanalytic Explorations* (pp. 183–188). London: Karnac, 1989.
Winnicott, D. W. (1989p). Psycho-neurosis in childhood. In: *Psychoanalytic Explorations* (pp. 64–72). London: Karnac, 1989.
Winnicott, D. W. (1989q). The psychology of madness: a contribution from psycho-analysis. In: *Psychoanalytic Explorations* (pp. 119–129). London: Karnac, 1989.
Winnicott, D. W. (1989r). Nothing at the centre. In: *Psychoanalytic Explorations* (pp. 49–52). London: Karnac, 1989.
Winnicott, D. W. (1989s). New light on children's thinking. In: *Psychoanalytic Explorations* (pp. 152–157). London: Karnac, 1989.
Winnicott, D. W. (1993a). *Talking to Parents*. Cambridge/Massachusetts: Perseus.
Winnicott, D. W. (1993b). The building up of trust. In: *Talking to Parents* (pp. 121–134). Cambridge/Massachusetts: Perseus.
Winnicott, D. W. (1993c). The development of a child's sense of right and wrong. In: *Talking to Parents* (pp. 105–110). Cambridge/Massachusetts: Perseus.
Winnicott, D. W. (1993d). Feeling guilty. In: *Talking to Parents* (pp. 95–104). Cambridge/Massachusetts: Perseus.
Winnicott, D. W. (1993e). What do we know about babies as cloth suckers? In: *Talking to Parents* (pp. 15–20). Cambridge/Massachusetts: Perseus.
Winnicott, D. W. (1996a). *Thinking about Children*. London: Karnac.
Winnicott, D. W. (1996b). The association for child psychology and psychiatry observed as a group phenomenon. In: *Thinking about Children* (pp. 235–254). London: Karnac.
Winnicott, D. W. (1996c). Autism. In: *Thinking about Children* (pp. 197–217). London: Karnac.
Wulff, M. (1946). Fetichism and object choice in early childhood. *Psychoanalytic Quarterly, 15*.
Zemeckis, R. (1994). *Forrest Gump*. Paramount Pictures: USA.

INDEX